Enterprise Java™ Computing

Managing Object Technology Series

Barry McGibbon, Series Editor
SIGS Publications, Inc.
New York, New York

1. What Every Software Manager Must Know to Succeed with Object Technology • *John D. Williams*
2. Managing Your Move to Object Technology: Guidelines and Strategies for a Smooth Transition • *Barry McGibbon*
3. The Object Primer: Application Developer's Guide to Object Orientation • *Scott W. Ambler*
4. Getting Results with the Object-Oriented Enterprise Model • *Thornton Gale and James Eldred*
5. Deploying Distributed Business Software • *Ted Lewis, Ph.D.*
6. The Blueprint for Business Objects • *Peter Fingar*
7. Object Technology Strategies and Tactics • *Gilbert Singer*
8. Upgrading Relational Databases with Objects • *Robert Vermeulen*
9. Building Object Applications That Work: Your Step-by-Step Handbook for Developing Robust Systems with Object Technology • *Scott W. Ambler*
10. CUC96: Component-Based Software Engineering • *Collected and Introduced by Thomas Jell*
11. Developing Business Objects • *Edited by Andy Carmichael*
12. Component-Based Development for Enterprise Systems: Applying The SELECT Perspective™ • *Paul Allen and Stuart Frost*
13. Developing Business Systems with CORBA • *Waqar Sadiq and Fred Cummins, J.D.*
14. Cognitive Patterns: Problem-Solving Frameworks for Object Technology • *Karen Gardner, Alex Rush, Michael Crist, Robert Konitzer, and Bobbin Teegarden*
15. Process Patterns: Building Large-Scale Systems Using Object Technology • *Scott W. Ambler*
16. Tried & True Object Development: Industry-Proven Approaches with UML • *Ari Jaaksi, Juha-Markus Aalto, Ari Aalto, and Kimmo Vättö*
17. Enterprise Architectural Patterns: Building Blocks of the Agile Company • *Michael A. Beedle*
18. NO BULL Object Technology for Executives • *William Perlman*
19. More Process Patterns: Delivering Large-Scale Systems Using Object Technology • *Scott W. Ambler*

21. Distributed Object Arechitectures with CORBA • *Henry Balen*
22. Enterprise Java™ Computing: Applications and Architectures • *Govind Seshadri*

Additional Volumes in Preparation

Enterprise Java™ Computing

Applications and Architectures

Govind Seshadri
with Gopalan Suresh Raj

PUBLISHED BY THE PRESS SYNDICATE OF THE UNIVERSITY OF CAMBRIDGE
The Pitt Building, Trumpington Street, Cambridge CB2 1RP, United Kingdom

CAMBRIDGE UNIVERSITY PRESS
The Edinburgh Building, Cambridge CB2 2RU, UK www.cup.cam.ac.uk
40 West 20th Street, New York, NY 10011-4211, USA www.cup.org
10 Stamford Road, Oakleigh, Melbourne 3166, Australia
Ruiz de Alarcón 13, 28014 Madrid, Spain

Published in association with SIGS Books

First published in 1999

Design and composition by David Van Ness
Cover design by Andrea Cammarata

Printed in the United States of America

A catalog record for this book is available from the British Library.

Library of Congress Cataloging-in-Publication Data is on record with the publisher.

ISBN 0 521 65712 1 paperback

For Mini and Arjun

About the Authors

Govind Seshadri is a leading Java technologist, whose work has been published in numerous journals. He is also a regular speaker on advanced Java development issues at technical conferences worldwide. Govind is the "Distributed Computing" columnist for *Java Report*, and a Senior Technical Architect for STR—a Chicago-based consultancy specializing in enterprise Java solutions. He can be reached at gseshadri@hotmail.com

Gopalan Suresh Raj is a senior analyst, software architect, and developer with expertise in multi-tiered systems development, enterprise component architectures, and distributed object computing. He is also an author, including contributions to *The Awesome Power of JavaBeans* (Manning Publications Co., 1998). Visit him at his popular Cornucopia Web site at http://www.execpc.com/~gopalan

Contents

Foreword

In early 1995, my language research led me to a new programming language from Sun that got me really excited—Java was simple yet had all of my favorite features from previous languages. Alas, at first I feared that Java would die because at that time most programmers loathed interpreted, garbage-collected languages (I cite Smalltalk as a good example). By mid-June 1995, however, Java exploded onto the programming scene. Now, even your mother has heard of Java—of course, my mother tells everyone that I invented Java.

There is one simple reason that programmers overcame their hatred of a Java-like language: Java provides for the seamless and invisible distribution of software across the Net and provides the best platform so far for doing commercial, distributed, network-based computing. The Java server-side APIs such as EJB, JDBC, Servlets, RMI, Serialization, etc... support the construction of distributed systems as never before. Aside from providing a standard, these libraries make it easy to manipulate data in relational databases, send objects to remote machines, invoke methods on objects across a network, build html interfaces on the fly, and so on. You can write server programs more robustly and more quickly in Java than in any other language. Heck, even a lowly socket connection, which takes a few lines in Java, used to take two pages of C code!

If you are going to build a system with a large server-side component, you need to read this book. Govind really knows what he's talking about as he has developed several large commercial applications using the APIs described herein; plus, he was one of the first MageLang Institute students back in 1996! This book has great content and contrary to many Java books I have seen, it is extremely well organized and well written. Govind provides great code samples that help you apply the Java APIs and that help you understand how the APIs such as JDBC and RMI can work together—it is not a Java syntax book. Besides, Govind is a friendly guy and claims to be nice to old people.

Terence Parr,
President and Lead Mage
MageLang Institute, Ltd.

Acknowledgments

This book got started with Richard Friedman, the President of SIGS Publications, asking me "So, would you be interested in writing a Java book for us?" My thanks to him for being a constant source of support and encouragement. I was fortunate to have Gopalan Raj as a contributing author on this book. Gopalan, a veritable oasis for the parched enterprise developer, makes his mark in a number of places, and I am grateful for his contributions. My special thanks to Lothlórien Homet, who is quite possibly the best editor in the business. Her energy, wit, and enthusiasm made all the difference. For technical review of early drafts, I'd like to thank Scott Isaacson from Novell. Yes, he did convince me rewrite a couple of chapters—and the book is all the better for it! For having agreed to write the foreword for this book, I thank Terence Parr, Chief Scientist of the MageLang Institute. I honed my Java skills a few years ago under the tutelage of the MageLang jGurus—and look what happened! Thanks are also due to my copy editor, Marcia Baker, and the book's designer, David Van Ness, for their alacrity in spite of the mind numbing deadlines. For making this book a reality, my thanks to the editors at Cambridge University Press—Lauren Cowles and Shamus McGillicuddy. Thanks also to Larry Podmolik, Rick Wilhelm, Mark Panthofer, and the crew at STR for sharing their Java expertise. Mr. Paul, now I understand why reading Shakespeare was so darn important. And for putting me on the straight and narrow, I owe thanks to Mr. Putappa. Thanks to my family, for everything. And yes, dad—it's all a matter of confidence! My heartfelt thanks go out to the original idea factory—my lovely wife Mini, and my son, Arjun, who was born with this book halfway complete. But for their support and understanding, you would not be reading this.

Introduction

Enterprise Java Computing: Applications and Architecture is all about understanding the basic building blocks that are necessary for developing any significant Java-based business application. This book offers an advanced introduction to most of the enterprise APIs found within the Java 2 platform—including JDBC, servlets, JNI, RMI, Java IDL and EJB. Since enterprise software developers typically have significant programming experience, this book assumes that the reader is well versed with Java syntax and understands the basics of web computing.

Ever since the introduction of the Java platform, there has been considerable debate regarding its applicability for building real-life business applications. Although much of the concern stemmed from partisan considerations, there were nonetheless some significant shortcomings. With the recent release of the Java 2 platform, however, one thing appears clear—Java has finally matured and entered into the mainstream of enterprise business computing.

This book takes a highly modular approach toward explaining the advanced enterprise APIs, and strives to present each chapter as a self-contained unit. Each chapter starts with a basic introduction of the enterprise technology being covered, and gradually moves on to cover more advanced topics. Consequently, the book can be read in any order the reader chooses. However, some of the material, which features the integration of multiple enterprise technologies (like JDBC and RMI, for instance), assume that the reader has acquired a basic understanding of the underlying technologies by having read the relevant chapters beforehand.

Conventions Used in This Book

Many of the chapters contain number-sequenced lists, which typically denote steps that should be carried out in sequence. This approach is widely used, especially when presenting a recipe-based solution for solving a fairly complex problem like developing an RMI application or an entity EJB. Sometimes, key words or terms may appear italicized. This usually denotes the usage of some new or important technical term. As is common with most computer books, the code examples here are represented in a different font than the regular text.

The accompanying CD-ROM contains all of the code examples listed in the book, packaged by order of chapter and application name. For example, the directory `cup\chap2\bugtrack` contains all of the Java source and class files, pertaining to the bugtrack example developed in Chapter 2. The CD-ROM also includes an evaluation copy of Cloudscape (formerly known as JBMS)—a full-fledged SQL92-compatible RDMS written in Java, from Cloudscape, Inc. I encourage you to use this software for trying out any of the database-oriented Java examples. All of the source code has been tested using Java 2 on Windows 98—although much of the software, being Java, is inherently platform-independent.

The book also contains numerous screen shots, diagrams, and line art, and the in-text references should provide a suitable explanation regarding their purpose.

Request for Comments

When writing a book on a rapidly evolving field like enterprise Java computing, some errors, inaccuracies and bugs are bound to show up. I would greatly appreciate if you could bring them to my attention by emailing me at `gseshadri@hotmail.com`. Also, please feel free to let us know what you liked about this book—and what you didn't. Your input will be taken seriously and will prove invaluable for guiding future editions of this book.

Chapter 1

Introduction to Enterprise Java Computing

From the beginning, Java has always been more than just another hot, new programming language. To those of us who delved into exploring Java beyond simple, Web-based applets, this was obvious. Apart from being an elegant and sophisticated object-oriented programming language, Java was also a serious computing platform. To a balkanized computing landscape, the prospect of designing platform-independent applications based on the "Write Once, Run Anywhere" (WORA) principle was simply too good to pass up.

This promise of WORA has retained the momentum behind the Java revolution. The latest release of the Java Development Kit, dubbed Java 2, has been over four years in the making. Java 2—nearly seven times as large as JDK 1.0—represents a quantum leap in terms of functionality compared to anything else we have seen before. With the release of Java 2, Java has finally entered the mainstream of enterprise application development.

This chapter first introduces you to the enterprise features of Java 2 and presents some benefits of using this platform.

Key Enterprise Technologies

The Java 2 platform offers some excellent features for writing large-scale, enterprise applications:

Java Database Connectivity (JDBC). Databases are at the core of almost all enterprise applications, so the success or failure of any enterprise application development environment eventually hinges on its ease of data access or lack thereof. Most readers who have dealt with data access issues under the Windows platform are probably familiar with Microsoft's Open Database Connectivity (ODBC) API for interfacing programs with Relational databases. ODBC is popular chiefly because of one critical feature—it makes the underlying database transparent to your programs. The advantage of this architecture is if your database changes, your programs needn't suffer a complete rewrite.

Consequently, it should not be surprising that the JDBC specification derives considerable inspiration from the ODBC architecture. Don't make the mistake of thinking JDBC is merely a Java wrapper around ODBC, however. Sun developed the JDBC API from ground zero in collaboration with numerous partners including IBM, Oracle, Sybase, and Informix, among others. The JDBC API, which is a core component of the Java 2 platform, defines classes for database connections, SQL statements, result sets, database metadata, and so forth. Although JDBC is still considered a rather low-level API, it is quite simple to use. The biggest advantage JDBC programs have over those written using ODBC (or anything else, for that matter) is they are platform and vendor independent. Using JDBC, you can quite literally make your enterprise data available "anytime, anyplace, anywhere." Chapter 2 gives you an in-depth look at JDBC technology and shows you how well suited the technology is for incorporating into Java programs as is.

Servlets. Servlets are server-side Java modules that seamlessly meld with a Web server, extending its functionality. Servlets are an excellent replacement for CGI programs and probably are the easiest and most effective way to introduce Java computing into your environment. Typically, servlets run within a servlet engine and, currently, most of the popular Web servers already come with a built-in servlet engine. Enabling nearly any Web server with a third-party servlet engine plug-in is also possible. Like conventional CGI scripts, the user-interface for a servlet can be either regular HTML forms or Java applets and it can communicate with browsers using HTTP. But therein ends the similarity because compared with CGI scripts, servlets are far and away a superior solution in nearly every sense. Unlike CGI scripts, servlets are secure memory resident, multithreaded, and they maintain client sessions. Servlets fully leverage the power of Java by extending enterprise technologies like RMI, CORBA, and EJB to the Web. Chapter 3 covers servlets in detail.

Java Native Interface (JNI). Although JNI is not considered part of the *Java Platform for the Enterprise*, it is, nonetheless, the standard mechanism for the integration of C/C++ code with Java. Java methods declared as *native* within a class may be implemented outside the Java environment as functions written in C or C++. These functions are then compiled into either a DLL or a shared object, depending on the platform, and are loaded by the Java classes into the environment at runtime. Currently, a great deal of interest exists in interfacing Java with older, procedural, C-based application systems. While a more elaborate technology like CORBA can be used for the same purpose, it is best suited for the more complex legacy applications. JNI, being Java friendly, works best for legacy integration work from within pure Java technologies like servlets or RMI servers. Note, using JNI, C/C++ applications can load a JVM and run Java classes within its context. Chapter 4 covers the JNI mechanism.

Remote Method Invocation (RMI). RMI brings the world of distributed object computing to Java's doorstep and elevates network programming to a much higher plane. With RMI, Java objects can easily invoke the methods of remote objects that may be running on a different host, as if they were locally available! Also, remote method invocations can send and receive nearly any valid Java object without having to worry about flattening it to a serial data stream. RMI automatically provides you with this feature by using the underlying *Object Serialization* mechanism. discussed in Chapter 5. RMI is especially useful for deployment as a multitier bridging mechanism; it can serve as an effective "glue" for integrating other enterprise Java technologies like JDBC and JNI. Additionally, RMI remote objects serving as wrappers to database and legacy system integration code are highly scalable because of the inherently distributed nature of the technology itself.

Some significant enhancements have been made to the RMI mechanism under Java 2, especially with the introduction of Remote Object Activation (ROA) and Custom Socket Types. Using the new ROA mechanism, your remote servers needn't be up and running all the time, consuming valuable system resources. The advantage of having clients dynamically instantiate ROA-enabled remote server objects "on the fly" makes building even more scalable distributed object networks possible. With Custom Socket Types, incorporating proprietary data encryption and compression protocols at the transport level is a simple matter. Chapter 6 takes an in-depth look at the major RMI features.

Java IDL. A closer look at some of the larger, mission-critical applications being deployed today reveals extensive integration with legacy systems. Although legacy systems can be integrated with Java using JNI, it relies upon the legacy code having a C/C++ callable interface. This makes it impractical for integration with large applications written in COBOL, for instance.

A tried and tested solution does exist for integrating legacy systems with object oriented applications, however—CORBA. The Common Object Request Broker Architecture (CORBA) is neither a language nor an API. Rather, CORBA is a set of well-defined standards that have gradually evolved for nearly a decade, clearly specifying the interaction between client and server objects. CORBA has broad industry support by way of the 700+ member companies of Object Management Group (OMG)—the CORBA standards bearer—and is fully ratified by the ISO.

At the heart of CORBA are two critical enabling technologies—the Interface Definition Language (IDL) and the Object Request Broker (ORB). The IDL is a purely declarative language and serves to define objects, including their attributes and available methods. Once the "wrapper objects" are defined for the legacy system using IDL—depending on your implementation language—the appropriate legacy language-specific precompiler can be applied on it to generate the CORBA-bindings or stubs. The developer can use these bindings to integrate the business logic, which may be part of the legacy code base.

The ORB is the essence of the CORBA paradigm. It provides the communications infrastructure for locating a remote object—irrespective of where it may reside on the network—and ferries service invocation requests and results. Also, because ORBs are standards-compliant, nothing prevents you from mixing-and-matching ORBs from myriad vendors, even across platforms. Using Java IDL and the included standards-compliant Java ORB, you can now develop distributed client or server applications in Java that can be seamlessly integrated with your existing CORBA infrastructure. Chapter 7 examines Java IDL and the integration of CORBA with Java applications.

Java Naming and Directory Interface (JNDI). Naming and directory services allow enterprise-wide access to a networked repository of information about users, machines, networks, and applications. The JNDI API is provided as a standard extension with Java 2 and acts as an interface to common enterprise naming and directory services. JNDI is not specific to any one protocol as such. It relies on service providers provided by specific vendors that can be integrated within a JNDI installation, thus allowing the Java client to speak multiple protocols like DNS, NDS, LDAP, or NIS. Chapter 8 covers JNDI as part of the discussion of Enterprise JavaBeans technology.

Enterprise JavaBeans (EJB). The JavaBeans specification defined a *client component model* for developing mostly visual applications. EJB takes a similar approach by defining a *server component model* for building large-scale, distributed systems. EJB frees the application developer to concentrate on programming only the business logic, while removing the need to write all the "plumbing" code typical of any enterprise application development scenario. For example, the enterprise developer no longer needs to write code that handles transactional behavior, security, connection pooling, or threading because the specification delegates this task to the EJB server vendor.

The EJBs containing the business logic are platform-independent and can be moved to a different, more scalable platform, if necessary, without any change in the EJBs per se. Another major highlight of the EJB specification is the support for ready-made components. This enables you to "plug and work" with off-the-shelf, third-party EJBs without having to develop or test them and without having detailed knowledge of their inner workings. Chapter 8 covers Enterprise JavaBeans technology in detail.

Using Java for Enterprise Application Development

The decision to choose a particular language or platform for deploying your mission critical business applications is a critical one. Over the years we have seen more than one hot new programming language offered as a panacea for the ills of application development swiftly thrown by the wayside. But still, Java is radically different than anything offered before. Here's why:

Java applications are architecture neutral. Few companies can claim to have a homogenized computing environment. Today, the typical enterprise computing landscape is a mutually incompatible melange of UNIX, Mac, and Windows platforms. Apart from having to rewrite multiple versions of the application for each platform supported, companies may spend significant time and resources in porting applications with every new version upgrade of the same platform itself. Java, with its promise of WORA, radically alters the status quo. Java applications are typically deployed in the platform-independent bytecode format. And, you can run your Java applications on nearly any platform, assuming the presence of a Java Virtual Machine on that platform.

Java can be used to develop zero-maintenance clients. Ask any IT manager. Developing enterprise applications is the *easy* part—the maintenance and support are what kill you. Browser-based Java applets are naturally maintenance-free because they are downloaded on an as-needed basis from a centralized repository. Although bandwidth- related issues may occur in deploying sophisticated applets over the Web, they are ideal for an intranet environment.

Java applications use a component-based architecture. Java client applications can be entirely composed using plug-and-play JavaBeans components using a visual builder or IDE. The Enterprise JavaBeans specification enables us to take a similar approach in using third-party components at the server level. Server-side components are especially powerful because they obviate the need for the enterprise developer to implement some of the more complex features typical of large-scale applications, including distributed transaction management, security, database connection pooling, persistence, and so forth.

Java applications are robust. Java applications are significantly more robust than ones written in C or C++. Because Java is a strongly typed language, most conditions like improper castings, initializations, and so forth are detected at compile time itself. Most of the common run-time bugs within large C/C++ programs can usually be traced to improper pointer handling. Because Java does enable the developer to explicitly use pointers, it automatically eliminates a significant source of bugs. In addition, Java developers needn't perform any memory management themselves. The automatic garbage collection mechanism handles this transparently for them, thus significantly reducing the possibility of hard-to-trace memory leaks. Java also comes with a highly evolved exception handling mechanism and can gracefully handle any potential error condition.

Java provides a secure computing environment. Although no software is bullet-proof, Java provides a much more secure computing environment compared to nearly any other programming language. By default, under Java 2, all Java code is considered "untrusted" and is run under the aegis of a security manager, which serves to provide a sandbox or boundary to the application context. If your Java application has to access resources like the local file system, network connections, other applications, and so on you must explicitly grant the necessary permissions by means of a security policy file. This is quite unlike, say, a typical Windows application, which once installed, has unfettered access to your entire system.

Java takes advantage of multiprocessor platforms. If your application is not multithreaded, it may be unable to take advantage of your platform's multiprocessor configuration. Thus, your applications may be using only a fraction of the available computing power and continue to perform poorly. Unfortunately, with conventional programming languages, no easy solutions exist. Few programming tasks are currently more challenging than writing good multithreaded applications in C or C++. In fact, the vast majority of the commercial software available today does not make any use of multithreading whatsoever. Java, however, brings the arcane world of multithreaded programming to the masses through a simple, high-level API. Multithreaded Java programs can do many things concurrently. For example, an applet can perform animation on a thread, while continuing to download additional images over the network on a different thread.

Everyone else is doing it. Java has long ceased to be just a programming language. In fact, Java is a veritable industry. Java is no longer the language of choice for just implementing simple Web-based applets. Today, Java is very much a part of the mainstream enterprise-computing scenario all over the world. If your company intends to be a player in the new Net-Economy, it cannot afford *not* to look at Java!

Summary

Java has come a long way since the first Web-based applets appeared over four years ago. Today, Java is more than just another hot programming language—it has evolved into a serious computing platform, which can be used to deploy large-scale, scalable, transactional, mission-critical business solutions. Advanced Java technologies like JDBC, Servlets, JNI, RMI, Java IDL, and Enterprise JavaBeans are the basic building blocks of any significant corporate business application.

Chapter 2

Java Database Connectivity

Let's face it. The success or failure of any enterprise application development environment eventually hinges on its ease of data access or lack thereof. A reason exists for this. Databases today form the inner core of any significant business application and with companies network-enabling their data repositories ever-rapidly, the need for efficient data access mechanisms is more imperative than ever.

If you have dealt with data access issues before, you probably are familiar with Microsoft's Open Database Connectivity (ODBC) standard, which is a C-based API for interfacing programs with Relational databases. ODBC is popular mainly because of one critical feature—it makes the underlying DBMS transparent to your programs. ODBC-enabled programs essentially provide a pass-through mechanism for SQL statements. The ODBC driver manager forwards the SQL statements to the appropriate vendor-supplied database driver that connects with the database, performs the action directed within the statement, and returns the results, if any. The advantage of this architecture is that now, if your database changes, your programs needn't suffer a complete rewrite. In fact, provided your database schema remains the same, all you have to do is simply load the driver for the new database. Thus, ODBC has rapidly evolved to become an industry standard and is supported by almost every database, not only on Windows platforms, but on much of UNIX as well.

Consequently, learning the Java Database Connectivity (JDBC) specification derives considerable inspiration from the ODBC architecture should not be surprising. At the same time, however, JDBC is a lot more than a mere Java version of ODBC. Javasoft developed the JDBC API from ground zero in collaboration with numerous partners, including IBM, Oracle, Sybase, and Informix, among others. The JDBC API is available as the `java.sql` package within any standard JDK distribution and defines classes for database connections, SQL statements, result sets, database metadata, and so forth.

Javasoft's original vision for JDBC was for it to serve as a base on which higher-level APIs and tools could be built by third-party vendors. Although JDBC is still considered a rather low-level API, it is quite simple to use and, as we shall soon see, well suited for incorporating into Java programs as is. The biggest advantage JDBC programs have over those written using ODBC (or anything else, for that matter) is they are platform- and vendor-independent. Using JDBC, you can quite literally make your enterprise data available anytime, anyplace, and anywhere!

This chapter starts with an overview of the JDBC architecture and continues to explain the various JDBC features for seamless Java/database integration. The chapter assumes the reader has a basic familiarity with SQL. Much of this chapter is based on the JDBC 1.0 API included within JDK 1.1. The last section explains the salient features of the upcoming JDBC 2.0 API, which is included within JDK 1.2.

JDBC Architecture

The JDBC API is divided into a user-level API for processing SQL statements and handling all application to JDBC Driver Manager communications, and a JDBC Driver API that database vendors use to interface their database drivers to Java. Figure 2-1

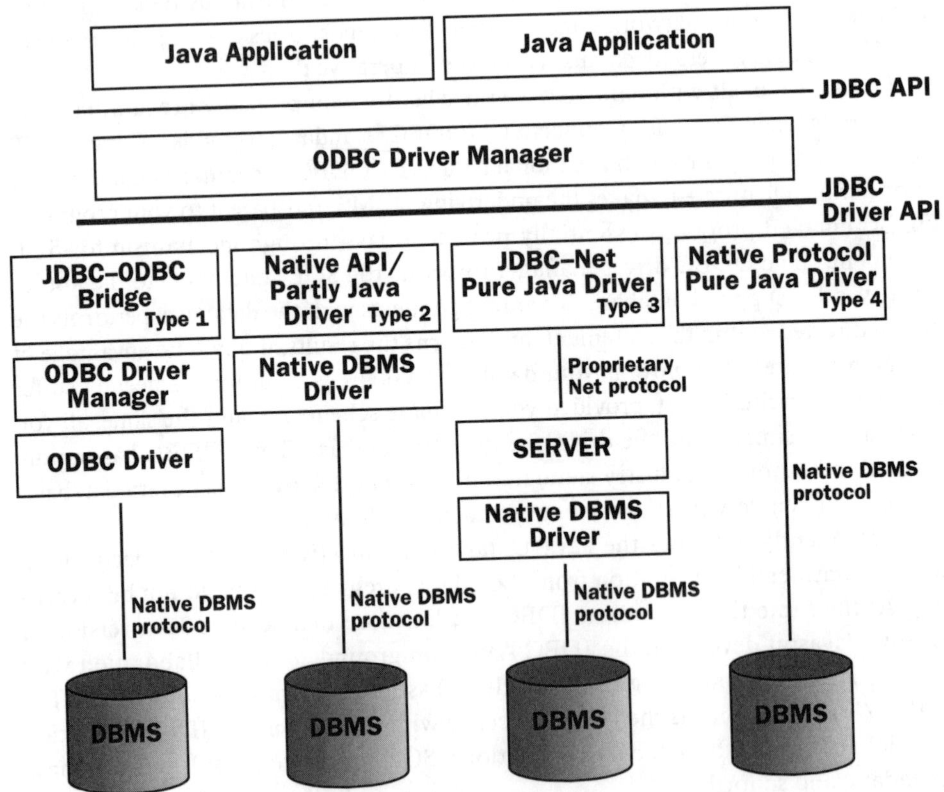

Figure 2-1: The JDBC architecture

gives us an overview of the JDBC architecture. The JDBC Driver Manager is the core of the JDBC architecture and serves to connect the Java application with one of the four different driver types, as well as to ferry any results back to the application.

Nearly every database engine offers its own unique set of extensions to standard SQL to differentiate itself in the marketplace. While making your statements strictly adhere to standard SQL is certainly desirable, doing so on all occasions is impossible. While JDBC API certainly prides itself in making the type of database transparent to the application, it should not be viewed as a "lowest common denominator" type of solution. You can certainly pass proprietary SQL statements to the underlying driver and as long as you have the proper vendor-supplied driver for the specific database engine, everything should be fine. When using third-party drivers, make certain to ensure they are JDBC-compliant. A driver is JDBC compliant when it supports at least the entry-level version of the SQL92 standard and passes the JDBC driver test suite that comes as part of the standard JDK distribution.

JDBC Driver Types

As you can see in Figure 2-1, JDBC drivers fall into one of four broadly defined categories. When shopping for a JDBC driver, knowing which type to look for is important because your vendor may have more than one type of JDBC driver for a given database. The categories the drivers may belong to are

Type 1: JDBC-ODBC bridge plus ODBC driver

Type 2: Native-API partly-Java driver

Type 3: JDBC-Net pure Java driver

Type 4: Native-protocol pure Java driver

The selection of a particular JDBC driver type pretty much impacts the overall system architecture for your application. For this reason alone, having a thorough understanding of the capabilities of each of them is crucial.

Type 1: JDBC-ODBC bridge plus ODBC driver

The JDBC-ODBC bridge driver is distributed as part of the JDBC package and essentially translates JDBC calls into ODBC. For many of the smaller databases, such as FoxPro or Access, using the JDBC-ODBC Bridge may be the only way to integrate them with Java. Additionally, this is also a good way to leverage your existing investment in your tried and tested ODBC drivers by reusing them with Java. However, Type 1 drivers are not suitable if your clients are in the form of applets. This is because ODBC drivers in the form of native code must be deployed on each of the client machines, for each database you intend to access. Type 1 drivers are best suited for deployment with two-tier applications running in a LAN environment, where maintenance of the client machines is not a significant logistical issue.

Type 2: Native-API partly Java driver

These drivers typically provide a Java wrapper to an existing vendor-supplied driver, which, in turn, implements a database-specific protocol like the Oracle Call Interface (OCI). Thus, Type 2 drivers transparently convert JDBC calls directly into a database-specific protocol and map results back to the JDBC API. Although Type 2 drivers do not make use of ODBC, they still require some native code in the form of the vendor-supplied driver to be installed on each client machine. For this reason, they are not recommended for use within applets. They can, however, be used within RMI servers or Java servlets, where the native code can be loaded with ease.

Type 3: JDBC-Net pure Java driver

Type 3 drivers do not require any native code to be installed at the client. This driver uses a published network protocol to communicate with a remote server, which in turn communicates with the required database using either ODBC or a vendor-supplied native database driver. Because Type 3 drivers are pure Java implementations, they are ideally suited for deployment within both applets and applications.

Type 4: Native-protocol pure Java driver

Type 4 drivers, like those of Type 3, are pure Java implementations. They essentially implement a vendor-specific database protocol and are highly database specific. A highlight of these drivers is they do not have to tunnel through additional layers imposed by either ODBC or native drivers. Consequently, Type 4 drivers usually tend to offer better performance when compared to others. Just like Type 3 drivers, they are suited for use within both applets and applications.

Selecting a JDBC Driver

Considering the myriad choices available, which JDBC driver would be the best fit for your system architecture? Let's examine the options a little closer.

- *Two-tier architecture; database client deployed as applets*: Type 1 and Type 2 drivers can be safely ruled out for use within applets. Both these types require native code, which needs to be preinstalled on the client machine. Type 3 drivers are unsuitable because they always work in conjunction with a middle-tier. Thus, your only option is to use a pure Java Type 4 driver. Note, however, applets can only connect back to the host from which they were downloaded. If your database server runs on a different host than the Web server (which is usually the case), you need to use a proxy server to forward the JDBC calls. Figure 2-2 shows the basic two-tier architecture with the database client deployed as an applet.

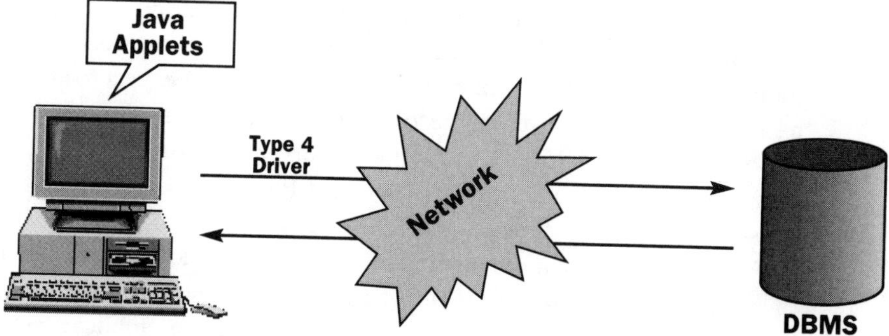

Figure 2-2: Two-tier architecture; database client deployed as applets

- *Two-tier architecture; database client deployed as an application*: Type 1, Type 2, or Type 4 drivers are suitable. Note, a Type 1 driver, in turn, uses an ODBC driver, which essentially accesses the database functionality at a lowest common denominator. Typically, any proprietary SQL extensions are not supported within an ODBC driver. If you need to harness the entire functionality of the database, your options narrow to a database-specific Type 2 or Type 4 driver. Figure 2-3 shows the basic two-tier architecture with the database client deployed as a Java application.

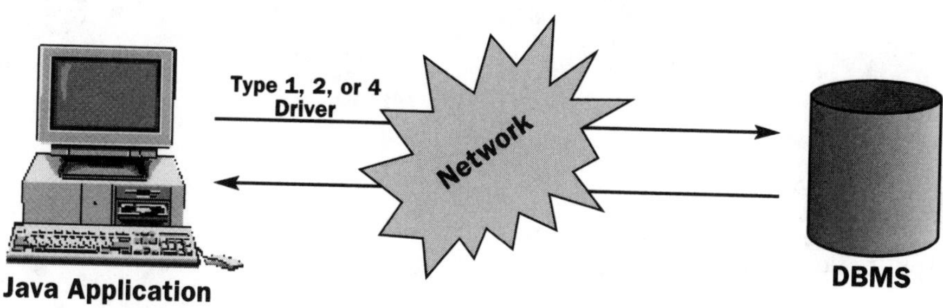

Figure 2-3: Two-tier architecture; database client deployed as application

- *Three-tier architecture; database client deployed as Java application or applets*: While nearly any type of driver can be used within the middle-tier, note ODBC drivers are usually not thread-safe. Your middle-tier must be able to service concurrent requests from multiple clients. This is imperative. If you do not use a thread-safe driver, you are essentially serializing database access and losing the tremendous advantage to be gained by deploying a multithreaded server. In this scenario, either a Type 2, Type 3, or Type 4 driver would work. You may be forced to use a Type 3 driver, especially if you are making use of an IDE that comes bundled with its own middleware. An example of this is the dbAnywhere server, which is part of Symantec's Visual Café environment. Note, Type 3 drivers are not particularly efficient because of the translation between the proprietary net-protocol and the database-specific protocol can be quite a performance drain. In my opinion, the only real value a Type 3 driver delivers is when you expect to access more than one database from within your client. If you expect to access just a single database, however, my recommendation is to consider using a high-performance Type 4 driver within an RMI server, CORBA server, or Servlet, as that enables you to deliver a 100 percent Pure Java solution end-to-end. Irrespective of which type of driver you choose, you can obtain additional performance gains by implementing database connection pooling and data-caching strategies within the middle-tier. Figure 2-4 shows a three-tier architecture with the database client deployed as an applet or application.

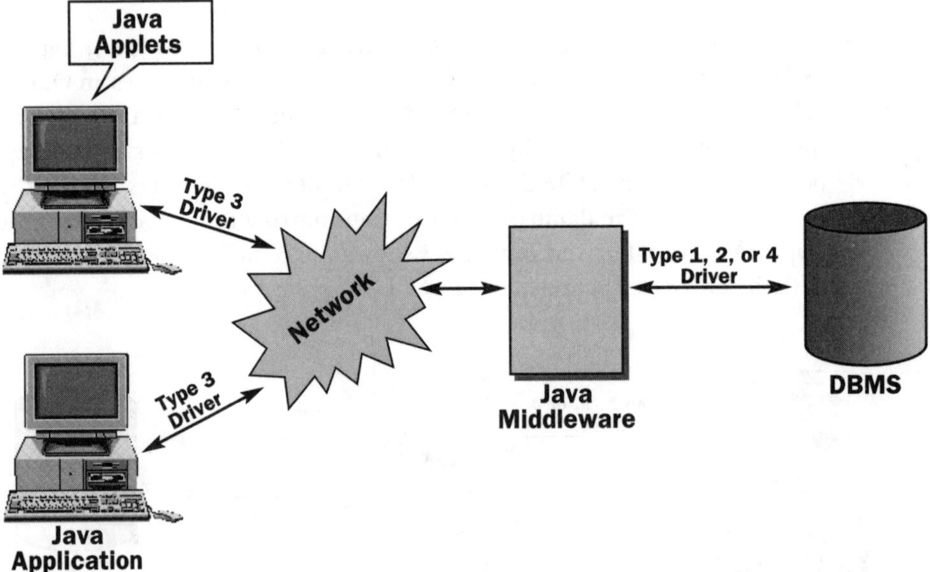

Figure 2-4: Three-tier architecture; database client deployed as applet or application

Once you finalize the driver type, you still must decide which driver to use within that category. Not a particularly simple task because not all JDBC drivers are made the same. From personal experience, I can say coming across, say, a Type 4 driver that is nearly twice as fast as some of its other competitors for the same database is not surprising! For this reason, while selecting a JDBC driver may seem like a fairly small matter in the overall scheme of things, it could potentially be what either makes or breaks your entire application.

Running some benchmarks with various JDBC drivers and obtaining some empirical data as it applies to your system architecture is always advisable. Do make it a point to use a test suite that will try and simulate the actual load factor your system may be subjected to as closely as possible. Even if you do finalize on a particular driver, considering the current state of flux in the driver marketplace, you should make it a point to retest your application with newer entrants periodically. Luckily for us, changing your JDBC driver is a reasonably simple matter, even after you have deployed your application because it does not involve extensive code changes.

> **Note**
>
> We are currently witnessing significant activity in the field of JDBC drivers, with vendors coming out with ever-more efficient drivers on almost a weekly basis. Sun maintains a Web page containing a master list of all the JDBC drivers and their vendors. Check it out periodically at:
>
> http://java.sun.com/products/jdbc/jdbc.drivers.html

JDBC URLs

As you know, a Uniform Resource Locator (URL) provides the location of a resource accessible locally or over the network. JDBC drivers make use of an URL-based naming scheme to talk to their target databases. Thus, by using URLs, you have the flexibility to access a remote database over a network, just like any other resource.

The standard syntax for JDBC URLs is

```
jdbc:<subprotocol>:<subname>
```

The first two segments—"jdbc" and "subprotocol"—are used by the JDBC Driver Manager to determine which particular driver to use. The rest of the URL is then used as input to the driver itself.

For instance, the URL:

```
jdbc:odbc:customer
```

accesses the customer database on the local machine by means of the JDBC-ODBC bridge.

You can also have a JDBC URL such as:

```
jdbc:msql://www.bigcat.com:1112/catalog
```

This causes the JDBC Driver Manager to use the locally installed mSQL driver, which, in turn, tries to establish a connection with the database "catalog" running on the host `www.bigcat.com` on port 1112.

Java/SQL Type Mappings

Before exploring the details of using the JDBC API, understanding the Java mappings for the standard SQL types, and vice versa, is important. Table 2-1 shows the default mappings for the same:

Table 2-1: Java/SQL Mappings

SQL Type	Java Type	Description
CHAR	string	Single character
VARCHAR	string	Variable length of chars up to 32K
LONGVARCHAR	java.io.InputStream	Extremely long (multimegabyte) strings
NUMERIC	java.math.BigDecimal	Absolute precision fixed point values for currency
DECIMAL	java.math.BigDecimal	Absolute precision decimal values for currency
BIT	boolean	Binary value (0 or 1)
TINYINT	byte	8-bit integer
SMALLINT	short	16-bit integer
INTEGER	int	Signed 32-bit integer
BIGINT	long	Signed 64-bit integer
REAL	float	Floating-point value
DOUBLE	double	Large floating-point value
FLOAT	float	Floating-point value
BINARY	byte[]	Array of binary values
VARBINARY	byte[]	Variable length array of binary values up to 32K
LONGVARBINARY	java.io.InputStream	Multi-megabyte length array of binary values
DATE	java.sql.Date	ISO-format date as "yyyy-mm-dd"
TIME	java.sql.Time	GMT time value in "hh-mm-ss" format
TIMESTAMP	java.sql.Timestamp	GMT time value with nanosecond field

Using the JDBC API

The JDBC API is implemented as the java.sql package and is a core component of the standard JDK distribution. It contains classes to handle all the fundamental issues involved with accessing relational data, including classes for locating and loading database drivers, establishing connections with remote data sources, executing SQL statements, and handling result sets. Next, you'll have an in-depth look at the actual mechanics of using the JDBC interface.

Loading a driver

The first thing you must do within any JDBC program is to load the appropriate driver that enables you to connect with your data source. Once a driver is loaded, it creates an instance of itself and automatically registers itself with DriverManager. You can, of course, load more than one driver if your application needs to access multiple databases. The responsibility of the driver manager is to use the appropriate driver for connecting with your data source, by using the protocol information found within the JDBC URL.

You can load a driver within your application in two ways. One simple way is to invoke the method Class.forName() and load the driver explicitly as:

```
String myDriver = "sun.jdbc.odbc.JdbcOdbcDriver";
Class.forName(myDriver);
```

The advantage of loading a driver this way is you can have your application read the driver name from an external configuration file. This enables you to switch drivers easily without having to recompile your application.

You can also specify a set of drivers to be loaded from the jdbc.drivers system property. This method can be especially useful if you need to use multiple drivers within your application.

For instance, you can start your application as:

```
java -Djdbc.drivers=com.bigdb.SqlDriver:sun.jdbc.odbc.JdbcOdbcDriver MyProgram
```

The class java.sql.DriverManager has two useful static methods, which may be handy when loading drivers.

You can set the maximum time all drivers can wait when attempting to log into a database by:

```
public static void setLoginTimeout(int seconds);
```

You can also obtain useful logging and tracing information output by the DriverManager and database drivers, by piping it to a log fileusing:

```
public static void setLogStream(PrintStream out);
```

To see the logging information on the console, you can have something like:

```
DriverManager.setLogStream(System.err);
```

Connecting to a database

Once the driver has been loaded, you can open a database connection and obtain a Connection object (shown in Listing 2-1) simply by calling the driver manager's static getConnection() method. At this point, you must provide the location of the data source via a JDBC URL, as well as other required information like remote hostname, username, and password. If your target database is an ODBC-compliant database, such as

Access or SQL Anywhere, having it properly configured and associated with a data source name is important. This is usually done via the ODBC option within the control panel on your Win32 platform. The following snippet shows how to establish a database connection with a previously configured ODBC data source bugtrack:

```
String url = "jdbc.odbc.bugtrack";
String user="dba";
String password="sql";
Connection dbCon=DriverManager.getConnection(url, user, password);
```

If the driver manager cannot find a matching driver registered within for the subprotocol specified in the JDBC URL, a SQLException is thrown.

Note

A situation may exist where more than one JDBC driver registered with the driver manager is capable of connecting to a given URL. Drivers always get registered in the order they are specified within the jdbc.drivers property. This is important to remember For instance, if you have a Type 3 driver specified before a Type 4 driver, assuming both can handle the subprotocol, the former will be used, even though using the latter may be more efficient. If you are registering drivers by specifying some within jdbc.drivers and loading others via Class.forName() calls, know that those specified within jdbc.drivers are registered first by the JDBC driver manager.

Listing 2-1: The Connection Interface

```
public interface Connection {
    //class constants
    public static final int TRANSACTION_NONE;
    public static final int TRANSACTION_READ_UNCOMMITTED;
    public static final int TRANSACTION_READ_COMMITTED;
    public static final int TRANSACTION_REPEATABLE_READ;
    public static final int TRANSACTION_SERIALIZABLE;
    //methods
    public abstract Statement createStatement() throws SQLException;
    public abstract PreparedStatement prepareStatement(String sql) throws SQLException;
    public abstract CallableStatement prepareCall(String sql) throws SQLException;
    public abstract String nativeSQL(String sql) throws SQLException;
    public abstract void setAutoCommit(boolean autoCommit) throws SQLException;
    public abstract boolean getAutoCommit() throws SQLException;
    public abstract void commit() throws SQLException;
    public abstract void commit() throws SQLException;
    public abstract void close() throws SQLException;
```

Listing 2-1: continued

```
        public abstract void close() throws SQLException;
        public abstract DatabaseMetaData getMetaData() throws SQLException;
        public abstract void setReadOnly(boolean readOnly) throws SQLException;
        public abstract boolean isReadOnly() throws SQLException;
        public abstract void setCatalog(String catalog) throws SQLException;
        public abstract String getCatalog() throws SQLException;
        public abstract void setTransactionIsolation(int level) throws SQLException;
        public abstract int getTransactionIsolation() throws SQLException;
        public abstract SQLWarning getWarnings() throws SQLException;
        public abstract void clearWarnings() throws SQLException;
   }
```

Executing SQL statements

Before you can start executing any SQL statements against the database, you first need to obtain a `Statement` object for your database session specified by the `Connection` object. Obtaining a `Statement` object is easy:

```
Statement stmt = dbCon.createStatement();
```

For illustrative purposes, I use a simple database, "BUGTRACK", which can be used for keeping track of the software faults within your application software. Tables 2-2 through 2-4 highlight the constituent tables of the sample database:

Table 2-2: The BUGS Table

BUG_ID	SUMMARY	PTY	STS	REPORT_DATE
1001	Browser crashes on startup	1	2	1998-07-12
1002	User bookmarks not saved	4	1	1998-08-14
1003	RMI does not work with MSIE	1	3	1998-08-11
1004	Java applets fail under Win 3.1	2	3	1998-08-24
1005	DB connection times out	3	1	1998-08-26

Table 2-3: The STATUS Table

STAT_CD	DESCRIPTION
1	Unassigned
2	In Progress
3	Resolved

Table 2-4: The PRIORITY Table

PRIOR_CD	DESCRIPTION
1	Critical
2	High
3	Medium
4	Low

The Statement interface provides three different methods for executing SQL statements: executeQuery(), executeUpdate(), and execute(). So, which one should you use? The return type from the method call determines that.

If you are executing SELECT statements that return a single result set, then you should use executeQuery(). If you want to execute any SQL Data Manipulation Language (DML) statement involving an INSERT, UPDATE, or DELETE, or any Data Definition Language (DDL) statements like CREATE TABLE, you should make use of executeUpdate(). For DML statements, the value returned from this method call is an integer, indicating the number of rows affected. If you passed a DDL statement as parameter, the value returned is always 0, because they do not directly affect rows within a table.

Situations may occur where the execution of a SQL statement may return more than one result set, more than one update count, or a combination of both. In such cases, you need to use the execute() method. A later section in this chapter covers execute().

The executeQuery method

As mentioned earlier, the simplest way to retrieve query information from a database is to invoke the executeQuery() method of the Statement object. This returns the results, if any, by means of a ResultSet object. Now, say you want to list all the critical faults within the BUGTRACK database using the JDBC API. You can do the same as follows:

```
ResultSet res = stmt.executeQuery("SELECT bug_id, summary, report_date FROM bugs
                WHERE pty=1");
```

After the method has been invoked, the ResultSet object will contain the following data:

BUG_ID	SUMMARY	REPORT_DATE
1001	Browser crashes on startup	1998-07-12
1003	RMI does not work with MSIE	1998-08-11

The ResultSet object can now be processed easily by calling some of the methods shown in Listing 2-2.

```
while (res.next()) {
    //process each row
    int bugid = res.getInt("bug_id");
    String summary = res.getString("summary");
    java.sql.Date d = res.getDate("report_date");
}
```

Listing 2-2: The ResultSet Interface

```
public interface ResultSet {
    public abstract boolean next() throws SQLException;
    public abstract void close() throws SQLException;
    public abstract boolean wasNull() throws SQLException;
    public abstract String getString(int columnIndex) throws SQLException;
    public abstract boolean getBoolean(int columnIndex) throws SQLException;
    public abstract byte getByte(int columnIndex) throws SQLException;
    public abstract short getShort(int columnIndex) throws SQLException;
    public abstract int getInt(int columnIndex) throws SQLException;
    public abstract long getLong(int columnIndex) throws SQLException;
    public abstract float getFloat(int columnIndex) throws SQLException;
    public abstract double getDouble(int columnIndex) throws SQLException;
    public abstract BigDecimal getBigDecimal(int columnIndex,int scale) throws
        SQLException;
    public abstract byte[] getBytes(int columnIndex) throws SQLException;
    public abstract Date getDate(int columnIndex) throws SQLException;
    public abstract Time getTime(int columnIndex) throws SQLException;
    public abstract Timestamp getTimestamp(int columnIndex) throws SQLException;
    public abstract InputStream getAsciiStream(int columnIndex) throws SQLException;
    public abstract InputStream getUnicodeStream(int columnIndex) throws SQLException;
    public abstract InputStream getBinaryStream(int columnIndex) throws SQLException;
    public abstract String getString(String columnName) throws SQLException;
    public abstract boolean getBoolean(String columnName) throws SQLException;
    public abstract byte getByte(String columnName) throws SQLException;
    public abstract short getShort(String columnName) throws SQLException;
    public abstract int getInt(String columnName) throws SQLException;
    public abstract long getLong(String columnName) throws SQLException;
    public abstract float getFloat(String columnName) throws SQLException;
    public abstract double getDouble(String columnName) throws SQLException;
    public abstract BigDecimal getBigDecimal(String columnName,int scale)
        throws SQLException;
    public abstract byte[] getBytes(String columnName) throws SQLException;
```

continues

Listing 2-2: continued

```
        public abstract Date getDate(String columnName) throws SQLException;
        public abstract Time getTime(String columnName) throws SQLException;
        public abstract Timestamp getTimestamp(String columnName) throws SQLException;
        public abstract InputStream getAsciiStream(String columnName) throws SQLException;
        public abstract InputStream getUnicodeStream(String columnName) throws
          SQLException;
        public abstract InputStream getBinaryStream(String columnName) throws
          SQLException;
        public abstract SQLWarning getWarnings() throws SQLException;
        public abstract void clearWarnings() throws SQLException;
        public abstract String getCursorName() throws SQLException;
        public abstract ResultSetMetaData getMetaData() throws SQLException;
        public abstract Object getObject(int columnIndex) throws SQLException;
        public abstract Object getObject(String columnName) throws SQLException;
        public abstract int findColumn(String columnName) throws SQLException;
    }
```

The executeUpdate method

If we want to update the STATUS table with a new entry called "Advisory", we have to invoke executeUpdate() as follows:

```
int count = stmt.executeUpdate("INSERT INTO status(stat_cd, description) VALUES
        (4,'Advisory')");
```

Assuming everything goes well, the method call initializes count to 1 and modifies the STATUS table as shown in the following:

STAT_CD	DESCRIPTION
1	Unassigned
2	In Progress
3	Resolved
4	Advisory

The execute method

Situations may occur where your program may have to deal with the execution of arbitrary SQL statements. In these cases, predicting whether your program should expect back an update count, a result set, or both, from the execution of the statement is difficult. In these cases, you must make use of the Statement.execute() method.

Statement.execute() works by returning a boolean to tell you the response type.

If it is true, it indicates the next result is a ResultSet, which can be obtained by calling Statement.getResultSet().

If it is false, it indicates the next result is an update count, which can be obtained by calling Statement.getUpdateCount(). A false value with an update count of –1 indicates no more results exist to retrieve.

The following code snippet demonstrates the handling of multiple result sets:

```
boolean res = stmt.execute(arbitrarySQLStatement);
int updateCnt = stmt.getUpdateCount();
while (res || (updateCnt != -1)) {
    if(res) {
        ResultSet rs = stmt.getResultSet();
        // process result set rs for query
    } else if(updateCnt != -1 && updateCnt !=0 ) {
        // process update count for DML statement
    } else if (updateCnt == 0) {
        // process for DDL statement or 0 rows updated
    }
    res = stmt.getMoreResults();
    updateCnt = stmt.getUpdateCount();
}
```

It is important to complete processing of the current ResultSet object before reexecuting another Statement object, as the methods shown in Listing 2-3 first close the calling Statement object's current result set if one is open.

Listing 2-3: The Statement Interface

```
public interface Statement {
    //methods
    public abstract ResultSet executeQuery(String sql) throws SQLException;
    public abstract int executeUpdate(String sql) throws SQLException;
    public abstract void close() throws SQLException;
    public abstract int getMaxFieldSize() throws SQLException;
    public abstract void setMaxFieldSize(int max) throws SQLException;
    public abstract int getMaxRows() throws SQLException;
    public abstract void setMaxRows(int max) throws SQLException;
    public abstract void setEscapeProcessing(boolean enable) throws SQLException;
    public abstract int getQueryTimeout() throws SQLException;
    public abstract void setQueryTimeout(int seconds) throws SQLException;
    public abstract void cancel() throws SQLException;
    public abstract SQLWarning getWarnings() throws SQLException;
    public abstract void clearWarnings() throws SQLException;
    public abstract void setCursorName(String name) throws SQLException;
    public abstract boolean execute(String sql) throws SQLException;
    public abstract ResultSet getResultSet() throws SQLException;
    public abstract int getUpdateCount() throws SQLException;
    public abstract boolean getMoreResults() throws SQLException;
}
```

Optimizing Queries with Prepared Statements

Before the database executes a SQL query, it first computes a strategy on how best to execute the query by parsing, compiling, and planning for the query. The query is executed only after the execution plan has been built. Now, if you are executing a rather popular query multiple times, by default, the database always goes through all the previously mentioned steps and repeatedly computes an execution plan each time it is executed. However, you can decrease the overhead by eliminating most of the steps required to compute an execution plan by making use of prepared statements. A *prepared statement* is essentially a precompiled SQL statement. Using prepared statements, you can parse, precompile, and plan for the query well in advance of its actual execution.

For example, consider the query that selects all rows matching a particular status and priority code from our BUGTRACK database. You can now precompile the query as a prepared statement as:

```
PreparedStatement ps = dbCon.prepareStatement("SELECT b.bug_id, b.summary,
    s.description, p.description, b.report_date FROM bugs b, status s, priority p WHERE
    s.stat_cd=? AND p.prior_cd=?");
```

Once you create the prepared statement as previously shown, the IN parameters, indicated by '?', have to be filled by in by the appropriate setXXX methods (shown in Listing 2-4), before the query can be executed.

By setting in the IN parameters as:

```
ps.setInt(1,3);
ps.setInt(1,1);
```

and executing the query with:

```
ResultSet rs = ps.executeQuery();
```

retrieves the following result set from the database:

BUG_ID	SUMMARY	STATUS. DESCRIPTION	PRIORITY. DESCRIPTION	REPORT_DATE
1003	RMI does not work with MSIE	Unassigned	Medium	1998-08-11

Once you have bound the IN parameters with data, you needn't rebind them for subsequent statements unless their value changes. This is especially useful if you have to deal with a large number of IN parameters because, now, you have to call the appropriate set() method to rebind only those that have changed. Do note, if your SQL statement contains any DML operations like an INSERT or UPDATE, you have to invoke the executeUpdate() method.

Listing 2-4: The PreparedStatement Interface

```
public interface PreparedStatement {
    public abstract ResultSet executeQuery() throws SQLException
    public abstract int executeUpdate() throws SQLException;
    public abstract void setNull(int parameterIndex, int sqlType) throws SQLException;
    public abstract void setBoolean(int parameterIndex, boolean x) throws SQLException;
    public abstract void setByte(int parameterIndex, byte x) throws SQLException;
    public abstract void setShort(int parameterIndex, short x) throws SQLException;
    public abstract void setInt(int parameterIndex, int x) throws SQLException;
    public abstract void setLong(int parameterIndex, long x) throws SQLException;
    public abstract void setFloat(int parameterIndex, float x) throws SQLException;
    public abstract void setDouble(int parameterIndex, double x) throws SQLException;
    public abstract void setBigDecimal(int parameterIndex, BigDecimal x) throws
        SQLException;
    public abstract void setString(int parameterIndex, String x) throws SQLException;
    public abstract void setBytes(int parameterIndex, byte x[]) throws SQLException;
    public abstract void setDate(int parameterIndex, Date x) throws SQLException;
    public abstract void setTime(int parameterIndex, Time x) throws SQLException;
    public abstract void setTimestamp(int parameterIndex, Timestamp x) throws
        SQLException;
    public abstract void setAsciiStream(int parameterIndex, InputStream x, int length)
        throws SQLException;
    public abstract void setUnicodeStream(int parameterIndex, InputStream x, int
        length) throws SQLException;
    public abstract void setBinaryStream(int parameterIndex, InputStream x, int length)
        throws SQLException;
    public abstract void clearParameters() throws SQLException;
    public abstract void setObject(int parameterIndex, Object x, int targetSqlType, int
        scale) throws SQLException;
    public abstract void setObject(int parameterIndex, Object x, int targetSqlType)
        throws SQLException;
    public abstract void setObject(int parameterIndex, Object x) throws SQLException;
    public abstract boolean execute() throws SQLException;
}
```

Note

JDBC makes no guarantees that the database engine will take advantage of the prepared statements and will not recompile queries when they are executed. You should consult your database reference guide and determine whether it supports precompiled SQL statements.

Calling Stored Procedures

Stored procedures are precompiled SQL program routines kept in the database itself, which can be called from external client applications. Using stored procedures is a clean way of partitioning your application and they are a natural fit to any N-tier computing strategy. Managing the security environment is usually a big concern for any enterprise application. Because your business logic is now stored and executed within the database, stored procedures allow a fine degree of control over their access.

Using stored procedures is better than using prepared statements. Stored procedures are not only faster, they can also be managed more easily. Modifying and optimizing your business logic within your database environment (by increasing caching limits, memory, and so forth) is far easier than finding ways to fine-tune at the middle layer.

You can call stored procedures from JDBC by using the `CallableStatement` object. For example, assume "LISTBUGS" is a stored procedure that accepts a status and priority code, and it returned a result set of the matching rows. LISTBUGS can be invoked as follows:

```
CallableStatement cs = dbCon.prepareCall("{ call LISTBUGS [(?, ?)] }");
cs.setInt(1,3); //set the IN param value for the status code
cs.setInt(1,1); //set the IN param value for the priority code
ResultSet rs = cs.executeQuery();
while (rs.next()) {
//process rows
}
```

Apart from result sets, stored procedures can also return values in two other ways. They can return a value from the call to the stored procedure itself or pass data back through parameters that are registered as either OUT or INOUT. Processing any returned result set before retrieving the OUT parameters is important. Listing 2-5 shows an extensive list of methods available for working with the `CallableStatement` object.

For example, consider a stored procedure, say, STOCKWATCH, that takes in 3 parameters—the first one for the stock symbol, the second for the day high, and the third for the day low. Assume STOCKWATCH also returns a value reflecting the current trading price of the stock.

We can then call the procedure as follows:

```
CallableStatement cs =dbCon.prepareCall("{? = call STOCKWATCH[(?,?,?)]}");
cs.registerOutParameter(1,java.sql.REAL); //register the ret value as OUT param
cs.registerOutParameter(3,java.sql.REAL); //register day high as OUT
cs.registerOutParameter(4,java.sql.REAL); //register day low as OUT
cs.setString(2,"SUNW"); //set the IN param value for stock symbol
cs.executeQuery();
float current = cs.getFloat(1); //retrieve OUT returned value
float high = cs.getFloat(3); //retrieve OUT param1
float low = cs.getFloat(4); //retrieve OUT param2
```

You can also call a stored procedure, which does not accept any parameters as:

```
CallableStatement cs =dbCon.prepareCall("{call someproc}");
```

Although numerous benefits exist to using stored procedures, some downsides exist, too. Currently, their implementation tends to be highly vendor-specific. If you overuse stored procedures, a danger always exists that you may be locked into using a particular database.

Listing 2-5: The CallableStatement Interface

```
public interface CallableStatement {
    public abstract void registerOutParameter(int parameterIndex, int sqlType)
        throws SQLException;
    public abstract void registerOutParameter(int parameterIndex, int sqlType, int scale)
        throws SQLException;
    public abstract boolean wasNull() throws SQLException;
    public abstract String getString(int parameterIndex) throws SQLException;
    public abstract boolean getBoolean(int parameterIndex) throws SQLException;
    public abstract byte getByte(int parameterIndex) throws SQLException;
    public abstract short getShort(int parameterIndex) throws SQLException;
    public abstract int getInt(int parameterIndex) throws SQLException;
    public abstract long getLong(int parameterIndex) throws SQLException;
    public abstract float getFloat(int parameterIndex) throws SQLException;
    public abstract double getDouble(int parameterIndex) throws SQLException;
    public abstract BigDecimal getBigDecimal(int parameterIndex, int scale)
        throws SQLException;
    public abstract byte[] getBytes(int parameterIndex) throws SQLException;
    public abstract Date getDate(int parameterIndex) throws SQLException;
    public abstract Time getTime(int parameterIndex) throws SQLException;
    public abstract Timestamp getTimestamp(int parameterIndex) throws SQLException;
    public abstract Object getObject(int parameterIndex) throws SQLException;
}
```

SQL Escape Syntax

Sometimes, the developer may have to execute SQL statements that contain SQL escape sequences. In such cases, the JDBC driver translates the escape sequences into database-specific code before it is sent to the database. This kind of processing enables you to keep your escape sequences relatively independent of the target database.

JDBC escape sequences are denoted by a keyword within curly braces and are of the form:

```
{keyword ... parameters ... }
```

From the previous section, you have already seen how the escape sequences can be used for invoking stored procedures. Table 2-5 shows some additional escape sequences supported by JDBC:

Table 2-5: JDBC Escape Sequences

Type	Escape Syntax	Example
Date	{d 'yyyy-mm-dd'}	{d '1998-01-01'}
Time	{t 'hh:mm:ss'}	{t '21:03:45'}
TimeStamp	{ts 'yyyy-mm-dd hh:mm:ss.f}	{ts '1998-12-12 12:00:00:0000}
Special Characters	{escape 'escape char')	SELECT fname, lname FROM cust WHERE lname = 'G\%' {escape '\'}
Functions	{fn functionName(args)}	{fn concat("Java", "Joe")}
Outer Joins	{oj outer-join-statement}	SELECT emp1.name, emp2.name FROM {oj employee emp1 LEFT OUTER JOIN employee emp2 ON emp1.mgr_id = emp2.emp_id}

Metadata

JDBC enables you to access schema information, either on the database as a whole or on a particular query result set. It provides you with two interfaces for the same: the `java.sql.DatabaseMetaData` and `java.sql ResultSetMetaData`. Obtaining information regarding the structure of the database is crucial, especially if you are a tools vendor who is writing, say, a generic data browser, which can be deployed on any platform and can work against any database!

You can easily obtain information regarding your database by first obtaining a `DatabaseMetaData` object from your `Connection` object, as:

```
DatabaseMetaData dmd = myCon.getMetaData();
```

The `DatabaseMetaData` API defines well over 100 methods (the relatively important ones are shown in Listing 2-6) that can be used for obtaining:

- Database and driver information
- Database limitations
- Information on supported database features and properties

For example, the database and driver information can be printed out as follows:

```
System.out.println("Database Name:" + dmd.getDatabaseProductName());
System.out.println("Driver Name:" +dmd.getDriverName());
```

Listing 2-6: The DatabaseMetaData Interface

```
public interface DatabaseMetaData {
    // partial listing of some important methods
    public abstract boolean allProceduresAreCallable() throws SQLException;
    public abstract boolean allTablesAreSelectable() throws SQLException;
    public abstract String getUserName() throws SQLException;
    public abstract boolean isReadOnly() throws SQLException;
    public abstract String getDatabaseProductName() throws SQLException;
    public abstract String getDatabaseProductVersion() throws SQLException;
    public abstract String getDriverName() throws SQLException;
    public abstract String getDriverVersion() throws SQLException;
    public abstract String getSQLKeywords() throws SQLException;
    public abstract String getNumericFunctions() throws SQLException;
    public abstract String getStringFunctions() throws SQLException;
    public abstract String getSystemFunctions() throws SQLException;
    public abstract String getTimeDateFunctions() throws SQLException;
    public abstract String getSearchStringEscape() throws SQLException;
    public abstract boolean supportsGroupBy() throws SQLException;
    public abstract boolean supportsLikeEscapeClause() throws SQLException;
    public abstract boolean supportsMultipleResultSets() throws SQLException;
    public abstract boolean supportsMultipleTransactions() throws SQLException;
    public abstract boolean supportsNonNullableColumns() throws SQLException;
    public abstract boolean supportsCoreSQLGrammar() throws SQLException;
    public abstract boolean supportsExtendedSQLGrammar() throws SQLException;
    public abstract boolean supportsANSI92EntryLevelSQL() throws SQLException;
    public abstract boolean supportsANSI92IntermediateSQL() throws SQLException;
    public abstract boolean supportsANSI92FullSQL() throws SQLException;
    public abstract boolean supportsOuterJoins() throws SQLException;
    public abstract boolean supportsFullOuterJoins() throws SQLException;
    public abstract String getSchemaTerm() throws SQLException;
    public abstract boolean supportsStoredProcedures() throws SQLException;
    public abstract int getMaxConnections() throws SQLException;
    public abstract int getDefaultTransactionIsolation() throws SQLException;
    public abstract boolean supportsTransactions() throws SQLException;
    public abstract boolean supportsTransactionIsolationLevel(int level) throws
        SQLException;
    public abstract ResultSet getProcedures(String catalog, String schemaPattern,
        String procedureNamePattern) throws SQLException;
    public abstract ResultSet getTables(String catalog, String schemaPattern, String
        tableNamePattern, String types[]) throws SQLException;
    public abstract ResultSet getTablePrivileges(String catalog, String schemaPattern,
        String tableNamePattern) throws SQLException;
```

continues

Listing 2-6: continued

```
        public abstract ResultSet getPrimaryKeys(String catalog, String schema, String
            table) throws SQLException;
        public abstract ResultSet getImportedKeys(String catalog, String schema, String
            table) throws SQLException;
    }
```

The ResultSetMetaData interface (shown in Listing 2-7) is used for obtaining metadata on result sets. For instance, you can obtain column information like column names, its type, and so forth, as well as information on the data itself, such as whether the data within a certain column is read-only.

Listing 2-7: The ResultSetMetaData Interface

```
    public interface ResultSetMetaData {
        public abstract int getColumnCount() throws SQLException;
        public abstract boolean isAutoIncrement(int column) throws SQLException;
        public abstract boolean isCaseSensitive(int column) throws SQLException;
        public abstract boolean isSearchable(int column) throws SQLException;
        public abstract boolean isCurrency(int column) throws SQLException;
        public abstract int isNullable(int column) throws SQLException;
        public abstract boolean isSigned(int column) throws SQLException;
        public abstract int getColumnDisplaySize(int column) throws SQLException;
        public abstract String getColumnLabel(int column) throws SQLException;
        public abstract String getColumnName(int column) throws SQLException;
        public abstract String getSchemaName(int column) throws SQLException;
        public abstract int getPrecision(int column) throws SQLException;
        public abstract int getScale(int column) throws SQLException;
        public abstract String getTableName(int column) throws SQLException;
        public abstract String getCatalogName(int column) throws SQLException;
        public abstract int getColumnType(int column) throws SQLException;
        public abstract String getColumnTypeName(int column) throws SQLException;
        public abstract boolean isReadOnly(int column) throws SQLException;
        public abstract boolean isWritable(int column) throws SQLException;
        public abstract boolean isDefinitelyWritable(int column) throws SQLException;
    }
```

Consider the following code that demonstrates some of the ResultSetMetaData methods. Assuming our target database is an ODBC data source, the example program shown in Listing 2-8 prints out the metadata for the BUGS table:

Listing 2-8: Displaying Database Metadata

```
    package cup.chap2.meta;
    import java.sql.*;
    public class MetaTest {
```

Listing 2-8: continued

```
        public static void main(String[] args) {
            try {
                Class.forName("sun.jdbc.odbc.JdbcOdbcDriver");
                String url = "jdbc:odbc:bugtrack";
                Connection con = DriverManager.getConnection(url,"dba","sql");
                Statement stmt = con.createStatement();
                ResultSet rs = stmt.executeQuery("SELECT * from bugs");
                ResultSetMetaData rmd = rs.getMetaData();
                for (int i=1;i<=rmd.getColumnCount();i++) {
                    String colName=rmd.getColumnName(i);
                    String colType=rmd.getColumnTypeName(i);
                    System.out.println(colName+":\t"+colType);
                }
                rs.close();
            } catch (Exception e) {
            System.out.println("Error processing metadata:"+e);
            e.printStackTrace();
            }
        }
    }
```

The real action lies within the code snippet shown in the following. Here, you first obtain the column count and then loop through each column, obtaining its type information:

```
for (int i=1;i<=rmd.getColumnCount();i++) {
    String colName=rmd.getColumnName(i);
    String colType=rmd.getColumnTypeName(i);
    System.out.println(colName+"\t\t"+colType);
}
```

If you were constructing a data browser, you could dynamically create the GUI controls for each table by using the information obtained from `getColumnDisplaySize()`.

The output of Lising 2-8 is

```
bug_id          INT
description     VARCHAR
priority        INT
status          INT
report_date     DATE
```

Transaction Management

A *transaction* is a set of one or more discrete SQL statements that can be treated as a unit and affect some change to the database. By default, the JDBC API performs implicit transaction management by opening a database connection in an autocommit mode and automatically commits each SQL statement execution by treating it as a complete transaction.

But what if you want to incorporate multiple SQL statements within a single transaction? In that case, you need to disable the autocommit feature and issue either a commit() or a rollback() call after the execution of your multiple SQL statements, depending on their outcome. Calling commit() makes permanent any database changes the SQL statement makes. If something goes awry, the changes can be discarded by calling rollback().

For example:

```
Connection myCon = DriverManager.getConnection(someURL);
//turn off the implicit transaction management
myCon.setAutoCommit(false);
Statement s = myCon.createStatement();
try {
    int x = s.executeUpdate(sqlStatementX);
    x = s.executeUpdate(sqlStatementY);
    x = s.executeUpdate(sqlStatementZ);
    //commits all statements executed since previous
    //commit or rollback call
    myCon.commit();
} catch (Exception e) {
    //rollback any database updates
    myCon.rollback();
}
```

As soon as the transaction ends, by default, a new one begins. Further, once a transaction is complete, all the resources associated with the connection—including statements, result sets, and locks—are released and can no longer be assumed valid.

All JDBC-compliant drivers must support transactions. You can easily determine whether your driver supports transaction management by querying the DatabaseMetaData object:

```
DatabaseMetaData dmd = myCon.getMetaData();
boolean supportsTransactions = dmd.supportsTransaction();
```

Transaction Isolation Levels

In a typical enterprise, tens, if not hundreds, of users are concurrently accessing the database. So, how does the database manage to keep the transactions of multiple users from overlapping one another? Consider the scenario shown in Figure 2-5, which demonstrates a classic problem known as "dirty read."

BUG_ID	SUMMARY	PTY	STS	REPORT_DATE
1001	Browser crashes on startup	1	2	1998-07-12
1002	User bookmarks not saved	4	1	1998-08-14
1003	RMI does not work with MSIE	1	3	1998-08-11
1004	Java applets fail under Win 3.1	2	3	1998-08-24
1005	DB connection times out	3	1	1998-08-26

```
SELECT * FROM bugs WHERE bug_id=1003
```

```
UPDATE bugs SET sts=2 WHERE bug_id=1002
UPDATE bugs SET sts=2 WHERE bug_id=1003
UPDATE bugs SET sts=2 WHERE bug_id=1004
```

Figure 2-5: "Dirty reads"

Here we have two users—*X* and *Y*—each executing their own transaction, but operating on the same table. Assuming the transaction of *Y* reads the value before *X* has committed or rolled back, is it still valid? This is an important question to answer, especially if you consider that the modified value read by *Y* will be invalid if *X* rolled back her transaction for some reason.

Well, this is where your database's transaction management features come in handy.

The `java.sql.Connection` class defines five transaction isolation levels:

- TRANSACTION_NONE: Transactions are not supported.
- TRANSACTION_READ_COMMITTED: Dirty reads are prevented; non-repeatable reads and phantom reads can occur.
- TRANSACTION_READ_UNCOMMITTED: Dirty reads, nonrepeatable reads, and phantom reads can occur.
- TRANSACTION_REPEATABLE_READ: Dirty reads and nonrepeatable reads are prevented; phantom reads can occur.
- TRANSACTION_SERIALIZABLE: Dirty reads, nonrepeatable reads, and phantom reads are prevented

The user must specify an appropriate transaction isolation level to indicate what level of care the database should exercise in resolving potential conflicts. For example, you can request the database to allow "dirty reads," by setting the isolation level as:

```
dbCon.setTransactionIsolation(TRANSACTION_READ_UNCOMMITTED);
```

Now, "dirty reads" are enabled for the rest of the connection session. You can also change the isolation level for only a single transaction by setting it just before the transaction begins and then resetting it once the transaction terminates. Changing the transaction isolation level in the midst of a transaction is not recommended, as this will immediately commit all the SQL statements executed up to that point.

Choosing the highest level of isolation for ensuring maximum data integrity may be tempting. But do remember, increasing isolation levels may make for more sluggish database interaction due to the extra overhead imposed by the locking mechanism. The developer must balance the need for performance with the need for data consistency before making a decision regarding the isolation level to use. The actual isolation level that can actually be supported depends on the capabilities of the underlying DBMS.

Implementing Connection Pools

Repeatedly opening and closing database connections each time a SQL statement needs to be executed can be expensive. Instead, a much more efficient solution is to cache the database connections and reuse them across successive transactions. Although JDBC 2.0 provides connection-caching features, if you are using a JDBC 1.0 compliant driver, you need to provide your own mechanism at the application level.

Listing 2-9 shows a simple implementation of a database connection pool.

Listing 2-9: Implementing a Simple Database Connection Pool

```
package cup.chap2.bugtrack;
import java.sql.*;
import java.util.Stack;
public class DBConnectionPool {
    private Stack connectionPool;
/**
    Construct a DB connection pool
**/
    private int num=0;
    public DBConnectionPool(String url, String driver,
        String user, String passwd, int numCon, boolean logging) {
        try {
            Class.forName(driver);
            connectionPool = new Stack();
            num = numCon;
            if (logging)
                DriverManager.setLogStream(System.out);
```

Listing 2-9: continued

```
            for (int i=0; i<numCon; i++) {
                connectionPool.push(DriverManager.getConnection(url, user,passwd));
            }
        } catch (SQLException e) {
            System.out.println("Error"+e);
        } catch (ClassNotFoundException e) {
            System.out.println(driver +" not found:"+e);
        }
    }
/**
    getConnection() obtains a database connection from the
    connection pool
**/
    public synchronized Connection getConnection() {
        try {
            if (connectionPool.empty()) return null;
            else return (Connection) connectionPool.pop();
        } catch (Exception e) {
            System.out.println("Error obtaining connection:"+e);
            e.printStackTrace();
        }
    }
/**
    freeConnection() releases a database connection back to the
    pool after use
**/
    public synchronized void freeConnection(Connection c) {
        connectionPool.push(c);
    }
/**
    close all cached database connections on garbage collection
**/
    public void finalize() {
        while (!connectionPool.empty()) {
                Connection c = (Connection) connectionPool.pop();
                c.close();
            }
    }
}
```

A Three-Tier Solution: Integrating RMI with JDBC

RMI servers can be an excellent middleware for the integration of database servers, especially in a predominantly Java-based computing environment. Now we'll take a closer look at a three-tier solution integrating RMI servers with databases. This section assumes the reader is familiar with the basics of RMI computing. If not, please read Chapter 6 on RMI computing first before continuing with this section.

Any RMI server has to implement a remote interface, which serves to advertise the remote functionality to the client. Listing 2-10 shows an example BugTrackInterface, which offers clients access to a single remote method bugtrack().

Listing 2-10: The BugTrackInterface Remote Interface

```
package cup.chap2.bugtrack;
import java.util.Vector;
import java.rmi.*;
public interface BugTrackInterface extends java.rmi.Remote {
    public Vector bugtrack(Vector queryData) throws RemoteException;
}
```

RMI servers can be easily integrated with remote database servers, as shown in Figure 2-6. Typically, multiple database connections are cached by maintaining a connection pool. The remote server then goes about obtaining a connection from the pool before executing any SQL statement and releases it back to the pool after use. Using an RMI model, deploying thin database clients is possible, as much of the real processing can be easily deployed at the middle tier. In our example server, shown in Listing 2-11, note the query itself is dynamically created based on the selected options passed from the client.

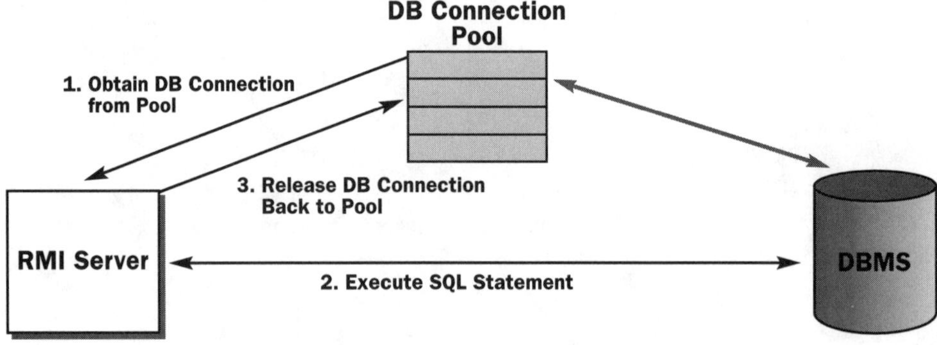

Figure 2-6: Integrating RMI servers with databases

Listing 2-11: The BugTrackServer RMI Server

```
package cup.chap2.bugtrack;
import java.rmi.*;
import java.rmi.registry.LocateRegistry;
import java.rmi.server.UnicastRemoteObject;
import java.util.*;
import java.sql.*;
public class BugTrackServer extends UnicastRemoteObject implements BugTrackInterface {
    private String name ;
    private Connection con ;
    DBConnectionPool myPool;

    public BugTrackServer (String serverName) throws RemoteException {
        super();
        name=serverName;
        myPool = new DBConnectionPool("jdbc:odbc:bugdb1",
            "sun.jdbc.odbc.JdbcOdbcDriver","dba","sql",5,false);
    }
/**
    bugtrack() dynamically creates and executes a query and
    returns the results back to the applet
**/
    public Vector bugtrack(Vector queryData) throws RemoteException {

        // obtain a connection from the pool
        Connection c = (Connection) myPool.getConnection();
        int statCd = ((Integer)queryData.elementAt(0)).intValue();
        int priorCd = ((Integer)queryData.elementAt(1)).intValue();
        int dateCd = ((Integer)queryData.elementAt(2)).intValue();
        String query="SELECT bug_id, summary, priority.description, status.description,
            report_date from bugs, status, priority where bugs.sts=status.stat_cd and
            bugs.pty=priority.prior_cd";
        if (statCd !=0 )query = query + " and status.stat_cd="+statCd;

        if (priorCd !=0 ) query = query + " and priority.prior_cd="+priorCd;
        if (dateCd !=0 ) {
            String from = (String)queryData.elementAt(3);
            String to = (String)queryData.elementAt(4);
            query = query + " and (bugs.report_date >= {d '"+from+"'} and
                bugs.report_date <= {d '"+to+"'} )";
        }
        ResultSet rs=null;
```

continues

Listing 2-11: continued

```
            Vector test =new Vector();
            Statement stmt=null;
            try {

                stmt = c.createStatement();
                rs = stmt.executeQuery(query);

                test.addElement(new Integer(0));
                while (rs.next()) {
                    String result = rs.getString(1)+" | "+rs.getString(2)+" | "+rs.getString(3)+"
                        | "+rs.getString(4)+" | "+(rs.getDate(5)).toString();
                    test.addElement(result.trim());
                }
            } catch (Exception e) {
                test.addElement(new Integer(1));
                test.addElement(e);
                System.out.println("Error:"+e);
            } finally {
                // release the connection back to the pool
                myPool.freeConnection(c);
            }
            return test;
        }
    /**
        main() creates a registry, and binds an instance of the
        remote object into the registry
    **/
        public static void main(String[] args) {
            System.setSecurityManager(new RMISecurityManager());
            try {
                System.out.println("BugTrackServer.main: creating registry");
                LocateRegistry.createRegistry(1099);
                System.out.println("BugTrackServer.main: creating server");
                BugTrackServer myBugTrackServer=new BugTrackServer("BugTrackServer");
                Naming.rebind("/BugTrackServer", myBugTrackServer);
                System.out.println("BugTrackServer bound in registry");
            }
            catch (Exception e) {
                System.out.println("Exception on bind: "+e);
            }
        }
    }
```

Listing 2-12 shows the client applet for our RMI server and enables a user to search the BUGS database on a variety of criteria like priority, status, and date ranges. Figure 2-7 shows the client applet after having conducted a successful search.

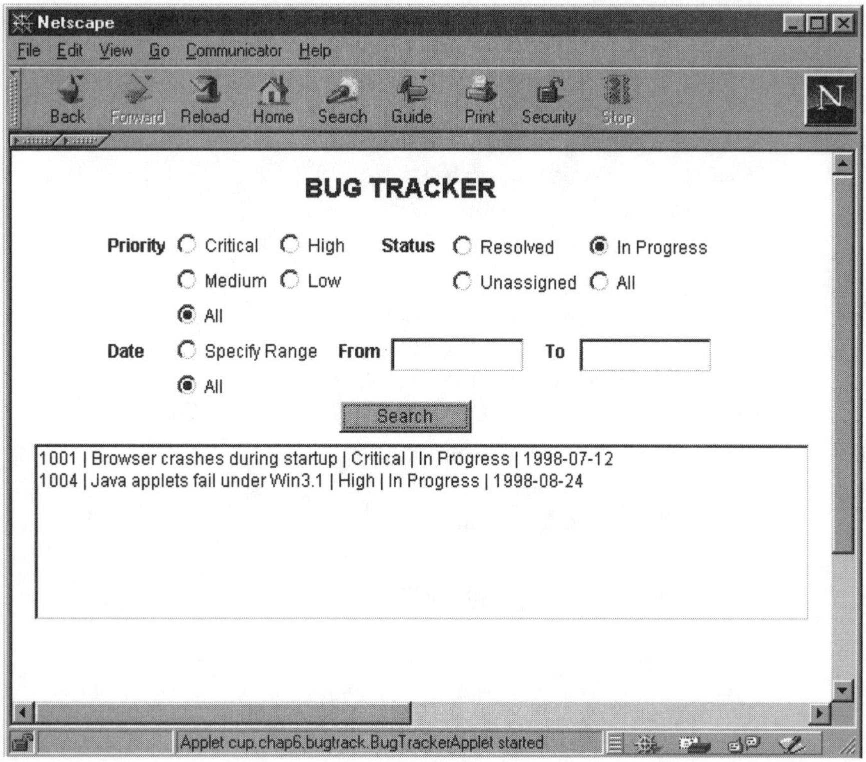

Figure 2-7: The BugTracker applet

Listing 2-12: The BugTrackerApplet RMI Client Applet

```
package cup.chap2.bugtrack;
import java.awt.*;
import java.applet.*;
import java.util.Vector;
import java.rmi.*;
import java.sql.*;
public class BugTrackerApplet extends Applet {
/**
    init() sets the layout for the applet, and
    creates a GUI. Don't worry too much about the
    GUI code...much of it was generated using an
    IDE. (Which is what you will be most likely
    be doing anyway!
**/
```

continues

Listing 2-12: continued

```
public void init() {
    setLayout(null);
    setSize(800,400);
    title = new java.awt.Label("BUG TRACKER");
    title.setBounds(198,6,136,24);
    title.setFont(new Font("SansSerif", Font.BOLD, 18));
    add(title);
    priorityLabel = new java.awt.Label("Priority");
    priorityLabel.setBounds(60,48,40,17);
    priorityLabel.setFont(new Font("Dialog", Font.BOLD, 12));
    add(priorityLabel);
    statusLabel = new java.awt.Label("Status");
    statusLabel.setBounds(252,48,40,17);
    statusLabel.setFont(new Font("Dialog", Font.BOLD, 12));
    add(statusLabel);
    gpPriority = new CheckboxGroup();
    rbCritical = new Checkbox ("Critical", gpPriority, false);
    rbCritical.setBounds(108,48,64,17);
    add(rbCritical);
    rbHigh = new Checkbox ("High", gpPriority, false);
    rbHigh.setBounds(180,48,48,17);
    add(rbHigh);
    rbMedium = new Checkbox ("Medium", gpPriority, false);
    rbMedium.setBounds(108,72,64,17);
    add(rbMedium);
    rbLow = new Checkbox ("Low", gpPriority, false);
    rbLow.setBounds(180,72,48,17);
    add(rbLow);
    gpStatus = new CheckboxGroup();
    rbComplete = new Checkbox ("Resolved", gpStatus, false);
    rbComplete.setBounds(300,48,88,19);
    add(rbComplete);
    rbInProgress = new Checkbox ("In Progress", gpStatus, false);
    rbInProgress.setBounds(396,48,88,19);
    add(rbInProgress);
    rbUnassigned = new Checkbox ("Unassigned", gpStatus, false);
    rbUnassigned.setBounds(300,72,88,19);
    add(rbUnassigned);
    rbAllPriority = new Checkbox ("All", gpPriority, true);
    rbAllPriority.setBounds(108,96,40,17);
    add(rbAllPriority);
    rbAllStatus = new Checkbox ("All", gpStatus, true);
```

Listing 2-12: continued

```
rbAllStatus.setBounds(396,72,40,19);
add(rbAllStatus);
dateLabel = new java.awt.Label("Date");
dateLabel.setBounds(60,120,32,17);
dateLabel.setFont(new Font("Dialog", Font.BOLD, 12));
add(dateLabel);
fromDate = new java.awt.TextField();
fromDate.setBounds(258,120,93,23);
add(fromDate);
toDate = new java.awt.TextField();
toDate.setBounds(390,120,93,23);
add(toDate);
dateLabel2 = new java.awt.Label("To");
dateLabel2.setBounds(366,120,24,17);
dateLabel2.setFont(new Font("Dialog", Font.BOLD, 12));
add(dateLabel2);
gpDate = new CheckboxGroup();
rbRange = new Checkbox ("Specify Range", gpDate, false);
rbRange.setBounds(108,120,104,17);
add(rbRange);
dateLabel3 = new java.awt.Label("From");
dateLabel3.setBounds(222,120,32,17);
dateLabel3.setFont(new Font("Dialog", Font.BOLD, 12));
add(dateLabel3);
rbAllDates = new Checkbox ("All", gpDate, true);
rbAllDates.setBounds(108,144,40,17);
add(rbAllDates);
buttonSearch = new java.awt.Button();
buttonSearch.setLabel("Search");
buttonSearch.setBounds(222,162,92,22);
buttonSearch.setBackground(new Color(12632256));
add(buttonSearch);
results = new java.awt.List(4);
add(results);
results.setBounds(8,192,544,120);

// register listeners
UserAction lUserAction = new UserAction();
buttonSearch.addActionListener(lUserAction);
SymItem lSymItem = new SymItem();
rbRange.addItemListener(lSymItem);
rbAllDates.addItemListener(lSymItem);
```

continues

Listing 2-12: continued

```
        results.addActionListener(lUserAction);
        try {
            // get hold of the remote object's stub
            server = (BugTrackInterface)
            Naming.lookup("rmi://"+getCodeBase().getHost()+"/BugTrackServer");
            System.out.println("rmi://"+getCodeBase().getHost()+"/BugTrackServer");
        } catch (Exception e) {
            System.out.println("Could not reach BugTrackServer");
        }

    }

    //controls
    Label title;
    Label priorityLabel;
    Label statusLabel;
    Checkbox  rbCritical;
    CheckboxGroup gpPriority;
    Checkbox  rbHigh;
    Checkbox  rbMedium;
    Checkbox  rbLow;
    Checkbox  rbComplete;
    CheckboxGroup gpStatus;
    Checkbox  rbInProgress;
    Checkbox  rbUnassigned;
    Checkbox  rbAllPriority;
    Checkbox  rbAllStatus;
    Label dateLabel;
    TextField fromDate;
    TextField toDate;
    Label dateLabel2;
    Checkbox  rbRange;
    CheckboxGroup gpDate;
    Label dateLabel3;
    Checkbox  rbAllDates;
    Button buttonSearch;
    java.awt.List results;
    BugTrackInterface server;
    class UserAction implements java.awt.event.ActionListener {
        public void actionPerformed(java.awt.event.ActionEvent e) {
            Object object = e.getSource();
            if (object == buttonSearch)
```

Listing 2-12: continued

```
                buttonSearch_ActionPerformed(e);
            }
        }
    /**
        Gather the user query params, perform the database lookup
        via the remote object, and append results to the list box
    **/
        void buttonSearch_ActionPerformed(java.awt.event.ActionEvent e) {
            results.clear();
            String status = gpStatus.getCurrent().getLabel();
            String priority = gpPriority.getCurrent().getLabel();
            String date = gpDate.getCurrent().getLabel();

            int statCd, priorCd;

            if (status.equals("Resolved")) statCd=3;
            else if (status.equals("In Progress")) statCd=2;
            else if (status.equals("Unassigned")) statCd=1;
            else statCd=0;
            if (priority.equals("Critical")) priorCd=1;
            else if (priority.equals("High")) priorCd=2;
            else if (priority.equals("Medium")) priorCd=3;
            else if (priority.equals("Low")) priorCd=4;
            else priorCd=0;
            Vector data = new Vector();
            data.addElement(new Integer(statCd));
            data.addElement(new Integer(priorCd));
            int dateCd=0;

            if (date.equals("Specify Range")) {
                dateCd=1;
                data.addElement(new Integer(dateCd));
                data.addElement(fromDate.getText());
                data.addElement(toDate.getText());
            } else data.addElement(new Integer(dateCd));
            try {
                Vector res = server.bugtrack(data);
                int errcode = ((Integer)res.elementAt(0)).intValue();
                if (errcode == 0 ) { //all ok
                for (int i=1; i< res.size();i++) {
                    String arow = (String) res.elementAt(i);
                    results.addItem(arow);
```

continues

Listing 2-12: continued

```
                }
            } else {
                Exception ex = (Exception) res.elementAt(1);
                results.addItem(ex.toString());
            }
        } catch (Exception e) {
            System.out.println("Error:"+e);
        }
    }
    class SymItem implements java.awt.event.ItemListener {
        public void itemStateChanged(java.awt.event.ItemEvent e) {
            Object object = e.getSource();
            if (object == rbRange)
                rbRange_ItemStateChanged(e);
            else if (object == rbAllDates)
                rbAllDates_ItemStateChanged(e);
        }
    }
    void rbRange_ItemStateChanged(java.awt.event.ItemEvent e) {
        fromDate.setText("yyyy-mm-dd");
        toDate.setText("yyyy-mm-dd");
    }
    void rbAllDates_ItemStateChanged(java.awt.event.ItemEvent e) {
        fromDate.setText("");
        toDate.setText("");
    }
}
```

Note

If you are running RMI under Java 2, you must use a security policy file to provide the RMI server with the necessary privileges. Refer to Chapter 6 for more information on creating a security policy file. Once a policy file has been created, you need to denote it when starting up the RMI server and rmiregistry as follows:

```
rmiregistry -J-Djava.security.policy=\somedir\policy
java -Djava.security.policy=\somedir\policy
    -Djava.rmi.server.codebase=somecodebase RMIserver
```

JDBC 2.0

Java 2 includes some advanced features for database integration in the form of the JDBC 2.0 API. Simply having an updated JDBC API is not enough, however. Of equal importance is for the developer to use an appropriate JDBC 2.0-compatible database driver. Considering the leeway driver vendors have in selectively implementing some of the newer features, the task of driver selection is now more important than ever.

JDBC 2.0 provides numerous upgrades to the existing API. The most significant changes relate to the way result sets and their associated cursors are handled. Now, it is possible to traverse a cursor in both directions, instead of only in the forward direction as with JDBC 1.0. You can also transparently update, delete, and insert into the database by simply making them to a result set. Other useful additions include the ability to carry out batch updates and support for SQL3 datatypes. The JDBC 2.0 API also specifies a standard extension package, `javax.sql`, which provides support for distributed transactions, a naming and directory interface (JNDI), connection pooling, and JavaBeans-based rowsets.

Implementing scrollable cursors

JDBC 1.0 enabled you to scroll the cursor associated with a result set in only the forward direction. If, for whatever reason, you need to access data your cursor had previously passed, you need to execute the query all over again. This is not efficient, especially if you are working with a large amount of data. With JDBC 2.0, you can now scroll cursors in either direction. Bidirectional scrolling is a prerequisite for building sophisticated data-aware JavaBeans components without adding the complexity of middleware specifically for data caching.

To enable this feature, you first have to create a scrollable `ResultSet` object as follows:

```
Statement stmt= dbCon.createStatement(ResultSet.TYPE_SCROLL_SENSITIVE,
     ResultSet.CONCUR_UPDATABLE);
```

The first argument to `createStatement()` denotes the type of result set produced and the second argument is used to indicate whether the result set is read-only or can be updated.

Three types of `ResultSet` objects can exist under JDBC 2.0:

- `TYPE_FORWARD_ONLY`: Creates a nonscrollable result set and the cursor can move only in the forward direction.
- `TYPE_SCROLL_SENSITIVE`: Result set's cursor is scrollable. Changes made to the open result set are transparently reflected in the database.
- `TYPE_SCROLL_INSENSITIVE`: Result set's cursor is scrollable. Changes made to the open result set are not reflected in the database until the result set is closed.

Result set behavior can be modified by two constants:

- CONCUR_READ_ONLY: Result set is read-only and cannot be updated.
- CONCUR_UPDATABLE: Result set can be modified. The database may also get concurrently updated with the changes depending on the type of result set used.

Now, let's perform a query against the example BUGTRACK database defined earlier:

```
ResultSet res = stmt.executeQuery("SELECT bug_id, summary, pty, sts FROM bugs");
```

You can move forward the cursor through the result set as usual:

```
while (res.next()) {
    //process each row
    int bugid = res.getInt("bug_id");
    String summary = res.getString("summary");
    int pty = res.getInt("pty");
    int sts = res.getInt("sts");
    System.out.println(bugid+"\t"+summary+"\t"+pty+"\t"+sts);
}
```

The output shows all the rows within the result set:

1001	Browser crashes on startup	1	2
1002	User bookmarks not saved	4	1
1003	RMI does not work with MSIE	1	3
1004	Java applets fail under Win 3.1	2	3
1005	DB connection times out	3	1

Because the result set was set up as scrollable, the cursor can also be moved backward. Note: Before you begin scrolling backward, the cursor should be placed after the last row in the result set.

```
res.afterLast(); //places cursor after last row
while (res.next()) {
    //process each row
    int bugid = res.getInt("bug_id");
    String summary = res.getString("summary");
    int pty = res.getInt("pty");
    int sts = res.getInt("sts");
System.out.println(bugid+"\t"+summary+"\t"+pty+"\t"+sts);
}
```

As expected, the output now shows the rows in reverse order:

1005	DB connection times out	3	1
1004	Java applets fail under Win 3.1	2	3
1003	RMI does not work with MSIE	1	3
1002	User bookmarks not saved	4	1
1001	Browser crashes on startup	1	2

Now, moving the cursor to nearly any desired row is easy. For instance, methods last(), afterLast(), first(), and beforeFirst() serve to move the cursor to the indicated row. You can also use the method absolute() and supply a row number to which you want the cursor to move. If the row number is positive, the cursor moves the given number from the start. If the row number is negative, the cursor moves the given number from the end.

For instance, using the previous result set as example,

```
res.absolute(2);
```

moves the cursor to the row:

1004	Java applets fail under Win 3.1	2	3

```
res.absolute(-2) ;
```

moves the cursor to the row:

1002	User bookmarks not saved	4	1

You can always verify on which row your cursor is located by using the methods isFirst(), isLast(), isBeforeFirst(), and isAfterLast(). These methods always return a boolean type. To obtain the exact row number, you can use the getRow() method:

```
res.absolute(2);
int row = res.getRow(); //returns 2
```

Updating result sets

Using JDBC 2.0, you can make database changes simply by updating rows within a result set, rather than executing a separate SQL statement for the same. The changes allowed include inserting new rows, deleting existing rows, and modifying column values. A result set can be updated only if it was created using the CONCUR_UPDATABLE constant.

Let's revisit our earlier query:

```
ResultSet res = stmt.executeQuery("SELECT bug_id, summary, pty, sts FROM bugs");
```

The result set now contains:

BUG_ID	SUMMARY	PTY	STS
1001	Browser crashes on startup	1	2
1002	User bookmarks not saved	4	1
1003	RMI does not work with MSIE	1	3
1004	Java applets fail under Win 3.1	2	3
1005	DB connection times out	3	1

Using JDBC 1.0, if you want to modify the priority of BUG_ID 1001 from 1 to 2, you would do it by executing a separate SQL statement:

```
stmt.executeUpdate("UPDATE bugs SET PTY=2, SET STS=3 WHERE bug_id = 1001");
```

Performing updates is much simpler under JDBC 2.0. First position the cursor on the row that needs to be updated and then call the appropriate `updateXXX()` method, depending on the datatype of the column whose value needs to be changed:

```
res.first();
res.updateInt("pty",2);
res.updateInt("sts",3);
res.updateRow();
```

The method `updateRow()` commits any changes made to the row to the database. Although you can cancel any changes to the row by invoking `cancelRowUpdates()`, this is effective only if called prior to committing the changes to the database.

Inserting new rows into tables is much easier using JDBC 2.0 than the older version. Consider the following JDBC 1.0 code snippet to insert a new row into the BUGS table:

```
stmt.executeUpdate("INSERT INTO bugs VALUES (1006, "Servlet crashes intermittently",
    2, 3,{d '1998-01-01'})");
```

You can insert new rows into the result set as well as the database in one swoop. Once the result set is obtained, you have to move the cursor to a buffer "insert row," which is available along with every `ResultSet` object, by calling `moveToInsertRow()`. The insert row is then updated by adding a value to each column as before. Once all the values have been updated, the changes are committed to both the result set and the database by calling `insertRow()`. Listing 2-13 shows the new functionality available for `ResultSet` processing under JDBC 2.0.

The following code segment demonstrates how we can add a new row to the BUGS table:

```
res.moveToInsertRow();
res.updateInt("bug_id",1006);
res.updateString("summary","Servlet crashes intermittently");
res.updateInt("pty",2);
res.updateInt("sts",3);
```

```
Date d = java.sql.Date.valueOf("1998-01-01");
res.updateDate("report_date",d);
res.insertRow();
```

If you fail to update a particular column explicitly, it will be initialized with a NULL. If the column cannot store NULL values, then a SQLException is thrown.

Deleting rows in JDBC 2.0 is easy. All you have to do is position the cursor on the row you want to delete and then call the deleteRow() method:

```
res.first(); //delete the first row from
res.deleteRow();//the result set and the database
```

Listing 2-13: JDBC 2.0 Additions to the ResultSet Interface

```
public interface ResultSet {
    //new JDBC 2.0 methods
    public Reader getCharacterStream(int columnIndex) throws SQLException;
    public Reader getCharacterStream(String columnName) throws SQLException;
    public BigDecimal getBigDecimal(int columnIndex) throws SQLException;
    public BigDecimal getBigDecimal(String columnName) throws SQLException;
    public boolean isBeforeFirst() throws SQLException;
    public boolean isAfterLast() throws SQLException;
    public boolean isFirst() throws SQLException;
    public boolean isLast() throws SQLException;
    public void beforeFirst() throws SQLException;
    public void afterLast() throws SQLException;
    public boolean first() throws SQLException;
    public boolean last() throws SQLException;
    public int getRow() throws SQLException;
    public boolean absolute(int row) throws SQLException;
    public boolean relative(int rows) throws SQLException;
    public boolean previous() throws SQLException;
    public void setFetchDirection(int direction) throws SQLException;
    public int getFetchDirection() throws SQLException;
    public void setFetchSize(int rows) throws SQLException;
    public int getFetchSize() throws SQLException;
    public int getType() throws SQLException;
    public int getConcurrency() throws SQLException;
    public boolean rowUpdated() throws SQLException;
    public boolean rowInserted() throws SQLException;
    public boolean rowDeleted() throws SQLException;
    public void updateNull(int columnIndex) throws SQLException;
    public void updateBoolean(int columnIndex, boolean x) throws SQLException;
    public void updateByte(int columnIndex, byte x) throws SQLException;
    public void updateShort(int columnIndex, short x) throws SQLException;
```

continues

Listing 2-13: continued

```
public void updateInt(int columnIndex, int x) throws SQLException;
public void updateLong(int columnIndex, long x) throws SQLException;
public void updateFloat(int columnIndex, float x) throws SQLException;
public void updateDouble(int columnIndex, double x) throws SQLException;
public void updateBigDecimal(int columnIndex, BigDecimal x) throws SQLException;
public void updateString(int columnIndex, String x) throws SQLException;
public void updateBytes(int columnIndex, byte[] x) throws SQLException;
public void updateDate(int columnIndex, Date x) throws SQLException;
public void updateTime(int columnIndex, Time x) throws SQLException;
public void updateTimestamp(int columnIndex, Timestamp x) throws SQLException;
public void updateAsciiStream(int columnIndex, InputStream x, int length)
   throws SQLException;
public void updateBinaryStream(int columnIndex, InputStream x, int length)
   throws SQLException;
public void updateCharacterStream(int columnIndex, Reader x, int length)
   throws SQLException;
public void updateObject(int columnIndex, Object x, int scale) throws SQLException;
public void updateObject(int columnIndex, Object x) throws SQLException;
public void updateNull(String columnName) throws SQLException;
public void updateBoolean(String columnName, boolean x) throws SQLException;
public void updateByte(String columnName, byte x) throws SQLException;
public void updateShort(String columnName, short x) throws SQLException;
public void updateInt(String columnName, int x) throws SQLException;
public void updateLong(String columnName, long x) throws SQLException;
public void updateFloat(String columnName, float x) throws SQLException;
public void updateDouble(String columnName, double x) throws SQLException;
public void updateBigDecimal(String columnName, BigDecimal x) throws SQLException;
public void updateString(String columnName, String x) throws SQLException;
public void updateBytes(String columnName, byte[] x) throws SQLException;
public void updateDate(String columnName, Date x) throws SQLException;
public void updateTime(String columnName, Time x) throws SQLException;
public void updateTimestamp(String columnName, Timestamp x) throws SQLException;
public void updateAsciiStream(String columnName, InputStream x, int length)
   throws SQLException;
public void updateBinaryStream(String columnName, InputStream x, int length)
   throws SQLException;
public void updateCharacterStream(String columnName, Reader reader, int length)
   throws SQLException;
public void updateObject(String columnName, Object x, int scale) throws
   SQLException;
public void updateObject(String columnName, Object x) throws SQLException;
public void insertRow()  throws SQLException;
```

Listing 2-13: continued

```
    public void updateRow() throws SQLException;
    public void deleteRow() throws SQLException;
    public void refreshRow() throws SQLException;
    public void cancelRowUpdates() throws SQLException;
    public void moveToInsertRow() throws SQLException;
    public void moveToCurrentRow() throws SQLException;
    public Statement getStatement() throws SQLException;
    public Object getObject(int i, Map map) throws SQLException;
    public Ref getRef(int i) throws SQLException;
    public Blob getBlob(int i) throws SQLException;
    public Clob getClob(int i) throws SQLException;
    public Array getArray(int i) throws SQLException;
    public Object getObject(String colName, Map map) throws SQLException;
    public Ref getRef(String colName) throws SQLException;
    public Blob getBlob(String colName) throws SQLException;
    public Clob getClob(String colName) throws SQLException;
    public Array getArray(String colName) throws SQLException;
    public Date getDate(int columnIndex, Calendar cal) throws SQLException;
    public Date getDate(String columnName, Calendar cal) throws SQLException;
    public Time getTime(int columnIndex, Calendar cal) throws SQLException;
    public Time getTime(String columnName, Calendar cal) throws SQLException;
    public Timestamp getTimestamp(int columnIndex, Calendar cal) throws SQLException;
    public Timestamp getTimestamp(String columnName, Calendar cal) throws
       SQLException;
}
```

Making batch updates

One of the more advanced features of JDBC 2.0 is the capability to submit multiple update statements to the database for processing as a single unit. This batch updating can be significantly more efficient compared to JDBC 1.0, where each update statement has to be executed separately.

Consider the following code segment demonstrating a batch update:

```
try {
    dbCon.setAutoCommit(false);
    Statement stmt= dbCon.createStatement();
    stmt.addBatch("INSERT INTO bugs "+
    "VALUES (1007, 'Server stack overflow', 1,2,{d '1999-01-01'})");
    stmt.addBatch("INSERT INTO bugs "+
    "VALUES (1008,'Cannot load DLL', 3,1,{d '1999-01-01'})");
    stmt.addBatch("INSERT INTO bugs "+
    "VALUES (1009,'Applet locks up',2,2,{d '1999-01-01'})");
```

```
        int[] updCnt = stmt.executeBatch();
        dbCon.commit();
    } catch (BatchUpdateException be) {
        //handle batch update exception
        int[] counts = be.getUpdateCounts();
        for (int i=0; I< counts.length; i++) {
          System.out.println("Statement["+i+"] :"+counts[i]);
        }
        dbCon.rollback();
    }
    catch (SQLException e) {
        //handle SQL exception
        dbCon.rollback();
    }
```

Before carrying out a batch update, disabling the auto-commit mode by calling `setAutoCommit(false)` is important. This way, you can rollback the batch transaction if one of the updates fail. When the `Statement` object is created, it is automatically associated a "command list," which is initially empty. We then add our SQL update statements to this command list, by making successive calls to the `addBatch()` method. On calling `executeBatch()`, the entire command list is sent over to the database and then executed in the order they were added to the list. If all the commands in the list are executed successfully, their corresponding update counts are returned as an array of integers. Please note, you always have to clear the existing batch by calling `clearBatch()` before creating a new one.

If any of the updates fail to execute within the database, a `BatchUpdateException` is thrown in response to it. In case a problem occurs in returning the update counts of each SQL statement, a `SQLException` is thrown to indicate the error.

Handling SQL3 datatypes

The next version of the ANSI/ISO SQL standard defines some new datatypes, commonly referred to as the *SQL3 types.* The following are the primary SQL3 types:

- STRUCT: This is the default mapping for any SQL structured type and is manifest by the `java.sql.Struct` type.
- REF: Serves as a reference to SQL data within the database. Can be passed as a parameter to a SQL statement. Mapped to the `java.sql.Ref` type.
- BLOB: Holds binary large objects. Mapped to the `java.sql.Blob` type.
- CLOB: Contains character large objects. Mapped to the `java.sql.Clob` type.
- ARRAY: Can store values of a specified type. Mapped to the `java.sql.Array` type.

You can retrieve, store, and update SQL3 types using the corresponding `getXXX()`, `setXXX()`, and `updateXXX()` methods defined in `ResultSet` interface, shown in Listing 2-1.

JDBC 2.0 standard extensions

The JDBC standard extensions will be available as part of the `javax.sql` package and provide support for some advanced features, including:

Rowsets: Rowsets essentially encapsulate a set of rows from some data source and can be created at design time using a GUI builder. By providing support for rowsets, Sun now allows JavaBeans components to make use of the JDBC API. Rowsets are fully serializable and can be persisted.

Java Naming and Directory Interface (JNDI): Using JNDI, database instances can register themselves into global directory service by using a logical name. Consequently, a JDBC application making use of JNDI can now specify this logical name to identify database instances instead of having to pass specific URLs to the JDBC driver manager. The advantage of such a mechanism is your application can be relatively free from having to know the database hostname and the exact driver type to use, well in advance.

Connection Pooling: Opening and closing database are among the most expensive database operations. Instead of having to perform this costly operation for each SQL statement execution, developers usually create a cache of open database connections, which are then reused by successive transactions. Under JDBC 1.0, connection pools had to be programmatically implemented by developers at the application level. JDBC 2.0 now provides us with this capability via the standard extension package.

Distributed Transaction Support: This feature allows JDBC drivers to support the standard two-phase commit protocol available with the Java Transaction Service. Distributed transaction support is a prerequisite for enabling Enterprise JavaBeans components to use JDBC functionality.

Summary

JDBC provides vendor- and platform-independent database connectivity. The JDBC API has been designed with simplicity in mind. JDBC drivers are broadly classified into four main types. Choosing an appropriate driver based on your system architecture is imperative, as this decision may ultimately drive overall system performance. The next generation of JDBC 2.0-compatible drivers promise to provide even greater speed and flexibility in accessing raltional databases.

Chapter 3

Deploying Java Servlets

One of the simplest and most effective ways of introducing Java into your computing environment is to make use of servlets. *Servlets* are essentially server-side Java modules that seamlessly meld with your Web server, extending its functionality. Support for servlets is provided through the javax.servlet package, which is provided as a standard Java extension.

Servlets have a lot in common with their client-side counterparts—applets. Like applets, servlets can be downloaded over a network from a different host and can dynamically "plug" into a Web server, if necessary. Of course, servlets conform to the Java sandbox security model when deployed in this fashion. Although servlets are protocol independent and can serve as middleware in a multitiered environment, their most common use is to serve as replacements for CGI scripts written in Perl, ASP, or C. As you will soon see for yourself, servlets can do everything CGI scripts can and a lot more.

You can run servlets under just about any Web server. If your Web server does not already support them natively, you can always servlet-enable it by adding on a "servlet engine." The example servlets in this chapter were developed using Sun's Java Servlet Development Kit (JSDK). JSDK is a freely available toolkit that contains a lightweight servlet engine, servletrunner, as well as the servlet extension packages.

This chapter should give you an in-depth understanding of the servlet architecture as well as their capabilities. To start with, you learn the benefits of using the servlets, their basic architectural model, and then examine how they can be developed using JSDK. Then you tackle some of the more advanced issues including session management, JDBC integration, RMI integration, and servlet-applet communication.

Why Servlets Are Better than CGI Scripts

Compared with CGI scripts, servlets are a far and away superior solution in just about every sense. To illustrate, let's take the servlet technology head-to-head against CGI on a variety of criteria that are pivotal for any effective Web deployment:

Performance: CGI was never meant to serve as a base for online transaction processing systems. CGI is not only stateless, it also creates considerable overhead because a separate process is spawned for each incoming request. Servlets, running under a single JVM, are loaded just once when invoked for the first time. After that, the memory resident servlet simply forks a new thread for each subsequent request. This feature also ensures servlets can easily support advanced features like database connection pooling and data caching. It's true most Web servers come with their own proprietary APIs to eliminate some of CGIs bottlenecks, but large-scale use of these is not without considerable risk and a surefire candidate for vendor lock-in.

Open standards: In these days of uncertainty, predicting whether today's leading Web server vendor will be around in a few years is difficult. Not a comforting thought, especially if you have made extensive use of their proprietary Web server APIs within your CGI programs. The Servlet API is a standard extension in JDK 1.2 and can be expected to be around at least as long as Java! Not to mention the simple fact that servlets can be used by a variety of Web servers on a variety of platforms without any changes.

Reusability: As we all know, any Java-based application is inherently capable of making optimal reuse of not only the extensive JDK, but also other third-party packages and user-defined object hierarchies. Discussing reuse with conventional CGI development is rather difficult because usually there is none. If you need to bolster your case for going the servlets way, contrast the chaotic melange of Perl or C-based cut-and-paste development with the simple elegance of a true object-oriented language. That alone should make servlets a shoo-in.

Simplicity: The Servlet API is conceptually simple and can be effectively wielded by anyone familiar with Java and CGI programming. As previously mentioned, any serious CGI programming involves making use of proprietary C-based Web server APIs. That programs using Web server extension APIs be as robust as possible is absolutely critical. An errant program may prove catastrophic, not just for the application, but for the entire Web server itself! Compared with the myriad benefits of using Java, mucking around with pointers and memory allocation issues is downright masochistic.

Functionality: Anything Java has, servlets have. This includes not only language features like automatic memory management, advanced networking, multithreading, and so forth., but also the real enterprise connectivity in the form of JNI, JDBC, EJB, RMI, and CORBA. Can anyone lay claim to the same level functionality with a CGI program written in Perl, ASP, or C?

Security: Servlets are written in Java, hence, they inherit the extensive Java security mechanisms. Servlets can enforce multilevel access privileges for the same servlet using Java's Access Control Lists (ACL) and can selectively enable only trusted users access to protected resources.

The Java Servlet Development Kit

To be able to compile and run your servlets, your environment must be configured to include the Servlet API and your Web server must be enabled with a servlet engine. As Figure 3-1 shows, the servlet engine extends the functionality of Web servers and servlets are actually run within this.

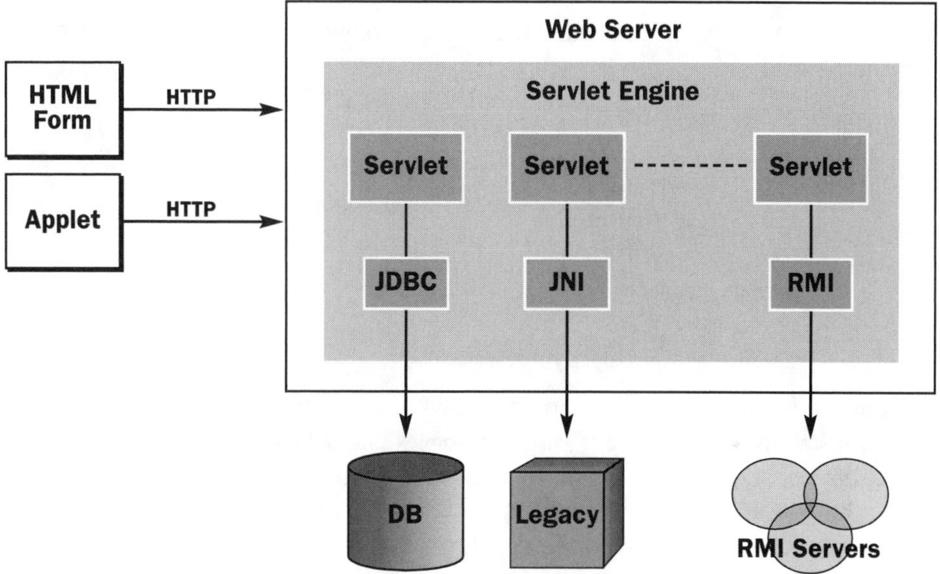

Figure 3-1: The Servlet architecture

Today, although numerous Web servers natively provide support for the standard Servlet API, some, like Microsoft's IIS do not. In such a situation, you must download one of the many servlet engines available and configure it for use with your specific Web server. For a comprehensive list of the various servlet engine implementations, look at:

http://java.sun.com/products/servlet/runners.html

A great way of getting started is to use Sun's freely available JSDK, which works with JDK 1.1 or 1.2. JSDK not only provides a development environment by making available the standard Servlet API, but also offers a simple servlet engine called servletrunner, for testing your servlets.

Using servletrunner

The JSDK is easy to install and configure. Assuming it is installed in the default location (I assume you are using a Win32 platform; if you are doing this under UNIX, please change the paths accordingly), you must add the location of servletrunner utility—c:\jsdk2.0\bin—to your PATH environment variable. To compile your servlets, you must also append the location of the Servlet API to your CLASSPATH. JSDK provides the servlet packages as a JAR file, which can be found in the default location c:\jsdk2.0\lib\jsdk.jar

Once your environment has been configured, the servletrunner can be started from the command line as

```
start servletrunner
```

By default, servletrunner listens on port 8080. If you wish, you can bind it to a different port by specifying it during startup. Numerous options can be specified with servletrunner:

```
Usage: servletrunner [options]
Options:
    -p port    the port number to listen on
    -b backlog    the listen backlog
    -m max    maximum number of connection handlers
    -t timeout    connection timeout in milliseconds
    -d dir    servlet directory
    -s filename    servlet property file name
```

Your servlets themselves need to be located in a specific directory, which under a default installation, would be c:\jsdk2.0\examples under Windows. Note, before you invoke any servlet, there is a corresponding entry for the same in the servlet.properties configuration file located in the same directory.

The servlet.properties has the following format:

```
#description of servlet
servlet.servlet-name.code=YourServlet
#optional initialization params for this servlet
servlet.servlet-name.initArgs=\
    username=someUser\
    password=somePassword
.
.
.
```

Once configured, the servlet can be executed from any browser using the URL:

```
http://hostname:port/servlet/servlet-name
```

Optionally, you can also pass initialization parameters that can be used by the servlet during startup. This can be done using the initArgs property. The value of the servlet.servlet-name.initArgs property holds the servlet's initialization parameters. The entire property must be specified as a set of name/value pairs. If multiple initialization parameters exist, they must be specified as a comma-delimited list as shown in the previous example.

Note

From my experience, it seems that servletrunner available within JSDK is a fairly lightweight implementation and is unsuitable for a demanding production environment. For deploying large servlet-based applications, you should consider enabling your Web server with one of the high-performance servlet engines commercially available or using an application server that supports servlets.

Understanding the Servlet Life Cycle

All the interfaces and classes for writing servlets are supported by two packages—javax.servlet and javax.servlet.http. Consider Listing 3-1 that demonstrates the implementation of a simple counter servlet:

Listing 3-1: The Counter Servlet

```
package cup.chap3.counter;
import java.io.*;
import javax.servlet.*;
import javax.servlet.http.*;
public class SimpleCounter extends HttpServlet {
private Integer count;
public void init (ServletConfig config) throws ServletException {
    // This method initializes the servlet and only gets call once.
    // Allocate all of the servlet resources here.
    super.init (config);
    count=new Integer(0);
}
public void doGet(HttpServletRequest servReq,
HttpServletResponse servRes) throws IOException {
    int localcount=0;
    servRes.setContentType("text/html");
    ServletOutputStream out = servRes.getOutputStream();
    synchronized (count) {
        count = new Integer(count.intValue() + 1);
        localcount=count.intValue();
    }
```

continues

Listing 3-1: continued

```
            out.println("<html><body><center><h3>");
            out.println("Number of hits for this page: "+localcount);
            out.println("</h3></center></body></html>");
        }
        public void destroy() {
            // Once this method is called then any instance
            //of this class can be garbage collected
            // Here is where all servlet resources can be deallocated.
            count=null;
        }
    }
```

As we can see from the previous program, the first thing any servlet must do is to import the servlet packages javax.servlet and javax.servlet.http. Also mandatory for any servlet is to implement the javax.servlet.Servlet interface (Listing 3-2), which contains methods for managing the servlet's behavior and handling its communication with external clients. Rarely does a servlet implement the Servlet interface directly, however. Although servlets may sometimes subclass GenericServlet (shown in Listing 3-3), most often, as in our example,

```
public class SimpleCounter extends HttpServlet {
    ...
}
```

they simply subclass HttpServlet (shown in Listing 3-4). Both GenericServlet and HttpServlet implement the Servlet interface.

Now, let's observe the behavior of the servlet when an external client makes a request. All servlets go through a three-stage lifecycle: *initialization*, *service,* and *destroy*, as shown in Figure 3-2.

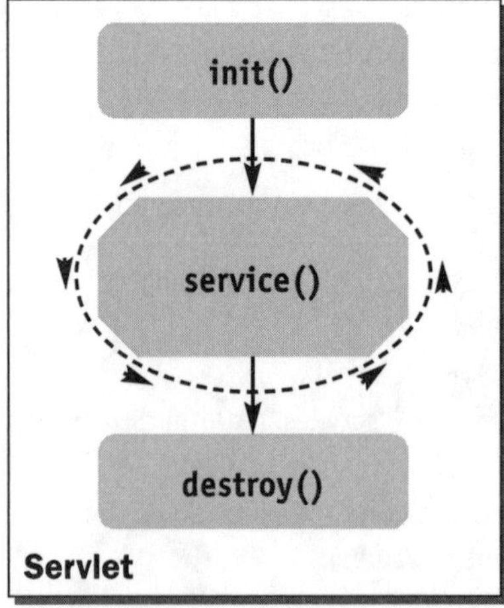

Figure 3-2: The servlet lifecycle

Listing 3-2: The javax.servlet.Servlet Interface

```
public interface Servlet {
    public abstract void init(ServletConfig config)
      throws ServletException;
    public abstract ServletConfig getServletConfig();
    public abstract void service(ServletRequest req,
      ServletResponse res) throws ServletException, IOException;
    public abstract String getServletInfo();
    public abstract void destroy();
}
```

Listing 3-3: The javax.servlet.GenericServlet Class

```
public class GenericServlet  implements Servlet {
    public ServletContext getServletContext();
    public String getInitParameter(String name);
    public Enumeration getInitParameterNames();
    public void log(String msg);
    public String getServletInfo();
    public void init(ServletConfig config) throws ServletException;
    public ServletConfig getServletConfig();
    public abstract void service(ServletRequest req,
      ServletResponse res) throws ServletException, IOException;
    public void destroy();
}
```

The first time a servlet is invoked by a client, it undergoes initialization, which includes setting defaults, initializing global data, loading external configuration data, and so forth. Initialization is performed by the `init(ServletConfig)` method and is invoked exactly once during the lifetime of the servlet. In this example:

```
public void init (ServletConfig config) throws ServletException {
    super.init (config);
    count=new Integer(0);
}
```

the initialization allocates an integer object and initialize it to zero. The initialization phase of the servlet helps us avoid the overhead of having to reallocate expensive resources for every invocation of the servlet. For instance, they are great for setting up a database connection pool, establishing connection with remote objects, or for initializing global data structures.

Listing 3-4: The javax.servlet.http.HttpServlet Class

```
public class HttpServlet extends GenericServlet {
    protected void doDelete(HttpServletRequest req,
        HttpServletResponse resp) throws ServletException, IOException;
    protected void doGet(HttpServletRequest req,
        HttpServletResponse resp) throws ServletException, IOException;
    protected void doOptions(HttpServletRequest req,
        HttpServletResponse resp) throws ServletException, IOException;
    protected void doPost(HttpServletRequest req,
        HttpServletResponse resp) throws ServletException, IOException;
    protected void doPut(HttpServletRequest req,
        HttpServletResponse resp) throws ServletException, IOException;
    protected void doTrace(HttpServletRequest req,
        HttpServletResponse resp) throws ServletException, IOException;
    protected long getLastModified(HttpServletRequest req);
    protected void service(HttpServletRequest req,
        HttpServletResponse resp) throws ServletException, IOException;
    public void service(ServletRequest req,
        ServletResponse res) throws ServletException, IOException;
}
```

Once the initialization is done, the service calls from clients are handled using the HTTP-based request and response paradigm, by executing the appropriate service method, as shown in Figure 3-3.

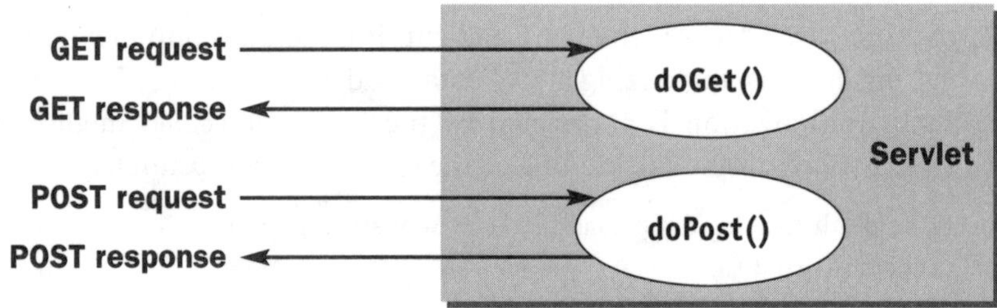

Figure 3-3: The request/response model

In this case, because the client accesses the servlet using the GET method, we have to provide an implementation for doGet():

```
public void doGet(HttpServletRequest servReq,
    HttpServletResponse servRes) throws IOException {
...
}
```

Note, the doGet() method receives two objects from the client. The HttpServletRequest object encapsulates the communication from the client to the servlet and the

HttpServletResponse object encapsulates the communication from the servlet back to the client. Because our example subclasses HttpServlet, we could have also implemented another HTTP-specific method like doPost() for the service cycle. We examine its use in later examples.

Before replying to the client, the first thing the doGet() method must do is to let the browser know we are sending back data in HTML format by setting the content's MIME type as:

```
servRes.setContentType("text/html");
```

Also interesting to observe is we synchronize access to the counter before we increment it as:

```
synchronized (count) {
    count = new Integer(count.intValue() + 1);
    localcount = count.intValue();
}
```

Note, servlets respond to a client's request in a multithreaded fashion. Instances may occur when your service methods need to access shared resources like instance or class variables, database connections, network connections, data files, and so forth. In such cases, it is imperative that the servlet developer synchronizes the access. Otherwise, you may have some other concurrently executing service method overwriting your changes. Figure 3-4 shows the output of the SimpleCounter servlet after it has been called three times, by repeatedly loading the URL http://hostname:8080/servlet/counter.

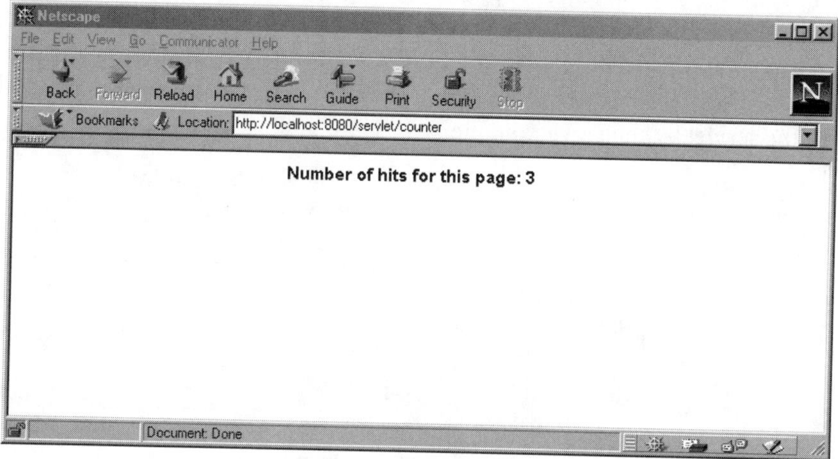

Figure 3-4: The SimpleCounter servlet

Once a servlet is no longer needed, it goes through the destroy cycle:

```
public void destroy() {
    count=null;
}
```

The destroy() method can get called either implicitly or explicitly. Either way, the developer must free all resources allocated to the servlet within the init() method like open file handles, database connections, and so forth. Once the destroy() method is called, the servlet can then be safely garbage collected.

Demonstrating Session-Tracking: The Shopping Cart Servlet

A prerequisite for implementing any kind of transaction processing system is the ability to maintain the state of the client, or its *session*, as it navigates through the various screens of the application. Servlets support state maintenance by creating a session object for each valid client and storing it at the server. But because numerous clients could be simultaneously accessing a servlet at any given point, it is critical that each session is "tracked" back to its originating client. The way the servlet session tracking mechanism works is fairly simple. When a user accesses the servlet for the first time, the user is assigned a new session object and a unique session ID is generated. This session ID is then sent as a cookie to the browser where it is stored. On subsequent requests, the browser's session ID cookie is transparently retrieved by the servlet and is used as a key to find the session object associated with that request. An important part of session tracking is the management of state information. Consequently, the session object supports the storage of additional state information within it in the form of name/value pairs. The only restriction is you can store and retrieve only valid Java objects from within a session object and not any primitive data types. As you can see from Figure 3-5, the state information itself is maintained outside the servlet by the servlet engine.

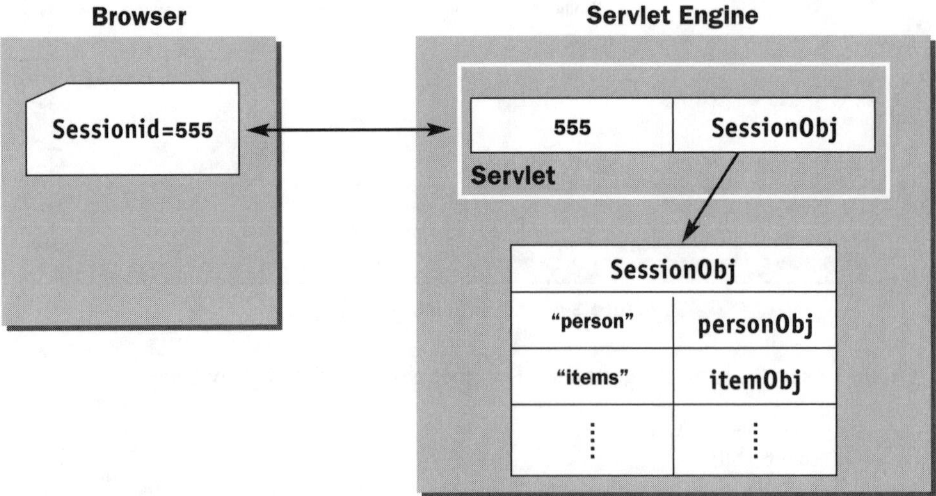

Figure 3-5: The HttpSession object

Storing cookies at the browser may not work at all times, however. For instance, for privacy reasons, the browser may have disabled the creation of cookies. In such cases, the session ID is supported at the client through URL rewriting.

To understand the details behind session tracking further, consider the shopping-cart servlet shown in Listing 3-5:

Listing 3-5: The Shopping Cart Servlet

```
package cup.chap3.shopping;
import java.io.*;
import java.util.*;
import javax.servlet.*;
import javax.servlet.http.*;
public class ShoppingServlet extends HttpServlet {
    public void init(ServletConfig conf) throws ServletException  {
        super.init(conf);
    }
    public void doGet (HttpServletRequest req, HttpServletResponse res)
    throws ServletException, IOException {
        PrintWriter  out;
        //set mime type
        res.setContentType("text/html");
        out = res.getWriter();
        boolean checkout = false;
        //obtain session object
        HttpSession session = req.getSession(true);
        if (session.isNew()) {
            String banner="Jambo World Music Imports";
            printHeader(out,banner,banner);
            printForm(out);
        }
        if (!session.isNew() &&
            (new Integer(req.getParameterValues("action")[0])).intValue()==3) {
                checkout=true;
        }
        if (!session.isNew() && !checkout) {
            String banner="Jambo World Music Imports";
            printHeader(out,banner,banner);
            printForm(out);
            //print shopping cart
            out.println("<P>");
            String del="";
            Vector buylist=(Vector)session.getValue("shopping.shoppingcart");
            int action=(new Integer(req.getParameterValues("action")[0])).intValue();
```

continues

Listing 3-5: continued

```
        switch (action) {
            case 2:   //delete an existing order
                del = req.getParameterValues("delindex")[0];
                int d = (new Integer(del)).intValue();
                buylist.removeElementAt(d);
              break;
            case 1:   // add to the shopping cart
                String cd = req.getParameterValues("CD")[0];
                String qty = req.getParameterValues("qty")[0];
                StringTokenizer t = new StringTokenizer(cd,"|");
                String album= t.nextToken();
                String artist = t.nextToken();
                String country = t.nextToken();
                String price = t.nextToken();
                Vector aCD = new Vector();
                aCD.addElement(album);
                aCD.addElement(artist);
                aCD.addElement(country);
                aCD.addElement(price);
                aCD.addElement(qty);
                //any previous buys?
                boolean match=false;
                if (buylist==null) {
                    //first order
                    buylist = new Vector();
                    buylist.addElement(aCD);
                } else { // not first buy
                    for (int i=0; i< buylist.size();i++) {
                        Vector anOrder = (Vector) buylist.elementAt(i);
                        String album1= (String)anOrder.elementAt(0);
                        String qty1 = (String) anOrder.elementAt(4);
                        if (album1.equals(album)) {
                            int n1 = (new Integer(qty1)).intValue();
                            int n = (new Integer(qty)).intValue();
                            n1 = n+n1;
                            qty1 = new Integer(n1).toString();
                            anOrder.setElementAt(qty1,4);
                            buylist.setElementAt(anOrder,i);
                            match = true;
                            break;
                        } //end of if name matches
                    } // end of for
```

Listing 3-5: continued

```
                if (!match) buylist.addElement(aCD);
            } // end of (buylist == null)
          default:  break;
        }
        int num_items = buylist.size();
        if (num_items >0) {
        out.println("<TABLE BORDER=1>");
        out.println("<TR><TD><B>ARTIST</B></TD><TD><B>ALBUM</B></TD>");
        out.println("<TD><B>COUNTRY</B></TD><TD><B>PRICE</B></TD>");
        out.println("<TD><B>QUANTITY</B></TD><TD></TD>  </TR>");
    }
    for (int i=0; i< num_items;i++) {
        Vector anOrder = (Vector) buylist.elementAt(i);
        String album = (String) anOrder.elementAt(0);
        String artist= (String)anOrder.elementAt(1);
        String country= (String)anOrder.elementAt(2);
        String price= (String)anOrder.elementAt(3);
        String qty = (String) anOrder.elementAt(4);
        String param1 = "<FORM NAME=Y ";
        param1 += "ACTION=http://localhost:8181/servlet/shopping ";
        param1 += "METHOD=GET><INPUT TYPE=SUBMIT VALUE=Delete> ";
        param1 += "<INPUT TYPE=HIDDEN NAME=delindex VALUE="+i+"> ";
        param1 += "<INPUT TYPE=HIDDEN NAME=action VALUE=2></FORM>";
        out.print("<TR><TD><B>"+album+"</B></TD>");
        out.println("<TD><B>"+artist+"</B></TD>";
        out.println("<TD><B>"+country+"</B></TD><TD><B>"+price+"</B></TD>");
        out.println("<TD><B>"+qty+"</B></TD><TD><TD>"+param1+"</TD></TR>");
    }
    session.putValue("shopping.shoppingcart", buylist);
    if (num_items >0) {
        out.println("</TABLE>");
        out.print("<P><FORM NAME=Z ");
        out.print("ACTION=http://localhost:8181/servlet/shopping ");
        out.println("METHOD=GET><INPUT TYPE=HIDDEN NAME=action VALUE=3> ");
        out.print("<INPUT TYPE=SUBMIT NAME=Checkout ");
        out.println("VALUE=Checkout></FORM>");
    }
    out.println("</CENTER><P>");
    out.println("<P><FONT SIZE=-6>");
    out.print("<br>Your first transaction was at: ");
    out.println((new Date(session.getCreationTime())).toString());
    print("<br>Your most recent transaction was at: ");
```

continues

Listing 3-5: continued

```
            out.println((new Date(session.getLastAccessedTime())).toString());
            out.println("</FONT><P>");
            out.flush();
        } //end of if (!session.isNew())
        if (checkout) {
            float total =0;
            String banner1="Jambo World Music Imports Checkout";
            String banner2= "Thank You for your order!";
            printHeader(out,banner1,banner2);
            out.println("<TABLE BORDER=1>");
            out.print("<TR><TD><B>ARTIST</B></TD><TD>");
            out.print("<B>ALBUM</B></TD><TD><B>COUNTRY</B></TD><TD>");
            out.print("<B>PRICE</B></TD><TD><B>QUANTITY</B></TD>");
            out.print("<TD></TD>      </TR>");
            Vector buylist =(Vector) session.getValue("shopping.shoppingcart");
            for (int i=0; i< buylist.size();i++) {
                Vector anOrder = (Vector) buylist.elementAt(i);
                String album = (String) anOrder.elementAt(0);
                String artist= (String)anOrder.elementAt(1);
                String country= (String)anOrder.elementAt(2);
                String price= (String)anOrder.elementAt(3);
                price = price.replace('$',' ');
                price = price.trim();
                String qty = (String) anOrder.elementAt(4);
                total += (new Float(price)).floatValue() * (new Integer(qty)).intValue();
                out.print("<TR><TD><B>"+album+"</B></TD><TD><B>"+artist+"
                    </B></TD>");
                out.print("<TD><B>"+country+"</B></TD><TD><B>"+price+"</B></TD>");
                out.println("<TD><B>"+qty+"</B></TD><TD></TD></TR>");
            }
            total += 0.005;
            String sum = new Float(total).toString();
            int n = sum.indexOf('.');
            sum = sum.substring(0,n+3);
            out.print("<TR><TD></TD><TD></TD><TD></TD>");
            out.print("<TD><B>"+"TOTAL"+"</B></TD><TD><B>$"+sum+"</B>
                </TD></TR>");
            out.println("</TABLE>");
            out.print("<P><BR><A HREF=http://localhost:8181/servlet/shopping>");
            out.println("Back to Jambo Home Page</A>");
            checkout=false;
            session.invalidate();
```

Listing 3-5: continued

```
        }
        out.println("</BODY>");
        out.println("</HTML>");
        out.close();
    }
    private void printHeader(PrintWriter out, String title, String header) {
        out.println("<HTML>");
        out.println("<HEAD>");
        out.println("<TITLE>"+title+"</TITLE>");
        out.println("</HEAD>");
        out.println("<BODY>");
        out.println("<P>");
        out.println("<CENTER>");
        out.println("<H1>");
        out.println(header);
        out.println("</H1><HR><P>");
    }
    private void printForm(PrintWriter out) {
        out.println("<FORM NAME=X ACTION=http://localhost:8181/servlet/shopping
            METHOD=GET>");
        //the items for your list box can easily be
        //sourced from a database using jdbc
        out.println("<P><B>CD:</B> ");
        out.println("<SELECT NAME=CD>");
        out.println("<OPTION SELECTED>---Select a CD---</OPTION>");
        out.println("<OPTION>Yuan | The Guo Brothers | China | $14.95</OPTION>");
        out.println("<OPTION>Drums of Passion | Babatunde Olatunji | Nigeria |
            $16.95</OPTION>");
        out.println("<OPTION>Kaira | Tounami Diabate| Mali | $16.95</OPTION>");
        out.println("<OPTION>The Lion is Loose | Eliades Ochoa | Cuba |
            $13.95</OPTION>");
        out.println("<OPTION>Dance the Devil Away | Outback | Australia |
            $14.95</OPTION>");
        out.println("<OPTION>Record of Changes | Samulnori | Korea | $12.95</OPTION>");
        out.println("<OPTION>Djelika | Tounami Diabate | Mali | $14.95</OPTION>");
        out.println("<OPTION>Rapture | Nusrat Fateh Ali Khan | Pakistan |
            $12.95</OPTION>");
        out.println("<OPTION>Cesaria Evora | Cesaria Evora | Cape Verde |
            $16.95</OPTION>");
        out.println("<OPTION>Ibuki | Kodo | Japan | $13.95</OPTION>");
        out.println("</SELECT>");
```

continues

Listing 3-5: continued

```
        out.println("<B>Quantity: </B><INPUT TYPE=HIDDEN NAME=action VALUE=1>
          <INPUT TYPE=TEXT NAME=qty SIZE=3 VALUE=1>
          <INPUT TYPE=SUBMIT NAME=Submit VALUE=Buy>");
        out.println("</FORM>");
      }
      public String getServletInfo() {
      return "Jambo World Music Imports Shopping Cart";
    }
  }
```

Note, a servlet can support session tracking only if it subclasses HttpServlet. If a servlet supports session tracking, the session object is always passed as part of the HttpServletRequest (shown in Listing 3-7) object to that servlet. As you can see, servlets provide support for the session objects by means of the HttpSession (shown in Listing 3-6) interface:

```
HttpSession session = req.getSession(true);
```

If a session has not already been established, the previous method returns a null. Otherwise, it returns a handle to the session object. Once you have a session object, determining whether the client is making a request for the first time is easy, as shown by:

```
(session.isNew()) {
        ...
}
```

Figure 3-6 shows the HTML form presented to the user accessing our shopping-cart servlet for the first time. The user can do one of three things—add a CD to the

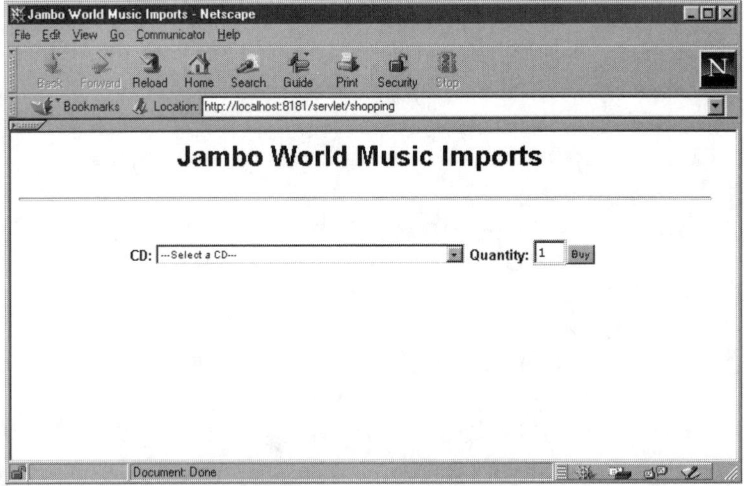

Figure 3-6: The ShoppingCart servlet

shopping cart, delete a CD from the cart, or, if at least one item is in the cart, proceed to the checkout counter.

The form data is posted to the servlet by means of the GET protocol and causes the doPost() method to be executed. Now, any named form control can be easily accessed within the servlet. The following line shows how the "action" element can be read from the posted form data:

```
req.getParameterValues("action")[0]
```

All the CDs selected by the user are stored within a Vector object, which is modified every time the user adds or deletes a CD from the shopping cart. Figure 3-7 shows a user who has added some items to the shopping cart.

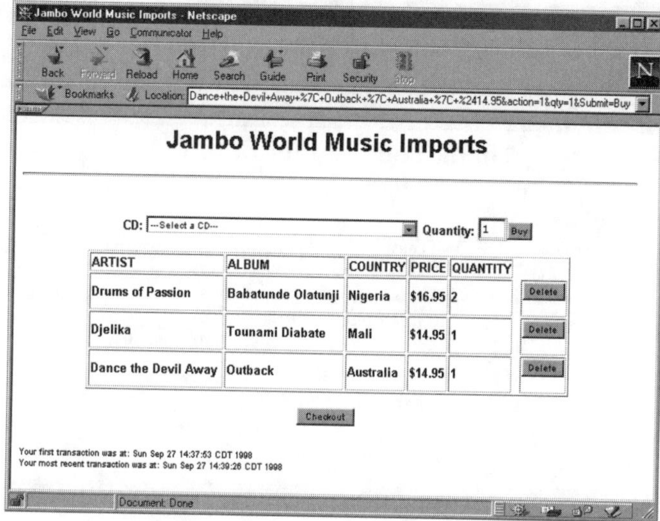

Figure 3-7: The ShoppingCart Servlet with Selections

Because the session object supports the storage of additional data as name/value pairs, we preserve the user's state across transactions by storing this Vector within the session object as:

```
session.putValue("shopping.shoppingcart", buylist);
```

The user's shopping cart is constantly refreshed after each action, be it an addition or a deletion. Retrieving a user's current state is easy as:

```
Vector buylist = (Vector) session.getValue("shopping.shoppingcart");
```

Remember, the session object may be shared by more than one servlet the user might access. Consequently, a possibility always exists that servlets may access or overwrite each other's session values. To minimize such namespace collisions between servlets, a good idea is always to prefix any value written to the session object with the name of the servlet.

The servlet communicates back to the browser via the `HttpServletResponse` (shown in Listing 3-8) object that is passed as a parameter to `doGet()`, after first obtaining an instance of `PrintWriter`:

```
out = res.getWriter();
```

When the user is done making all the selections, the "checkout" option can be used to finish the session. Notice the session is invalidated as:

```
session.invalidate();
```

The user's "buy list" is then displayed and the final bill is computed. Figure 3-8 shows the result of a checkout operation.

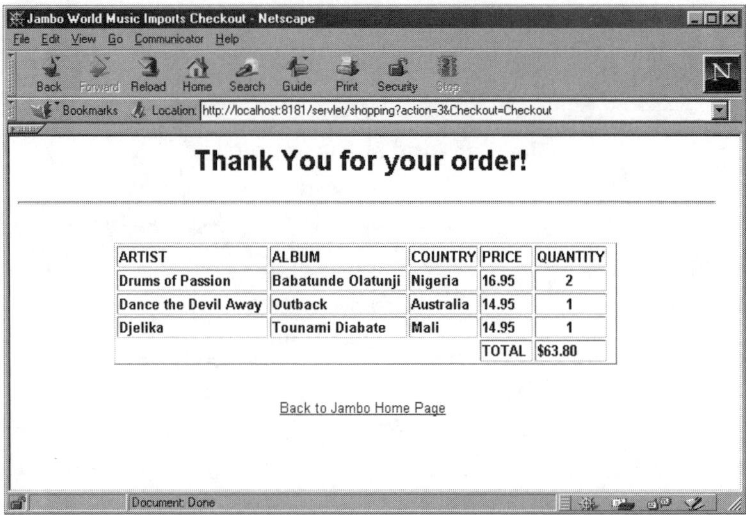

Figure 3-8: The ShoppingCart Servlet on Checkout

Listing 3-6: The javax.servlet.http.HttpSession Interface

```
public interface HttpSession {
    public abstract String getId();
    public abstract HttpSessionContext getSessionContext();
    public abstract long getCreationTime();
    public abstract long getLastAccessedTime();
    public abstract void invalidate();
    public abstract void putValue(String name, Object value);
    public abstract Object getValue(String name);
    public abstract void removeValue(String name);
    public abstract String[] getValueNames();
    public abstract boolean isNew();
}
```

Listing 3-7: The javax.servlet.http.HttpServletRequest Interface

```
public interface HttpServletRequest extends ServletRequest {
    public abstract Cookie[] getCookies();
    public abstract String getMethod();
    public abstract String getRequestURI();
    public abstract String getServletPath();
    public abstract String getPathInfo();
    public abstract String getPathTranslated();
    public abstract String getQueryString();
    public abstract String getRemoteUser();
    public abstract String getAuthType();
    public abstract String getHeader(String name);
    public abstract int getIntHeader(String name);
    public abstract long getDateHeader(String name);
    public abstract Enumeration getHeaderNames();
    public abstract HttpSession getSession(boolean create);
    public abstract String getRequestedSessionId();
    public abstract boolean isRequestedSessionIdValid();
    public abstract boolean isRequestedSessionIdFromCookie();
    public abstract boolean isRequestedSessionIdFromUrl();
}
```

Listing 3-8: The javax.servlet.http.HttpServletResponse Interface

```
public interface HttpServletResponse extends ServletResponse {
    public abstract void addCookie(Cookie cookie);
    public abstract boolean containsHeader(String name);
    public abstract void setStatus(int sc, String sm);
    public abstract void setStatus(int sc);
    public abstract void setHeader(String name, String value);
    public abstract void setIntHeader(String name, int value);
    public abstract void setDateHeader(String name, long date);
    public abstract void sendError(int sc, String msg) throws IOException;
    public abstract void sendError(int sc) throws IOException;
    public abstract void sendRedirect(String location) throws IOException;
    public abstract String encodeUrl(String url);
    public abstract String encodeRedirectUrl(String url);
}
```

HttpSessionBindingListener Interface

Objects that implement the HttpSessionBindingListener interface can get notification on being bound and unbound from a HttpSession.

When an object is bound within a session via HttpSession.putValue(), an instance of HttpSessionBindingEvent communicates the event to the valueBound() method, identifying the session into which the object is bound.

Similarly, when an object is unbound from the session due to a call to HttpSession.removeValue(), an instance of HttpSessionBindingEvent communicates the event to the valueUnbound() method, identifying the session from which the object is unbound.

The following code example demonstrates the use of HttpSessionBindingListener:

```
class SomeSessionObj implements HttpSessionBindingListener {
        ...
        public void valueBound(HttpSessionBindingEvent event) {
           //obtain the name associated with the object
           //within a HttpSesssion
           String str = event.getName();
           HttpSession session = event.getSession();
           ...
        }
        public void valueUnbound(HttpSessionBindingEvent event) {
           //cleanup
           ...
        }
}
```

Using Cookies for Client-Side Persistency

From the early days of the Web, cookies have been used for enabling session management with HTTP and HTTPS protocols. *Cookies* are essentially a small amount of state information that can be stored within the browser by any server replying with the appropriate HTTP response headers. To name a few applications, cookies are routinely used for storing user preferences, automating security user sign on facilities, and holding transaction data within shopping-cart applications.

Typically, all cookie information gets stored as name/value pairs. Consider the following code segment, which creates a cookie and initializes it with login information:

```
String login = request.getParameter("login");
Cookie loginCookie = new Cookie("login", login);
```

You can do a lot with cookies and the javax.servlet.http.Cookie class provides a number of methods for setting a cookie's values and attributes, as shown in Listing 3-9.

Listing 3-9: The javax.servlet.http.Cookie Class

```
public class Cookie extends Object implements Cloneable {
    public Cookie(String name, String value);
    public void setComment(String purpose);
    public String getComment();
    public void setDomain(String pattern);
    public String getDomain();
    public void setMaxAge(int expiry);
    public int getMaxAge();
    public void setPath(String uri);
    public String getPath();
    public void setSecure(boolean flag);
    public boolean getSecure();
    public String getName();
    public void setValue(String newValue);
    public String getValue();
    public int getVersion();
    public void setVersion(int v);
    public Object clone();
}
```

For instance, documenting the purpose of a specific cookie by setting its comment field is always useful:

```
loginCookie.setComment("This is used to keep the user login persistent");
```

Before setting a cookie at the browser, specifying its lifetime or how long it can be persisted at the client is important. The age of a cookie must be specified in seconds. For instance:

```
int age=60*60*24*10; //10 days
loginCookie.setMaxAge(age);
```

sets the maximum lifetime of the cookie as ten days. If a negative age is specified, as in:

```
loginCookie.setMaxAge(-1);
```

you are opting for the default behavior, which is to delete the cookie when the user shuts down the browser.

A cookie can be deleted by setting its age to zero, as

```
loginCookie.setMaxAge(0);
```

Cookies are set when they are sent as headers of the response to the client. Once you have created the loginCookie, you can easily set it as:

```
response.addCookie(loginCookie);
```

Once a cookie has been set, it can be easily retrieved during a subsequent servlet access as browsers pass them back as a part of the HTTP request headers.

To retrieve any cookie, you must retrieve all the cookies as:

```
Cookie[] cookies = request.getCookies();
```

Once you access the array of cookie objects, you can then search to find the cookie you want:

```
for(i=0; i < cookies.length; i++) {
     Cookie aCookie = cookie[i];
     if (aCookie.getName().equals("login") {
        String loginvalue = aCookie.getValue();
     }
}
```

Note, only those cookies actually stored by a specific server are returned to it—you cannot access any cookies set by a different host.

One of the longstanding problems with using cookies is they do not enjoy consistent support among all the browsers. Even when they are, you cannot always rely upon them being available—users are increasingly disabling their browsers from storing any cookie information out of privacy considerations. For this reason, providing some additional means for enabling state persistence is always preferable.

> **Note**
>
> A limit exists on the size as well as on the number of cookies that can be stored within a browser. Most browsers impose a four-kilobyte restriction on the size of the cookie. Additionally, each host can store a maximum of 20 cookies.

The SingleThreadModel Interface

The default behavior of a servlet dictates your service methods like doGet() or doPost() be thread-safe. You may remember from the servlet lifecycle that clients concurrently invoking a servlet result in the dispatch of the service method within a new thread. Consequently, it is imperative for the developer to synchronize access manually to any shared data from within the service methods. But in most cases, this is easier-said than done—manual data synchronization is both a tedious task and highly error-prone. We can provide automatic synchronization for servlets, however, and make them thread-safe simply by implementing the Servlet APIs SingleThreadModel interface.

SingleThreadModel is an empty interface. Any servlet implementing it is guaranteed that no two separate threads will invoke its service method concurrently. Instead, the Web server now maintains a pool of servlet instances in memory and has each incoming service invocation dispatched by one of the free servlet instances, as shown in Figure 3-9.

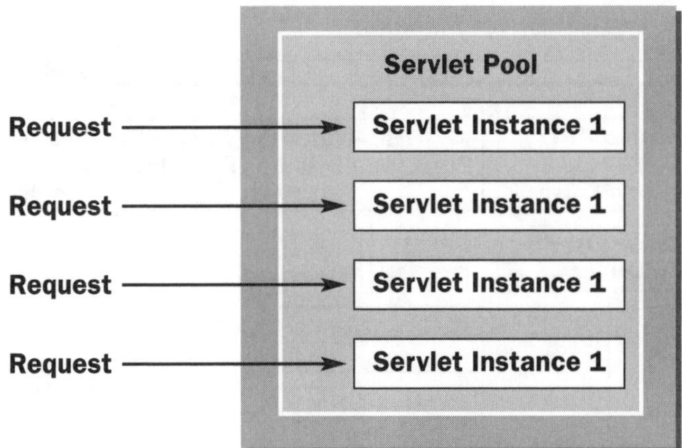

Figure 3-9: Servlet implementing the SingleThreadModel

By default, most servlet engines create a pool of seven servlet instances in memory for any servlet that implements SingleThreadModel. This default number may, however, be changed using the servlet engine's configuration screen. Developers should strictly regulate the number of servlets implementing SingleThreadModel, as using too many may negatively affect your site performance.

Although this mechanism has inherent benefits because it is not constrained by costly access synchronization, it may not be useful in situations where the servlet needs to maintain its state, as in page-hit counters, and so forth.

Integrating Servlets with JDBC

Servlets are commonly used as middleware for database integration. They are a fast and stable platform. As a standard Java extension, they can also reuse the functionality found within the entire JDBC API, as shown in Figure 3-10. Further, the servlet architecture itself facilitates the easy implementation of advanced features like database connection pooling and data caching.

A three-tier example

Listing 3-10 demonstrates a servlet implementation for a simple query processor. It is assumed the reader has an understanding of JDBC concepts and has already Chapter 2.

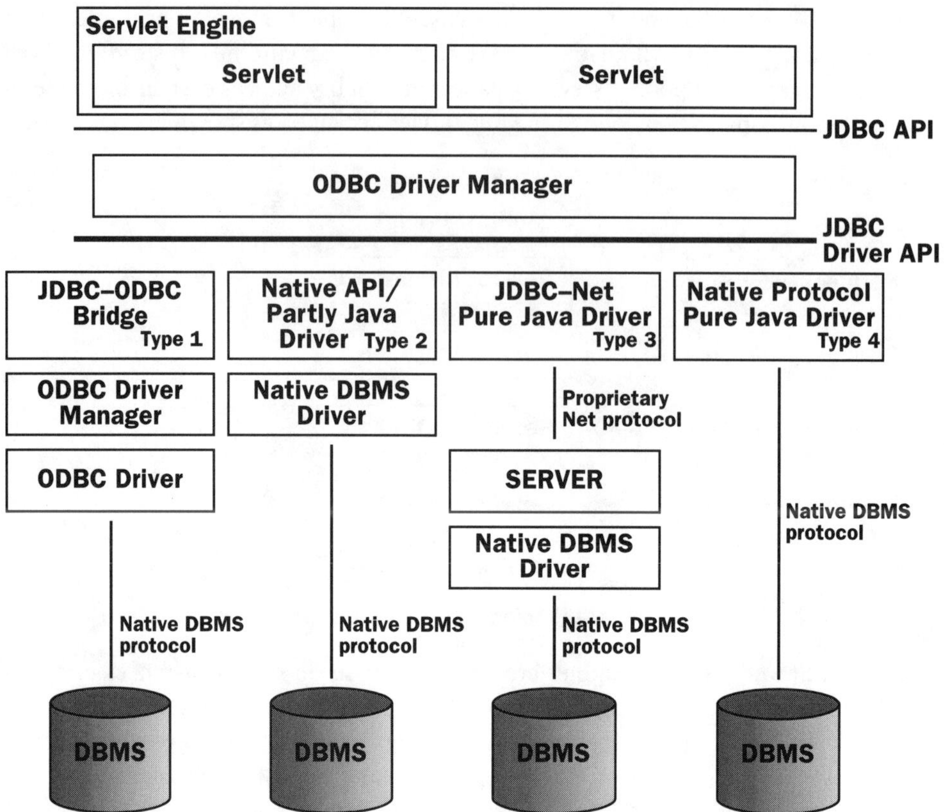

Figure 3-10: Integrating Servlets with Databases

Listing 3-10: Servlet/Database Integration Using JDBC

```
package cup.chap3.db;
import java.sql.*;
import java.io.*;
import java.util.*;
import javax.servlet.*;
import javax.servlet.http.*;
public class DBServlet extends HttpServlet implements SingleThreadModel {
    private Connection con=null;
    public void init(ServletConfig conf) throws ServletException {
      super.init(conf);
      try {
        Class.forName("sun.jdbc.odbc.JdbcOdbcDriver");
        String url = "jdbc:odbc:bugdb";
        con =DriverManager.getConnection(url,"dba","sql");
      } catch (Exception e) {
        System.out.println(e);
      }
```

Listing 3-10: continued

```
    }
    public void doGet(HttpServletRequest req, HttpServletResponse res)
    throws ServletException, IOException {
        PrintWriter   out;
        res.setContentType("text/html");
        out = res.getWriter();
        displayHeader(out);
        displayQueryInterface(out);
        displayFooter(out);
    }
    public void doPost(HttpServletRequest req, HttpServletResponse res)
    throws ServletException, IOException {
        PrintWriter   out;
        res.setContentType("text/html");
        out = res.getWriter();
        String query = req.getParameter("query");
        try {
            Statement stmt = con.createStatement();
            ResultSet rs = stmt.executeQuery(query);
            displayHeader(out);
            displayQueryInterface(out);
            out.println("<TABLE BORDER CELLPADDING=8 CELLSPACING=4>");
            displayResultSet(rs, out);
            out.println("</TABLE>");
            displayFooter(out);
            rs.close();
        } catch (Exception e) {
            System.out.println(e);
        }
    }
    private void displayHeader(PrintWriter out) {
        out.println("<HTML>");
        out.println("<HEAD><TITLE>General Purpose Query Processor</TITLE></HEAD>");
        out.println("<BODY>");
        out.println("<CENTER>");
    }
    private void displayQueryInterface(PrintWriter out) {
        out.println("<FORM METHOD=POST ACTION=http://localhost:8181/servlet/dbservlet>");
        out.println("Please Input Your Query: <INPUT NAME=query SIZE=40>");
        out.println("<INPUT TYPE=SUBMIT VALUE='Submit Query'>");
        out.println("</FORM>");
    }
```

continues

Listing 3-10: continued

```
private void displayFooter(PrintWriter out) {
    out.println("</CENTER>");
    out.println("</BODY>");
    out.println("</HTML>");
    out.close();
}
private void displayResultSet(ResultSet rs, PrintWriter out) throws SQLException {
    ResultSetMetaData metaData = rs.getMetaData();
    int cols =metaData.getColumnCount();
    out.println("<TR>");
    for(int i=1;i<=cols;++i) {
        out.println("<TH> "+metaData.getColumnName(i)+" </TH>");
    }
    out.println("</TR>");

    while (rs.next()) {
        out.println("<TR>");
        for (int i=1; i<=cols; i++) {
            displayColumnData(rs, out, metaData.getColumnType(i), i);
        }
        out.println("</TR>");
    }
}
private void displayColumnData(ResultSet rs, PrintWriter out, int columnType, int col)
throws SQLException  {
    switch(columnType) {
        case Types.CHAR:
        case Types.VARCHAR:
        case Types.LONGVARCHAR:
            String s = rs.getString(col);
            out.println("<TD>" + s + "</TD>");
            break;
        case Types.NUMERIC:
        case Types.DECIMAL:
            java.math.BigDecimal num = rs.getBigDecimal(col, 10);
            out.println("<TD>" + num.toString() + "</TD>");
            break;
        case Types.INTEGER:
            int i = rs.getInt(col);
            out.println("<TD>" + new Integer(i) + "</TD>");
            break;
        case Types.BIGINT:
```

Listing 3-10: continued

```
            long bigi = rs.getLong(col);
            out.println("<TD>" + new Long(bigi) + "</TD>");
            break;
        case Types.SMALLINT:
            short smalli = rs.getShort(col);
            out.println("<TD>" + new Integer(smalli) + "</TD>");
            break;
        case Types.TINYINT:
            byte tinyi = rs.getByte(col);
            out.println("<TD>" + new Integer(tinyi) + "</TD>");
            break;
        case Types.REAL:
            float real = rs.getFloat(col);
            out.println("<TD>" + new Float(real) + "</TD>");
            break;
        case Types.FLOAT:
        case Types.DOUBLE:
            double longreal = rs.getDouble(col);
            out.println("<TD>" + new Double(longreal) + "</TD>");
            break;
        case Types.BIT:
            boolean bit = rs.getBoolean(col);
            out.println("<TD>" + new Boolean(bit) + "</TD>");
            break;
        case Types.BINARY:
        case Types.VARBINARY:
        case Types.LONGVARBINARY:
            byte[] longbin = rs.getBytes(col);
            out.println("<TD>" + new String(longbin, 0) + "</TD>");
            break;
        case Types.DATE:
            java.sql.Date date = rs.getDate(col);
            out.println("<TD>" + date.toString() + "</TD>");
            break;
        case Types.TIME:
            java.sql.Time time = rs.getTime(col);
            out.println("<TD>" + time.toString() + "</TD>");
            break;
        case Types.TIMESTAMP:
            java.sql.Timestamp ts = rs.getTimestamp(col);
            out.println("<TD>"+ ts.toString() + "</th>");
            break;
```

continues

Listing 3-10: continued

```
            }
        }
        public void destroy() {
            try {
                con.close();
            } catch (Exception e) {
                System.out.println(e);
            }
        }
    }
```

As you can see, integrating databases with servlets is fairly straightforward. Our example DBServlet basically receives and executes arbitrary SQL query statements. On successful execution, the ResultSet object is displayed in a table format, after undergoing any necessary conversion. We assume the queries, in this case, pertain to the BUGTRACK database shown in Chapter 2.

The init() method of any data-access servlet is responsible for initializing the servlet, loading the required database driver, and creating a Connection instance with the target database. Establishing a database connection is a highly resource intensive process and takes a big bite of overall server performance. Luckily, with servlets, we needn't face the overhead of reconnecting with the database each time we need to perform a query. Because the init() is executed just once during the lifetime of the servlet, we can simply reuse the cached database connection within our service methods. Typically, most data-access servlets create a database connection pool from within init() and reuse those connections from within the service methods, as shown in Figure 3-11. For the sake of simplicity, however, our example servlet opens just a single connection with the database.

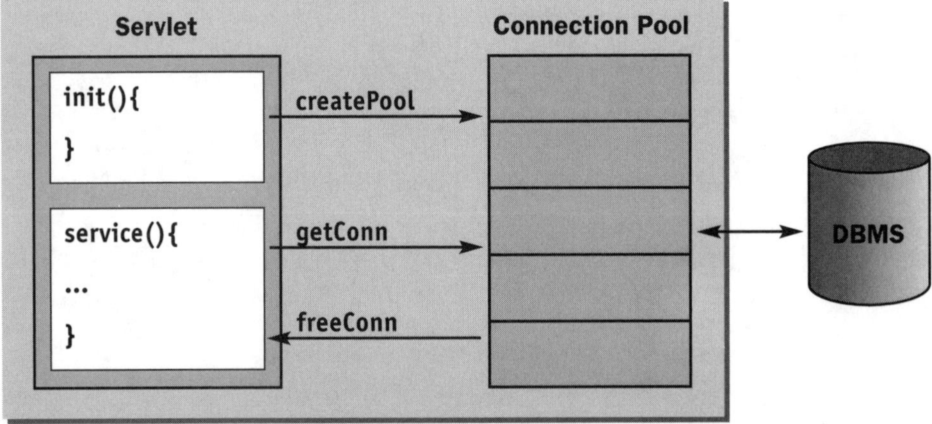

Figure 3-11: Servlet using a database connection pool

Also, because we assume our target database is Access, we load the included JDBC-ODBC Bridge driver and register it with the JDBC Driver Manager as:

```
Class.forName("sun.jdbc.odbc.JdbcOdbcDriver");
```

Also, note the JDBC URL used for obtaining the connection:

```
String url = "jdbc:odbc:bugdb";
```

If the target database is accessed using the JDBC-ODBC Bridge driver, the initial part of the URL must always be jdbc:odbc. The third component, bugdb, indicates the ODBC data source. Thus, setting up the target database as a valid ODBC data source on the host machine before executing the servlet is important.

Servlets, by default, are executed on a separate thread for each incoming request by the servlet engine. In such a scenario, it is critical that any shared resources are synchronized. For instance, in our example, we would have to synchronize access to the cached Connection object. Instead of dealing with complex issues related to multithreaded access, simply indicating the servlet will function in a single-threaded mode may be better, by implementing the SingleThreadModel interface as:

```
public class DBServlet extends HttpServlet implements SingleThreadModel
```

DBServlet implements the doGet() as well as the doPost() methods. In the example, doGet() is invoked when the servlet is accessed for the first time by its URL as http://hostname:port/servlet/dbservlet.

The doGet() method simply presents an HTML form interface, enabling the user to submit a SQL query statement. Observe the form is submitted via HTTP POST back to DBServlet. When this happens, the query statement is automatically passed to the doPost(). This method is both responsible for performing the query and displaying the result set, and for again presenting the HTML form interface, thus enabling the user to perform additional queries.

Once the result set is obtained as:

```
Statement stmt = con.createStatement();
ResultSet rs = stmt.executeQuery(query);
```

it is passed to the method displayResultSet()for display in HTML table format. Because we are building a dynamic query processor, we do not have any advance knowledge regarding the result set, including the column names, their types, and so forth . For display and formatting purposes, we must first obtain the ResultSetMetaData object as:

```
ResultSetMetaData metaData = rs.getMetaData();
```

The following code segment shows how we can go about displaying the column headings for the result set table:

```
int cols =metaData.getColumnCount();
out.println("<TR>");
for(int i=1;i<=cols;++i) {
    out.println("<TH> "+metaData.getColumnName(i)+" </TH>");
}
out.println("</TR>");
```

The actual query data itself is displayed by iterating through the result set object:

```
while (rs.next()) {

        out.println("<TR>");
        for (int i=1; i<=cols; i++) {
           displayColumnData(rs, out, metaData.getColumnType(i), i);
        }
        out.println("</TR>");
}
```

Note, displayColumnData() is invoked to retrieve the actual column value from the result set and to map it from the SQL type to its corresponding Java type, before displaying it.

Figure 3-12 shows the result set upon executing the query "select bug_id summary, detail, pty, sts, report_date from bugs".

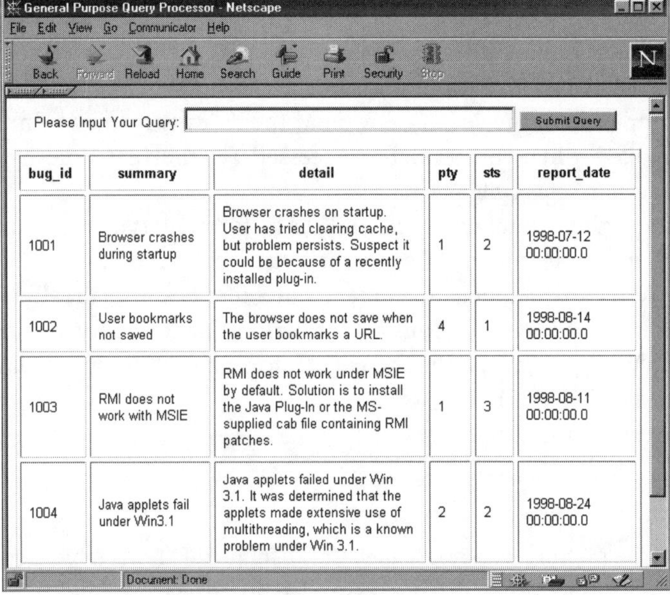

bug_id	summary	detail	pty	sts	report_date
1001	Browser crashes during startup	Browser crashes on startup. User has tried clearing cache, but problem persists. Suspect it could be because of a recently installed plug-in.	1	2	1998-07-12 00:00:00.0
1002	User bookmarks not saved	The browser does not save when the user bookmarks a URL.	4	1	1998-08-14 00:00:00.0
1003	RMI does not work with MSIE	RMI does not work under MSIE by default. Solution is to install the Java Plug-In or the MS-supplied cab file containing RMI patches.	1	3	1998-08-11 00:00:00.0
1004	Java applets fail under Win3.1	Java applets failed under Win 3.1. It was determined that the applets made extensive use of multithreading, which is a known problem under Win 3.1.	2	2	1998-08-24 00:00:00.0

Figure 3-12: Integrating Servlets with JDBC

Tips for servlet/JDBC integration

- Avoid synchronizing your service methods as they execute your servlets in a single-threaded environment:

```
public synchronized void doPost(HttpServletRequest req,
        HttpServletResponse res) throws IOException, ServletException {
            ...
            //access any shared data in a threads-safe fashion
}
```

- Although the previous snippet may seem like a quick and easy way of ensuring servlets are thread-safe when accessing shared data, it completely ignores Java's powerful multithreading model. A better approach is to synchronize access explicitly to shared data from within the service methods as:

```
public void doPost(HttpServletRequest req,     HttpServletResponse res)
        throws IOException, ServletException {
    synchronized(sharedObject) {
        ...
          //access/modify the shared object
    }
        ...
}
```

- Use cached PreparedStatement objects wherever possible. A prepared statement is essentially a precompiled SQL statement. By creating the prepared statements for the most frequently used SQL queries within the servlet's init() method, you can obtain some performance gains. This should be more apparent for high-traffic sites, where even small gains quickly add up due to the call volume.
- For low-traffic sites, you can cache a database connection within init() and have the servlet implement SingleThreadModel. This automatically creates a pool of data-access servlets with established database connections to service your clients in a thread-safe mode. For high-traffic sites, you can create a database connection pool within your init() method and run your servlets in the default, fully multithreaded mode. You can also use a pooling database driver to create and manage the database connection pool automatically, if one is available for your database. Always ensure your destroy() method closes any open database connections.
- Use stored procedures to implement complex SQL logic. Stored procedures are faster than dynamic SQL and minimize network traffic for high-volume applications.
- You can have a transaction span multiple page requests or even multiple servlets by storing the Connection instance within your HTTPSession. Then, at any given point, you can extract your Connection instance and perform an explicit commit or rollback, depending on the situation. Database connections stored within HTTPSession must always be wrapped within some class that implements HttpSessionBindingListener. This enables you to receive notification when the object is unbound from the session, enabling you to close the connection gracefully.

Integrating Servlets with RMI

Using RMI servers, you can deploy your business objects across multiple machines, enabling highly scalable, distributed, and multiprocessor configurations. With RMI, all your business logic is effectively transformed into a set of distributed services, which can be seamlessly invoked from nearly any computer within your enterprise. Although RMI works great in a pure Java environment, significant challenges exist in presenting a unified interface to these distributed services to non-Java clients like XML and HTML-based interfaces. And that's where servlets come in. Servlets are an excellent technology for effectively integrating an enterprise's distributed object services with the Web. Two different ways exist to make available RMI servers to browser-based HTML clients.

- The servlet can act as a client to one or more distributed RMI servers.
- The RMI server itself can be modified to service both regular RMI clients and HTML clients.

Let's look at both of the previous scenarios in more detail. Before proceeding further, however, you may want to go through the chapter on RMI computing to understand the basics of distributed object computing in Java.

Servlets as RMI clients

Significant advantages exist to integrating RMI servers by having servlets serve as RMI clients. Most notably, servlets finally enable you to reuse your distributed object infrastructure with HTML clients, without having to make any changes to the RMI servers themselves per se. Additionally, as shown in Figure 3-13, because a single servlet can integrate multiple RMI servers, you can now present a unified Web-based interface to your distributed objects, which are typically deployed across multiple machines within your enterprise. This architecture also helps you overcome a rather constricting security limitation imposed upon conventional browser-based RMI clients. For instance, RMI applets can communicate with remote servers that run only on the host from which the applets were downloaded from and no other.

Note, RMI computing over the Web takes a significant performance hit when both the client and server are operating behind firewalls. This is because the RMI traffic is tunneled through HTTP and relies upon a CGI program to perform call forwarding on the server-side. (Readers seeking details can find them in the chapter on RMI computing.) In such a scenario, using servlets to mediate the conversation may be more efficient, as this is significantly more efficient than CGI.

Now, let's look at a concrete example. Listing 3-11 shows the remote interface, `TempConverterInterface`, containing methods for performing temperature conversions between Celsius and Fahrenheit. The RMI server, `TempConverterServer`, implementing this interface is shown in Listing 3-12.

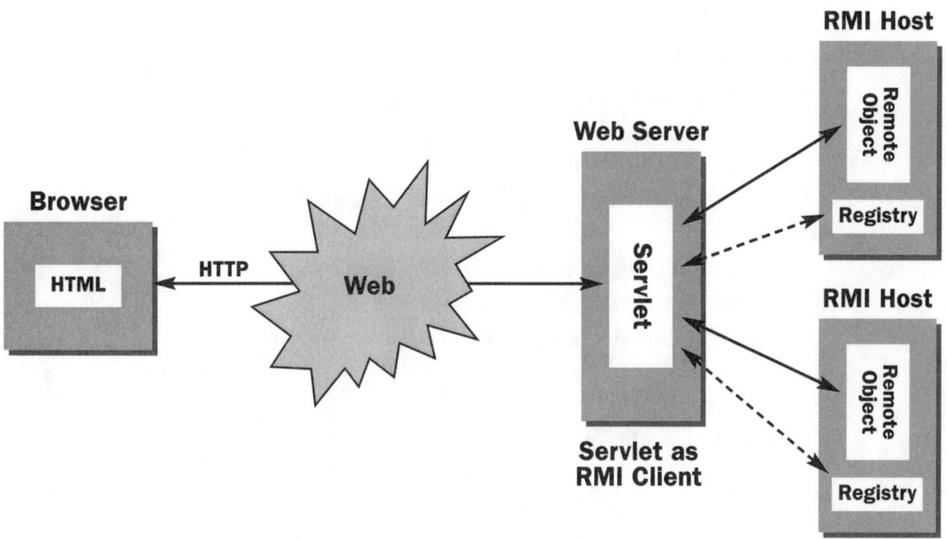

Figure 3-13: Servlets as RMI Clients

Listing 3-11: Servlets as RMI Clients: The Remote Interface

```
package cup.chap3.rmiservlet;
import java.rmi.*;
import java.rmi.server.*;
public interface TempConverterInterface extends Remote {
    public int fToC(int f) throws RemoteException;
    public int cToF(int c) throws RemoteException;
}
```

Listing 3-12: Servlets as RMI Clients: The RMI Server

```
package cup.chap3.rmiservlet;
import java.rmi.*;
import java.rmi.server.*;
public class TempConverterServer extends UnicastRemoteObject
        implements TempConverterInterface {
    public TempConverterServer () throws RemoteException {
        super();
    }
    public int fToC(int f) throws RemoteException {
        float c = (f-32)*5/9;
        Float cel = new Float(c);
        return cel.intValue();
    }
    public int cToF(int c) throws RemoteException {
        float f = (c+32)*9/5;
```

continues

Listing 3-12: continued

```
            Float fahren = new Float(f);
            return fahren.intValue();
        }
        public static void main(String[] args) {
         System.setSecurityManager(new RMISecurityManager());
         try {
            TempConverterServer tempServer =new TempConverterServer();
            Naming.rebind("/TempServer", tempServer);
            System.out.println("TempServer bound in registry");
         }
           catch (Exception e) {
          System.out.println(e);
         }
        }
    }
```

You can compile the RMI server previously shown, generate the stub and skeleton files, and install it as shown in the RMI chapter. Listing 3-13 shows the servlet that acts as a client an RMI server.

Listing 3-13: Servlets as RMI Clients

```
package cup.chap3.rmiservlet;
import java.io.*;
import javax.servlet.*;
import javax.servlet.http.*;
import java.rmi.*;
//before servlet startup include path of jdk , . and servlets dir
//before registry &  rmi server startup include path of jdk , .
public class RMIServlet extends HttpServlet {

    public TempConverterInterface tempServer =null;
    private int convDegrees ;
    private String cDegrees =null;
    private String fDegrees =null;
    public void init(ServletConfig config) throws ServletException {
       super.init(config);
    System.out.println("Within Init");
       try {
         if (System.getSecurityManager() == null)
         System.setSecurityManager(new RMISecurityManager());
         tempServer = (TempConverterInterface)
         Naming.lookup("rmi://remotehost/TempServer");
```

Listing 3-13: continued

```
        } catch (Exception e) {
            System.out.println("Error obtaining remote reference to TempServer");
            System.out.println(e);
        }
    }

    public void doPost(HttpServletRequest req,HttpServletResponse res)
    throws IOException{
        res.setContentType("text/html");
        String option = req.getParameter("convert");
        if (option.equals("ftoc")) {
            fDegrees = req.getParameter("degrees");
            int arg = new Integer(fDegrees).intValue();
            convDegrees = tempServer.fToC(arg);
        } else if (option.equals("ctof")) {
            cDegrees = req.getParameter("degrees");
            int arg = new Integer(cDegrees).intValue();
            convDegrees = tempServer.cToF(arg);
        }
        ServletOutputStream out = res.getOutputStream();
        display(out);
    }

    public void doGet(HttpServletRequest req, HttpServletResponse res)
    throws IOException {
        res.setContentType("text/html");
        ServletOutputStream out = res.getOutputStream();
        display(out);
    }
    private void display(ServletOutputStream out) throws IOException {
        out.println("<HTML><HEAD><TITLE>RMI/Servlet Integration Demo");
        out.println("</TITLE></HEAD>");
        out.println("<BODY>");
        if (cDegrees != null) {
            out.println("<H1>"+cDegrees+"&deg; C = "+convDegrees+"&deg; F</H1>");
            cDegrees=null;
        } else if (fDegrees != null) {
            out.println("<H1>"+fDegrees+"&deg; F = "+convDegrees+"&deg; C</H1>");
            fDegrees=null;
        }
        out.println("<FORM METHOD=POST
            ACTION=http://host:port/servlet/rmiservlet>");
```

continues

Listing 3-13: continued

```
            out.println("<INPUT TYPE=radio NAME=convert
               VALUE=ftoc CHECKED>Fahrenheit to Celsius");
            out.println("<br>");
            out.println("<INPUT TYPE=radio NAME=convert
               VALUE=ctof>Celsius to Fahrenheit");
            out.println("<br>");
            out.println("<INPUT TYPE=text NAME=degrees>");
            out.println("<P>");
            out.println("<INPUT TYPE=submit VALUE=Convert>");
            out.println("</FORM></BODY></HTML>");
            out.close();
        }
    }
```

You may have noticed some interesting modifications that have been made to the init() method of RMIServlet. For example:

```
if (System.getSecurityManager() == null)
  System.setSecurityManager(new RMISecurityManager());
```

A servlet must always have an installed security manager before attempting to load a reference to the RMI server across the network. The security manager sandboxes any downloaded stub classes and ensures they do not cause any security breaches.

Before the servlet can issue any RMI calls, it needs to obtain a reference to the remote object in the form of an RMI stub file from the naming server on the remote machine. This is done by invoking:

```
tempServer = (TempConverterInterface)
Naming.lookup("rmi://remotehost/TempServer");
```

The Naming.lookup() call is successful only if an entry is within the rmiregistry on the remote machine for the remote server. Otherwise, an exception is thrown indicating a lookup failure. Note, we must obtain the stub for the remote server just once, as it is cached and reused by the servlet for successive RMI calls.

Assuming you have aliased RMIServlet as /servlet/rmiservlet within your servlet engine, the servlet can be executed by loading the URL:

```
http://host:port/servlet/rmiservlet
```

The method doGet() gets called by default and simply presents the HTML form-based interface to the user. Notice the form is submitted via HTTP POST back to the same servlet rmiservlet. When this happens, the doPost() method is executed, which, in turn, extracts the posted form data and, depending on the chosen option, invokes the appropriate RMI call using the cached RMI stub. The results are then displayed by calling display().

Listing 3-14 shows a conventional RMI client that can be used for testing your RMI server.

Listing 3-14: RMI Client

```
package cup.chap3.rmiservlet;
import java.rmi.*;
public class TempClient {
    public static void main(String[] args) {
      try {
    if (System.getSecurityManager() == null)
        System.setSecurityManager(new RMISecurityManager());
        TempConverterInterface tempServer = (TempConverterInterface)
          Naming.lookup("/TempServer");
        int fahren = 30;
        int cel = 30;
        int c = tempServer.fToC(fahren);
        int f = tempServer.cToF(cel);
        System.out.println(cel + " degrees Celsius = "+f+" degrees Fahrenheit");
        System.out.println(fahren + " degrees Fahrenheit = "+c+" degrees Celsius");
      }
      catch (Exception e) {
        System.out.println(e);
      }
    }
}
```

Note

If you are running RMI under Java 2, you need to use a security policy file to provide the client and server programs with the necessary privileges. Refer to Chapter 6 for more information on creating a security policy file. Once a policy file has been created, you need to denote it when starting up the RMI client, server, and rmiregistry as follows:

```
rmiregistry -J-Djava.security.policy=\somedir\policy
java -Djava.security.policy=\somedir\policy
   -Djava.rmi.server.codebase=somecodebase RMIserver
java -Djava.security.policy=\somedir\policy RMIclient
```

RMIlets—servlets as remote objects

In the previous section, you saw how easy it was to implement a servlet as an RMI client. An equally exciting possibility is to have a servlet behave as an RMI distributed object. The single biggest advantage of setting up a servlet as an RMI object (I prefer to call these RMI server/servlet hybrids *RMIlets*) is that now, the servlet can be subject to asynchronous updates by some back-end RMI server or client, without having to resort to inefficient polling strategies. This feature is most useful when the servlet is responsible for providing dynamic content like stock quotes or breaking news. An RMIlet can be updated instantaneously—as soon as the data becomes available at the remote server—either via callbacks or by the server acting as a client to the RMIlet. Of course, an RMIlet can also service myriad clients, as shown in Figure 3-14, because it can seamlessly communicate using the HTTP protocol, in addition to JRMP or IIOP. Although this is possible, I would not recommend accessing an RMIlet using RMI clients due to servlet lifecycle issues. Listing 3-15 implements an RMIlet by implementing the `TempConverterInterface` remote interface shown earlier in Listing 3-11.

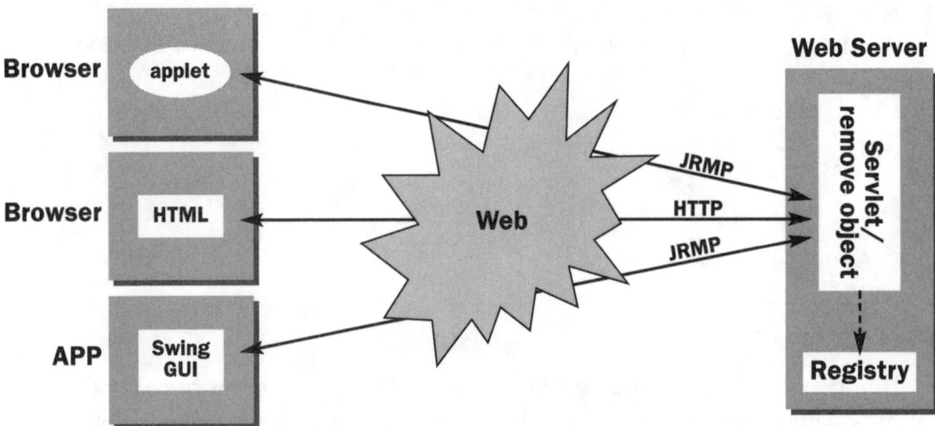

Figure 3-14: A simple "RMIlet"

Listing 3-15: Implementing an RMIlet

```
package cup.chap3.rmiservlet;
import java.io.*;
import javax.servlet.*;
import javax.servlet.http.*;
import java.rmi.*;
import java.rmi.registry.*;
import java.rmi.server.*;
public class RMIlet extends HttpServlet
implements Remote, Serializable, TempConverterInterface {
    //public TempConverterInterface tempServer =null;
```

Listing 3-15: continued

```
    private int convDegrees ;
    private String cDegrees =null;
    private String fDegrees =null;
    private Registry registry =null;
    public void init(ServletConfig config) throws ServletException {

    super.init(config);
        System.out.println("Within Init");
        try {
            UnicastRemoteObject.exportObject(this);
            bindInRegistry();
        } catch (Exception e) {
            System.out.println(e);
        }
    }

    public void doPost(HttpServletRequest req,HttpServletResponse res)
    throws IOException{
        res.setContentType("text/html");
        String option = req.getParameter("convert");
        if (option.equals("ftoc")) {
            fDegrees = req.getParameter("degrees");
            int arg = new Integer(fDegrees).intValue();
            convDegrees = fToC(arg);
        } else if (option.equals("ctof")) {
            cDegrees = req.getParameter("degrees");
            int arg = new Integer(cDegrees).intValue();
            convDegrees = cToF(arg);
        }
        ServletOutputStream out = res.getOutputStream();
        display(out);
    }
    public void doGet(HttpServletRequest req, HttpServletResponse res)
    throws IOException {
        res.setContentType("text/html");
    ServletOutputStream out = res.getOutputStream();
        display(out);
    }
    private void display(ServletOutputStream out) {
        try {
        out.println("<HTML><HEAD><TITLE>RMI/Servlet Integration Demo");
        out.println("</TITLE></HEAD>");
```

continues

Listing 3-15: continued

```
        out.println("<BODY>");
        if (cDegrees != null) {
            out.println("<H1>"+cDegrees+"&deg; C = "+convDegrees+"&deg; F</H1>");
            cDegrees=null;
        } else if (fDegrees != null) {
            out.println("<H1>"+fDegrees+"&deg; F = "+convDegrees+"&deg; C</H1>");
            fDegrees=null;
        }
        out.println("<FORM METHOD=POST
            ACTION=http://localhost:8080/servlet/rmilet>");
        out.println("<INPUT TYPE=radio NAME=convert VALUE=ftoc CHECKED>
            Fahrenheit to Celsius");
        out.println("<br>");
        out.println("<INPUT TYPE=radio NAME=convert
            VALUE=ctof>Celsius to Fahrenheit");
        out.println("<br>");
        out.println("<INPUT TYPE=text NAME=degrees>");
        out.println("<P>");
        out.println("<INPUT TYPE=submit VALUE=Convert>");
        out.println("</FORM></BODY></HTML>");
        out.close();
        } catch (IOException e) {
            System.out.println("Err:"+e);
        }
    }
    public int fToC(int f) throws RemoteException {
        float c = (f-32)*5/9;
        Float cel = new Float(c);
        return cel.intValue();
    }
    public int cToF(int c) throws RemoteException {
        float f = (c+32)*9/5;
        Float fahren = new Float(f);
        return fahren.intValue();
    }

public void bindInRegistry() {
    try {
        registry = LocateRegistry.getRegistry(1099);
    } catch (Exception e) {
        registry = null;
    }
```

Listing 3-15: continued

```
        if (registry ==null) {
            try {
                registry = LocateRegistry.createRegistry(1099);
            } catch (Exception e) {
                System.out.println(e);
            }
        }
        try {
            registry.rebind("TempServer",this);
        } catch (Exception e) {
            System.out.println(e);
        }
    }

    public void destroy() {
            try {
                registry.unbind("TempServer");
            } catch (Exception e) {
                System.out.println(e);
            }
        }
}
```

The servlet is compiled and deployed as usual. The only extra step that must be carried out here is the generation of the RMI stub and skeleton by applying rmic on the compiled class.

> **Note**
>
> If you are running this example under Java 2, you need to use a policy file and start up rmiregistry separately by indicating the policy file. Refer to the security note in the previous section for details.

Consider the declaration of RMIlet:

```
public class RMIlet extends HttpServlet
implements Remote, Serializable, TempConverterInterface {
...
}
```

An RMIlet must implement the remote interfaces that serve to advertise the remote functionality. Observe the RMIlet is essentially a servlet that can still receive and respond to requests from clients using HTTP, as well as conform to the servlet lifecycle. The servlet also becomes a de facto RMI server when it exports itself as a remote object using the static UnicastRemoteObject.exportObject() method when it is first loaded:

```
public void init(ServletConfig config) throws ServletException {
    ...
    try {
        UnicastRemoteObject.exportObject(this);
        bindInRegistry();
     } catch (Exception e) {
     ...
    }
}
```

The UnicastRemoteObject.exportObject() invocation causes the RMIlet to bind itself to a random port, set the base transport protocol as TCP/IP, and start listening for incoming client calls on that port. Note, although the RMI server functionality is created at this point, the RMIlet is unavailable to service an RMI client, as it is not yet bound within rmiregistry.

The call to the local method bindInRegistry() essentially serves to bind the generated RMI stub of the RMIlet into the rmiregistry. Note, if the rmiregistry is not already available, it is created from within this method, before any binding takes place.

The remote methods:

```
public int fToC(int f) throws RemoteException {
    ...
}
public int cToF(int c) throws RemoteException {
    ...
}
```

essentially fulfill the contract required by the remote interface TempConverterInterface. These remote methods are accessible by RMI clients and made available to HTML clients by their inclusion within the service method.

The doGet() service method is invoked if the client makes a HTTP GET request and the user is presented with a HTML form interface. If the client performs a POST operation, the doPost() receives the input parameters, performs the necessary temperature conversions by calling either the fToC() or cToF() method and outputs the results as HTML.

Also, note, because the destroy() method is automatically called when the servlet is unloaded by the servlet engine, you have to unbind any existing reference for the RMIlet within rmiregistry.

Figure 3-15 shows the output after the remote object has been invoked by a HTML client.

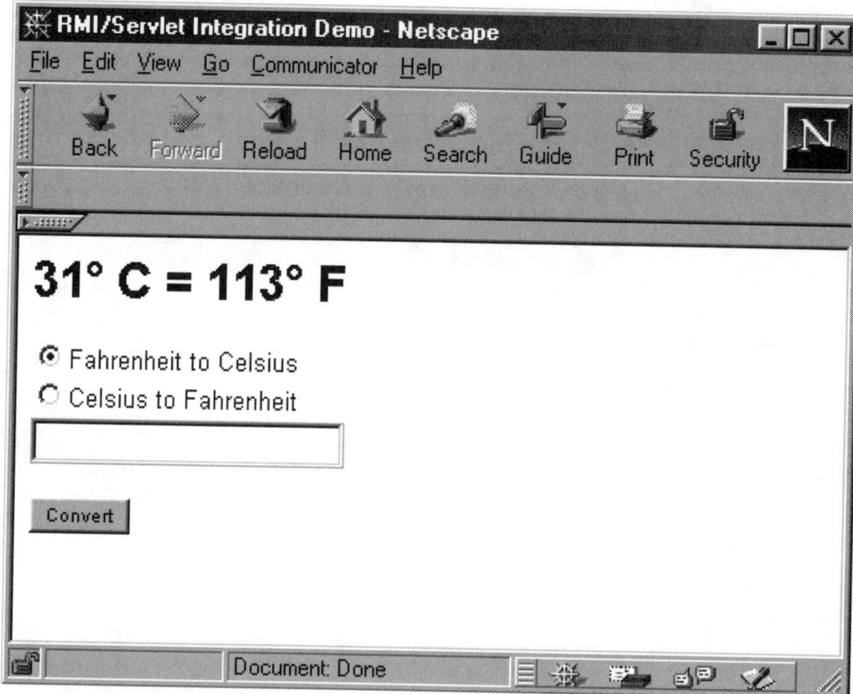

Figure 3-15: Accessing the remote object from an HTML client

Applet-Servlet Communication Using Object Serialization

So far, you have seen servlets used in conjunction with browser-based HTML clients. While this is by far their most common application, servlets can also serve as a middle-tier for any Java applet or application, as shown in Figure 3-16.

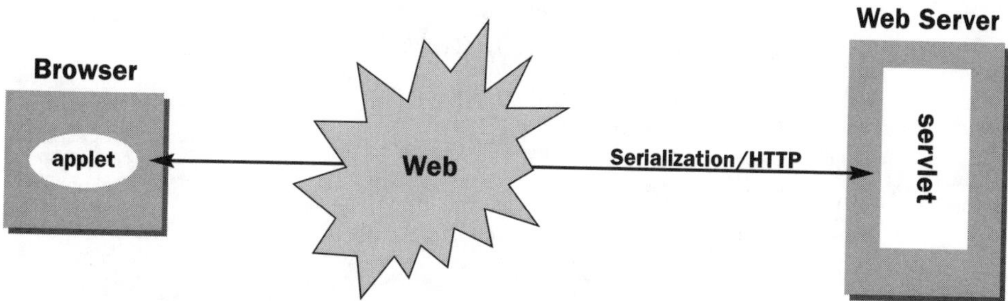

Figure 3-16: Applet-Servlet communication using serialization

Listings 3-16 and 3-17 demonstrate a scenario where an applet communicates with a servlet by passing Java objects using serialization.

Listing 3-16: Applet/Servlet Communication—The Guest Book Applet

```
package cup.chap3.applet;
import java.awt.*;
import java.applet.*;
import java.net.*;
import java.util.*;
import java.io.*;
public class GuestBook extends Applet
{
    public void init()
    {
        //generated by an ide
        setLayout(null);
        setSize(583,285);
        name = new java.awt.TextField();
        name.setBounds(128,12,276,27);
        add(name);
        email = new java.awt.TextField();
        email.setBounds(128,48,276,27);
        add(email);
        guests = new java.awt.TextArea();
        guests.setBounds(28,104,379,163);
        add(guests);
        signButton = new java.awt.Button();
        signButton.setLabel("Sign GuestBook");
        signButton.setBounds(432,24,133,33);
        signButton.setBackground(new Color(12632256));
        add(signButton);
        readButton = new java.awt.Button();
        readButton.setLabel("Read GuestBook");
        readButton.setBounds(432,164,133,33);
        readButton.setBackground(new Color(12632256));
        add(readButton);
        lblName = new java.awt.Label("Name");
        lblName.setBounds(72,16,44,23);
        add(lblName);
        lblEmail = new java.awt.Label("Email");
        lblEmail.setBounds(72,52,44,23);
        add(lblEmail);
        SymMouse aSymMouse = new SymMouse();
        signButton.addMouseListener(aSymMouse);
        readButton.addMouseListener(aSymMouse);
    }
```

Listing 3-16: continued

```
java.awt.TextField name;
java.awt.TextField email;
java.awt.TextArea guests;
java.awt.Button signButton;
java.awt.Button readButton;
java.awt.Label lblName;
java.awt.Label lblEmail;
class SymMouse extends java.awt.event.MouseAdapter
{
    public void mouseClicked(java.awt.event.MouseEvent event)
    {
        Object object = event.getSource();
        if (object == signButton)
            signButton_MouseClicked(event);
        else if (object == readButton)
            readButton_MouseClicked(event);
    }
}
void signButton_MouseClicked(java.awt.event.MouseEvent event)
{
URLConnection uc = null;

try {
    uc = new URL("http://localhost:8080/servlet/guestbook").openConnection();
    uc.setDoOutput(true);
    uc.setDoInput(false);
    uc.setUseCaches(false);
    uc.setRequestProperty("Content-type", "application/octet-stream");
    ObjectOutputStream objOut = new ObjectOutputStream(uc.getOutputStream());
    Vector param = new Vector();
    param.addElement(name.getText());
    param.addElement(email.getText());
    objOut.writeObject(param);
    objOut.flush();
    objOut.close();
    name.setText("");
    email.setText("");
    //uc=null;
} catch (Exception e) {
    System.out.println(e);
}
}
```

continues

Listing 3-16: continued

```
        void readButton_MouseClicked(java.awt.event.MouseEvent event)
        {
        URLConnection uc = null;
        Vector results=null;
         try {
           uc=new URL("http://host:port/servlet/guestbook").openConnection();
                 uc.setDoOutput(false);
                 uc.setDoInput(true);
                 uc.setUseCaches(false);
                 uc.setRequestProperty("Content-type", "application/octet-stream");
             ObjectInputStream objIn = new
             ObjectInputStream(uc.getInputStream());
             results=(Vector) objIn.readObject();
             objIn.close();
           } catch (Exception e) {
             System.out.println(e);
           }
           guests.setText("");
           for (int i=0;i< results.size();i++) {
             Vector guestinfo = (Vector) results.elementAt(i);
             String gstName = (String) guestinfo.elementAt(0);
             String gstEmail = (String)guestinfo.elementAt(1);
             guests.append("Name: "+gstName+"\n");
             guests.append("Email: "+gstEmail+"\n");
             guests.append("----------------------------------\n");
           }
        }
}
```

Our GuestBook applet can do one of two things—it can add an entry to the GuestBookServlet or retrieve its contents—depending on whether the user chooses to sign or read the guest book.

If the user selects to sign the guest book, the applet firstly opens a connection with the servlet as:

```
uc =new URL("http://host:port/servlet/guestbook").openConnection();
```

Because performing a "sign" operation involves sending data from the applet to the servlet, it is carried out via a "POST" operation from the applet. Consequently, setting the appropriate URLConnection parameters is important:

```
uc.setDoOutput(true);
uc.setDoInput(false);
uc.setUseCaches(false);
```

Because we are sending across a stream of binary data to the servlet, we must reflect the same within the content-type property before actually writing out the data, as the Netscape browser seems to require this:

```
uc.setRequestProperty("Content-type", "application/octet-stream");
```

The applet then simply sends the data to the servlet using object serialization:

```
ObjectOutputStream objOut =new ObjectOutputStream(uc.getOutputStream());
Vector param = new Vector();
param.addElement(name.getText());
param.addElement(email.getText());
objOut.writeObject(param);
```

Reading the contents of `GuestBookServlet` is equally straightforward. After opening a connection with the servlet and setting the appropriate `URLConnection` and content-type properties, the data can be read from the servlet using serialization as:

```
ObjectInputStream objIn= new objectInputStream(uc.getInputStream());
results=(Vector) objIn.readObject();
```

Listing 3-17: Applet/Servlet Communication—The Guest Book Servlet

```
package cup.chap3.applet;
import java.io.*;
import javax.servlet.*;
import javax.servlet.http.*;
import java.util.Vector;
public class GuestBookServlet extends HttpServlet implements SingleThreadModel {
    Vector guestCache;

    public void init(ServletConfig config) throws ServletException {
        super.init(config);
        guestCache = new Vector();
    }

    public void doPost(HttpServletRequest req,HttpServletResponse res)
    throws IOException{

        ObjectInputStream objIn =
            new ObjectInputStream(req.getInputStream());
        Vector data=null;
        try {
            data = (Vector) objIn.readObject();
        } catch (Exception e) {
            System.out.println(e);
        }
```

continues

Listing 3-17: continued

```
        guestCache.addElement(data);
        objIn.close();
    }
    public void doGet(HttpServletRequest req, HttpServletResponse res)
    throws IOException
    {
        res.setContentType("application/octet-stream");
        ObjectOutputStream objOut = new
        ObjectOutputStream(res.getOutputStream());
        objOut.writeObject(guestCache);
        objOut.close();
    }
}
```

The design of GuestBookServlet is quite simple. To keep things simple and to avoid dealing with multithreaded issues, the servlet implements the SingleThreadModel interface. Notice we also keep the contents of the guest book loaded in memory using the Vector object guestCache.

The GuestBookServlet services both GET and POST operations performed by an applet by implementing the corresponding doGet() and doPost() methods.

When the applet "signs" the guest book, the data is picked up by the doPost() method, which, in turn, unmarshals the HTTP-encapsulated serialized data and adds it to guestCache as:

```
data = (Vector) objIn.readObject();
guestCache.addElement(data);
```

When the applet performs a "read" operation, the servlet's doGet() method is automatically triggered and the contents of guestCache is sent over to the applet using object serialization as:

```
objOut.writeObject(guestCache);
```

Figure 3-17 shows the contents of a sample guest book.

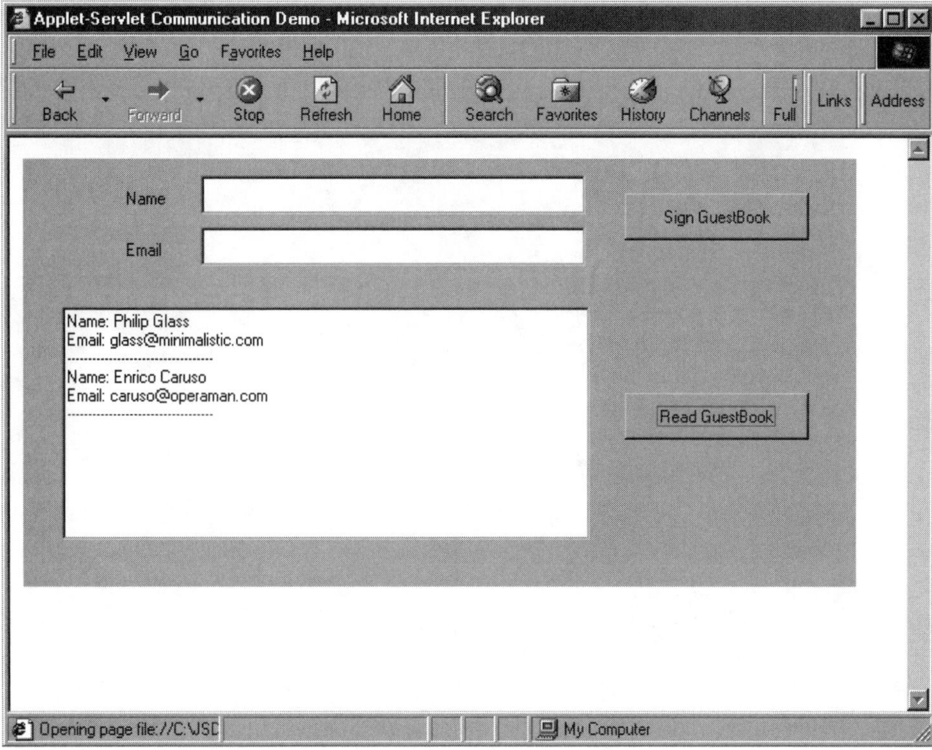

Figure 3-17: The Guest Book applet

Summary

Servlets are quite possibly the easiest way to introduce your enterprise to the world of server-side Java computing. Using servlets, an enterprise can significantly enhance the capabilities of their web server, without having to resort to proprietary solutions. Servlets, unlike CGI scripts, are highly scalable due to their inherently multithreaded nature, and are secure, since they run only within the context of the servlet engine. Furthermore, since servlets can maintain sessions, they enable us to develop browser-based client/server systems, communicating using HTTP. Since servlets are written in Java, they naturally leverage the power of all the enterprise Java APIs, including JDBC, JNI, RMI, Java IDL and Enterprise JavaBeans.

Chapter 4

Melding Java with Legacy Systems Using JNI

The Java Native Interface (JNI) is an integral part of JDK 1.1 and Java 2, and it is the only standard mechanism for the integration of C/C++ code with Java. This chapter discusses the integration of C/C++ software with Java through detailed programming examples. Also covered are important issues like multithreaded programming and exception handling from within native methods. Note, as of JDK 1.1, the JVM is shipped in the form of a DLL or shared library, depending on the platform. Consequently, C/C++ programs can now load a JVM and run Java classes within its context. Readers can gain an insight into this advanced feature by the coverage of the Introspection API at the end of this chapter.

A great deal of interest currently exists in interfacing Java with older, procedural, C-based application systems. Note, all example native programs in this chapter are implemented in C. Using the tips provided, however, they can easily be converted to C++. Also note, the chapter refers to the term "DLL" rather freely. In this context, DLL not only implies Dynamic Link Library (for Win32 systems), but is also synonymous with "shared library" (for UNIX-based systems), unless otherwise explicitly mentioned.

Introducing Native Methods

What exactly is a native method? Simply put, *native methods* are methods not implemented in Java itself, but in a different language like C or C++. The methods themselves are compiled into a DLL, which is loaded by the Java program at runtime.

Why do we need native methods?

Even though you may have already taken the "100% Pure Java" pledge, numerous compelling reasons exist for taking a hybrid approach to Java development:

- *Time to market*: The primary reason for using native methods is to shorten the "time to market" in moving legacy systems to the Web. Companies have significant investments in tried and tested mission-critical application systems that have gradually matured over the years and they are loath to rewrite them. Far easier is to place an object-oriented wrapper around the legacy services and make them available through a Java server than to reinvent the wheel.
- *Proprietary software*: Proprietary enterprise software systems come with their own APIs. True, many vendors like SAP, BAAN, PeopleSoft, and so forth are already providing or have plans to provide Java APIs in the future. But still, some time may occur before the smaller software vendors catch up with the Java revolution. If your vendor does not currently provide a Java API, wrapping its APIs as native methods may be your only solution for proprietary software/Java integration.
- *Legacy code*: Using native methods, a Java wrapper can be placed around legacy code, allowing it to be integrated with enterprise Java technologies like servlets, RMI, and CORBA.
- *Platform services*: Java, because of its inherent cross-platform nature, provides support for only the lowest common denominator level of functionality on all platforms. If your application needed access to any system services or platform-dependent features, you have to use native methods.
- *Hardware devices*: Most peripheral devices and plug-in cards usually come with their own C-based APIs. If you need to provide your Java applications direct access to, say, a scanner or a graphics accelerator, you need native methods.
- *Speed*: Some people argue that time-critical tasks must be implemented as native methods for optimal performance. Introducing non-Java code for the sake of speed alone is inadvisable. Java execution speeds have made tremendous gains with widespread availability of high-performance JVMs and JIT-compilers. If execution speed is paramount, consider deploying your Java application as a native binary instead.

Disadvantages of native methods

The Java paradigm was meant to be "100 percent pure" and exacts a rather steep price from those breaking the pledge.

- *Portability*: The most obvious disadvantage is Java programs making use of native methods lose their portability. If your application has to run on a different platform, the native code must also be ported to the new platform.
- *Difficulty*: Placing Java wrappers around procedural systems rely upon the successful identification of data abstractions in the legacy code base—not an easy task.
- *Complexity*: Developing real-life applications by making extensive use of native methods is not easy. Application developers have to be proficient not only in Java, but also in C or C++.
- *Security*: Programs using native methods are not as secure as pure Java applications. Java technologists please note: native programs run outside the sandbox and are not subject to the constraints of the Java security model.
- *Deployment*: Numerous browser security restrictions exist for applets that make use of native methods. For instance, only signed applets can make use of native methods.

Current support for native methods

Although the JNI is the de facto standard for implementing native methods, numerous other proprietary interfaces exist that serve the same purpose. But, unfortunately, none of the other contenders can be expected to implement uniformly across all JVMs.

- *J/Direct*: Microsoft's J/Direct interface is currently the most significant rival to the JNI standard. A highlight of J/Direct is it completely does away with the stub and wrapper files necessary for integration with JNI. In fact, developers can directly invoke methods found within any Win32 DLL from Java without having to write any C-wrapper code! Although using the J/Direct interface may seem to make integration under Windows simpler, remember: your Java programs may well be restricted to the Microsoft JVM. Those still interested can obtain complete details at: http://www.microsoft.com/java/resource/jdirect.htm
- *Java/COM interface*: Microsoft's Java/COM interface essentially exposes a subset of the Win32 API via COM interfaces and allows their access from within Java programs. Much of what was achieved by the Java/COM interface has been obviated with the introduction of J/Direct. Support for the Java/COM interface is available only under Microsoft JVMs.
- *RNI*: The Raw Native Interface is yet another proprietary Microsoft specification for the integration of native code with Java. RNI is a fairly low-level API. Using this, developers can wrap Win32 API calls within a custom DLL

and invoke the wrapper functionality from within Java. RNI seems surprisingly similar to Sun's NMI—the JDK 1.0 standard for native methods.

- *JDK 1.0 Native Method Interface (NMI)*: Initially, NMI was promoted by Sun as the standard native method interface under JDK 1.0. But this standard did anything but take off. NMI offered direct access to the JVM in the form of C structures - itself not a very robust architecture in the first place. Inefficient garbage collection, as well as numerous other VM inconsistencies further compounded the problem. Although backward compatibility for NMI is still provided by JDK 1.1, Sun has pretty much shied away from this interface. In fact, no promise exists NMI will even be available within future versions of the JDK. The message to those intent on using native methods is clear: Use JNI!

JNI Design Goals

The JNI architecture is well-thought out and easily meets all its stated design goals:

- *Binary compatibility*: JNI programs are "binary compatible" across all JVMs on a given platform. This implies you can compile your application for a certain JVM and run the application using a different vendor's JVM (on the same platform), as long as both JVMs implement JNI. Although this sounds like a fairly obvious need, embedding native code within Java introduces some strange peculiarities. For instance, this feature was absent in the NMI under JDK 1.0 because vendors followed different memory layouts for their native code at runtime.
- *Protected Access*: Unlike the NMI in JDK 1.0, JNI does not provide native programs with direct access to JVM internals. All JVM access is highly protected and regulated by means of the JNI "accessor functions". These C-based functions also empower JNI applications with a high degree of functionality.
- *Improved garbage collection*: The garbage collection mechanism has been vastly improved under JNI, compared to earlier implementations. This makes for much more stable programs by reducing hard-to-track memory leaks.

What Can You Do with JNI?

Using JNI, you can do almost anything with native methods that can be done using regular Java methods. For instance, you can

- Pass any Java object/primitive data type as a parameter to native methods.
- Return any Java object/primitive data type from a method call.
- Create, update, and inspect Java objects from native methods.
- Invoke Java methods from native methods.

- Load Java classes and examine them.
- Throw Java exceptions from native methods.
- Implement monitor-based synchronization to support multithreaded access.

The remainder of this chapter examines in detail the various JNI facilities that help us perform the previously mentioned tasks.

Understanding the JNI Life Cycle

Contrary to popular perception, you needn't be a rocket scientist to master JNI programming. In fact, JNI development follows a well-defined life-cycle and is shown in Figure 4-1.

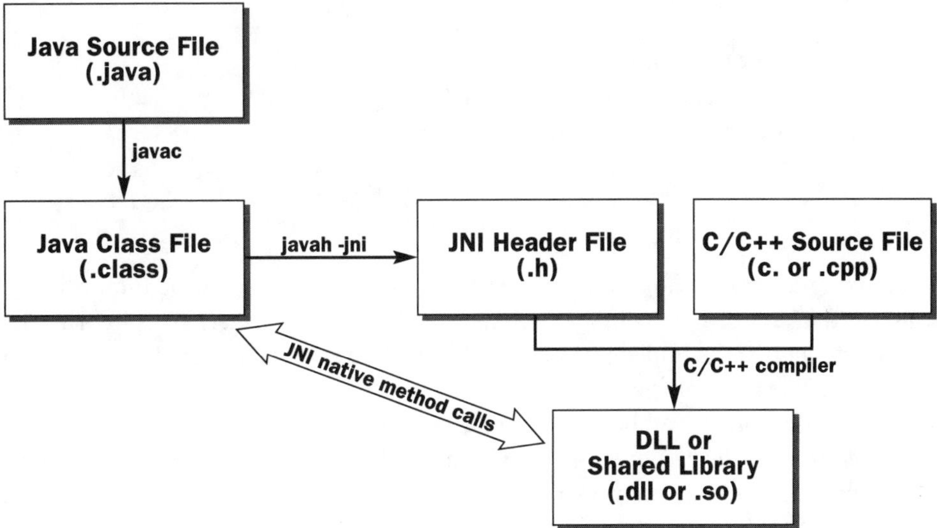

Figure 4-1: The JNI Life-Cycle

Nearly any JNI program can be implemented by closely adhering to the following six-step program:

1. Write the Java code.
2. Compile the Java code.
3. Generate the JNI-style header file.
4. Implement the native method.
5. Create the shared library or DLL.
6. Run the Java program.

Now, we explore in detail the intricacies of JNI programming by means of the perennial favorite—the "Hello World" example shown in Listing 4-1.

1. Write the Java code

Listing 4-1: A Simple JNI Example

```
/**
    JNIHelloWorld.java
    Demonstrating a simple native method invocation
**/
public class JNIHelloWorld {
    // declare the native method
public native void sayHello();
// load the library containing the native method implementation
static {
System.loadLibrary("helloworld");
}
public static void main(String[] args) {
JNIHelloWorld testJNI = new JNIHelloWorld();
//invoke native method
testJNI.sayHello();
}
}
```

Looking at the previous example, some things may seem out of the ordinary. Observe the keyword native in the declaration of method sayHello(). This informs the Java compiler that the implementation of this method is found externally, in the form of a DLL. The static block containing System.loadLibrary("helloworld") loads the DLL containing the native method implementation during runtime.

The System.loadLibrary() method behavior depends on the platform on which it runs. For instance, if the example were run on a Win32 platform, the DLL HELLOWORLD.DLL would get loaded. If the example were run on a Solaris platform, the shared library libhelloworld.so would be loaded.

2. Compile the Java source

Nothing different here. Compile the Java source as usual:

```
javac JNIHelloWorld.java
```

3. Generate the JNI-style header file

The javah header generator is available as part of Java 2 and is applied to the class file containing the native method declarations.

```
javah -jni JNIHelloWorld
```

Specifying the -jni flag is important. Otherwise, the javah utility generates header and stub files for the older JDK 1.0 native method interface instead of the JNI-style header file. Listing 4-2 shows the generated JNI header file, JNIHelloWorld.h

Listing 4-2: The JNI Header File

```
/* DO NOT EDIT THIS FILE - it is machine generated */
#include <jni.h>
/* Header for class JNIHelloWorld */
#ifndef _Included_JNIHelloWorld
#define _Included_JNIHelloWorld
#ifdef __cplusplus
extern "C" {
#endif
/*
 * Class:     JNIHelloWorld
 * Method:    sayHello
 * Signature: ()V
 */
JNIEXPORT void JNICALL Java_JNIHelloWorld_sayHello (JNIEnv *, jobject);
#ifdef __cplusplus
}
#endif
#endif
```

The name of the generated header file is always SomeClass.h, assuming your native methods are defined within SomeClass.java. Observe the generated function prototype for the native method sayHello(). Two parameters are passed by default to every native method by the JVM. The first, JNIEnv, is the JNI interface pointer (shown in Figure 4-2), which serves as a handle to the accessor function table. Please note, JNIEnv is a thread-specific data structure.

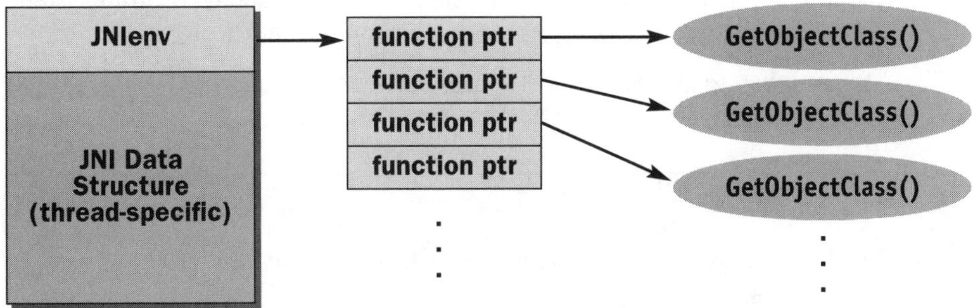

Figure 4-2: The JNI interface pointer

The second argument, jobject, is equivalent to this in C++ and is a handle to the instance which invoked the native method. Please note, if this was a static method, we would have a handle to the class itself passed in the form of a jclass object, instead of the jobject.

The included file, jni.h, is part of the standard JDK 1.1 distribution. It defines JNI data structures like JNIEnv, jobject, and so forth.

4. Implement the native method

Now, let's provide the implementation for our native method within a C source file, say, JNIHelloWorld.c, shown in Listing 4-3. Observe the prototype for our native implementation function is borrowed from the previously generated JNI header file.

Listing 4-3: The HelloWorld Native Implementation

```
/** JNIHelloWorld.c
**/
#include "JNIHelloWorld.h"
JNIEXPORT void JNICALL Java_JNIHelloWorld_sayHello(JNIEnv *env, jobject this) {
    printf("Hello World...welcome to JNI!\n");
}
```

The power of native methods stems from their capability to harness the power and features of the implementation language completely—be it C or C++. In the current example, printing a simple greeting should help get a basic understanding of the bridge between Java and C/C++.

5. Create the shared library or DLL

For Solaris platforms, you can create a shared library, such as libhellowworld.so as follows:

```
cc -G JNIHelloWorld.c -I $JAVAHOME/include -I$JAVAHOME/include/solaris
-o libhelloworld.so
```

Here, $JAVAHOME refers to the location where the JDK is installed on your system. For Win32 platforms, you can create a DLL HELLOWORLD.DLL as follows:

```
cl -I$JAVAHOME\include -I$JAVAHOME\include\win32 -LD JNIHelloWorld.c -
    FeHELLOWORLD.DLL
```

Note

Win32: the DLL implementing the native method functionality must be found within the system PATH.

Solaris: The JVM searches the environment variable LD_LIBRARY_PATH for the location of the shared library that needs to be loaded.

6. Run the Java program

The Java program is run as usual. Invoking

```
java HelloWorld
```

produces loads and executes our native method producing

```
Hello World...Welcome to JNI!
```

Mapping Between Java and C Data Types

One of the problems that has significantly affected the portability of conventional C/C++ programs has been the primitive data types such as float, int, char, and so forth are highly platform-dependent. For instance, an int type on some systems could be defined as 8-bits, and on others, as 16-bits. To avoid this problem, JNI defines platform-independent types like jint, jchar, jlong, and so forth, which developers can use within their native programs. The JNI header file, jni.h, in turn, contains the platform-specific mappings to their equivalent data types by means of typedef statements.

When passing data between Java and native programs, note that all primitive data types are passed by value and Java objects, strings, and arrays are always passed by reference. Table 4-1 shows the Java primitives and their equivalent JNI types. Table 4-2 gives a listing of the data types passed by reference.

Table 4-1: Data Types Passed by Value

Java Type	C Type
boolean	jboolean
byte	jbyte
char	jchar
short	jshort
int	jint
long	jlong
float	jfloat
double	jdouble

Table 4-2: Data Types Passed by Reference

Java Type	C Type
class	jclass
Object	jobject
string	jstring
Object []	jobjectArray
String []	jstringArray
boolean []	jbooleanArray
byte []	jbyteArray
char []	jcharArray
short []	jshortArray
int []	jintArray
long []	jlongArray
float []	jfloatArray
double []	jdoubleArray

Accessing Java Objects from Native Methods

This section examines how the value of any Java object can be retrieved and reset from within a native method. As mentioned before, the JNI functions play a pivotal role in any interaction between the native and Java worlds. Accessing Java objects from within native methods is a fairly straightforward process: you simply invoke the appropriate JNI functions in the proper sequence for seamless interaction.

Accessing instance data

A recipe exists for just about any type of JNI interaction. In this case, the general guidelines for accessing instance data are

- Get the class type of the invoking object, using the GetObjectClass() function.
- Obtain the target field ID by passing the class name, field name, and signature to the GetFieldID() function.
- Use the appropriate GetxxxField()/SetxxxField() functions to get/set your target object field.
- Convert any retrieved object field as needed.

Listing 4-4—JNIObjAccess.java—demonstrates how a native method can access the contents of a Java object. Here, our Java class declares a single native method, askJNI(), which accepts a String argument and returns back a String type. The main method simply serves to instantiate an object of type JNIObjAccess, and invokes the native method askJNI().

Listing 4-4: Demonstrating Object Access

```
/**
    JNIObjAccess.java
    This program demonstrates a native method that
    accepts a parameter and returns a value back to
    the invoking object
*/
public class JNIObjAccess {
    public String name = "Java Joe";
    public native String askJNI(String msg);
    static {
        System.loadLibrary("JNIObjectAccess");
    }
    public static void main(String[] args) {
        JNIObjAccess ex1 = new JNIObjAccess();
        String msg = "Unleash the power of JNI!";
```

Listing 4-4: continued

```
        String jniSays = ex1.askJNI(msg);
        System.out.println(jniSays);
    }
}
```

Now, look at the C implementation, JNIObjAccess.c, shown in Listing 4-5, for our native method, askJNI. Remember, the prototype for the function declaration Java_JNIObjAccess_askJNI (JNIEnv *env, jobject this, jstring arg) is obtained from the generated header file, as in the first example. Again, note the first two arguments: the handle to the accessor function table JNIEnv and the jobject handle to the Java instance are passed by default to every native method. The third argument, jstring, is the Java String passed to the native method.

Listing 4-5: Accessing Java Objects from C

```
/**
    JNIObjAccess.c
    Native method implementation
    demonstrating basic string manipulation
*/
#include "JNIObjAccess.h"
JNIEXPORT jstring JNICALL
Java_JNIObjAccess_askJNI (JNIEnv *env, jobject this, jstring arg) {
    char retstr[100];
    /* convert from unicode to UTF-8 */
    const char *msg =(*env)->GetStringUTFChars(env,arg,0);
    /* obtain the value of "name" within the invoking object */
    jclass jc = (*env)->GetObjectClass(env,this);
    jfieldID jf =(*env)->GetFieldID(env,jc,"name","Ljava/lang/String;");
    jstring nameStr =(jstring)(*env)->GetObjectField(env,this,jf);
    const char *name = (*env)->GetStringUTFChars(env,nameStr,0);
    /*create the new string */
    sprintf(retstr, "%s - %s",name, msg);
    /* free memory to avoid leakage*/
    (*env)->ReleaseStringUTFChars(env,msg,0);
    (*env)->ReleaseStringUTFChars(env,name,0);
    /* return new string by wrapping it within a Java string object*/
    return ((*env)->NewStringUTF(env,retstr));
}
```

Strings are stored quite differently in Java compared to C. For instance, while Java strings are stored as arrays of 16-bit Unicode characters, C strings are null-terminated arrays of 8-bit characters. Hence, making the necessary format changes is important when passing string types between the two languages. Luckily, JNI provides an extensive set of functions for working with string data. The line

```
const char *msg =(*env)->GetStringUTFChars(env,arg,0);
```

converts the Java string into a constant array of UTF characters. The Unicode Text Format (UTF) is an 8-bit code that is compatible with ASCII.

Informing the JVM when you are done with using any UTF string is important, so the memory allocated for its storage can be garbage-collected. This is accomplished by calling

```
(*env)->ReleaseStringUTFChars(env,msg,0);
```

Note, the presence of a `GetStringUTFChars()` without a matching `ReleaseStringUTFChars()` is a sure sign of a memory leak.

Much of the remaining program simply follows the previously mentioned recipe for object access from native methods. Finally, the result is sent back to the invoking Java method by creating a new Java string from the native string buffer.

```
return ((*env)->NewStringUTF(env,retstr));
```

On executing the program, the native method returns the string:

```
Java Joe - Unleash the power of JNI!
```

> **Note**
>
> Native method programming is less cumbersome in C++. Also, the `JNIEnv` pointer is not passed in the parameter list during the invocation of any JNI function.
>
> For instance, the JNI function invocation in the previous example:
>
> ```
> const char *name = (*env)->GetStringUTFChars(env,nameStr,0);
> ```
>
> when translated into C++ becomes
>
> ```
> const char *name = env->GetStringUTFChars(nameStr,0);
> ```

Tables 4-3 and 4-4. show the various JNI functions that can be used for accessing Java objects. An appropriate function is called depending on the data type of the target Java field.

Accessing static data

Static data can be accessed from within native methods similar to instance data. The difference lies in making use of different JNI functions specific to handling static data types. The general guidelines for accessing static data are

- Get the class type of the invoking object using `GetObjectClass()`.
- Obtain the target FieldID by passing the class name, field name, and signature to `GetStaticFieldID()`.

- Use the appropriate GetStaticField()/SetStaticField() functions to get/set the object field.
- Convert any retrieved object field as needed.

Table 4-3: GetXXXField() JNI Functions

GetFieldRoutineName()	Native Type	Java Type
GetObjectField()	jobject	Object
GetBooleanField()	jboolean	boolean
GetByteField()	jbyte	byte
GetCharField()	jchar	char
GetShortField()	jshort	short
GetIntField()	jint	int
GetLongField()	jlong	long
GetFloatField()	jfloat	float
GetDoubleField()	jdouble	double

Table 4-4: SetXXXField() JNI Functions

SetFieldRoutineName()	Native Type	Java Type
SetObjectField()	jobject	Object
SetBooleanField()	jboolean	boolean
SetByteField()	jbyte	byte
SetCharField()	jchar	char
SetShortField()	jshort	short
SetIntField()	jint	int
SetLongField()	jlong	long
SetFloatField()	jfloat	float
SetDoubleField()	jdouble	double

Suppose, in the previous example, JNIObjAccess.java, name was statically defined as:

```
public static String name = "Java Joe";
```

Our native implementation is now slightly different and needs the following changes:

```
jfieldID jf = (*env)->GetStaticFieldID(env,jc,"name",
    "Ljava/lang/String;");
jstring nameStr = (jstring)
    (*env)->GetStaticObjectField(env,this,jf);
```

Tables 4-5 and 4-6 show the various JNI functions that can be used for accessing static Java objects. An appropriate function is called, depending on the data type of the target Java field.

Table 4-5: GetStaticXXXField() JNI Functions

GetStaticFieldRoutineName()	Native Type	Java Type
GetStaticObjectField()	jobject	Object
GetStaticBooleanField()	jboolean	boolean
GetStaticByteField()	jbyte	byte
GetStaticCharField()	jchar	char
GetStaticShortField()	jshort	short
GetStaticIntField()	jint	int
GetStaticLongField()	jlong	long
GetStaticFloatField()	jfloat	float
GetStaticDoubleField()	jdouble	double

Table 4-6: SetStaticXXXField() JNI Functions

SetStaticFieldRoutineName()	Native Type	Java Type
SetStaticObjectField()	jobject	Object
SetStaticBooleanField()	jboolean	boolean
SetStaticByteField()	jbyte	byte
SetStaticCharField()	jchar	char
SetStaticShortField()	jshort	short
SetStaticIntField()	jint	int
SetStaticLongField()	jlong	long
SetStaticFloatField()	jfloat	float
SetStaticDoubleField()	jdouble	double

Obtaining JVM Type Signatures

Before you access any object or invoke a Java method from within a native method, you must first obtain its unique field or method identifier. This is done by supplying the appropriate JNI function with the JVM signature of the target object or method. Table 4-7 summarizes the encoding scheme within the JVM for Java data types.

Table 4-7: JVM Type Signatures

Signature	Java Type
Z	boolean
B	byte
C	char
S	short
I	int
J	long
F	float
D	double
Lfully-qualified-class;	fully-qualified-class
[type	type[]
(arg-types)return-type	method-type
V	void

Although Table 4-7 may prove useful for a quick lookup when formulating method or field signatures, developers needn't memorize its contents. Far simpler is to make use of the Java class file disassembler—javap—to generate the internal type signatures for any Java class file.

For example, applying javap to our previous example as:

```
javap -private -s JNIObjAccess
```

generates

```
private java.lang.String name;
        /*  Ljava/lang/String;  */
private native java.lang.String askJNI(java.lang.String);
        /*  (Ljava/lang/String;)Ljava/lang/String;  */
```

The output of javap displays every Java method or field belonging to the class—with each member followed by its corresponding internal JVM signature enclosed within comments.

By default, javap displays signatures for all class entities with public scope. Hence, specifying the -s and -private options to javap is important, as they also help display signatures for static and private fields and methods.

Note

Developers need to pay special attention when denoting the type signatures for Java classes. The signature for any Java class is always:

```
Lfully_qualified_classname;
```

For instance, the signature for the class `com.cup.MyTestClass` is:

```
Lcom/cup/MyTestClass;
```

A mistake made all too often when denoting the type signature for a Java class is omitting the semicolon after the class name.

Similarly, for Java methods, note you must not include any spaces between the parameter signatures. For instance, the signature for the Java method:

```
int compute(MyTestClass x, int[] y)
```

would be

```
"(Lcom/cup/MyTestClass;[I)I"
```

Accessing Java Arrays

JNI does not enable you to access Java arrays directly from within native methods. Instead, you must make use of JNI functions to iterate through the array and to access the individual array elements. The general guidelines for working with Java arrays are

- First, obtain the size of the array using `GetArrayLength()` function.
- Second, iterate through the array, obtaining each element by using the appropriate `GetxxxArrayElement()` function, depending on the element data type.
- Third, if you need to update an array element, use the correct `SetxxxArrayElement()` function.

Listings 4-6 and 4-7 are a good example of how arrays are handled by native methods. The example Java class initializes an array of strings, invokes the native method `nativestuff()` by passing this array as an argument, and then prints the modified array. As denoted in Table 4-2, remembering Java arrays are passed by reference is important. Any change made to them within native methods get automatically reflected within Java on return.

Listing 4-6: Demonstrating Array Access

```
/**
    JNIArrayAccess.java
    Java source demonstrating the passing of
    array types to native methods
```

Listing 4-6: continued

```
*/
public class JNIArrayAccess {
    private native void nativestuff(String[] strArray);
    static {
        System.loadLibrary("Example2");
    }
public static void main(String[] args) {
        String[] strArray = new String[4] ;
        strArray[0]= "This";
        strArray[1]= "is";
        strArray[2]= "a";
        strArray[3]= "test!";
        JNIArrayAccess x = new JNIArrayAccess();
        x.nativestuff(strArray);
        for (int i=0; i<strArray.length; i++) {
            System.out.println(strArray[i]);
        }
    }
}
```

Listing 4-7: Accessing Java Arrays from C

```
/**
    JNIArrayAccess.c
Native  implementation demonstrating manipulation of
array types within native methods
*/
#include " JNIArrayAccess.h"
JNIEXPORT void JNICALL Java_ JNIArrayAccess _nativestuff (JNIEnv *env, jobject obj,
        jobjectArray objArray) {
    const char *str ;
    char retstr[100] ;
    jint i;
    jstring newstr;

    /* determine the size of the array */
    jsize len = (*env)->GetArrayLength (env,objArray);
    /* loop through the entire array */
    for ( i=0; i< len; i++) {
        /* obtain each element and update it's value */
        javaStr=(jstring) (*env)->GetObjectArrayElement(env,objArray,i);
        str = (*env)->GetStringUTFChars(env,javaStr,0);
        sprintf(retstr, "JNI SAYS: %s",str);
```

continues

Listing 4-7: continued

```
            newstr = (*env)->NewStringUTF(env,retstr);
            (*env)->SetObjectArrayElement( env,objArray,i,newstr);
            (*env)->ReleaseStringUTFChars(env,str,0);
        }
    }
```

On executing the program, the Java string array that was modified by the native method now reads

```
JNI Says: This
JNI Says: is
JNI Says: a
JNI Says: test!
```

The previous approach is the only way to deal with Java Object arrays, although it also works with arrays of primitive data elements. JNI offers some specialized functions exclusively for working with arrays of primitive data elements, however, which may prove more efficient.

Consider the following sample native method, `doubleSalary()`, which doubles the value of all the elements within a float array.

```
JNIEXPORT void JNICALL Java_ExampleClass_doubleSalary
(JNIEnv *env, object this, jfloatArray salary) {

jint FACTOR = 2;
jint i;

jsize s = (*env)->GetArrayLength(env,salary);
     jfloat *arr=(*env)->GetFloatArrayElements(env,salary,0);
     for (i=0;i<s;i++) {
        arr[i] *= FACTOR;
     }
(*env)->ReleaseFloatArrayElements(env,salary,arr, 0);
     return;
}
```

We can obtain a pointer to the elements of the array by calling

```
jfloat *arr=
     (*env)->GetFloatArrayElements(env,salary,0);
```

Now, JNI ensures that `arr` points to an array of floats stored in some nonvolatile region of the memory, by making a separate copy of the array if necessary. Accessing the array elements by traversing a pointer is considerably more efficient than retrieving them one at a time. Also possible is to read and modify the array elements directly, as shown by:

```
arr[i] *= FACTOR;
```

Note, the GetFloatArrayElements() function "locks" the memory region storing the array, thus preventing access by the JVM garbage collector. Also, the pointer arr may actually be pointing to a copy of the original array, in which case, any changes will be reflected back in the original only upon "unlocking" this memory. Hence, it is important to free this region explicitly by calling

```
(*env)->ReleaseFloatArrayElements(env,salary,arr, 0);
```

Tables 4-8 show the various JNI functions that can be used for accessing arrays of primitive Java elements.

Table 4-8: Functions for Accessing Arrays of Primitive Elements

JNI Function	Primitive Array Data Type
GetBooleanArrayElements()	boolean
GetByteArrayElements()	byte
GetCharArrayElements()	char
GetShortArrayElements()	short
GetIntArrayElements()	int
GetLongArrayElements()	long
GetFloatArrayElements()	float
GetDoubleArrayElements()	double

Accessing Java Methods from Native Methods

We take for granted that a Java object's regular methods can invoke each other—the situation is not too different with native methods.

Accessing instance methods

As always, a cookbook approach is ready, which should make the process of invoking any Java method from within a native method a cinch:

- Get the class type of the invoking Java object using GetObjectClass().
- Obtain the method identifier of Java method you want to invoke by calling GetMethodID().
- Initialize any method parameters for this Java method.
- Invoke the Java method by calling the appropriate CallxxxMethod() function depending on the return type.
- Convert the returned object field if necessary for use within the native method.

Now, look at a fairly detailed example. First, two Java classes—Employee (Listing 4-8) and its subclass, Manager (Listing 4-9)—are defined. Nothing is unusual about either class: both have a simple print() method to display themselves. The Employee class also has a giveRaise() method to increment the salary field. Observe that the constructor for Manager accepts an Employee object, as well as a bonus amount.

Listing 4-8: The Employee Class

```
/**
    Employee.java
    This is the class that is passed to the
    native method in Example3.java
*/

public class Employee {
    public Employee (String name, String title, double salary) {
        this.name =name;
        this.title=title;
        this.salary=salary;
    }
    public void giveRaise(double raise) {
        salary += raise;
    }
    public void print() {
        System.out.println("NAME:"+name);
        System.out.println("TITLE:"+title);
        System.out.println("SALARY:"+salary);
    }
    String name;
String title;
double salary;
}
```

Listing 4-9: The Manager Class

```
/**
    Manager.java
    This is the class that is returned by the
    native method in Example3.java
*/
public class Manager extends Employee {
    public Manager (Employee emp, double bonus) {
        super(emp.name,emp.title,emp.salary);
        this.bonus = bonus;
    }
```

Listing 4-9: continued

```
        public void print() {
        super.print();
            System.out.println("BONUS:"+bonus);
        }
        double bonus;
    }
```

Finally, programs CallJava.java (shown in Listing 4-10) and CallJava.c (shown in Listing 4-11), demonstrate the use of the Employee and Manager classes within native methods. We pass an instance of the Employee class to the native method promoteEmployee(), which, in turn, creates and returns an instance of the Manager class back to the invoking object.

Listing 4-10: Invoking Java Methods from Native Methods

```
/**
    CallJava.java
    This program demonstrates the usage of user
    defined classes with native methods. We pass an
    instance of the Employee class to our native method,
    which in turn, creates and returns an instance of the
    Manager class back to the invoking object.
*/
public class CallJava {
    private native Manager promoteEmployee(Employee empObj);
    static {
        System.loadLibrary("CallJava");
    }
    public static void main(String[] args) {
        Employee empObj = new Employee("Java Joe",
            "Java Engineer",45000.00);
        System.out.println("Before JNI invocation");
        empObj.print();
        CallJava jniCallJava= new CallJava();
        Manager newManager =
            (Manager) jniCallJava.promoteEmployee(empObj);
        System.out.println("\nAfter JNI invocation");
        newManager.print();
    }
}
```

Listing 4-11: Creating and Returning Java Objects from C

```
/**
    CallJava.c
    This native implementation demonstrates how we
    can receive and return complex Java objects from
    within native methods. We also see how native
    methods can not only invoke methods of the parent
    object, but instantiate arbitrary Java objects.
*/
#include "CallJava.h"
JNIEXPORT jobject JNICALL Java_CallJava_promoteEmployee
(JNIEnv *env, jobject obj, jobject empObj) {
    jclass clsEmp;
    jclass clsManager;
    jobject jo;
    jmethodID ctorManager ;
    jmethodID giveRaise;
    jstring newTitle;
    /* update the title field of the Java object passed to native method */
    clsEmp = (*env)->GetObjectClass(env,empObj);
    jo = (jobject)(*env)->GetFieldID(env,clsEmp,"title",
                    "Ljava/lang/String;");
    newTitle = (*env)->NewStringUTF(env, "Java Programming Manager");
    (*env)->SetObjectField(env,empObj,jo,newTitle);
    /* invoke the giveRaise method for the Employee object */
    giveRaise = (jmethodID)
        (*env)->GetMethodID(env,clsEmp,"giveRaise","(D)V");
    (*env)->CallVoidMethod(env,empObj,giveRaise, 10000.00);
    /* create and return an instance of the Manager class */
    clsManager =(jclass)(*env)->FindClass(env,"Manager");
    ctorManager = (jmethodID) (*env)->GetMethodID(env,clsManager,
        "<init>","(LEmployee;D)V");
    jo =(*env)->NewObject(env, clsManager,ctorManager, empObj,12000.00);
    return(jo);
}
```

On running the Java program, you see "Java Joe" is rewarded with a promotion as well as a bonus!

```
Before JNI Invocation
NAME: Java Joe
TITLE: Java Engineer
SALARY: 45,000.00
After JNI Invocation
```

```
NAME: Java Joe
TITLE: Java Programming Manager
SALARY: 55,000.00
BONUS: 12,000.00
```

Table 4-9 shows the various JNI functions that can be used for invoking Java methods from within native methods.

Table 4-9: CallxxxMethod Functions for Invoking Java Methods

CallMethodRoutineName()	Native Type	Java Type
CallVoidMethod()	void	void
CallObjectMethod()	jobject	Object
CallBooleanMethod()	jboolean	boolean
CallByteMethod()	jbyte	byte
CallCharMethod()	jchar	char
CallShortMethod()	jshort	short
CallIntMethod()	jint	int
CallLongMethod()	jlong	long
CallFloatMethod()	jfloat	float
CallDoubleMethod()	jdouble	double

Accessing static methods

Static Java methods are invoked in a manner similar to calling instance methods. The general guidelines outlined in the following give more details:

- Get the class type of the invoking Java object using `GetObjectClass()`.
- Obtain the method identifier of Java method you want to invoke by calling `GetStaticMethodID()`.
- Initialize any method parameters for this Java method.
- Invoke the Java method by calling the appropriate `CallStaticxxxMethod()` function (shown in Table 4-10) depending on the return type. Please note, for this function, you have to pass the `class` object to which the method belongs and not the implicit parameter object, as in the case of an instance method.
- Convert the returned object field if necessary for use within the native method.

Table 4-10: Static Java Methods

CallMethodRoutineName()	Native Type	Java Type
CallStaticVoidMethod()	void	void
CallStaticObjectMethod()	jobject	Object
CallStaticBooleanMethod()	jboolean	boolean
CallStaticByteMethod()	jbyte	byte
CallStaticCharMethod()	jchar	char
CallStaticShortMethod()	jshort	short
CallStaticIntMethod()	jint	int
CallStaticLongMethod()	jlong	long
CallStaticFloatMethod()	jfloat	float
CallStaticDoubleMethod()	jdouble	double

JNI Exception Handling

Native methods, like regular methods, are capable of raising arbitrary Java exceptions. Additionally, native methods can either choose to interrogate and handle these exceptions from within the native implementation itself or simply throw them back to the invoking Java object.

Numerous JNI functions choose to report an abnormal state by returning an error code and posting a Java exception. Also, exceptions may be thrown in numerous other cases, such as exceeding array bounds, passing incorrect types for method arguments, and so forth.

Although invoking most JNI functions with an exception pending may lead to completely unpredictable behavior, the following JNI functions can be used safely, even with an exception pending.

```
throwable ExceptionOccurred(JNIEnv *env)
```

returns the exception object if an exception is pending and, otherwise, returns NULL

```
void ExceptionDescribe(JNIEnv *env)
```

prints the pending exception to `stderr` for diagnostic or debugging purposes

```
void ExceptionClear(JNIEnv *env)
```

clears any exception currently pending.

Once your native code has determined an exception is, indeed, pending by having invoked `ExceptionOccurred()`, then basically two ways exist to handle it:

- The native code can simply pass control back to the invoking Java object by means of a `return()` statement and have the exception handled within Java.
- The pending exception can be cleared by invoking `ExceptionClear()` and doing the exception handling within the native method itself. This approach is useful if the exception occurs early within a native method and you anticipate further JNI function invocations.

You can throw nearly any valid Java exception by using one of the following JNI functions:

```
Throw(JNIEnv *env, jobject obj)
```

accepts a `java.lang.Throwable` object as a parameter and causes the exception to be posted within the current thread

```
ThrowNew(JNIEnv *env, jclass excepClass, const char *msg)
```

accepts a valid subclass of type `java.lang.Throwable` and posts the exception initialized with the diagnostic `msg`.

Please note, `Throw()` and `ThrowNew()` simply serve to post the exception within the native method. The actual Java exception is thrown by JVM only when the native method returns.

For example, consider the following native code segment, which throws a user-defined `NegativeNumberException` back to the calling Java program:

```
if (students < 0) {
     (*env)->ThrowNew(env,
(*env)->FindClass(env, "NegativeNumberException",
          "Number of students must be greater than zero"
               );
     return;
} else {
     avg_score = total_score/students;
}
```

In a completely hopeless situation, your native method can raise an unrecoverable fatal error and terminate the JVM after printing a diagnostic to `stderr`, by invoking

```
FatalError(JNIEnv *env, char *msg)
```

Note

You cannot throw a Java exception in your C++ code, as it is currently impossible to distinguish between C++ and Java exceptions

Your native code must not throw any C++ exceptions

Use SignalError() to throw a Java exception

```
SignalError(NULL, "java/lang/OutOfMemoryError", "Failed to create string.");
```

Multithreaded Programming with JNI

Native methods can certainly be accessed by more than one thread concurrently from within Java. But, as with regular methods, if your native methods access any shared data, they must be synchronized.

The easiest way to ensure that only one thread executes the body of the native method is to indicate it is synchronized:

```
public synchronized native void someNativeMethod();
```

Locking out an entire method may not be the most optimal solution, especially considering that synchronized methods run considerably slower compared to non-synchronized methods. Instead, it may be more efficient to lock specific objects selectively within native code.

Readers may already be familiar with synchronized blocks within Java methods. For instance, a shared object may be synchronized within a Java method as:

```
synchronized (someObj) {
...
}
```

JNI offers similar data-locking functionality by way of two monitor-based functions:

```
jint MonitorEnter(JNIEnv *env, jobject obj);
jint MonitorExit(JNIEnv *env, jobject obj);
```

MonitorEnter() increments an internal counter associated with the monitor for a particular object, for each time a given thread enters the monitor. A thread can effectively lock an object and gain control of its monitor only if the monitor is not already being held by a different thread. If another thread already owns the monitor, then the current thread simply waits until the monitor is released.

Each call to MonitorExit() has the effect of decreasing the counter of the monitor for the locked object. An object is freed by the current thread when its monitor's counter reaches zero.

Because native methods can invoke regular Java methods, you can also make use of the methods Object.wait(), Object.notify(), and Object.notifyAll() for synchronization.

Let's examine the details of synchronizing native methods by means of the classic producer/consumer example. In a producer/consumer situation, the producer typically generates some data and then places it into a buffer. The duty of the consumer is to consume the data as soon as it is placed in the buffer. The problem is not as easy as it sounds—especially if the producer and consumer run within independent threads running asynchronously. The producer/consumer threads must be synchronized; this is critical. Otherwise, you may be faced with a situation known as a *race condition*, which occurs when either of the following situations is encountered:

- A consumer is running faster than the producer, causing it to read the same data twice.
- A producer may be faster, causing it to overwrite the buffer before it has been read by the consumer.

Proper synchronization is imperative for avoiding race conditions. Then, the consumer reads the data only once and only as soon as something has been produced by the consumer, and not otherwise.

In the example, our startup class NativeProducerConsumer, (shown in Listing 4-12) creates a MsgBuffer object and starts up two asynchronous threads for a producer and a consumer, after passing them the MsgBuffer object. The Producer and Consumer classes, both of which extend Thread, share data through the msg field of the MsgBuffer class. We ensure two asynchronously running threads also cannot access the MsgBuffer at the same time. The Consumer can access MsgBuffer only if the available flag, (set by the Producer) is true, indicating new data is ready for pickup.

This synchronization actually occurs within the produce() and consume() native methods (shown in Listing 4-13) of the MsgBuffer class and is implemented using the wait() and notifyAll() methods.

When new data is available, the Producer thread calls the produce() native method of the MsgBuffer. The produce() method loops in a wait state if the available flag is still set true, indicating any data previously placed in the msg buffer is yet to be picked up by Consumer. If available is false, produce() sets the msg buffer with the data, prints it, sets available to true, indicating new data is ready to be consumed and calls notifyAll(), waking up any waiting Consumer threads.

Similarly, the Consumer thread remains in a wait loop until the available flag turns true, indicating the Producer thread has populated the MsgBuffer. Once the Consumer breaks out of the wait state, it accesses msg in the MsgBuffer, "consumes" it, sets the available flag to false, and wakes up any waiting Producer threads by calling notifyAll().

Listing 4-12: The JNI-based Producer/Consumer Example

```
class MsgBuffer {
    static {
        System.loadLibrary("jnithreads");
    }
        private String msg;
        private boolean available = false;

        public native void consume() ;
        public native void produce(int i);
        public void setTrue() {
            this.available = true;
        }
        public void setFalse() {
            this.available = false;
        }
}
class Producer extends Thread {
            private MsgBuffer MsgBuffer;
            public Producer(MsgBuffer buf) {
                MsgBuffer = buf;
            }
            public void run() {
                for (int i = 1; i < 11; i++) {
                    MsgBuffer.produce(i);
                try {
                    sleep((int)(Math.random() * 100));
                } catch (InterruptedException e) { }
                }
        }
}
class Consumer extends Thread {
            private MsgBuffer MsgBuffer;
            public Consumer(MsgBuffer buf) {
                MsgBuffer = buf;
            }
            public void run() {
                for (int i = 1; i < 11; i++) {
                        MsgBuffer.consume();
                    }
            }
}
public class NativeProducerConsumer {
```

Listing 4-12: continued

```
            public static void main(String[] args) {
                MsgBuffer c = new MsgBuffer();
                Producer p1 = new Producer(c);
                Consumer c1 = new Consumer(c);
                p1.start();
                c1.start();
            }
}
```

Listing 4-13: C Program Demonstrating JNI-synchronization

```
#include "MsgBuffer.h"
#include <stdio.h>
JNIEXPORT void JNICALL Java_MsgBuffer_consume(JNIEnv *env, jobject this) {
    jclass jc;
    jfieldID jf1;
    jfieldID jf2;
    jboolean avail;
    jmethodID jmet1;
    jmethodID jmet2;
    jmethodID jmet3;
    jmethodID jmet4;
    jstring msg;
    const char *msgBuffer;
    jc = (*env)->GetObjectClass(env, this);
    jf1 = (*env)->GetFieldID(env,jc,"msg","Ljava/lang/String;");
    jf2 = (*env)->GetFieldID(env,jc,"available","Z");
    jmet1 = (*env)->GetMethodID(env,jc,"wait","()V");
    jmet2= (*env)->GetMethodID(env,jc,"notifyAll","()V");
    jmet3 =(*env)->GetMethodID(env,jc,"setTrue","()V");
    jmet4 =(*env)->GetMethodID(env,jc,"setFalse","()V");

    while (!(*env)->GetBooleanField(env,this,jf2)) {
        (*env)->CallVoidMethod(env,this,jmet1);
    }
    (*env)->CallVoidMethod(env,this,jmet4);
    msg = (jstring) (*env)->GetObjectField(env,this,jf1);
    msgBuffer = (*env)->GetStringUTFChars(env,msg,0);
    printf("Consumer obtained:%s\n",msgBuffer);

    /* important to lock object before calling notifyAll
        to prevent IllegalMonitorStateException
        from getting thrown
```

continues

Listing 4-13: continued

```
    */
    (*env)->MonitorEnter(env,this);
    (*env)->CallVoidMethod(env,this,jmet2);
    (*env)->MonitorExit(env,this);
}
JNIEXPORT void JNICALL Java_MsgBuffer_produce(JNIEnv *env, jobject this, jint i) {
    jclass jc;
    jfieldID jf1;
    jfieldID jf2;
    jboolean avail;
    jmethodID jmet1;
    jmethodID jmet2;
    jmethodID jmet3;
    jmethodID jmet4;
    jstring newmsg;
    char buf[100];

    jc = (*env)->GetObjectClass(env, this);
    jf1 = (*env)->GetFieldID(env,jc,"msg","Ljava/lang/String;");
    jf2 = (*env)->GetFieldID(env,jc,"available","Z");
    jmet1 = (*env)->GetMethodID(env,jc,"wait","()V");
    jmet2= (*env)->GetMethodID(env,jc,"notifyAll","()V");
    jmet3 =(*env)->GetMethodID(env,jc,"setTrue","()V");
    while ((*env)->GetBooleanField(env,this,jf2)) {
       (*env)->CallVoidMethod(env,this,jmet1);
    }
    sprintf(buf,"Message #%d",i);
    newmsg = (*env)->NewStringUTF(env,buf);
    (*env)->SetObjectField(env,this,jf1,newmsg);
    printf("Producer created:%s\n",buf);

    (*env)->CallVoidMethod(env,this,jmet3);
    /* important to lock object before calling notifyAll
       to prevent IllegalMonitorStateException
       from getting thrown
    */
    (*env)->MonitorEnter(env,this);
    (*env)->CallVoidMethod(env,this,jmet2);
    (*env)->MonitorExit(env,this);
}
```

Output

```
Producer created: Message #1
Consumer obtained: Message #1
Producer created: Message #2
Consumer obtained: Message #2
Producer created: Message #3
Consumer obtained: Message #3
Producer created: Message #4
Consumer obtained: Message #4
Producer created: Message #5
Consumer obtained: Message #5
        .
        .
        .
```

Using the Invocation API

The advent of JDK 1.1 has finally made available the power of Java to the teeming masses of C/C++ developers. Because the JVM is now shipped as a DLL, it can easily be loaded and initialized by any C/C++ application making use of JNI's Invocation API, shown in Figure 4-3. The Invocation API is of significant importance because, now, a native application potentially has access to some advanced features of Java—including RMI, JDBC, CORBA, and so forth.

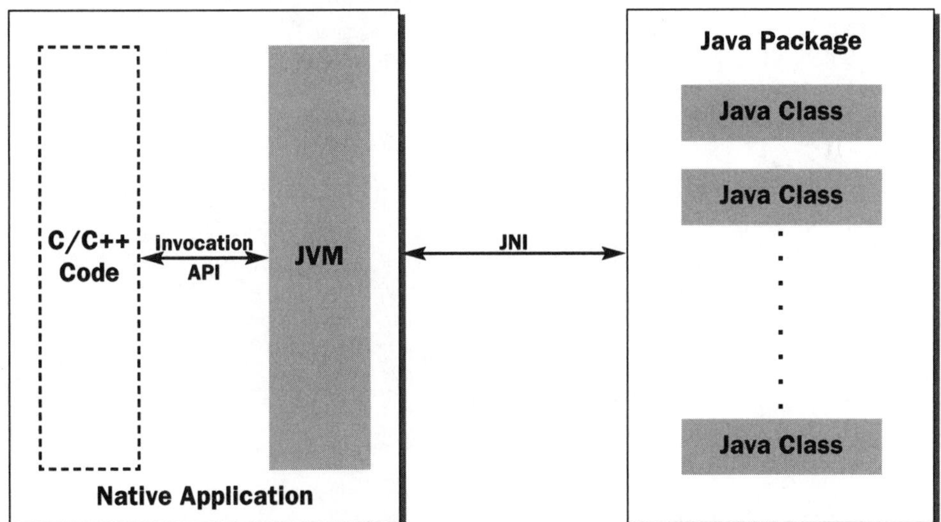

Figure 4-3: The Invocation API

Consider Listing 4-13 that implements a simple Java class HelloC:

Listing 4-14: The HelloC Example

```
/** HelloC.java
    Example Java class which is loaded by the C
    program using the Invocation  API
**/
public class HelloC {
    public void sayHello() {
       System.out.println("Hello C...this is
       Java speaking!");
    }
}
```

We can now easily load and create an instance of the previous Java class from any native application making use of the Invocation API. Listing 4-15 demonstrates a C program, which after loading and initializing the JVM, loads and creates an instance of our test Java class—HelloC. It then goes on to execute the sayHello() method on this newly created instance.

Listing 4-15: Using the Invocation API

```
/**
    CallJava.c
    Using the JNI's  Invocation API, it is
possible for C/C++ program to seamlessly
    load the JVM and execute Java classes within it.
This program demonstrates how a C program can
instantiate a JVM, load the HelloC class, create
an object, and invoke its methods.
*/

#include <jni.h>
#ifdef _WIN32
#define PATH_SEPARATOR ';'
#else /* UNIX */
#define PATH_SEPARATOR ':'
#endif
/* set location of our test java class HelloC  here*/
#define USER_CLASSPATH "."
main() {
    JNIEnv *env;
    JavaVM *jvm;
    JDK1_1InitArgs vm_args;
    jint result;
    jclass cls;
    jobject jo;
```

Listing 4-15: continued

```
        jmethodID ctorCls;
        jmethodID mid;
        char classpath[1000];
        /* indicate version number if you use JDK1.1.2 and beyond */
        vm_args.version = 0x00010001;
        JNI_GetDefaultJavaVMInitArgs(&vm_args);
        /* Append local classpath to the end of default system classpath */
        sprintf(classpath, "%s%c%s",
        vm_args.classpath, PATH_SEPARATOR, USER_CLASSPATH);
        vm_args.classpath = classpath;
        /* Create the Java VM */
        result = JNI_CreateJavaVM(&jvm,&env,&vm_args);
        if (result < 0) {
            fprintf(stderr, "Can't create Java VM\n");
            exit(1);
        }
        /* load the test class */
        cls = (*env)->FindClass(env, "HelloC");
        if (cls == 0) {
            fprintf(stderr, "Can't find class HelloC\n");
            exit(1);
        }
        /* instantiate an object  of this class*/
        ctorCls = (jmethodID) (*env)->GetMethodID (env,cls,"<init>","()V");
        jo =  (*env)->NewObject(env, cls,ctorCls);
        /* invoke the method */
        mid = (*env)->GetMethodID(env, cls, "sayHello", "()V");
        if (mid == 0) {
            fprintf(stderr, "Can't find HelloC.sayHello\n");
            exit(1);
        }
        (*env)->CallVoidMethod(env, jo, mid);
        (*jvm)->DestroyJavaVM(jvm);
}
```

Note

If you are running the program on a Win32 platform, please note the location of your JVM implementation DLL—javai.dll—must be present within the system PATH. On Solaris, the location of the shared library—libjava.so—must be added to LD_LIBRARY_PATH.

The C program must be compiled and linked with the standard JNI libraries before it can be run. On Win32, you can compile using the MS Visual C++ compiler:

```
cl -I$JAVA_HOME\include -MT invoke.c -link $JAVA_HOME\lib\javai.lib
```

For Solaris, use

```
cc -I$JAVA_HOME/include -L$JAVA_HOME/lib-ljava invoke.c
```

A run of the previous program results in the following output:

```
Hello C...this is Java speaking!
```

The Invocation API is quite powerful and provides extensive support for multi-threaded access. As mentioned before, the JNI interface pointer `JNIEnv` is thread-specific and cannot be cached or used across multiple threads. Hence, any new native thread needing access to the Java VM must first attach itself to the JVM and obtain a different JNI interface pointer by calling `AttachCurrentThead()`. Native threads can detach themselves from Java threads by calling `DetachCurrentThread()`.

Summary

Although the JNI is an extremely powerful interface, it is can be complex for large-scale legacy systems integration. This is mainly due to the lack of a sophisticated Java development environment for integration of native code. It is certainly possible to use JNI within signed applets, provided the shared libraries are preinstalled on the client machines. It is also interesting to note that applications written in C/C++ can instantiate a JVM and interpret Java class files within its context, thereby extending their functionality.

Chapter 5

Object Serialization

A fundamental need of any object-oriented application is *persistency*, which can be defined as preserving the state of objects beyond the lifetime of the programs that instantiated them. Although this may appear simple, providing object persistency has always been a challenge in most other object-oriented languages like C++, Smalltalk, and so forth.

Meaningful object persistency involves a lot more than simply reading and writing out its data elements from a text file. In addition, any such mechanism must not only have the capability to handle evolution of the object schema through versioning and support object validation, it must also be robust and secure.

Luckily for us, ever since the advent of JDK 1.1, Java has provided developers with a lightweight persistency solution in the form of Object Serialization. This chapter takes an in-depth look at the intricacies of this remarkably powerful, but nonetheless easy-to-use, mechanism. We examine how objects can be saved to files and distributed over a network, and look more closely at techniques for object compression, validation, and encryption. Note, much of what you learn in this chapter should serve as a solid foundation for the understanding of other enterprise Java technologies like RMI, EJB, and so forth.

Fundamentals of Object Serialization

Java has for long allowed developers to read and write primitive data types such as int, char, and so forth from streams. Now, with the Object Serialization mechanism, you can just as easily read and write entire objects from any file or network input/output stream.

Serializing an object essentially involves encoding its state in a structured way within a bytearray. Once serialized, the bytearray can be saved to a file or distributed over a network through a socket-based connection or by using RMI. A highlight of the serialization process is it also encodes enough information about the object type within the bytestream, allowing the original object to be easily recreated. The process of recreating a copy of the original object from the bytestream is known as *deserialization*. Figure 5-1 gives us a high-level view of the common deployment strategies for serialized objects.

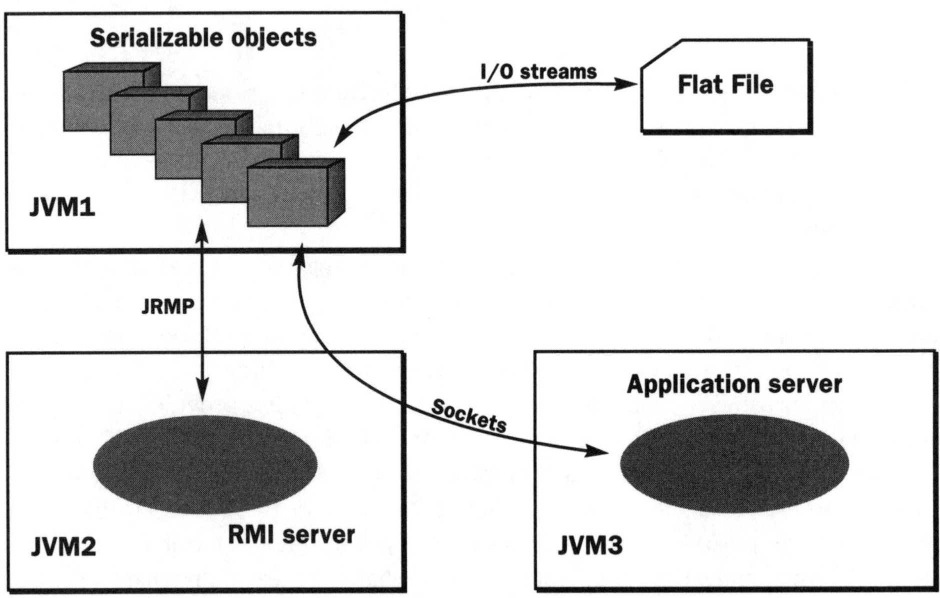

Figure 5-1: Strategies for deploying serialized objects

So, how is this magic implemented? From the developer's perspective, much of it is transparent. For an object to be serializable, it must implement either the java.io.Serializable or java.io.Externalizable interface. Although implementing Serializable should be sufficient for most applications, note that Externalizable gives the developer complete control over the serialization process.

Once a class is serializable, all subtypes of the class are also automatically serializable. Also, much of the power of serialization is derived because it reads and writes complete graphs of objects at a time. For instance, you can serialize an entire linked-list or some such complex data structure by issuing a single method call.

Any serializable class can read and write its instances using the methods supplied by java.io.ObjectInputStream and java.io.ObjectOutputStream, which extend java.io.InputStream and java.io.OutputStream, respectively. Objects are written to an ObjectOutputStream using its writeObject() method. Similarly, objects are read from an ObjectInputStream using its readObject() method.

The Serializable Interface

A common application of the serialization mechanism is to provide lightweight persistency for Java objects by saving them to a flat-file. Java developers who have grappled with the challenge of preserving an object's state under JDK 1.0 cannot help but be amazed by the newfound simplicity of serialization. Let's look more closely at an example demonstrating how objects can be written to and restored from flat-files.

As mentioned before, the easiest way to make an object serializable is to ensure it implements the java.io.Serializable interface in the class declaration. Listing 5-1 shows a class that does exactly that:

Listing 5-1: A Simple Serializable Class

```
package cup.chap5.fileio;
import java.io.*;
public class Person implements Serializable {
    private int id;
    private String name;
    private String dept;
    public Person(int id, String name, String dept) {
        this.id = id;
        this.name = name;
        this.dept = dept;
    }
    public void print() {
        System.out.println("Id: "+id);
        System.out.println("Name: "+name);
        System.out.println("Department: "+dept);
        System.out.println("----");
    }
}
```

Now our Person class is capable of being serialized. Note, the java.io.Serializable interface is an empty interface and does not declare any methods or fields. It simply serves to indicate to the compiler that objects of any class implementing this interface may be serialized.

Also, what is imperative is the fields within our Person class must all be serializable. Because the primitive Java data types—as well as the type wrapper classes—are by default serializable, we can use them without any problems. If we had references to any other user-defined objects within the Person class, however, it would be necessary for their classes to implement either the Serializable or Externalizable interface.

> **Note**
>
> If any constituent field of a class implementing Serializable cannot be serialized, a NotSerializableException is immediately thrown.

Consider Listing 5-2, which demonstrates how objects can be saved to a flat-file:

Listing 5-2: Writing Serialized Objects to a File

```
package cup.chap5.fileio;
import java.io.*;
import java.util.Vector;
public class PersistEmployees {
    public static void main(String[] args) {
        Vector  employees = new Vector();
        employees.addElement(new Person(100,"Henri Dikongue","Marketing"));
        employees.addElement(new Person(101,"Jerry Murphy","Product Development"));
        employees.addElement(new Person(102,"Dr. Remmy Ongala","Research"));
        employees.addElement(new Person(103,"Katie Cooder","Marketing"));
        employees.addElement(new Person(104,"Pat Guzman","Product Development"));
        try {
            FileOutputStream fos = new FileOutputStream("empdata.ser");
            ObjectOutputStream oos = new ObjectOutputStream(fos);
            oos.writeObject(employees);
            oos.flush();
            oos.close();
        } catch (IOException e) {
            System.out.println("Error during object serialization:"+e);
        }
    }
}
```

To make things a bit interesting, let's persist a Vector type initialized with a bunch of Person objects. In this case, we needn't worry about the Vector implementing Serializable. Being a core component of the JDK, it does so by default. Because using the suffix ".ser" is customary for any file containing the serialized data for a Java bean or object, we will read and write our serialized from a local file, empdata.ser.

As previously noted, the ObjectOutputStream object must be attached to some OutputStream object when it is created. In this case, because we want to write the object to a data file, we must first create a FileOutputStream object. Persisting the object itself is simply a matter of calling writeObject() and flushing the buffer. Note, the ObjectOutputStream class implements the ObjectOutput interface. Because ObjectOutput, in turn, extends the DataOutput interface, which defines methods like writeInt(), writeChar(), and so forth basic data types can also be written to the stream.

Listing 5-3 shows how read the data file and deserialize the FileInputStream to yield a copy of the previously persisted Vector object:

Listing 5-3: Reading Serialized Objects from a File

```
package cup.chap5.fileio;
import java.io.*;
import java.util.Vector;
import java.io.*;
public class ReadEmployees {
    public static void main(String[] args) {
        Vector employees = new Vector();
        try {
            FileInputStream fis = new FileInputStream("empdata.ser");
            ObjectInputStream ois = new ObjectInputStream(fis);
            employees = (Vector) ois.readObject();
            ois.close();
        //print out all the employees
            for (int i=0; i< employees.size();i++) {
                Person emp = (Person) employees.elementAt(i);
                emp.print();
            }
        } catch (Exception e) {
            System.out.println("Error during object Deserialization:"+e);
        }
    }
}
```

We can read objects from a stream by making use the readObject() method found in the ObjectInputStream class. The ObjectInputStream object is instantiated by attaching it to some InputStream. In this case, because we are obtaining our input stream from a file, we must attach it to an instance of FileInputStream.

Consider the line:

```
employees = (Vector) ois.readObject();
```

A call to readObject() always returns an instance of type Object, so it is critical that you always cast the resulting object to its proper type before use. But cases may still exist where you may not have knowledge of the class type read from the stream until run time. In such cases, if the class name cannot be resolved by calling the getClass() method, you can make use of the Reflection API to obtain the class information.

Note, the ObjectInputStream class implements the ObjectIntput interface. Because ObjectInput, in turn, extends the DataInput interface which defines methods like readInt(), readChar(), and so forth basic data types can also be read from the stream.

After obtaining the Vector object, we can iterate through it, retrieving and printing each of the constituent Person objects. The resulting output is

```
Id: 100
Name: Henri Dikongue
Department: Marketing
----
Id: 101
Name: Jerry Murphy
Department: Product Development
----
Id: 102
Name: Dr. Remmy Ongala
Department: Research
----
Id: 103
Name: Katie Cooder
Department: Marketing
----
Id: 104
Name: Pat Guzman
Department: Product Development
----
```

Handling object references

Consider an example of object references. Look closely at the following snippets:

```
public Language {
    public Language(...) {
        ...
    }
...
}
public Country {
    Language lingua_franca;
    public Country(Language l, ...) {
        ...
    }
    ...
}
Language french = new Language(...);
```

```
Country congo = new Country(french, ...);
Country algeria = new Country(french, ...);
Country france = new Country(french, ...);
```

What do you think happens when countries that refer to the same Language object are serialized? You may think multiple copies of the Language object get written out to the stream. But, interestingly enough, that is not the case. The ObjectOutputStream keeps track of each unique object written to the stream within a *known object table* and assigns each of them a serial number. Thus, if a previously written object appears again on the stream, instead of writing the entire object to the stream, the serialization mechanism writes out just its "handle" or serial number (taken from the known object table) to the stream.

The procedure is reversed when reading the objects. The ObjectInputStream keeps track of all objects read in and assigns a serial number to each one. So, when it later reads in a handle from the stream, it simply replaces it with the corresponding object reference from its internal known object table. Both the ObjectInputStream and ObjectOutputStream retain their states until the streams are explicitly closed.

A need may exist to rewrite an object's modified state to the stream a second time. In such situations, it is important first tocall the reset() method from ObjectOutputStream, selectively zapping the known object table's memory of having previously written the object to the stream.

Protecting sensitive information

Having all of an object's fields automatically converted to a bytestream for security reasons may not be desirable. Note, once the state of an object has been serialized, Java's security mechanisms are no longer applicable. If you are distributing serialized objects over a network using sockets or RMI, remember, by default, serialized data is always transmitted as clear text. Even if your fields were tagged private within the original object, it does not matter. Any party intercepting the bytestream can not only read the data, but can also potentially alter it in malicious ways.

The ideal solution would be to encrypt the bytestream when distributing objects over a network. But this is usually a fairly complex task, suited only for specialized use. Also, fields may exist within your Java objects that serve a useful purpose only within the context of a particular JVM. For instance, these may include local file handles, local thread handles, handles to native methods, and the like. Serializing these fields and passing their state to a different JVM makes no sense.

You can use the transient keyword for tagging such sensitive objects and fields, preventing them from getting serialized. Marking any field as such prevents its state from being written or restored from a stream. When transient fields are read from a stream, they are set to their default values. You can reinitialize these fields yourself, however, using custom serialization techniques described in later sections.

Also worth noting is the serialization mechanism handles an object's static data in a manner similar to fields marked transient and static fields are automatically skipped over when creating bytestream.

Implementing Custom Serialization

We have seen that a class can be totally transparent from the serialization process simply by implementing the Serializable interface. But if necessary, any Serializable class can customize the serialization process by defining the following two methods within:

```
private void writeObject(java.io.ObjectOutputStream out) throws IOException ;
private void readObject(java.io.ObjectInputStream in) throws IOException,
    ClassNotFoundException ;
```

Custom serialization techniques can be especially useful for initializing transient fields. As mentioned in the previous section, an object's transient and static fields are not written out to the output stream during the serialization process. So, when the input object stream is, in turn, read to recreate the object, any such fields are initialized to their default Java values. For instance, a Java String is initialized to null, int to 0, and so on. Although this feature is convenient, it may land up placing the object in an invalid state. Reinitializing the transient and static fields to some acceptable values is imperative, depending on the other state information for the object.

Listings 5-4 and 5-5 demonstrate how a valid object state can be maintained by overriding the readObject() and writeObject() methods. Our serializable class ValidPerson does not write out the field contact during serialization as it is marked transient. On deserialization, however, readObject() reinitializes contact to some valid value, after taking into account other state information for the object. The example also demonstrates how additional data can be written to the stream during customization. Here, we write out a Date object when the object is serialized. We then extract this Date object on deserialization and use it to determine the amount of time the object was passive.

Listing 5-4: Serializable Class Implementing Custom Serialization

```
package cup.chap5.validation;
import java.io.*;
import java.util.Date;
public class ValidPerson implements Serializable {
    private int id;
    private String name;
    private String dept;
    private transient String contact;
    public ValidPerson(int id, String name, String dept) {
        this.id = id;
        this.name = name;
        this.dept = dept;
        this.contact = resolveContact(dept);
    }
```

```
    private void writeObject(ObjectOutputStream oos) throws IOException {
        try {
                oos.defaultWriteObject();
                oos.writeObject(new Date());
            } catch(IOException e) {
                System.out.println("Error in writeObject:"+e);
            }
    }
    private String resolveContact(String d) {
        String tel="";
        if (d.equals("Marketing")) tel = "(212) 242-4343";
        else if (d.equals("Research")) tel = "(312) 322-4200";
        else if (d.equals("Product Development")) tel = "(650) 843-1210";
        else tel = "(800) 214-9943";
        return tel;
    }
    private void readObject(ObjectInputStream ois) throws IOException,
                ClassNotFoundException {
        try {
                ois.defaultReadObject();
                System.out.println("Validating Person<"+this.name+">");
                this.contact = resolveContact(this.dept);
                Date oldDate = (Date) ois.readObject();
                Date newDate = new Date();
                long oldtime = oldDate.getTime();
                long newtime = newDate.getTime();
                long inactive =newtime - oldtime;
                System.out.println("Object was passive for "+
                    new Long(inactive).toString() + " ms");
                } catch(Exception e) {
                System.out.println("Error in readObject:"+e);
            }
    }
    public void print() {
        System.out.println("Id: "+id);
        System.out.println("Name: "+name);
        System.out.println("Department: "+dept);
        System.out.println("Contact: "+contact);
        System.out.println("----");
    }
}
```

Listing 5-5: Demonstrating Custom Serialization

```
package cup.chap5.validation;
import java.io.*;
public class ValidPersonDemo {

    public static void main(String[] args) {
        ValidPerson tintin =
            new ValidPerson(100,"TinTin","Marketing");
        try {
            FileOutputStream fos =
                new FileOutputStream("demo");
            ObjectOutputStream oos =
                new ObjectOutputStream(fos);
            oos.writeObject(tintin);
            oos.flush();
            oos.close();
        } catch (IOException e) {
            System.out.println("Error during object serialization"+e);
        }
    try {
        Thread.sleep(5000); //sleep for 5 seconds
            FileInputStream fis =
                new FileInputStream("demo");
            ObjectInputStream ois = new ObjectInputStream(fis);
            ValidPerson someone =
                (ValidPerson) ois.readObject();
            //print it out
                someone.print();
        } catch (Exception e) {
            System.out.println("Error during object
            deserialization"+e);
        }
    }
}
```

When implementing the writeObject() method, observe that the default object must be the first one written by invoking defaultWriteObject(). Similarly, when implementing readObject(), the default object must be the first one read by calling defaultReadObject().

Also worth noting is, with custom serialization, a class is responsible for only its own fields—and not for those of its superclasses.

On compiling and running Listing 5-5, we see the output:

```
Validating Person<TinTin>
Object was passive for 5160 ms
Id: 100
Name: TinTin
Department: Marketing
Contact: (212) 242-4343
```

Transmitting Objects over Sockets

Serialization raises network programming in Java to a much higher level. Much of the power and flexibility is derived from the fact that now, the developer is absolved from the responsibility of having to convert the objects to some format suitable for transmission and to reconvert the received stream into Java objects. Instead, you can now simply read and write Java objects from a network stream. This approach also imparts a tremendous amount of flexibility to the client and the server entities. Now, every time the underlying object model for the exchanged data changes, you needn't retrofit your entire application protocol to reflect the changes. You just continue to exchange the modified objects as usual.

A client/server example

The code examples shown in Listings 5-6, 5-7, and 5-8 demonstrate how a serialized object can be seamlessly exchanged over a socket connection. Do observe the profound similarities between writing and reading an object from an underlying network stream, and a file stream as demonstrated earlier.

Listing 5-6: Serializable Class for Client/Server Communication

```
package cup.chap5.sockets;
import java.io.Serializable;
public class Person implements Serializable {
    private String name;
    private int age;
    private String[] bigone;
    public Person(String n, int a) {
        name =n;
        age =a;
        bigone = new String[10000];
        for (int i=0; i<10000;i++)
            bigone[i] = "This is String:"+i;
    }
```

continues

Listing 5-6: continued

```
        public void setAge(int n) {
            age =n;
        }
        public void setName(String n) {
            name=n;
        }
        public void print() {
            System.out.println("NAME IS:"+name);
            System.out.println("AGE IS:"+age);
        }
    }
```

Listing 5-7: Client for Transmitting Objects over Sockets

```
package cup.chap5.sockets;
import java.io.*;
import java.net.*;
import java.util.*;
public class SerialClient {
    public static void main(String[] args) {
        Person me=null;
        Socket client=null ;
        ObjectOutputStream objOut=null ;
        ObjectInputStream objIn=null ;
        try {
            me = new Person("Joe",30);
            client = new Socket("somehost",34145);
            objOut = new ObjectOutputStream(client.getOutputStream());
            objIn = new ObjectInputStream(client.getInputStream());
            me.print(); //before
            long marker1 = new Date().getTime();
            objOut.writeObject(me);
            me = (Person) objIn.readObject();
            long marker2= new Date().getTime();
            long  diff =  marker2- marker1;
            System.out.println("Transfer took: "+ new Long(diff).toString()+" ms");
            me.print(); //after
        } catch (Exception e) {
            System.out.println("Client error:"+e);
        }
    }
}
```

Listing 5-8: Server for Transmitting Objects over Sockets

```
package cup.chap5.sockets;
import java.net.*;
import java.io.*;
import java.util.*;
public class SerialServer extends Thread {
    private Socket channel;
    private ObjectOutputStream objOut;
    private ObjectInputStream objIn;
    public SerialServer(Socket s) {
        channel =s;
        try {
            objOut = new ObjectOutputStream(channel.getOutputStream());
            objIn = new ObjectInputStream(channel.getInputStream());
        } catch (Exception e) {
            System.out.println("Could not create channel with client"+e);
        }
    }
    public void run() {
        Person aPerson=null;
        try {
            aPerson = (Person) objIn.readObject();
            aPerson.print();
        } catch (Exception e) {
            System.out.println("error on read:"+e);
        }
        try {
            aPerson.setName("King Kong");
            aPerson.setAge(100);
            objOut.writeObject(aPerson);
        } catch (Exception e) {
            System.out.println("error on write");
        }
    }
    public static void main(String arg[]) {
        try {
            ServerSocket server = new ServerSocket(34145);
            while (true) {
                Socket channel = server.accept();
                SerialServer newSerial = new SerialServer(channel);
                newSerial.start();
            }
```

continues

Listing 5-8: continued

```
            } catch (Exception e) {
                System.out.println("Error on accept:"+e);
            }
        }
    }
```

Notice Person class contains a rather large array, bigone, which has an adverse impact on the efficacy of the network communication. On running the server and client programs as:

```
start java cup.chap5.sockets.SerialServer
java cup.chap5.sockets.SerialClient
```

the client, SerialClient, send across a Person object to the server, SerialServer. The server modifies the received object and echoes it back to the client, which simply prints it out. SerialClient also prints out the total time (in ms) taken for the entire cycle to complete. The output of a typical run is shown in the following:

```
NAME IS:Joe
AGE IS:30
Transfer took: 13350 ms
NAME IS:King Kong
AGE IS:100
```

You can experiment with increasing the size of the array bigone and see a rather significant increase in the turnaround time. This exercise proves that although the serialization protocol may be convenient and programmer-friendly, it is not efficient. In particular, serialization must be judiciously used when dealing with large objects.

Transmitting objects over compressed sockets

While the serialization mechanism may seem particularly slow in dealing with large objects, ways to make your client/server communication significantly more efficient exist. An obvious way of wringing the most out of the available bandwidth is to compress the network traffic. Luckily for us, with Java, we don't have to venture into implementing any complicated data compression protocols. The JDK's java.util.zip package provides us with a couple of streams-based classes—GZIPInputStream and GZIPOutputStream—and makes the job of reading and writing compressed data a cinch.

Listings 5-9 and 5-10 demonstrate how a serialized object can be seamlessly exchanged over a compressed socket connection:

Listing 5-9: Client for Transmitting Compressed Objects over Sockets

```
package cup.chap5.sockets;
import java.io.*;
import java.net.*;
import java.util.zip.*;
```

Listing 5-9: continued

```
import java.util.*;
public class CompressSerialClient {
    public static void main(String[] args) {
        try {
            Person me=null;
            Socket client=null ;
            ObjectOutputStream objOut=null ;
            ObjectInputStream objIn=null ;
            GZIPOutputStream os =null;
            ByteArrayOutputStream baos =null;
            GZIPInputStream is =null;
            ByteArrayInputStream bais =null;
            me = new Person("Joe",35);
            client = new Socket("somehost",34145);
            os = new GZIPOutputStream (client.getOutputStream());
            baos = new ByteArrayOutputStream();
            objOut = new ObjectOutputStream(baos);
            me.print(); //before
            long marker1= new Date().getTime();
            objOut.writeObject(me);
            baos.writeTo(os);
            os.finish();
                                                    Stream());
            [illegible]
            [illegible]
            StringBuffer sb =new StringBuffer();
            while ((bytesRead = is.read (buffer)) != -1) {
                sb.append(new String(buffer,0,bytesRead));
            }
                is.close();
                bais = new ByteArrayInputStream(sb.toString().getBytes());
                objIn = new ObjectInputStream(bais);
                me = (Person) objIn.readObject();
                long marker2= new Date().getTime();
                long  diff =  marker2- marker1;
                System.out.println("Transfer took: "+new Long(diff).toString()+" ms");
                me.print(); //after
        } catch (Exception e) {
            System.out.println("Client error:"+e);
        }
    }
}
```

Listing 5-10: Server for Transmitting Compressed Objects over Sockets

```
package cup.chap5.sockets;
import java.net.*;
import java.io.*;
import java.util.*;
import java.util.zip.*;

public class CompressSerialServer extends Thread {
    private Socket channel;
    private ObjectOutputStream objOut;
    private ObjectInputStream objIn;
    private GZIPInputStream is;
    private ByteArrayInputStream bais;
    private ByteArrayOutputStream baos;
    private GZIPOutputStream os;
    public CompressSerialServer(Socket s) {
        channel =s;
    }
    public void run() {
        Person aPerson=null;
        try {
            is = new GZIPInputStream (channel.getInputStream());
        } catch (Exception e) {
            System.out.println("Could not set compression stream");
        }
    StringBuffer sb = new StringBuffer();
    byte buffer[] = new byte[1024];
    int bytesRead;
    try {
        while ((bytesRead = is.read (buffer)) != -1) {
            sb.append(new String(buffer,0,bytesRead));
        }
        bais = new ByteArrayInputStream(sb.toString().getBytes());
        objIn = new ObjectInputStream(bais);
        aPerson = (Person) objIn.readObject();
        aPerson.print(); //server received this
        } catch (Exception e) {
            System.out.println("error on read:"+e);
        }
        try {
            os = new GZIPOutputStream (channel.getOutputStream());
            baos = new ByteArrayOutputStream();
```

Listing 5-10: continued

```
            objOut = new ObjectOutputStream(baos);
            aPerson.setName("King Kong");
            aPerson.setAge(101);
            objOut.writeObject(aPerson);
            baos.writeTo(os);
            os.finish();
        } catch (Exception e) {
            System.out.println("error on write:"+e);
        }
    }
    public static void main(String arg[]) {
        try {
            ServerSocket server = new ServerSocket(34145);
            while (true) {
                Socket channel = server.accept();
                CompressSerialServer newSerial =
                new CompressSerialServer(channel);
                newSerial.start();
            }
        } catch (Exception e) {
            System.out.println("Error on accept:"+e);
        }
    }
}
```

You can run the client and server programs as:

```
start java cup.chap5.sockets.CompressSerialServer
java cup.chap5.sockets.CompressSerialClient
```

The output of a typical run is shown in the following:

```
NAME IS:Joe
AGE IS:35
Transfer took: 1480 ms
NAME IS:King Kong
AGE IS:101
```

The compression may add some overhead to the overall CPU requirements of your application. But, as you can see, the potential savings in bandwidth should more than offset any such expense.

Advanced Serialization

For most applications, implementing the Serializable interface and letting the serialization be performed automatically by the object stream classes should suffice. If necessary, however, the developer can take complete control of the encoding and decoding process of an object. Many instances exist where it is imperative to have this level of flexibility. For example, you may be interested in writing out the data in some predefined format. Or your classes may need to be augmented with some proprietary authentication or encryption mechanisms. To enable this, classes must define their own proprietary serialization mechanism by implementing the java.io.Externalizable interface.

The externalizable interface

Unlike Serializable, Externalizable is not an empty interface and classes implementing it must provide definition for the following methods, with their signatures exactly as shown:

```
public void writeExternal(ObjectOutputStream out) throws IOException;
public void readExternal(ObjectInputStream in) throws IOException,
    ClassNotFoundException;
```

When implementing the Externalizable interface, your classes are not only responsible for serializing their own fields, but also for ensuring the constructor for the superclass, if any, gets invoked. This is a critical step we took for granted earlier on because it was automatically done for us behind the scenes. In this case, if the superclass constructor is not explicitly called, then it is simply not sent out as part of the serial data.

Also mandatory is for Externalizable classes to implement a public no-argument constructor. This is the first thing invoked by readExternal() when reconstructing the object. If the no-arg constructor is absent, then an InvalidClassException exception is thrown.

Note

You may have noticed both writeExternal and readExternal have public scope. This implies some client object can potentially bypass some of the Java sandbox mechanisms and overwrite or gain access to the state of the Externalizable object. As a general rule of thumb, a class should implement Externalizable interface only if the object contains nonsensitive information.

Authenticating serialized objects using message digests

Thus far, you have seen how easy it is to serialize Java objects. But behind this facade of simplicity lurks some serious issues involving the security and integrity of the serialized object stream itself. The object bytestream, by default, is always transmitted as clear text when distributing serialized objects over a network connection. Anyone intercepting the network traffic can alter the state of the object in potentially malicious ways. Serialized objects saved to a data file are even more susceptible to tampering. It is a simple matter for anyone with access to an editor to make changes to the prevailing state of a serialized object.

Most nontrivial objects must have some level of authentication upon deserialization. One of the most effective authentication mechanisms currently available is by computing "message digests" for the objects. A message digest is a cryptographically secure digital fingerprint for a given block of data, generated by supplying an arbitrary sized bytearray (the message) as input to a message digest algorithm.

Some of the better-known algorithms for this purpose include the Secure Hash Algorithm (SHA-1)—the current National Institute for Standards and Technology (NIST) standard—and MD5 from MIT, both of which are currently supported by Java.

For our demonstration, we make use of SHA-1. The digest obtained from this algorithm is always a 20-byte data packet, regardless of the size of the original data. The generated digest can be considered "unique" for all practical purposes. The probability of someone forging a signature is computationally unfeasible, considering they have 2^{120} possible choices to contend with for any given message. Further, the digest itself does not reveal anything about the message used to generate it. Typically, the integrity of a bytestream is ensured using a combination of message digests and data encryption. For the sake of simplicity, we will not encrypt the bytestream in our example. However, the following section covers the topic of encrypting serialized objects.

Listing 5-11 shows the class AuthPerson, which implements the Externalizable interface and demonstrates message digest-based authentication. Here, the class authenticates itself by comparing the fingerprint of the serialized data read from an input stream with the original fingerprint for the object.

Listing 5-11: Demonstrating the Externalizable Interface

```
package cup.chap5.externalization;
import java.io.*;
import java.security.*;
public class AuthPerson implements Externalizable {
    private int id;
    private String name;
    private String dept;
    public AuthPerson() {
    //no-arg constructor
```

continues

Listing 5-11: continued

```
    }
    public AuthPerson(int id, String name, String dept) {
        this.id = id;
        this.name = name;
        this.dept = dept;
    }
    public void writeExternal(java.io.ObjectOutput out)
        throws IOException {
        ByteArrayOutputStream baos = new ByteArrayOutputStream();
        DataOutputStream dos = new DataOutputStream(baos);
        try {
            dos.writeInt(id);
            dos.writeUTF(name);
            dos.writeUTF(dept);
            byte[] hash = computeHash(baos.toByteArray());
            out.writeObject(new String(baos.toByteArray()));
            out.writeObject(new String(hash));
        } catch (Exception e) {
            System.out.println("error on writeExternal:"+e);
        }
    }
    public void readExternal(java.io.ObjectInput in)
        throws IOException, ClassNotFoundException {
        String streamData = (String) in.readObject();
        String originalHash = (String) in.readObject();
        byte[] tmpHash = computeHash(streamData.getBytes());

        if (!originalHash.equals(new String(tmpHash))) {
            throw new java.io.StreamCorruptedException();
        }
        ByteArrayInputStream bais =new ByteArrayInputStream(streamData.getBytes());
        DataInputStream dis = new DataInputStream(bais);
        id = (int) dis.readInt();
        name= (String) dis.readUTF();
        dept = (String) dis.readUTF();
    }
    private byte[] computeHash(byte[] data) {
        MessageDigest algorithm=null ;
        try {
            algo= MessageDigest.getInstance("SHA-1");
        } catch (NoSuchAlgorithmException e) {
            System.out.println(e.toString());
```

Listing 5-11: continued

```
                System.exit(1);
            }
            algorithm.reset();
            return (algorithm.digest(data));
        }
        public void print() {
            System.out.println("Id: "+id);
            System.out.println("Name: "+name);
            System.out.println("Department: "+dept);
            System.out.println("----");
        }
    }
```

As mentioned earlier, the serialization and deserialization of Externalizable classes is handled by writeExternal() and readExternal() methods, respectively. In Listing 5-11, writeExternal() first converts the object's fields into a bytearray and supplies it as input to the method computeHash(), which, in turn, computes and returns its message digest. Within computeHash(), MessageDigest.getInstance("SHA-1") basically initializes and returns a message digest object implementing the SHA-1 algorithm. The digest itself is obtained by the statement algorithm.digest(data), which is returned. WriteExternal() then writes out the bytearray, as well as its fingerprint, to the object output stream.

The authentication of the serialized object takes place within readExternal(), which first reads in the bytestream, as well as its original "fingerprint". It then invokes computeHash() to obtain a new digest for the received bytestream. If the serialized data can considered authentic if the received and newly computed digests match. Otherwise, readExternal() throws a StreamCorruptedException, indicating an authentication failure.

Encrypting Serialized Objects via Sealed Objects

While serialization is a convenient feature, it should be noted that the resultant bytestream poses some significant security challenges. For instance, if your serialized objects are saved to a file or sent over a network connection, the data is represented as clear text. An obvious solution for ensuring data privacy would be to encrypt the bytestream. While numerous approaches for enabling Java with encryption capabilities have been proposed in the past, most have relied on utilizing proprietary third-party libraries, and in some cases, even native code. In this section, we will examine the details of encrypting objects using the Java Cryptography Extension (JCE) 1.2 package. The JCE complements Java 2's java.security package, and implements numerous popular encryption algorithms like DES and RSA, amongst other things. However, the JCE is not distributed as part of Java 2 due to the restrictive policies of the U.S. Department of Commerce towards the export of encryption technology. Currently, however, JCE was downloadable by U.S. and Canadian residents from Sun's Java Developer Connection page at http://developer.java.sun.com/developer/earlyAccess/jdk12/jce.html

Using JCE, we can convert any serializable object into a *sealed object* by wrapping them within an instance of the `javax.crypto.SealedObject` class. As the name probably suggests, a sealed object encrypts the object's serialized data using a key derived from a cryptographic algorithm like DES, thus preserving its privacy. Sealed objects are serializable and can be written to and read from object input/output streams as usual.

A sealed object can be decrypted to yield the original object—but only if you make use of the same encryption algorithm and key used to encrypt it.

In this section, we create a sealed object by using a secret-key, derived from a user-supplied password and a cryptographic algorithm. This type of encryption is also known as *Password-Based Encryption (PBE)* because it makes use of a user-supplied password at runtime to perform the encryption/decryption.

Listing 5-13 creates a `Vector` of `Account` (as shown in Listing 5-12) objects and writes it out to disk after encrypting it as a `SealedObject`.

Listing 5-12: Account Containing Sensitive Data

```
package cup.chap5.encryptio;
public class Account implements java.io.Serializable {
    private int accountNum;
    private String owner;
    private float balance;
    public Account(int num, String name, float amt) {
        accountNum =num;
        owner = name;
        balance = amt;
    }
    public void print() {
        System.out.println("Account Number: "+accountNum);
        System.out.println("Owner: "+owner);
        System.out.println("Balance: $"+balance);
        System.out.println("----");
    }
}
```

Listing 5-13: Creating a SealedObject

```
package cup.chap5.encryptio;
import java.io.*;
import java.util.Vector;
import javax.crypto.*;
import javax.crypto.spec.*;
public class EncryptObject {
    public static void main(String[] args) {
    Vector  accounts =new Vector();
        accounts.addElement(new Account(100,"Chris Raine",65000.64f));
        accounts.addElement(new Account(101,"Jerry Murphy",120000.45f));
        accounts.addElement(new Account(102,"Dr. Remmy Ongala",30403.32f));
        accounts.addElement(new Account(103,"Scott Mottet",3234.31f));
        accounts.addElement(new Account(104,"Scott Stieber",43453.44f));
        try {
            // Salt
            byte[] salt = {
                (byte)0xc7, (byte)0x73, (byte)0x21, (byte)0x8c,
                (byte)0x7e, (byte)0xc8, (byte)0xee, (byte)0x99
            };
            // Iteration count
                int count = 20;
            // Create PBE parameter set
                PBEParameterSpec pbeParamSpec =new PBEParameterSpec(salt, count);
                if ((System.getProperty("passwd")) == null) {
                System.out.println("Usage: java-Dpasswd=yourpassword
                                    cup.chap5.encryptio.EncryptObject");
                    System.exit(0);
                }
                PBEKeySpec keySpec = new PBEKeySpec(
                                    (System.getProperty("passwd")).toCharArray()
                );
                SecretKeyFactory keyFac =SecretKeyFactory.getInstance("PBE");
                SecretKey sKey = keyFac.generateSecret(keySpec);
                // Create PBE Cipher
                Cipher cipher =Cipher.getInstance("PBEWithMD5AndDES");
                // Initialize PBE Cipher with key and parameters
                cipher.init(Cipher.ENCRYPT_MODE, sKey, pbeParamSpec);
                FileOutputStream fos =
                new FileOutputStream("encryptaccts.ser");
                ObjectOutputStream oos =
                new ObjectOutputStream(fos);
```

continues

Listing 5-13: continued

```
                // do the sealing
                SealedObject so =new SealedObject(accounts, cipher);
             oos.writeObject(so);
             oos.flush();
        } catch (Exception e) {
            System.out.println("Error during encryption:"+e);
        }
    }
}
```

Consider the following constructor for creating a SealedObject:

```
public SealedObject(Serializable obj, Cipher c) throws IOException, IllegalBlockSizeException
```

As you can see, the first thing to do is come up with the appropriate cipher instance:

```
SecretKeyFactory keyFac =
     SecretKeyFactory.getInstance("PBE");
SecretKey sKey = keyFac.generateSecret(keySpec);
Cipher cipher = Cipher.getInstance("PBEWithMD5AndDES");
cipher.init(Cipher.ENCRYPT_MODE, sKey, pbeParamSpec);
```

Note, placing the cipher in encryption mode first, before using it to obtain our SealedObject instance is important. The cipher is also initialized with the PBE key, as well as the salt and iteration count. The sealed object itself is then obtained by applying the cipher on the serializable accounts object:

```
SealedObject so = new SealedObject(accounts, cipher);
```

Listing 5-14, shows the decryption of the SealedObject to yield the original serialized object.

Listing 5-14: Decrypting a SealedObject

```
package cup.chap5.encryptio;
import java.io.*;
import java.util.Vector;
import javax.crypto.*;
import javax.crypto.spec.*;
public class DecryptObject {
     public static void main(String[] args) {
        try {
            // Salt
            byte[] salt = {
            (byte)0xc7, (byte)0x73, (byte)0x21, (byte)0x8c,
            (byte)0x7e, (byte)0xc8, (byte)0xee, (byte)0x99
        };
```

Listing 5-14: continued

```
            // Iteration count
            int count = 20;
            // Create PBE parameter set
            PBEParameterSpec pbeParams =new PBEParameterSpec(salt, count);
            String passwd = System.getProperty("passwd");
            if (passwd == null) {
               System.out.print("Usage: java -Dpasswd=yourpassword
               cup.chap5.encryptio.DecryptObject");
               System.exit(0);
            }
            PBEKeySpec keySpec =new PBEKeySpec(passwd.toCharArray());
            SecretKeyFactory keyFac =SecretKeyFactory.getInstance("PBE");
            SecretKey sKey = keyFac.generateSecret(keySpec);
            // Create PBE Cipher
            Cipher cipher =Cipher.getInstance("PBEWithMD5AndDES");
            // Initialize PBE Cipher with key and parameters
            cipher.init(Cipher.DECRYPT_MODE, sKey, pbeParams);
            FileInputStream fis =
               new FileInputStream("encryptaccts.ser");
            ObjectInputStream ois = new ObjectInputStream(fis);
            SealedObject so = (SealedObject) ois.readObject();
            Vector accounts = (Vector) so.getObject(cipher);
            //print out all the employees
            for (int i=0; i< accounts.size();i++) {
               Account acct = (Account) accounts.elementAt(i);
               acct.print();
            }
         } catch (Exception e) {
            System.out.println("Error during decryption:"+e);
         }
      }
   }
```

Because the SealedObject is a serialized object, it can easily be read from the object input stream as:

```
SealedObject so = (SealedObject) ois.readObject();
```

Before we can decrypt the SealedObject we need to use the cipher initialized with the same secret key, which was used to encrypt the original object. Thus, we recreate it here by supplying the same salt, iteration count, and password. Observe that the cipher also must be initialized to be in decrypt mode. The sealed object is then decrypted as:

```
Vector accounts = (Vector) so.getObject(cipher);
```

Understanding Object Versioning

Nothing is immutable—least of all a Java class. So, what happens to the persisted objects of some class, if the class definition changes? For instance, we may have added a few new fields or changed the signature of a method. Does it mean the previously serialized objects cannot be recovered? Well, this is where the need comes in for object versioning.

Versioning serialized classes

The serialization process uses a unique identification value to keep track of the persisted objects. When a `Serializable` or `Externalizable` object is saved, it's fully-qualified class name and the Stream Unique IDentifier (SUID) of the class is written out to the stream. The SUID is a unique 64-bit hash and is obtained by applying the SHA-1 message digest algorithm to the serialized class, including its name, field types, and method signatures. This step is important because it prevents the data persisted by one class from being read by another class with the same name. For any class to be able to read successfully from an object stream, its SUID must match the SUID of the serialized data in the stream.

But, as we all know, class definitions are usually in a state of flux. As new versions of the application are released existing classes evolve, causing fields to get added or dropped and method signatures to change. This results in a different SUID for the class, making it incompatible with serialized data persisted for previous versions of the same.

So, how do we enable different versions of a class to continue to exchange data with each other? When dealing with multiple versions of a class, basically two issues must be addressed:

- Newer versions should be able to continue to read serialized data persisted by older versions of the class.
- Newer versions should write out serialized data in a format compatible with older versions of the class.

Compatible and incompatible changes

If a newer version must be compatible with an older version, the newer version must abide by the rules for compatible and incompatible changes.

A compatible change is one that can be made to a new version of the class, which still keeps the stream compatible with older versions of the class. Examples of compatible changes are

- Addition of new fields or classes does not affect serialization, as any new data in the stream is simply ignored by older versions. When the instance of an older version of the class is deserialized, the newly added field is set to its default value.

- You can field change access modifiers like private, public, protected or package, as they are not reflected to the serial stream.
- You can change a transient or static field to a nontransient or nonstatic field, as it is similar to adding a field.
- You can change the access modifiers for constructors and methods of the class. For instance, a previously private method can now be made public, an instance method can be changed to static, and so forth. The only exception is you cannot change the default signatures for readObject() and writeObject() if you are implementing custom serialization. The serialization process looks at only instance data and not at the methods of a class.

Changes that would render the stream incompatible are

- Once a class implements the Serializable interface, you cannot later make it implement the Externalizable interface because this will result in the creation of an incompatible stream.
- Deleting fields can cause a problem. Now, when the object is serialized, an earlier version of the class would set the old field to its default value because nothing was available within the stream. Consequently, this default data may lead the newly created object to assume an invalid state.
- Changing a nonstatic into static or nontransient into transient is not permitted, as it is equivalent to deleting fields.
- You also cannot change the field types within a class, as this would cause a failure when attempting to read in the original field into the new field.
- You cannot alter the position of the class in the class hierarchy. Because the fully qualified class name is written as part of the bytestream, this change will result in the creation of an incompatible stream.
- You cannot change the name of the class or the package it belongs to, as that information is written to the stream during serialization.

Using serialver

As mentioned earlier, when an object is serialized, its fully qualified class name, as well as the 64-bit SUID, is written to the stream. Later, when a class attempts to read the serialized object, its SUID must match that of the serialized object; otherwise, an InvalidClassException is thrown.

But therein lies the problem—because, when classes evolve, so do their SUIDs. Luckily, a solution is at hand in the form of serialver—a utility provided by the JDK, which enables us to generate the SUID of a Java class file. If the output of serialver is included within a class file, then that class is now compatible with all its persisted objects and can be used to read back the same, even though the class definition itself may undergo some mutation down the road.

For instance, running

```
serialver cup.chap5.io.Person
```

generates

```
cup.chap5.io.Person: static final long serialVersionUID =3734178553292263588L;
```

Now, you can continue to read the Person objects even with future versions of the class, as long as they have the "old" SUID embedded within them as:

```
static final long serialVersionUID =3734178553292263588L;
```

This works because a class—before it reads the serialized data from the stream—first checks for the presence of the serialVersionUID field within. If found, its value is written to the stream, instead of one being calculated on the fly. Because the SUID values should now match, no problem would occur in reading in the serialized data.

Using a GUI version of serialver is probably easier, which can be enabled by the -show option. Figure 5-2 shows the output of serialver applied to the Person class.

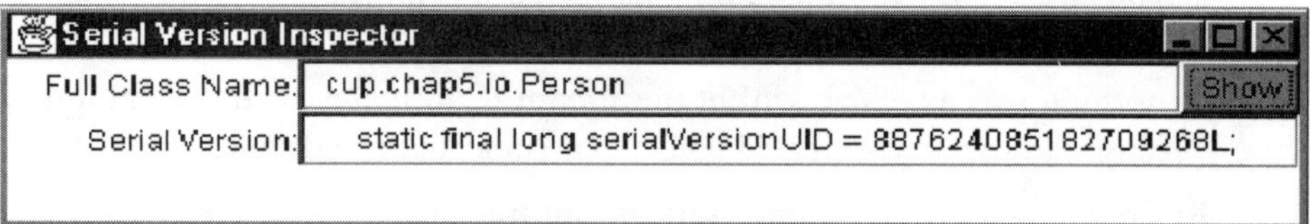

Figure 5-2: GUI version of serialver

Once the window appears, simply type in the name of a fully qualified class name to obtain its SUID. The entire line can then be cut and pasted within the class that needs versioning.

Serialization—Advantages and Disadvantages

The biggest advantage of serialization is it is easy to use and can be customized. Serialized classes can support coherent versioning and are flexible enough to allow gradual evolution of your application's object schema. If necessary , the serialized stream can be encrypted, authenticated, and compressed, supporting the needs of secure Java computing. The serialization mechanism plays a pivotal role in Java and is here to stay. Simply too many critical technologies rely on it—including RMI, JavaBeans, and EJB.

Serialization poses a few limitations as well, however. It should ideally not be used with large-sized objects, as it offers significant overhead. Large objects also significantly increase the memory requirements of your application because the object input/output streams cache live references to all objects written to or read from the stream until the stream is closed or reset. Consequently, the garbage collection of these objects can be inordinately delayed. Also, note the Serializable interface does not offer fine-grained control over object access—although you can somewhat circumvent this issue by, instead, implementing the complex Externalizable interface. Further, because serialization does not offer any transaction control mechanisms per se, it is unsuitable for use within applications needing concurrent access without making use of additional APIs.

Interestingly enough, serialization can also be used as a mechanism for exchanging objects between Java and C++ libraries, using third-party vendor libraries (like RogueWave's Tools.h++) within C++.

Summary

Java objects can easily be converted into a byte stream if they implement either the java.io.Serializable or java.io.Externalizable interface. Once an object is deemed serializable, it can be persisted to a data file, exchanged over a network socket connection, or can be used with RMI. It is also possible to encrypt the serialized data by creating sealed objects.

Chapter 6

Remote Method Invocation

Before the advent of JDK 1.1, designing complex networked applications was a rather cumbersome task at best—mainly because we had to apply age-old procedural networking idioms like sockets-based programming to an object-oriented computing environment. As any seasoned developer will agree, sockets-based network programming is an extremely laborious task. Here, all client/server communication must be mediated by a user-defined application protocol, which serves to define the precise byte-oriented sequence of the message. A client object must not only be responsible for creating the message, but also must bear the logic to decipher the response from the server. And, likewise, for the server objects!

But all that's history. Now, Java's Remote Method Invocation (RMI) technology—a core component of JDK 1.1 and Java 2—brings the world of distributed object computing to Java's doorstep and elevates network programming to a much higher plane. With RMI, Java objects can easily invoke the methods of *remote objects* as if they were locally available. The amazing part is the remote objects may be under the jurisdiction of an entirely different JVM, running on a different host halfway around the world. Also, because you interact with an RMI object much like a local object, remote methods can send and receive nearly any valid Java object without having to worry about flattening it to a serial data stream. RMI automatically provides you with this feature by using the underlying Object Serialization mechanism. The communication between the RMI client and server itself is facilitated by the Java Remote Method Protocol (JRMP).

RMI is especially useful for deployment as a multitier bridging mechanism and can serve as an effective "glue" for integrating other enterprise Java technologies, such as JDBC and JNI, as indicated in Figure 6-1. RMI remote objects, serving as wrappers to database and legacy system integration code, are also highly scalable because of the inherently distributed nature of the technology itself.

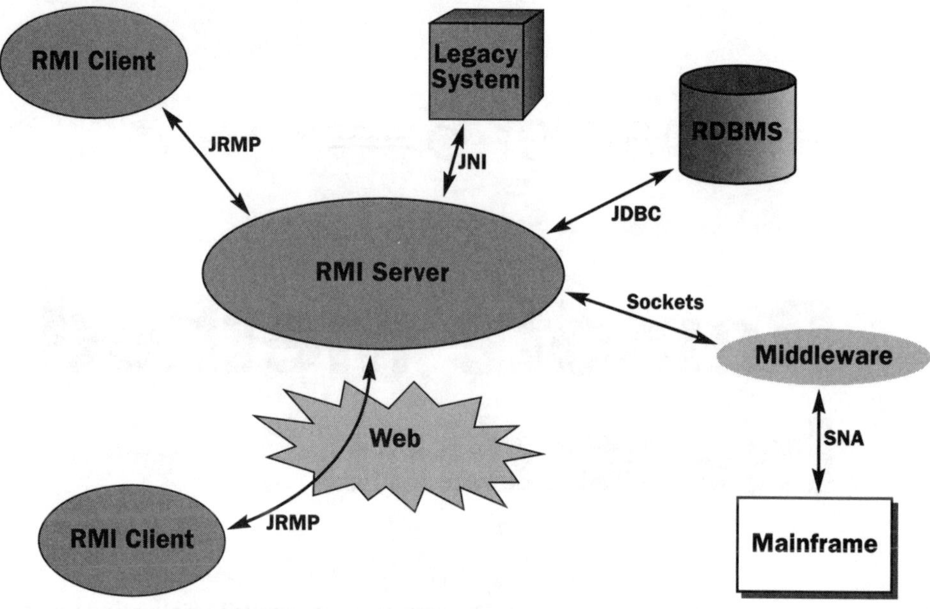

Figure 6-1: Distributed Object Computing Using RMI

This chapter provides a comprehensive introduction to distributed object computing using RMI and strives to demonstrate most of the features through concrete examples. The author assumes the reader has an understanding of the Java Serialization mechanism.

Developing an RMI System: A Stepwise Approach

Conceptually, the RMI development life-cycle is fairly straightforward and follows a series of well-defined steps.

1. Define the remote interface.
2. Develop the remote object by implementing the remote interface.
3. Develop the client program.
4. Compile the Java source files.
5. Generate the client stubs and server skeletons.
6. Start the RMI registry.
7. Start the remote server objects.
8. Run the client

Now, let's look beneath the hood of RMI with a detailed example.

Here, a simple remote server is implemented that returns an Employee object if its ID matches the one queried by the RMI client. The general RMI architecture is shown in Figure 6-2.

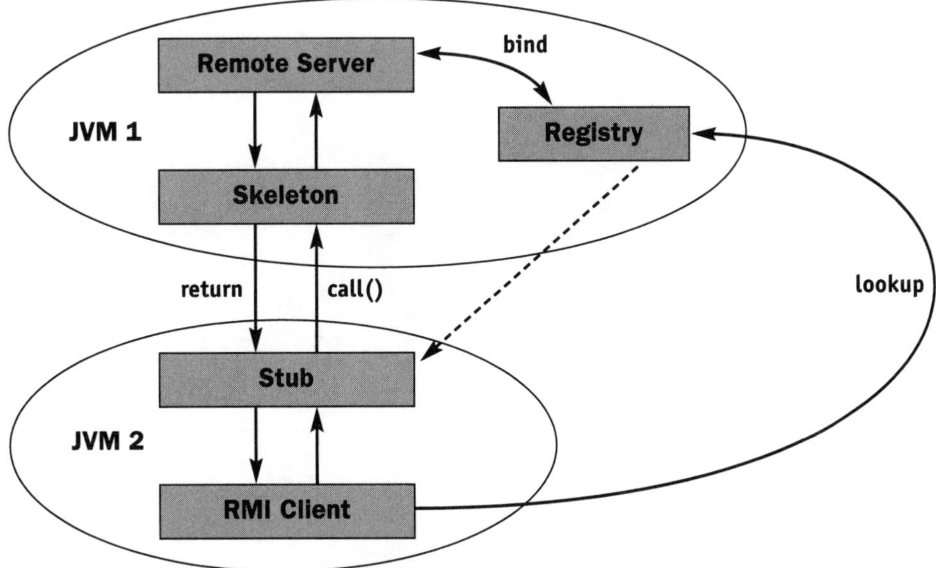

Figure 6-2: The RMI architecture

1. Define the remote interface

The services or methods offered by the remote object are advertised via a remote interface. An important characteristic of any remote object is the complete implementation of the defined remote interface. The code shown in Listing 6-1 defines the remote interface for this remote object.

Listing 6-1: Remote Interface for the Employee Server

```
package cup.chap6.rmiexample;
public interface EmployeeInterface extends java.rmi.Remote {
    public Employee lookup(int empID) throws java.rmi.RemoteException;
}
```

Some common rules must be followed when defining remote interfaces.

- First, all remote interfaces have to extend java.rmi.Remote or some other interface that directly extends it. The java.rmi.Remote interface is used to identify all remote objects by the RMI system.
- Second, each method within the remote interface has to declare the java.rmi.RemoteException in its throws clause—in addition to any other application specific exceptions—and to have public scope. This is used to trap any exception that may transpire during the distributed processing.

- Third, during RMI calls, all primitive data types and local objects are passed by value. You may remember, in a local method invocation, Java always passes a reference to the object. However, all remote objects (those that implement the java.rmi.Remote interface) are passed by reference.

Now, observe the Employee class shown in Listing 6-2, whose instance is returned by the remote object.

Listing 6-2: The Employee Class

```
package cup.chap6.rmiexample;
public class Employee implements java.io.Serializable {
    private int id;
    private String department;
    private String name;
    public Employee(int empID, String dept, String n) {
       id = empID;
       department = dept;
       name = n;
    }
    public int getId() {
       return id;
    }
    public void print() {
       System.out.println("ID: "+id);
       System.out.println("Department: "+department);
       System.out.println("Name: "+name);
    }
}
```

The class declaration may be the only thing that seems unusual about Employee:

```
public class Employee implements java.io.Serializable
```

Any Java class passed as a parameter to a remote object or returned from a remote method invocation needs to implement the Serializable interface. This is because RMI makes use of the Object Serialization facility (which was covered in detail in the previous chapter) to flatten or *marshal* objects into a serial stream and later reconstruct the object or *unmarshal* objects from the stream. Apart from having to implement the Serializable interface, you needn't do anything more to exchange objects between the client and the server. All the dirty work is taken care of by the underlying RMI subsystem. Now, for a greater appreciation of the power of serialization, briefly contemplate the challenges faced by a sockets-based programmer to implement the same.

2. Develop the remote object by implementing the remote interface

Listing 6-3 implements the remote interface to give the remote object—FortuneServer :

Listing 6-3: The EmployeeServer Remote Object

```
package cup.chap6.rmiexample;
import java.rmi.*;
import java.rmi.server.UnicastRemoteObject;
public class EmployeeServer extends UnicastRemoteObject implements EmployeeInterface {
    private String srvname ;
    private Employee[] employees = {
        new Employee(100,"Human Resources", "Jenny Jenkins"),
        new Employee(101,"Product Development", "Karl Schenke"),
        new Employee(102,"Product Development","Ter Parr"),
        new Employee(103,"Product Development","Rusty Harris")
    };
    public EmployeeServer (String serverName)throws java.rmi.RemoteException {
        super();
        srvname=serverName;
    }
    public Employee lookup(int empID) throws RemoteException {
        for (int i=0;i<employees.length;i++)
            if (empID == employees[i].getId())
                return employees[i];
        return null;
    }
    public static void main(String[] args) {
        System.setSecurityManager(new RMISecurityManager());
        try {
            EmployeeServer myEmployeeServer = new EmployeeServer("EmployeeServer");
            Naming.bind("/EmployeeServer", myEmployeeServer);
            System.out.println("EmployeeServer bound in registry");
        }
        catch (Exception e) {
            System.out.println("Exception on bind "+e.toString());
            System.out.println(e.printStackTrace());
        }
    }
}
```

Consider

```
public class EmployeeServer extends UnicastRemoteObject implements EmployeeInterface {
    ...
}
```

A remote server object usually directly or indirectly extends

```
java.rmi.server.UnicastRemoteObject
```

which provides the functionality needed to create and make available the remote object to external clients. (Remote objects can also be created using the static method `UnicastRemoteObject.exportObject()`, which we examine when implementing RMI callbacks.) This operation essentially serves to define a singleton remote object that uses a TCP-based transport for communication. Also, note, a remote server object can implement any number of remote interfaces, enabling us to create a generic remote object that can service different RMI clients.

Observe the constructor for our remote object:

```
public EmployeeServer (String serverName)throws java.rmi.RemoteException{
    super();
    srvname=serverName;
}
```

Here, `super()` invokes the constructor for `java.rmi.server.UnicastRemoteObject` that binds the server to an anonymous port and starts to listen for incoming calls on that port. Also necessary is for the constructor to trigger a `java.rmi.RemoteException` condition if sufficient network resources are unavailable as it attempts to export the remote object.

The remote object has to provide an implementation for every method that appears in the remote interface it implements. Observe, in our method

```
public Employee lookup(int empID) throws RemoteException {
    ...
}
```

we throw a `RemoteException`, as defined in the remote interface. This way, the calling client program can get to know when something goes awry at the remote object via the familiar Java exception handling mechanism. Our remote object can also implement other methods, beyond what appears in the remote interface, but these methods would be strictly local to the host JVM and cannot be accessed from outside it.

Now, look more closely at the main body of our remote object. Consider:

```
System.setSecurityManager(new RMISecurityManager());
```

The `main()` method of our remote object must always instantiate some user-defined security manager or the `RMISecurityManager` in order to ensure that any remotely loaded stubs and classes behave themselves. If you do not have a security manager in place, then stub classes can be loaded only from the local file system as defined by CLASSPATH. One should note that there are always some inherent risks in downloading arbitrary RMI classes over the network, especially if it is coming from some non authenticated source - the installed security manager notwithstanding. As an additional precaution, you can disable arbitrary class downloading by setting the property `java.rmi.server.useCodeBaseOnly` to true - in which case, the classes will be downloaded only from the locally defined codebase.

The line:

```
EmployeeServer myEmployeeServer =new EmployeeServer("EmployeeServer");
```

creates a new instance of the remote object and binds it to an anonymous port on the host machine. At this point, the remote object is ready to listen for any incoming calls.

Before a client can invoke a method on a remote object, it must first be able to locate it easily over the network and obtain a reference to the remote object. Thus, it is necessary for all remote objects to be registered first within a registry or namespace, which serves to advertise them to any network client. Toward this, the RMI system provides a URL-based registry that enables you to bind a URL, in the form `rmi://hostname:portnumber/remoteobjectname`, to the remote object, where "remoteobjectname" can be any user-defined string literal identifying the object in question. The `java.rmi.Naming` class offers methods through which a remote object can be registered. In the example,

```
Naming.bind("/EmployeeServer", myEmployeeServer);
```

has the effect of binding a reference to the remote object to the URL `/FortuneServer`. Remember, you currently can bind remote objects only if they are running on the same host as the RMI registry itself.

Note

Your remote server objects must register themselves within the RMI registry using unique names; this is critical. If you invoke `Naming.bind()` with the designated name already in use, an exception will be thrown. If you expect to host a large number of remote objects on your system, first create a good naming convention to prevent this name clashing. If necessary, you can replace an existing remote object handle within the registry with a different object by invoking `Naming.rebind()` instead of `Naming.bind()`.

By default, the current host is assumed if it is omitted from the URL. Also note, the RMI registry runs on port 1099 by default on the server. You can have more than one RMI registry running on the same host, albeit on different ports. Thus, you can have different registries contain bindings for different groups of remote objects. If you have more than one RMI registry or if the default one is started on a different port, the port information should be reflected when binding the URL. Another important point to remember is the RMI registry within JDK 1.1 is nonpersistent. If it crashes for whatever reason, you must rebind all the remote objects within it all over again to make them available to remote clients.

3. Develop the client program

Listing 6-4 demonstrates the client applet for our RMI server.

Listing 6-4: RMI Client Application

```
package cup.chap6.rmiexample;
import java.awt.*;
import java.applet.*;
import java.rmi.*;
public class RMIClient {
    public static void main(String[] args) {
        if (args.length <1 ) {
            System.out.println("Usage: java
            cup.chap6.rmiexample.RMIClient <empid>");
            System.exit(-1);
        }
        try {
            EmployeeInterface empReference =(EmployeeInterface)
                    Naming.lookup("/EmployeeServer");
            int id = new Integer(args[0]).intValue();
            Employee emp = empReference.lookup(id);
            if (emp != null) {
                emp.print();
            } else {
                System.out.println("No employees matching ID:"+id);
            }
        } catch (Exception e) {
            System.out.println(e.toString());
            System.out.println(e.printStackTrace());
        }
    }
}
```

Look at the RMI client program. You can see the all-important statement here is

```
EmployeeInterface empReference =(EmployeeInterface)
Naming.lookup("/EmployeeServer");
```

As mentioned earlier, before a client can invoke a method from a remote object, the client must first obtain a reference to it. This is done by querying the RMI registry on the remote server with the name given to our remote object when it was stored in the registry. The reference to the remote object is passed back in the form of a stub file (more on this later) because it has the necessary information for suitably dispatching the method invocation to the remote implementation. Notice, once the remote reference is obtained, invoking a remote method is no different from invoking a local one.

4. Compile the Java source files

Assuming your Java source files are located in some directory "sourcedir," they can be compiled using the javac compiler to yield our example package cup.chap6.rmiexample containing the class files for the client application and remote RMI server.

```
javac -d . Employee.java
javac -d . EmployeeInterface.java
javac -d . EmployeeServer.java
javac -d . RMIClient.java
```

This creates Employee.class, EmployeeInterface.class, EmployeeServer.class, and RMIClient.class in the path /sourcedir/cup/chap6/rmiexample/

5. Generate the client stubs and server skeletons

The rmic compiler, provided by the JDK 1.1 and Java 2, is used to generate the client stubs and server skeletons for the remote objects. The stub/skeleton layer acts as the glue that integrates the application layer with the rest of the RMI system, as shown in Figure 6-3. A *stub* is a client-side proxy for the remote object and implements all the interfaces supported by the remote object. So, when a client invokes a remote method, the call is first forwarded to the stub. The stub is responsible for sending the remote call over to the server-side skeleton. It does this by first opening a socket to the remote server, serializing or *marshaling* the object parameters, and forwarding the data stream to the skeleton. A skeleton contains a method that receives the remote calls, *unmarshals* or deserializes the parameters, and invokes the actual remote object implementation. Stubs and skeleton classes are determined and loaded dynamically as needed at runtime.

Figure 6-3: The RMI stub/skeleton layer

For this example, running rmic on our remote object class file as:

```
rmic -d . cup.chap6.rmiexample.EmployeeServer
```

generates EmployeeServer_Stub.class and EmployeeServer_Skel.class into the path /somedir/cup/chap6/rmiexample/

Note

The RMI implementation within Java 2 does not need a server skeleton, as the stub can directly communicate with the remote object. If you know for certain all your clients will be running Java 2, you can run rmic with the -v1.2 option to prevent the generation of stub files. Otherwise, you can use the -vcompat option to create files that works with both Java versions.

6. Start the RMI registry

On UNIX systems, the RMI registry can be started and run in the background as:

```
rmiregistry&
```

On Windows, you have to type in from the command line:

```
start rmiregistry
```

The rmiregistry is uses port 1099 by default. You can also bind rmiregistry to a different port by indicating the new port number as:

```
rmiregistry <new port>
```

If you bind rmiregistry to a different port, then you must also modify the Naming.lookup() call within your remote object appropriately by supplying the new port number within.

Note

One of the more common mistakes is to start up the RMI registry from a window where the CLASSPATH includes the classes for the remote server in its path. Consequently, this causes the RMI registry to ignore the java.rmi.server.codebase setting for the server. The registry must contain the location of the remote object classes in an HTTP URL-encoded format, so when this information is sent to the client, the classes can then be downloaded via an HTTP server. If the registry does not send the location of the stub files in an HTTP URL-encoded format, the client has no way to download the class files dynamically for the remote object and throws a java.lang.ClassNotFoundException. To avoid this situation, before your start RMI registry, always ensure the CLASSPATH variable, if present, does not include the location of any downloadable classes.

Every RMI server running on a given host has a handle or reference to itself present in a "yellow-pages"-like name server (aka, the rmiregistry) running on the same host. Note, the rmiregistry does not maintain a persistent store of the remote objects. If it must be restarted for whatever reason, then the remote objects have to be rebound within it all over again.

Java 2 Security Policy Files

Under JDK 1.0 and 1.1, locally resident code loaded from the CLASSPATH was completely trusted. With Java 2, however, we have to grant privileges explicitly even for those classes loaded from the CLASSPATH. This is because, although a Java application may be signed, different applications need varying levels of access to system resources. Just because you may have installed a Java application you downloaded from the Web locally on your machine, does not imply it should have complete access to your enterprise network resources. While the new security model is quite a departure from the old "all-or-nothing" approach, it is extremely flexible. Now, every Java application can be executed with a highly granular level of control over its operations like file access, network use, and so forth.

Thus, in Java 2, a Java application must first obtain information regarding its privileges and the security policy it must adhere through a policy file. This is usually a text file with multiple permissions in a predefined format, representing some level of access to a system resource. Obviously, because not all applications enjoy the same privileges, more than one policy file can exist.

For instance, the contents of the policy file can be:

```
grant {
    permission java.security.AllPermission;
};
```

Note, granting java.security.AllPermission should be done with caution, as it implies your Java code can run pretty much with the Java 2 security features disabled. Typically, we would allow Java code to have all permissions only during the testing phase, when we just want to get something up and running in a hurry.

For instance, the policy file shown in the following:

```
grant {
   permission java.io.FilePermission "/temp/*", "read","write";
   permission java.net.SocketPermission "somehost.somedomain.com:999", "connect";
   permission java.net.SocketPermission "*:1024-65535", "connect,accept";
   permission java.net.SocketPermission "*:80", "connect";
};
```

1. allows the Java code to read/write any files only under the /temp directory, including any subdirectories,
2. allows all Java classes to establish a network connection with the host "somehost.somedomain.com" on port 999,
3. allows classes to connect to or accept connections on unprivileged ports greater than 1024, on any host, and
4. allows all classes to connect to the HTTP port 80 on any host.

The topic of creating policy files and assigning resource permissions is an extensive one. You can obtain complete details by looking at the following links:

http://java.sun.com/products/jdk/1.2/docs/guide/security/PolicyFiles.html
http://java.sun.com/products/jdk/1.2/docs/guide/security/permissions.html

If you are running this example under Java 2, you also need a "security policy" file, denoting the level of security and permissions for your remote objects to carry out various operations like socket creation, and so forth. The RMI registry must now be started giving the location of the policy file as:

```
start rmiregistry -J-Djava.security.policy=C:\somedir\policy
```

7. Start the remote server objects

Assuming your RMI classes are stored within some subdirectory named "ex1" located directly underneath the "document-root" of your Web server, you can start up the remote server object under JDK 1.1 as:

```
start java -Djava.rmi.server.codebase=http://hostname/ex1/
    cup.chap6.rmiexample.EmployeeServer
```

If you are starting up your RMI server under Java 2, you also need to set the `java.security.policy` property and indicate the location of the policy file that sets the security level upon server startup:

```
start java -Djava.rmi.server.codebase=http://hostname/ex1/
    -Djava.security.policy=c:\somedir\policy cup.chap6.rmiexample.EmployeeServer
```

Although you nearly always specify the codebase as a http URL when deploying your server in a production mode, you can test the RMI client and server on the same host by including all classes within the CLASSPATH or by specifying a local file-based URL.

The `java.rmi.server.codebase` property specifies the location of the stub and other user-defined classes that need to be downloaded at runtime by the remote client. To boost performance by minimizing the number of network connections made by the client, you can package the stubs and user-defined classes into a single JAR file and specify it within the codebase. If the codebase specifies a directory instead of a JAR file, howw-ever, you must always include the trailing slash at the end of the codebase URL.

Starting Your Server Using javaw

Instead of using the Windows command start, you can make use of the Windows JDK utility `javaw` to fire-up the Java interpreter as a separate process and run your RMI server in the background. But, personally speaking, I prefer using the `start` command. The `start` command is far easier to terminate a Java process that was initiated using start than `javaw`. Also, if you are in a debugging mode, seeing any diagnostic messages that may be printed to the console is nearly impossible if you initiated the remote server process using `javaw`.

8. Run the client

A restriction exists for RMI applets, imposed by the applet security manager. The RMI server must run on the same machine that hosts the Web server because applets can connect only with the host from which they were downloaded. This restriction can be circumvented if the applets are signed. RMI applications can, however, connect with servers running anywhere on the network.

Also true is support for RMI has historically been rather inconsistent among browsers. For this reason, I highly recommended you run RMI applets on browsers enabled with the Java PlugIn. The Java PlugIn essentially replaces the browsers JVM with the standard Sun JRE—thus offering a common Java environment across browsers. Of course, if your RMI client is an application instead of an applet, then no similar deployment considerations exist.

You should be able to run your RMI client under JDK 1.1 as:

```
java cup.chap6.rmiexample.RMIClient 103
```

or, under Java 2 as:

```
java -Djava.security.policy=c:\somedir\policy
     cup.chap6.rmiexample.RMIClient 103
```

producing the output:

```
ID: 103
Department: Product Development
Name: Rusty Harris
```

Do We Need an HTTP Server for RMI?

Typically, unless you have previously placed the RMI server's stub classes—as well as any other user-defined classes—within the client's CLASSPATH, they need to be dynamically retrieved from the remote server host. Because RMI makes use of the HTTP protocol to retrieve classes dynamically, it is necessary to have a Web server for this purpose running on the remote host. This is a requirement for both RMI applets and applications. You can use any HTTP server like Apache or Jigsaw for this purpose. Additionally, Sun provides a simple "class server" implementation exclusively for use with RMI at:

ftp://ftp.javasoft.com/pub/jdk1.1/rmi/class-server.zip

Understanding Remote Polymorphism

One of the more interesting features of RMI is its support for remote polymorphism. This essentially means different objects may be downloaded in response to a RMI call, even though the implementation for these objects may not be available at the client. Remote polymorphism provides designers with great flexibility by enabling them to declare rather generic methods within their interfaces, whose behavior may be subject to modification at runtime. In addition, remote polymorphism is a prerequisite if you are to apply any sophisticated design patterns in a distributed context.

To understand this powerful concept further, let's extend the `Employee` class, shown in Listing 6-2 in the previous section, to create the `Manager` and `Developer` subclasses shown in Listing 6-5 and 6-6, respectively. Notice both these subclasses basically override the `Employee's print()` method and add an extra instance variable.

Listing 6-5: The Manager Class

```
package cup.chap6.rmiexample;
public class Manager extends Employee {
    private String officeLocation;
    public Manager(int empID, String dept, String nme, String locn) {
        super(empID,dept,nme);
        officeLocation=locn;
    }
    public void print() {
        super.print();
        System.out.println("Office Location: "+officeLocation);
    }
}
```

Listing 6-6: The Developer Class

```
package cup.chap6.rmiexample;
public class Developer extends Employee {
    private String faveDrink;
    public Developer(int empID, String dept, String nme, String beverage) {
        super(empID,dept,nme);
        faveDrink=beverage;
    }
    public void print() {
        super.print();
        System.out.println("Favorite Drink: "+faveDrink);
    }
}
```

Now, we modify the EmployeeServer remote object shown earlier in Listing 6-3 by adding some Manager and Developer instances to the employees array. Now, you can have an instance of either of the subtypes returned, assuming their ID matches that of the search criterion.

```
private Employee[] employees = {
    new Employee(100,"Human Resources", "Jenny Jenkins"),
    new Employee(101,"Product Development", "Karl Schenke"),
    new Manager(102,"Product Development","Ter Parr","E124"),
    new Developer(103,"Product Development","Rusty Harris","Jolt Cola")
};
```

The RMI server can be recompiled and started as usual. Now, if the RMI client is run with the input 103 as before, the remote object's lookup() method does something different—instead of returning an instance of Employee, it now returns a matching instance of the Developer subtype. The RMI subsystem then recognizes the Developer class is a valid subclass of Employee and returns both the classes to the client after serializing them. Later, when the client then invokes the print() method on Employee, it actually executes the overridden print() method of the Developer subclass. Note, neither the remote interface nor the RMI client had to be modified to effect this behavior.

Implementing RMI Callbacks

Simply having a remote object whose methods can be invoked by distributed client objects is insufficient for some of the more complex interactions. For instance, applications supporting any kind of collaborative functionality (chat rooms, bulletin-board systems, and so forth) need to implement a peer-to-peer relationship between the interacting client and server objects.

One of the more elegant ways to enable the remote server to asynchronously communicate with the client is to use callbacks. But again, what is a callback? Event-driven programming in languages like C have traditionally used function pointers to pass around references to functions that are then asynchronously invoked in response to some "event," be this a timer going off, a mouse click, or something of the sort. Java makes use of interfaces to give programmers access to the same functionality in an object-oriented world. Here, the interface defines the methods that may be invoked by any object with access to the interface. Of course, the real "functionality" itself is present within some other object that implements this interface and this is simply "called back" by the target object.

Implementing callbacks, however, poses a fair challenge in the best of situations, especially so in a distributed object-computing environment like RMI.

Luckily, the steps you must follow to implement RMI callbacks have a lot in common with those needed to implement the simple remote server object seen previously. The key difference is, now, you also have to set up the client applet or application as a remote object (for example, make it implement some remote interface) and, somehow, register its reference with the remote server object. This way, the server can asynchronously invoke the remote methods of any connected client in the same way the client can asynchronously invoke the methods implemented within the remote server objects. The general architecture for an RMI system implementing callbacks is shown in 6-4.

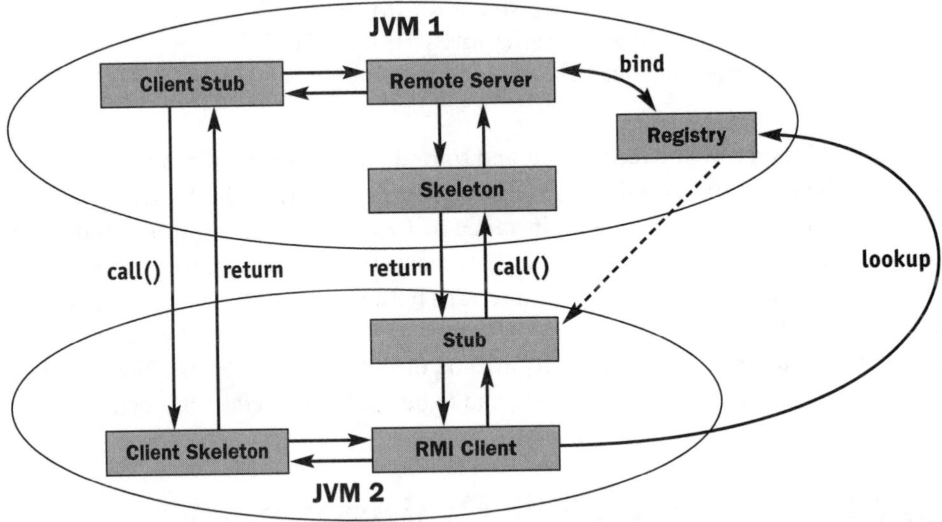

Figure 6-4: An RMI system implementing callbacks

Developing an RMI system with callbacks

Developing an RMI system that implements callbacks is similar to the RMI life-cycle we saw earlier, but with a few additional steps.

1. Specify the remote client interface.
2. Specify the remote server interface.
3. Develop the remote server object by implementing the remote server interface.
4. Develop the client application or applet by implementing the remote client interface.
5. Compile the Java source files for the RMI client and server.
6. Generate the stubs and skeletons for the RMI client and server objects.
7. Start the remote server object.
8. Run the client applet after creating a HTML file for the RMI client.

In our example, the remote server object—QuoteServer—maintains a list of quotes. Our RMI client applet—QuoteApplet—can make additions to this list of quotes anytime, in an asynchronous manner. Finally, the use of RMI callbacks is demonstrated by having the server object periodically select a quote from its list in random fashion and update each of the connected client objects in an asynchronous manner.

Now, let's take a closer look at the necessary steps for implementing the previous example:

1. Specify the remote client interface

Any RMI client applet or application that exports itself as a remote object needs to implement a remote client interface. This is what enables the server object to invoke the client functionality in an asynchronous manner via callbacks.

Listing 6-7: Remote Interface for Client Object

```
package cup.chap6.rmicallback;
/**
This defines the methods available to the
server for remote invocation as callbacks
*/
public interface QClientInterface extends java.rmi.Remote {
        public void refreshClient(String q) throws java.rmi.RemoteException;
}
```

The refreshClient() method defined in Listing 6-7 serves to define how each remote client object can be "notified" or updated by the server object asynchronously.

2. Specify the remote server interface

The remote server interface shown in Listing 6-8 serves to specify the functionality implemented by the server object, which is then made accessible to a client via remote methods invocations.

Listing 6-8: Remote Interface for Server Object

```
package cup.chap6.rmicallback;
public interface QServerInterface extends java.rmi.Remote {
     public void addQuote(String quote) throws java.rmi.RemoteException;
     public void setQClientInterface(QClientInterface c) throws java.rmi.RemoteException;
}
```

Our remote server interface lists two methods available to client RMI objects. The addQuote() method is used by remote clients to update the list of quotes and the setQClientInterface() method is used by clients to "register" themselves with the server object.

3. Develop the remote server object by implementing the remote server interface

Consider the implementation for the remote server object, shown in Listing 6-9.

Listing 6-9: Implementation for Remote Server Object

```
package cup.chap6.rmicallback;
import java.rmi.*;
import java.rmi.server.UnicastRemoteObject;
import java.rmi.registry.LocateRegistry;
import java.util.*;
public class QuoteServer extends UnicastRemoteObject implements
        QServerInterface, Runnable {
    private Vector clientele; //tracks all connected clients
    private QClientInterface myQClientInterface;
    private Vector quoteList; //maintains updatable list of quotes
    private QClientInterface myClientObj;
    private Thread clientThread=null;
    private static int counter=0;
    public QuoteServer ()  throws java.rmi.RemoteException {
        super();
        // create and initialize the quote list
        quoteList = new Vector();
        quoteList.addElement("Climb mountains to see lowlands");
        quoteList.addElement("If you want the rainbow, put up with the rain");
        quoteList.addElement("Smooth seas do not make skilful sailors");
        clientele = new Vector();
    }
    public  void setQClientInterface(QClientInterface c) throws RemoteException {
        synchronized (clientele) {
            clientele.addElement(c);
        }
        if (clientThread == null) {
            clientThread = new Thread(this, "clientThread");
            clientThread.start();
        }
    }
    private void doIt() {
        synchronized (clientele) {
            Vector backup = (Vector) clientele.clone();
            int seed;
            while ((seed = new Random().nextInt()) <=0) ;
                seed = seed % quoteList.size();
```

Listing 6-9: continued

```
                String data = quoteList.elementAt(seed)+ ": "+ ++counter;
                for (int i=0; i < clientele.size(); i++) {
                    myClientObj = (QClientInterface) clientele.elementAt(i);
                    try {
                        //update the client asynchronously via callback
                        myClientObj.refreshClient((String) data );
                    } catch (RemoteException e) {
                        System.out.println("client must have disconnected!");
                        //get rid of the remote reference for disconnected client
                        backup.removeElement(myClientObj);
                        if (backup.size() <= 0) {
                            //no more clients- so stop server thread
                            clientele = (Vector) backup.clone();
                            Thread dummy = clientThread;
                            clientThread = null;
                            dummy.stop();
                        }
                    }
            }
            clientele = (Vector) backup.clone();
        } //end syncronization on clientele
    }
    public void run() {
        while (true) {
            try {
                //sleep for a second
                Thread.currentThread().sleep(1000);
            } catch (Exception e) {
                        }
            doIt();
        }
    }
    public void addQuote(String quote) throws RemoteException {
        synchronized (quoteList) {
            //update quote list
            quoteList.addElement(quote);
        }
    }
    public static void main(String[] args) {
        System.setSecurityManager(new RMISecurityManager());
        try {
            System.out.println("QuoteServer.main: creating registry");
```

continues

Listing 6-9: continued

```
            LocateRegistry.createRegistry(1099);
            System.out.println("QuoteServer.main: creating server");
            QuoteServer myQuoteServer=new QuoteServer();
            System.out.println("QuoteServer.main: binding server ");
            Naming.rebind("/QuoteServer", myQuoteServer);
            System.out.println("QuoteServer bound in registry");
        } catch (Exception e) {
            System.out.println("Exception on binding QuoteServer");
            System.out.println(e.toString());
        }
    }
}
```

Observe the implementation of the remote server object. Note, the RMI registry can also be started from within a server, if necessary, as demonstrated by the line:

```
LocateRegistry.createRegistry(1099);
```

Of course, it is important to see that an instance of the registry is not already running on the host or else an exception will be thrown.

Our remote server creates two `Vector` objects—`quoteList` for the quotes and `clientele`—to maintain references to all the connected remote RMI client objects.

The remote method `setQClientInterface()` is called by every remote client first and it serves to register a handle for the client within the remote server. Note, every client connection results in the creation of a new thread within the server, which serves to update the client periodically by invoking the `refreshClient()` callback. Any client can asynchronously update the synchronized `quoteList` vector maintained by the server by simply invoking `addQuote()`.

The server object also demonstrates the management of client handles stored within `clientele`, as clients connect/disconnect from the remote server.

4. Develop the client application or applet by implementing the remote client interface

Listing 6-10 demonstrates how the client applet can export itself as a remote object.

Listing 6-10: RMI Client Applet Implementing Callbacks

```
package cup.chap6.rmicallback;
import java.rmi.*;
import java.rmi.server.*;
import java.util.Random;
import java.awt.*;
import java.applet.*;
public class QuoteApplet extends Applet implements QClientInterface {
```

Listing 6-10: continued

```
public void init() {
    setLayout(null);
    setSize(426,237);
    label = new java.awt.Label("Input Quote:");
    label.setBounds(12,24,72,24);
    add(label);
    sendButton = new java.awt.Button();
    sendButton.setLabel("Send");
    sendButton.setBounds(348,24,60,24);
    sendButton.setBackground(new Color(12632256));
    add(sendButton);
    quotes = new java.awt.TextArea();
    quotes.setBounds(36,60,372,156);
    add(quotes);
    myQuote = new java.awt.TextField();
    myQuote.setBounds(84,24,252,28);
    add(myQuote);
    SymAction lSymAction = new SymAction();
    sendButton.addActionListener(lSymAction);
    try {
        //by exporting the client object, turn it into a
        //remote object
        UnicastRemoteObject.exportObject(this);
    } catch (Exception e) {
        System.out.println("Could not export client remote object");
        System.out.println(e);
    }
    try {
        //obtain the remote server object's reference by interrogating the
        //rmi registry
        srvQuote = (QServerInterface)
            Naming.lookup("//"+getCodeBase().getHost()+"/QuoteServer");
        srvQuote.setQClientInterface(this);
    } catch (Exception e) {
        System.out.println("Could not set client interface at server");
        System.out.println(e.toString());
    }
}
public void refreshClient(String q) throws java.rmi.RemoteException {
    //this is the callback method implementation
        quotes.append(q+"\n");
}
```

continues

Listing 6-10: continued

```
        java.awt.Label label;
        java.awt.Button sendButton;
        java.awt.TextArea quotes;
        java.awt.TextField myQuote;
        QServerInterface  srvQuote=null;
        class SymAction implements java.awt.event.ActionListener {
            public void actionPerformed(java.awt.event.ActionEvent e) {
                Object object = e.getSource();
                if (object == sendButton)
                    sendButton_ActionPerformed(e);
            }
        }
        void sendButton_ActionPerformed(java.awt.event.ActionEvent e){
            try {
                //update the remote server object with a new quote
                srvQuote.addQuote((String)myQuote.getText());
            } catch (Exception e) {
                System.out.println(e.toString());
            }
            myQuote.setText("");
        }
}
```

Unlike remote server objects, clients implementing callbacks neither need to run a registry nor even to register itself into one. A client applet can simply export itself as a remote object by calling:

```
UnicastRemoteObject.exportObject(this);
```

How is the server able to contact the remote client object if no RMI registry process is running at the client host? Consider the line:

```
srvQuote.setQClientInterface(this);
```

Here, the client uses the remote server method to pass along a reference to itself to the server. This handle is later used by the server as a proxy for the remote client object itself.

5. Compile the Java source files for the RMI client and server

As with the example in the earlier section, your Java class files must be made available under some directory within the document root of your Web server. Assuming you have all the Java source files within $DOCUMENT_ROOT/ex2, you can compile them by going to that directory and executing

```
javac -d . QClientInterface.java
javac -d . QServerInterface.java
```

```
javac -d . QuoteServer.java
javac -d . QuoteApplet.java
```

This creates the package cup.chap6.rmicallback containing the classes QClientInterface.class, QServerInterface.class, QuoteServer.class, and QuoteApplet.class

6. Generate the stubs and skeletons for the RMI client and server objects

Because you now have the client and server are remote objects, you need to generate the stubs and skeleton files for both of them.

From within $DOCUMENT_ROOT/ex2, invoke

```
rmic -d . cup.chap6.rmicallback.QuoteServer
rmic -d . cup.chap6.rmicallback.QuoteApplet
```

This generates the server skeletons and client stubs for the client and server remote objects within $DOCUMENT_ROOT/ex2/cup/chap6/rmicallback/

QuoteServer_Stub.class and QuoteServer_Skel.class are the client stubs and server skeletons for the remote server object.

QuoteApplet_Stub.class and QuoteApplet_Skel.class are the same for the remote client object.

7. Start the remote server object

Start the remote server object from within $DOCUMENT_ROOT/ex2 as:

```
(For JDK 1.1)
java -Djava.rmi.server.codebase=http://hostname/ex2/
     cup.chap6.rmicallback.QuoteServer &
(For Java 2)
java -Djava.rmi.server.codebase=http://hostname/ex2/
     -Djava.security.policy=c:\somedir\policy
     cup.chap6.rmicallback.QuoteServer &
```

8. Run the client applet after creating a HTML file for the RMI client

Because Java applets are always embedded within an HTML file, you must create one to send across the QuoteApplet.class to the browser, as shown in Listing 6-11.

Listing 6-11: HTML File for RMI Applet Implementing Callback

```
<html>
<body>
<applet codebase="." code="cup.chap6.rmicallback.QuoteApplet.class" width=500
     height=300>
</applet>
</body>
</html>
```

Figure 6-5 shows the RMI applet implementing callbacks executing within Java Plug-In enabled Netscape and Microsoft browsers:

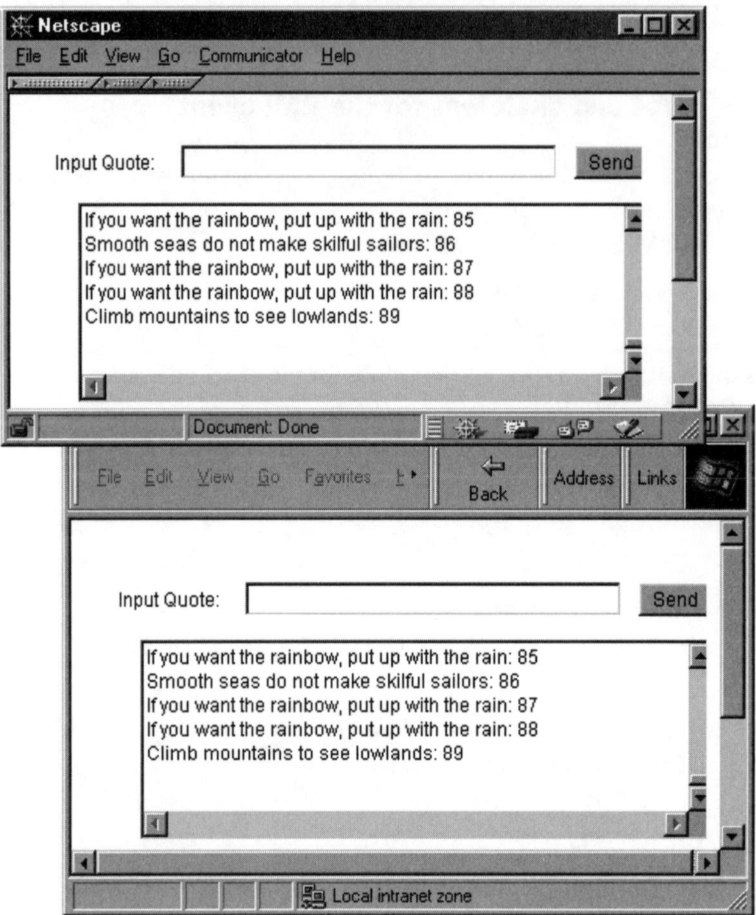

Figure 6-5: RMI applet implementing callbacks

We see our client RMI applet not only has the capability to perform asynchronous updates on the remote server object, but the applet itself is also periodically updated with a randomly selected quote by the remote server object. Some restrictions exist with deploying RMI applets that implement callbacks, however. For instance, they cannot be used across firewalls. RMI makes use of HTTP tunneling to get through firewalls. HTTP is a stateless protocol and does not offer a suitable transport for callbacks.

Distributed Garbage Collection

One of the highlights of RMI is Java's garbage collection mechanism is extended to cover even remote objects. The RMI subsystem implements a reference counting-based distributed garbage collection (DGC) algorithm to implement memory management at the remote server. The DGC works by having the remote server keep track of all the RMI clients connected to it at any given time. When a client obtains a reference to the remote server, the DGC mechanism marks the remote object as dirty; when a client drops the reference, the remote object is marked as clean. All remote objects free of any references are then periodically garbage collected.

The unreferenced interface

Although the DGC mechanism transparently takes care of memory management needs at the remote server, situations may occur where you must be notified immediately as soon as the server has no live references. For instance, you may want to release valuable resources explicitly—like database and network connections—and perform other "housekeeping" activities, before the garbage collector kicks in.

Any remote object implementing the java.rmi.server.Unreferenced interface can get immediate notification via the unreferenced() method, as soon as no clients are holding a live reference to the remote object. The following snippet demonstrates a typical implementation:

```
public class RemoteImpl extends UnicastRemoteObject implements
        SomeRemoteInterface, Unreferenced {
    public RemoteImpl() {
        super();
        ...
        //allocate resources here
    }
    ...
    public void unreferenced() {
        ...
        //perform "housekeeping" activities here
        //by freeing previously allocated resources
    }
}
```

The leaseValue property

When an RMI client obtains a reference to the remote object, the reference is live for the default lease term of ten minutes. If a client does not refresh the connection to the remote object before the lease term expires, the reference is consider dead and the remote object may be subject to garbage collection. The lease term, however, can be easily changed and is controlled by setting the system property `java.rmi.dgc.leaseValue` in milliseconds. For example, starting up the remote server `MyRemoteServer` as:

```
java -Djava.rmi.dgc.leaseValue=300000 MyRemoteServer
```

resets the lease value to five minutes.

You should ensure the lease interval is not too short because the client automatically renews the lease when it is halfway expired. Otherwise, the client needlessly consumes significant network bandwidth in repeatedly renewing a lease.

Working with Firewalls

Firewalls are an inescapable reality for networked applications, which have to operate beyond the sheltering confines of an Intranet. Without them, enterprise LANs would be wide open to nearly every hacker on the Web. Firewalls typically block most incoming traffic before they reach the enterprise LAN, unless the traffic is intended for certain "well-known ports," used by common enterprise applications like HTTP, SMTP, FTP, and so forth. You may wonder how RMI traffic gets across firewalls, considering that, by default, the JRMP protocol opens dynamic socket connections between the client and server. Well, RMI makes use of HTTP tunneling to burrow through firewalls by encapsulating RMI calls within an HTTP POST request. Much of the underlying mechanism is transparent to the user; the RMI client, the server or both can be behind a firewall.

Consider the scenario shown in Figure 6-6, where the RMI client is communicating with a remote server outside of the firewall. Here, we make the assumption the firewall proxy can forward data to arbitrary ports and the RMI registry is listening on a well-known port on the remote host.

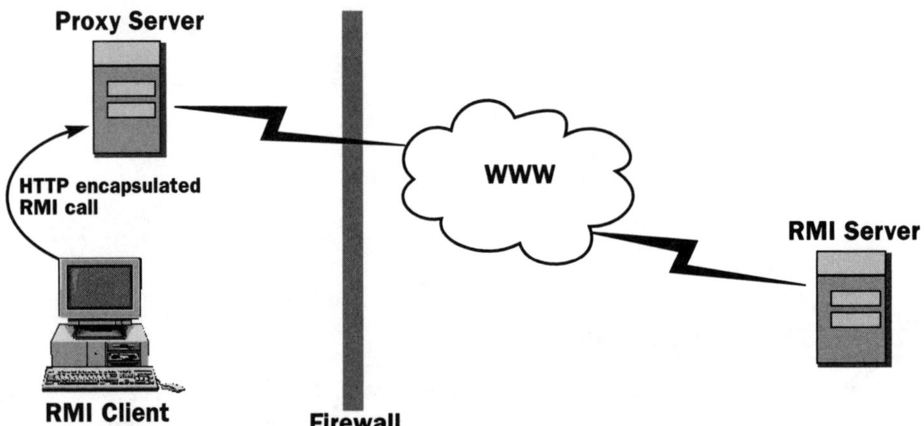

Figure 6-6: RMI client communicating with server outside firewall

When the RMI client tries to open a connection with the remote server, the call is blocked at the firewall. Once this happens, the client automatically retries by encapsulating the RMI call data within an HTTP POST request, with the POST header being of the form:

```
http://<hostname>:<port>
```

Because the HTTP protocol is recognized by the firewall, it is allowed to get through to the outside and is sent directly to the port on which the remote server is listening by the firewall proxy server. At the remote server, the incoming HTTP-encapsulated call is automatically decoded and dispatched, with the reply sent back again as HTTP-encapsulated data.

The setup is slightly different for the scenario shown in Figure 6-7, when both the RMI client and server are behind firewalls or when the firewall proxy can forward data only to the well-known HTTP port 80.

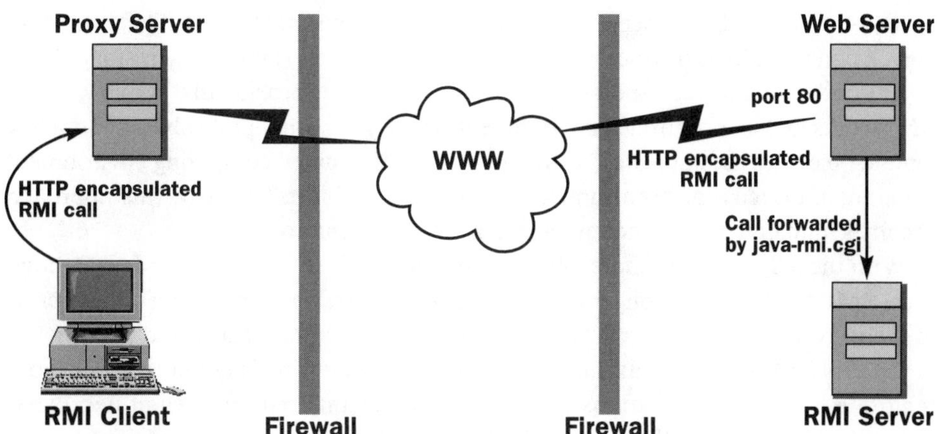

Figure 6-7: Firewall scenario with both RMI client and server behind firewalls

Now, the client can no longer send HTTP encapsulated calls to arbitrary ports because the remote object is also running behind a firewall. Instead, the HTTP POST header is of the form:

```
http://<hostname>:80/cgi-bin/java-rmi?forward=<port>
```

This causes the execution of the CGI script `java-rmi.cgi`, which invokes a local JVM and forwards the RMI call to the designated port. The `java-rmi.cgi` program, which is available as part of the JDK distribution, must be located within the Web server's cgi-bin directory and configured with the path of Java interpreter. Also, in both the previous scenarios, the RMI server must specify the host's fully qualified domain name during startup to avoid DNS resolution problems, as:

```
java.rmi.server.hostname=myhost.mydomain.com
```

Although RMI has a built-in mechanism for overcoming firewalls, a significant performance degradation is imposed by the HTTP encapsulation. For this reason, a client can, optionally, simply disable HTTP encapsulation by setting:

```
java.rmi.server.disableHttp=true
```

Remote Object Activation

Few deny that RMI is one of the most useful and powerful Java technologies currently around. But, still, some glaring lacunae are within the RMI architecture, as currently implemented under JDK 1.1. For instance, under JDK 1.1, each of the remote objects must be started manually prior to their use by the remote clients. Additionally, if any of the remote objects crash during operation—although they can be restarted all over again—they loses all instance data and a client cannot resume "where it left off." Also note, having hundreds of resource-intensive remote objects running in memory all the time is highly inefficient, especially if they are only used occasionally. While it is true RMI works fine in a controlled environment where you would probably run just a few remote objects, what happens if your enterprise's distributed computing environment demands hundreds, or even thousands, of remote objects? Clearly, this approach becomes unmanageable rather quickly in a real-life scenario.

With the help of the Remote Object Activation (ROA) feature under Java 2, however, RMI developers no longer have to worry about starting up remote objects prior to their invocation. Now, by extending `java.rmi.activation.Activatable` and making use of the new RMI activation daemon `rmid`, your RMI servers register information about remote object implementations that should be instantiated only when necessary, rather than be running all the time. The ROA mechanism accomplishes this by what is known as *lazy activation*. Lazy activation implies that the passive remote object is activated by `rmid` by loading its constituent classes into a JVM only upon the receipt of the client's first remote method invocation, and not until then. If need be, we can also supply persistence or initialization data during activation, allowing the remote object to reestablish its state information. Choosing to make your remote objects is strictly a server-side decision; RMI clients don't care whether the remote objects are activatable or not.

The best way to understand ROA is to see it in action. Because all remote objects need to implement some remote interface, let us first declare a remote interface `CountInterface` (shown in Listing 6-12) containing a single method `getCount()`. This method basically enables a client to obtain a count of the number of times the remote object has been accessed. Our example remote object which implements `CountInterface`, `CountServer` (shown in Listing 6-13), demonstrates how we can maintain a running count of the number of accesses by RMI clients. Here, `CountServer` is an activatable object whose instantiation is deferred until the first remote method invocation. Further, it makes use of the `MarshalledObject` to recreate any previously persisted data.

Listing 6-12: Remote Interface for Activatable Remote Object

```
package cup.chap6.activation;
import java.rmi.*;
public interface CountInterface extends Remote {
    public Integer getCount() throws RemoteException;
}
```

Consider the code for our activatable remote object, `CountServer`, shown in Listing 6-13.

Listing 6-13: Activatable Remote Object

```
package cup.chap6.activation;
import java.rmi.*;
import java.rmi.activation.*;
import java.io.*;
public class CountServer extends Activatable implements CountInterface {
    private Integer count;
    private File storage;
    public CountServer(ActivationID id, MarshalledObject data)
      throws RemoteException, ClassNotFoundException, IOException {
        super(id, 0);
        // The MarshalledObject is used to pass any previously
        // persisted state information
        storage = (File) data.get();
        if (storage.exists()) {
            // If MarshalledObject is a serialized file, then use the
            // state info within that to initialize the object
            this.restoreState();
        } else {
            // Remote object is starting for the first time
            count = new Integer(0);
        }
    }
    public Integer getCount() throws RemoteException {
      this.saveState();
      return count;
    }
    private void restoreState() throws IOException, ClassNotFoundException {
      File f = storage;
        try {
            FileInputStream fis = new FileInputStream(f);
            ObjectInputStream ois = new ObjectInputStream(fis);
            count = (Integer)ois.readObject();
            ois.close();
```

continues

Listing 6-13: continued

```
            } catch (Exception e) {
                System.out.println("Exception: "+e);
            }
        }
        private synchronized void saveState() {
            FileOutputStream fos = null;
            ObjectOutputStream oos = null;
            File f  = storage;
            try {
                fos = new FileOutputStream(f);
                oos = new ObjectOutputStream(fos);
                count = new Integer(count.intValue()+1);
                oos.writeObject(count);
                oos.close();
            } catch (IOException e) {
                System.out.println("Exception: "+e);
            }
        }
    }
```

Consider the line:

```
public class CountServer extends Activatable implements CountInterface
```

A remote object can be activatable by simply extending the `Activatable` class.

Observe the constructor for `CountServer`. This is called by the activation daemon `rmid` when a new instance of this remote object needs to be created:

```
public CountServer(ActivationID id, MarshalledObject data)
    throws RemoteException, ClassNotFoundException, IOException {
...
}
```

The constructor here serves two purposes: it registers the remote object with the activation system and then exports it on an anonymous port. The `MarshalledObject` parameter here can contain any serialized object. In this case, we use it to supply the filename for some previously persisted state information, which, if valid, we use to initialize the state of the remote object. The great thing about using the `MarshalledObject` is, now, your remote objects can preserve state even between successive restarts.

The `ActivationID` is passed in by `rmid`, represents a unique identifier for the remote object to be activated, and includes a remote reference to the object's activator.

The remote object provides an implementation for the method `getCount()`, which increments a counter specifying the number of times the object was accessed. The method also serializes the count data and persists it to the file passed as the `MarshalledObject`, before returning the information to the client.

Before activatable remote objects can be instantiated, the rmid and rmiregistry services must be correctly initialized with information regarding the activatable remote objects. First, we need to initialize rmid with some URL-based information, which will allow it to locate and load the remote object's constituent classes before instantiating them. Second, we must register a remote reference for the activatable class (an instance of the generated stub class) within the rmiregistry and associate it with an URL-based identifier. This configuration work is usually performed by a separate setup, or bootstrap class, executed for each activatable object. The bootstrap class usually terminates once it is done with supplying the rmid and rmiregistry with the necessary configuration information.

Listing 6-14 demonstrates the bootstrap program for our activatable remote object.

Listing 6-14: Bootstrap Program for Activatable Remote Object

```
package cup.chap6.activation;
import java.rmi.*;
import java.rmi.activation.*;
import java.util.Properties;
import java.io.File;
public class Bootstrap {
    // This class registers information about the CountServer
    // class with rmid and the rmiregistry
    //
    public static void main(String[] args) throws Exception {
       CountInterface counter;
       System.setSecurityManager(new RMISecurityManager());
       String location = "http://host:port/activation/";
       Properties props = new Properties();
       // Because of the Java 2 security model, file writing has to be
       // explicitly allowed
       props.put("java.security.policy","/policy");
       ActivationGroupDesc.CommandEnvironment ace = null;
       ActivationGroupID agi=
       ActivationGroup.getSystem().registerGroup(
             new ActivationGroupDesc(props, ace));
       // Indicate filename we want to persist as the Marshalled object
       MarshalledObject data= new MarshalledObject(new File("/Count.ser"));
       ActivationDesc desc = new ActivationDesc
          (agi, "cup.chap6.activation.CountServer", location, data);
       counter = (CountInterface)Activatable.register(desc);
       //bind within rmiregistry
       Naming.rebind("/CountServer", counter);
       System.exit(0);
    }
}
```

Once we have created a policy file (the AllPermission one works fine for testing), we need to initialize the java.security.policy property with its location. Assuming it has been created in the root directory (C:\ on Windows), we can do the same by having:

```
props.put("java.security.policy","/policy");
```

Consider:

```
MarshalledObject data=
    new MarshalledObject(new File("/Count.ser"));
```

Here, the MarshalledObject is indicated as being a File—Count.ser—that is created in the root directory. Our activatable remote object to store the serialized count data uses this File object. Although we could probably have hardcoded the filename within the remote object itself, MarshalledObject provides a flexible mechanism for passing any initialization data to the remote object.

The line:

```
ActivationDesc desc = new ActivationDesc
    (agi, "cup.chap6.activation.CountServer", location, data);
```

creates an ActivationDesc object that stipulates the fully qualified class name for the activatable remote object, the location of its code, the object's group identifier, and any initialization data. This information is conveyed to the activation daemon—rmid—by:

```
counter = (CountInterface)Activatable.register(desc);
```

Of course, if a client has to locate our remote object, it must first be found within the RMI registry. We bind the reference for the remote object within the registry and permit its access via a URL-based name through:

```
Naming.rebind("/CountServer", counter);
```

Listing 6-15 shows the client program, which is used to access the activatable remote object. Each time a client makes a remote method invocation, the activatable remote object updates its counter and stores the state in the form of serialized data to the file specified by the MarshalledObject.

Listing 6-15: Client Program for the Activatable Remote Object

```
package cup.chap6.activation;
import java.rmi.*;
public class RMIClient {
    public static void main(String args[]) {
        try {
            CountInterface counter = (CountInterface)Naming.lookup("/CountServer");
            Integer result = (Integer)counter.getCount();
```

Listing 6-15: continued

```
            System.out.println("Number of accesses for
                    the remote object: "+result.toString());
        } catch (Exception e) {
            System.out.println("Exception: " + e);
        }
    }
}
```

On running RMIClient repeatedly, you should see the following output:

```
Number of accesses for the remote object: 1
Number of accesses for the remote object: 2
Number of accesses for the remote object: 3
    .
    .
    .
```

Even if you shut down and restart the CountServer, the remote object still maintains the access count. This is because the previous state is read in from the serialized file and is used to initialize the remote object via MarshalledObject.

Implementing Custom Sockets

Under normal circumstances, communication between RMI clients and servers takes place using TCP-based sockets—provided by java.net.Socket—and used by the default RMI socket factories. Although regular TCP-sockets are fine for most situations, instances may occur where you want to use a different protocol for the transport layer. For example, the default TCP-sockets do not provide adequate security for the communication channel. This could cause concern—especially for electronic commerce applications—that may be deployed over the Web and exercise little or no control over the route sensitive data-like credit card information may take before reaching its eventual destination. Nearly anyone along the way could potentially read your sensitive data and infringe upon your privacy.

An obvious solution to preserve the privacy of the communication channel in such a situation is to encrypt the data stream. Although approaches to enable RMI applications with encryption have been proposed in the past, most have relied upon using proprietary third-party libraries and, in some cases, even native code, directly within your applications. With the release of Java 2, however, it is now certainly possible to design more elegant solutions. The enhanced version of RMI enables you to replace the default TCP socket easily with a custom socket type of your own creation. Now, by serving your proprietary sockets via a custom socket factory, your RMI transport layer can use a non-TCP or custom transport protocol running over IP. Although custom sockets are typically deployed for enabling encryption, they can also be used to provide specialized functionality like data compression, authentication, and so forth. Figure 6-8 shows a typical configuration for an RMI system which implements multiple custom socket types.

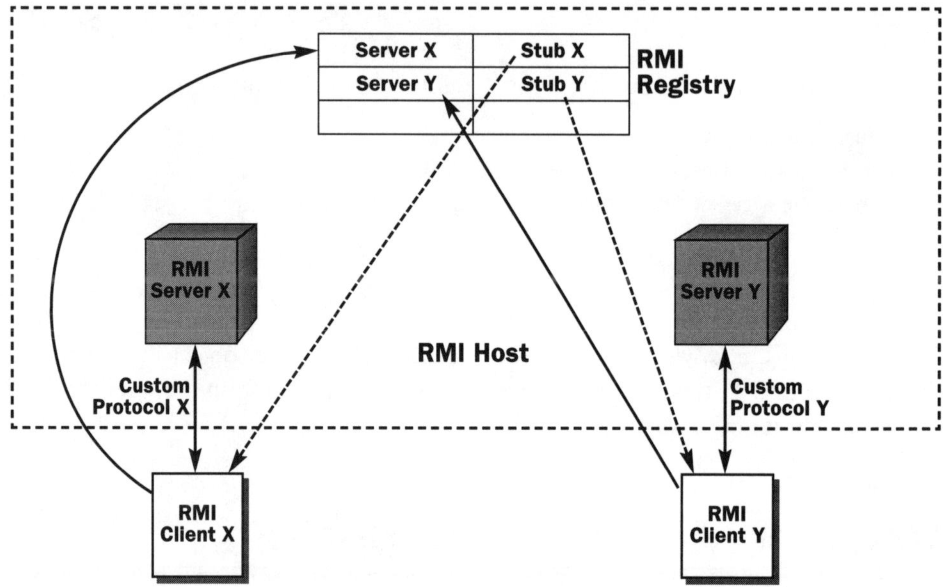

Figure 6-8: An RMI system implementing multiple custom socket types.

Significant activity has occurred in the field of Java encryption lately and, currently, numerous cryptographic packages are available for effectively securing Java network communication. Unfortunately, though, the U.S. Department of Commerce classifies all high-grade encryption software as "munitions" and bans the export of the same outside the U.S. and Canada. (Looks like not only Java developers consider the keyboard to be mightier than the sword!) If you are outside of North America, you can still secure your Java applications by using a non-American cryptographic provider who is exempt from any such embargo.

The rot13 Cipher

In this section, we look at a step-by-step approach toward developing a custom socket type capable of basic encryption. Then we examine the details of securing RMI client/server communication by replacing the default RMI socket factory with a custom socket factory that serves our encrypted sockets. To keep things simple (and avoid being sued by the Department of Commerce for any potential export violations), we will not use any "real-life" cryptosystems. Instead, we will use a specific version of the venerable "Caesar cipher" developed by the Roman emperor Julius Caesar himself, over two millennia ago.

Some believe Julius Caesar communicated with his friends using a simple monoalphabetic substitution cipher, where the plain text letter was replaced by the ciphertext three places down the alphabet. (For instance, the letter C was replaced by the letter F, and so on. Of course, unlike us, good old Julius used the Roman alphabet consisting of 24 letters, but you get the picture.) Although the Caesar cipher may have once been effective in communicating messages vital to national security, its use today is predominantly within Usenet newsreaders for encrypting risqué postings that might offend some readers. Most newsreaders implement the `rot13` algorithm, which is a simple Caesar cipher-based mechanism replacing each letter in the text with another one, which is thirteen places forward or backward in the alphabet. Hence, the `rot13` version of "The butler did it!" becomes "Gur ohgyre qvq vg!" A major advantage of `rot13` over `rot(N)` is, for some, *N* is self-inverse—the same code can be used for encoding and decoding the message. The `rot13` substitution table is shown in Table 6-1.

Table 6-1: rot13 Encoding

PLAINTEXT	A	B	C	D	E	F	G	H	I	J	K	L	M
CIPHERTEX	N	O	P	Q	R	S	T	U	V	W	X	Y	Z
PLAINTEXT	N	O	P	Q	R	S	T	U	V	W	X	Y	Z
CIPHERTEXT	A	B	C	D	E	F	G	H	I	J	K	L	M

The entire process of deploying custom sockets with RMI applications can be summarized in a few concise steps:

1. Create your custom socket type.
2. Create a custom client-side socket factory by implementing `RMIClientSocketFactory`.
3. Create a custom server-side socket factory that implements `RMIServerSocketFactory`.
4. Enable the RMI server with the custom client and server socket factories.
5. Select your custom socket type as the transport protocol.

Now, we examine the details of each of the previous steps and deploy a custom socket that implements `rot13` encryption.

1. Create the custom socket implementing rot13 encryption

As mentioned before, by defining a custom socket type, we can control the nature of the data flow at the RMI transport level. Although any IP-based protocol can be used at the transport layer, in this case, we develop a custom socket that provides rot13 encryption atop TCP/IP and, consequently, subclass java.net.Socket. To create a custom socket, we must

a. Create a suitable Input Stream for the custom socket.

b. Create a suitable Output Stream for the custom socket.

c. Create the custom socket by extending java.net.Socket.

d. Create a ServerSocket subclass that supports our custom socket.

Now we examine each of the previous steps in detail:

a. Create a suitable input stream for the custom socket

In Listing 6-17, Rot13InputStream extends FilterInputStream and basically serves to decode the previously encoded data. Notice this is done by having the read() methods of the Rot13InputStream return data after it has been read from the underlying InputStream, with each valid English letter shifted forward 13 times by invoking the rot13() method. The rot13 constants, shown in Listing 6-16, are used to determine the number of shifts while encoding/decoding the data, as well as ferreting out all lowercase or uppercase English letters from the data stream.

Listing 6-16: rot13 Encryption Constants

```
package cup.chap6.rot13;
public interface Rot13Constants {
    public static final int ROT13KEY = 13;
    public static final int UPPERCASE_A = 65;
    public static final int UPPERCASE_Z = 90;
    public static final int LOWERCASE_A = 97;
    public static final int LOWERCASE_Z = 122;
}
```

Listing 6-17: Input Stream for the Custom Socket

```
package cup.chap6.rot13;
import java.io.*;
public class Rot13InputStream extends FilterInputStream
    implements Rot13Constants {
    public Rot13InputStream(InputStream in) {
       super(in);
    }
```

Listing 6-17: continued

```
    public int read() throws IOException {
      int x = in.read();
    if (x >=UPPERCASE_A && x <=UPPERCASE_Z)
      x = rot13(x);
    else if (x >=LOWERCASE_A && x <= LOWERCASE_Z) {
        char up = Character.toUpperCase((char)x);
        x =(int)Character.toLowerCase((char)rot13((int)up));
      }
      return x;
    }
    private int rot13(int code) {
      int encoded = code + ROT13KEY;
      if (encoded >UPPERCASE_Z)
        encoded = UPPERCASE_A + (encoded % UPPERCASE_Z) -1;
      return encoded;
    }
    public int read(byte b[], int off, int len) throws IOException {
        int numBytes = in.read(b, off, len);
        if (numBytes <= 0)
          return numBytes;
        int i = 0;
        for(; i < numBytes; i++) {
        int num = (int)b[off+i];
        if (num >=UPPERCASE_A && num <=UPPERCASE_Z) {
          int decodedChar = rot13(num);
          b[off+i] = (byte)decodedChar;
        } else if (num >=LOWERCASE_A && num <= LOWERCASE_Z) {
          int decodedChar=
          rot13((int)Character.toUpperCase((char)b[off+i]));
          b[off+i] = (byte)Character.toLowerCase((char)decodedChar);
        }
      }
      return i;
    }
}
```

b. Create a suitable output stream for the custom socket

In Listing 6-18, Rot13OutputStream serves to encrypt the communication channel. By extending FilterOutputStream, Rot13OutputStream encrypts the outgoing data a byte at a time by invoking the write() methods before writing them out to the underlying

OutputStream. Notice the same rot13() method is used for both encoding and decoding a given letter by shifting it 13 times forward.

Listing 6-18: Output Stream for Custom Socket

```
package cup.chap6.rot13;
import java.io.*;
public class Rot13OutputStream extends FilterOutputStream
    implements Rot13Constants {
    public Rot13OutputStream(OutputStream out) {
        super(out);
    }
    private int rot13(int code) {
        int encoded = code + ROT13KEY;
    if (encoded >UPPERCASE_Z)
        encoded = UPPERCASE_A + (encoded % UPPERCASE_Z) -1;
    return encoded;
    }
    public void write(int x) throws IOException {
        if (x >= UPPERCASE_A && x <= UPPERCASE_Z)
            x = rot13(x);
        else if (x >= LOWERCASE_A && x <= LOWERCASE_Z) {
            char up = Character.toUpperCase((char)x);
            x = (int)Character.toLowerCase((char)rot13((int)up));
        }
        out.write(x);
        out.flush();
    }
    public void write(byte b[], int off, int len) throws IOException {
        for (int i = 0; i < len; i++)
        write((int)b[off + i]);
    }
}
```

c. Create your custom socket by extending java.net.Socket

Our custom socket, Rot13Socket (shown in Listing 6-19) makes use of the previously defined input/output stream classes to provide rot13-based encryption capabilities to the RMI communication channel. Here, because we are layering the encryption on top of TCP/IP, we can simply subclass java.net.Socket and override the methods that directly manipulate the input and output streams to implement our custom socket. Notice we also explicitly flush our custom output stream to ensure all the encoded data is sent before the socket is closed.

Listing 6-19: Custom Socket Implementing rot13 Encryption

```
package cup.chap6.rot13;
import java.io.*;
import java.net.*;
import java.util.*;
public class Rot13Socket extends Socket {
    private InputStream in = null;
    private OutputStream out = null;
    public Rot13Socket() throws IOException {
        super();
    }
    public Rot13Socket(String host, int port) throws IOException  {
        super(host, port);
    }
    public synchronized InputStream getInputStream()throws IOException {
        if (in == null)
            in = new Rot13InputStream(super.getInputStream());
        return in;
    }
    public synchronized OutputStream getOutputStream()
        throws IOException {
        if (out == null)
            out = new Rot13OutputStream(super.getOutputStream());
        return out;
    }
    public synchronized void close() throws IOException {
        OutputStream o = getOutputStream();
        o.flush();
        super.close();
    }
}
```

d. Create a ServerSocket subclass that supports your custom socket

You need to ensure the RMI system provides server sockets to support your custom socket. Listing 6-20 shows the implementation of a subclass of `ServerSocket` that supports the previously developed `rot13` custom socket. Notice all `Rot13ServerSocket` must do is override the `accept()` method to ensure it instantiates a socket of type `Rot13Socket` instead of the default type `Socket`.

Listing 6-20: Server Socket Supporting the Custom Socket

```
package cup.chap6.rot13;
import java.io.*;
import java.net.*;
public class Rot13ServerSocket extends ServerSocket {
    public Rot13ServerSocket(int port) throws IOException {
        super(port);
    }
    public Socket accept() throws IOException {
        Socket s = new Rot13Socket();
        implAccept(s);
        return s;
    }
}
```

2. Create a custom client-side socket factory by implementing RMIClientSocketFactory.

Listing 6-21 shows a client-side RMI socket factory developed by implementing the RMIClientSocketFactory interface. A client-side socket factory is responsible for supplying the RMI runtime with sockets of the appropriate type. Consequently, we must override the createSocket() method to ensure our client socket factory is capable of generating Rot13Socket sockets, in addition to the default type java.net.Socket.

Notice within the createSocket() method, we can also call the default RMISocketFactory's createSocket() method. This way, CaesarClientSocketFactory can still generate a regular TCP socket if the "rot13" option is unspecified. Because our client socket factory classes must be downloaded to the client, they also need to implement the Serializable interface.

Listing 6-21: Client Socket Factory Supporting the Custom Socket

```
package cup.chap6.rot13;
import java.io.*;
import java.net.*;
import java.rmi.server.*;
public class CaesarClientSocketFactory
    implements RMIClientSocketFactory, Serializable {
    private static RMISocketFactory defaultFactory =
        RMISocketFactory.getDefaultSocketFactory();
    private String protocol;
    public CaesarClientSocketFactory(String protocol) {
        this.protocol = protocol;
    }
public Socket createSocket(String host, int port)
    throws IOException {
```

Listing 6-21: continued

```
            if (protocol.equals("rot13"))
               return new Rot13Socket(host, port);
            else {
               System.out.println("Using default tcp sockets");
               return defaultFactory.createSocket(host, port);
            }
         }
      }
```

3. Create a custom server-side socket factory that implements RMIServerSocketFactory

Listing 6-22 shows the server-side RMI socket factory, which ensures our RMI servers are capable of generating Rot13Socket type sockets. This is developed by implementing the RMIServerSocketFactory and Serializable interfaces. We also must override the createServerSocket() method to ensure our server socket factory is capable of generating sockets of type Rot13Socket, in addition to the default type java.net.Socket.

Listing 6-22: Server Socket Factory Supporting the Custom Socket

```
package cup.chap6.rot13;
import java.io.*;
import java.net.*;
import java.rmi.server.*;
public class CaesarServerSocketFactory
   implements RMIServerSocketFactory, Serializable {
   private static RMISocketFactory defaultFactory =
      RMISocketFactory.getDefaultSocketFactory();
   private String protocol;
   public CaesarServerSocketFactory(String protocol) {
   this.protocol = protocol;
   }
   public ServerSocket createServerSocket(int port)
      throws IOException {
      if (protocol.equals("rot13")) {
         System.out.println("encoding channel");
         return new Rot13ServerSocket(port);
      } else {
         System.out.println("using default socket protocol");
         return defaultFactory.createServerSocket(port);
      }
   }
}
```

4. Enable the RMI server with the custom client and server socket factories

Now that we have implemented the custom socket, as well as the client and server factories required for creating it, let's develop a simple RMI application that communicates using it. Consider the remote interface Soothsayer (shown in Listing 6-23), which is implemented by the remote object SoothsayerImpl (shown in Listing 6-24).

Listing 6-23: The Soothsayer Interface

```
package cup.chap6.rot13;
public interface Soothsayer extends java.rmi.Remote {
    String seekCounsel(String name) throws java.rmi.RemoteException;
}
```

Listing 6-24: The SoothsayerImpl Remote Object

```
package cup.chap6.rot13;
import java.io.*;
import java.rmi.*;
import java.rmi.server.*;
public class SoothsayerImpl extends UnicastRemoteObject
    implements Soothsayer {
        public SoothsayerImpl(String protocol) throws RemoteException {
            super(0, new CaesarClientSocketFactory(protocol),
            new CaesarServerSocketFactory(protocol));
        }
        public String seekCounsel(String name) throws RemoteException {
            return name+": Beware the Ides of March!";
        }
        public static void main(String[] args) {
            if (System.getSecurityManager() == null)
            System.setSecurityManager(new RMISecurityManager());
        try {
        SoothsayerImpl obj = new SoothsayerImpl("rot13");
        Naming.rebind("/Soothsayer", obj);
        System.out.println("Soothsayer bound in registry");
    } catch (Exception e) {
        System.out.println("SoothsayerImpl err: " + e.toString());
        }
    }
}
```

Assuming you are familiar with the basics of RMI computing, the only thing that may seem unusual about SoothsayerImpl is its constructor:

```
super(0, new CaesarClientSocketFactory(protocol),
    new CaesarServerSocketFactory(protocol));
```

Here we invoke the constructor of UnicastRemoteObject, while passing along the client and server socket factories, which are capable of generating sockets of type Rot13Socket. If we had simply invoked the constructor as super(), our RMI server would have then communicated using the default TCP sockets.

5. Select your custom socket type as the transport protocol

Because we can design socket factories capable of serving more than one type of custom socket, a good practice is to indicate explicitly the custom socket type that should be created by the factories. For instance, by using the "rot13" option within our example, we can cause the client and server socket factories to generate our custom rot13 encryption socket, instead of the vanilla TCP sockets:

```
SoothsayerImpl obj = new SoothsayerImpl("rot13");
```

Listing 6-25 shows the client code. Notice that apart from instantiating an RMI security manager, the client does not require any further modification to use custom sockets, which is something really cool about RMI! Our example client here is an application; if it were an applet, you would also have to deploy it as a signed applet with the appropriate permissions for it to download the client RMI socket factory and generate a custom socket.

Listing 6-25: RMI Client Program

```
package cup.chap6.rot13;
import java.rmi.*;
public class MyClient {
    public static void main(String args[]) {
        if (System.getSecurityManager() == null)
        System.setSecurityManager(new RMISecurityManager());
        try {
            Soothsayer obj = (Soothsayer) Naming.lookup("/Soothsayer");
        String advice = obj.seekCounsel("Caesar");
            System.out.println(advice);
        } catch (Exception e) {
            System.out.println("MyClient exception: " +e.getMessage());
            e.printStackTrace();
        }
    }
}
```

6. Run the application

The RMI example can be compiled in the usual manner, as:

```
javac -d . *.java
rmic -d . cup.chap6.rot13.SoothsayerImpl
```

Java 2 dictates RMI applications should be run only in conjunction with a policy file that sets the security environment. Although a detailed discussion on security policies is beyond the scope of this book, you can place the following permission snippet within a file called "policy" and use it for testing purposes:

```
grant {
    // Allow everything for now
    permission java.security.AllPermission;
};
```

Use the previous permission with great caution because it permits your application to do what it likes and disables much of the security sandbox features. Also, note we have to indicate a security policy file for starting both the RMI client and server and the rmiregistry:

```
start rmiregistry  -J-Djava.security.policy=/somedir/policy
start  java -Djava.security.policy=/somedir/policy cup.chap6.rot13.SoothsayerImpl
java -Djava.security.policy=/somedir/policy cup.chap6.rot13.MyClient
```

After you start up your RMI server and it is bound within the registry, you see the welcoming message "Soothsayer bound in registry," which indicates your server is ready to receive any incoming calls.

Once the client obtains a reference to the remote object, the seekCounsel() remote method is invoked. The following output may seem trivial but, remember, the rot13 protocol provided by our custom socket was used for the RMI transport:

Caesar: Beware the Ides of March!

Jini Technology

Jini is probably one of the most exciting Java technologies introduced by Sun during 1998. Inspired by the genius of Sun's chief scientist, Bill Joy, Jini is astounding in its scope and potential implications. Fundamentally, Jini is a distributed-object computing technology and is all about ubiquitous network-centric computing. Jini also relies heavily upon Java 2 RMI because all low-level communication is handled using that protocol.

In the world of Jini computing, just about everything is a distributed object. The distributed services available are not restricted to conventional database and transactional services. They may also include the capabilities of network enabled hardware devices like printers, fax machines, telephones, digital cameras, disk drives, TV's, and so forth.

But how does a TV or a disk drive become a distributed object? That small detail is handled by the Jini architecture. Jini objects—be they software or hardware entities—need to implement the core Jini technology. Being an amazingly compact Java binary of around 48K, this core can easily be incorporated within any Java software by implementing the Jini class library or it can be embedded at the device level within almost any hardware containing a JVM.

Jini obviously seems to derive much of its inspiration from that ubiquitous appliance—the common telephone—and hopes to make using any Jini-enabled device just as simple. In fact, the only external interfaces for Jini-enabled devices are a power cord and a telephone plug! Consequently, Jini-enabled devices are network-enabled by literally plugging them into one, much like you would a conventional telephone. Sun even has a new phrase for this spontaneous networking: "Plug and Work!"

How Jini works

Jini is all about providing users ubiquitous access to resources—be they hardware devices or software objects—within a dynamic, distributed Jini system or djinn. Each resource can, in turn, offer multiple services; for instance, a fax machine can offer a faxing service, a hard disk can offer a storage service, a compression object can offer data compression service, and so forth. Jini also terms this networked agglomeration of software and hardware entities as a federation. Figure 6-9 shows a typical Jini system consisting of numerous software and hardware services.

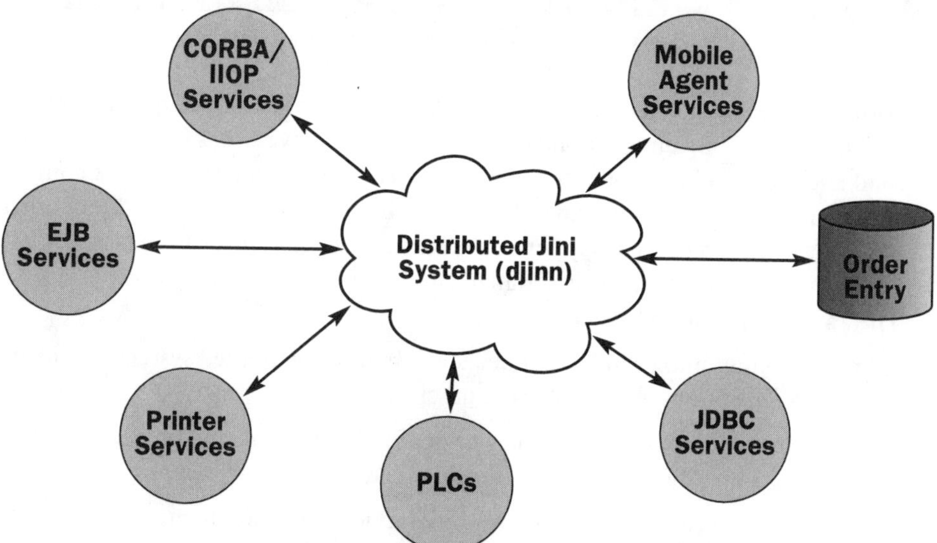

Figure 6-9: A distributed Jini system

The main goals of Jini are

- To enable users to share services and resources over a network.
- To provide users the ability to access resources anywhere easily on the network, even though the network location of the user may constantly change.
- To simplify the task of creating and managing network devices, software services, and users.

The three major components that make up a running Jini system (shown in Figure 6-10) are

1. The Jini Client—Anything that would like to make use of the Jini service
2. The Service Locator—Anything that acts as a Locator/Trader/Broker between the service and the client, and is used to find services in a distributed Jini system.
3. The Jini Service—Any entity that can be used by a client program or another service (for example, a printer, a VCR, or a software entity like an EJB service)

Jini Client	Service Locator	Jini Service
	Jini Technology	
	Java Technology	
	Operating System	
	Network Transport	

Figure 6-10: The basic architecture of a Jini system

Although the Jini spec is independent of the protocol used for network communication, the current implementation is based on TCP/IP. Java's socket support is used to send and receive object code that will be moved around among the three components. Typically, objects in one Java Virtual Machine (JVM) invoke objects on other JVMs using any protocol that supports Java Remote Method Invocation (Java/RMI) like semantics. The object code is serialized and marshaled over the wire.

The Jini specification also defines

- A Programming Model that helps you build a distributed system organized as a federation of Jini services and clients.
- A Runtime Infrastructure that resides on the network and provides mechanisms for adding, removing, locating, and accessing services.

The runtime Infrastructure is used by Jini Services to make themselves available when they join the network. It is also used by clients to locate and contact Jini services. The runtime infrastructure consists of support for discovery, join, and lookup.

The Runtime Infrastructure resides in the Lookup services and in Jini-enabled devices. Lookup services are the central organizing mechanism for Jini-based systems. When a device is plugged into a network, it registers its services with a Lookup service. The device and its services are now part of a federation. When a client wants to locate a Jini service to assist with some task, it consults a Jini Lookup service.

Lookup services organize the Jini services they contain into groups. A group is a set of registered services identified by a string. `"Corporate EJB Servers"` group can be services offered by all EJB Servers running in a Company's local area network. Similarly `"EOI Dept Printers"` group can be services offered by all Printers on the EOI Dept. local network. A *service* can be a member of multiple groups. Multiple Lookup services can also maintain the same *group*. Redundancy can make a Jini system more fault-tolerant.

The runtime services

The Runtime Infrastructure enables Jini services to register with Lookup services through a process called discovery and join. Discovery is the process by which a Jini-enabled device locates Lookup services on the network and obtains references to them. Join is the process by which a device registers the services it offers with Lookup services. The runtime infrastructure enables clients to locate and contact services through a process called lookup.

Discovery

Discovery is used by both the Jini services and Lookup Locator services to announce their presence on a distributed Jini network. Jini services use this to obtain Lookup service proxies, while Lookup services use this to announce their presence on the network. The discovery process uses three types of subprotocols, depending on the state a Jini component is in. They are

- Multicast Request Protocol—used by a new Jini service to call anonymous Lookup services on a LAN using multicast UDP
- Multicast Announcement Protocol—used by Lookup services to announce their presence on a LAN using multicast UDP
- Unicast Request Protocol—used by Jini services contacting far Lookup services using Unicast TCP

These subprotocols use four types of packets:

- Multicast Request Packet
- Multicast Announcement Packet
- Unicast Request Packet
- Unicast Response Packet—used by both request protocols

Unicast discovery protocol

Unicast discovery can be used for Lookup services that reside outside the LAN and the address on which they run are already known. Unicast discovery is done using the `LookupLocator` class located in the `net.jini.core.discovery` package.

The `LookupLocator` class has two f methods `getHost()` and `getPort()`, which are useful in multicast situations to retrieve the hostname the Locator is sitting on and its port number. Unicast discovery involves two steps: the discovering entity sends out a Unicast request and then the Lookup service responds with a Lookup service registrar object.

The following example code shows how Unicast discovery is done using the `LookupLocator` class.

Listing 6-26: Unicast Discovery Using the LookupLocator Class

```
LookupLocator lookup = new LookupLocator("jini://execpc.com/~gopalan");
LookupLocator lookup2 = new LookupLocator("jini://localhost/", 80);
ServiceRegistrar registrar = lookup.getRegistrar();
```

Multicast Announcement protocol

The Multicast Announcement protocol is used by Lookup services to announce their presence on the network. This is used whenever a Lookup service is started or a new one becomes available after a network failure. The message the Lookup service sends out with an announcement contains the service ID of this Lookup service, the IP address, the port number where the Unicast discovery of this Lookup service is located, and the list of groups it manages.

Multicast Request protocol

If the location of a Lookup service is unknown, a broadcast search must be made for one. Multicast Request protocol is to discover Lookup services that belong to one or more groups. The class `LookupDiscovery` in the package `net.jini.discovery` is used for broadcast searches. The listener should implement the `DiscoveryListener` interface. A typical source module used for Multicast Request is shown in the following.

Listing 6-27: A Typical Source Module Used for Multicast Request

```
public void setup (boolean check) {
    String[] groups = {new String (""), new String ("public")};
    try {
        discoverLookup = new LookupDiscovery (groups);
        discoverLookup.addDiscoveryListener(this);
    } catch(IOException e) {
        // a socket problem during startup
        e.printStackTrace ();
    }
}
public void run () {
```

Listing 6-27: continued

```
        int priority = Thread.currentThread ().getPriority ();
        Thread.currentThread ().setPriority(Thread.MIN_PRIORITY);
        while (!discovered); // busy waiting
        Thread.currentThread ().setPriority (priority);
    }
    public void discovered (DiscoveryEvent e) {
        System.out.println("EchoServer:  discovered...");
        ServiceRegistrar[] registrar = e.getRegistrars ();
        lookupRegistrar = (ServiceRegistrar) registrar [0];
        discovered = true;
    }
    public void discarded (DiscoveryEvent e) {
        // so be it
        System.out.println("EchoServer:  discarded...");
    }
```

The discovering Jini service drops a multicast UDP presence announcement onto a well-known port. Each announcement contains a list of names of groups the Jini service is interested in joining, the IP address and port number where the service can be contacted by Lookup services, and the list of Lookup services it has heard from already. Lookup services monitor the well-known port for presence of any announcement packets. As soon as a Lookup service receives a presence announcement, it inspects the list of group names contained in the packet. If the Lookup service maintains any of these groups, it contacts the sender of the packet directly. The Discovering Jini service, uses the Unicast discovery protocol to obtain a "Lookup Service Registrar."

Join

Discovery provides the Lookup service proxies to the Jini service. The join process is used to register the Jini service proxy at the Lookup service through the Lookup service proxy obtained in discovery. Once registered, the Lookup service contains an entry corresponding to its serviceID and its attributes.

Listing 6-28: The Join Process

```
    /*
        Create the attributes (an array of entry objects) that describe
        this server and use it to register this server with the lookup
        service. JoinManager finds and registers with the lookup service.
        ============================================================ */
        Entry [] aeAttributes;
        JoinManager joinmanager;
        EchoServer myServer;
        aeAttributes = new Entry []{
```

continues

Listing 6-28: continued

```
        new ServiceInfo(PRODUCT,
                        MANUFACTURER,
                        VENDOR,
                        VERSION,
                        null, null),
        new BasicServiceType("EchoServer")
    };
    myServer = new EchoServer ();
    joinmanager = new JoinManager (myServer, aeAttributes, myServer,
                    new LeaseRenewalManager ());
```

Once a Jini service discovers a Lookup service, it can register its own services on that Lookup service using the join process. The Jini service connects to the Lookup service through the service registrar object it received from the Lookup service in the discovery process. Through the service registrar object, the Jini service sends information about itself to the Lookup service. The Lookup service stores the uploaded information from the Jini service and associates that service with its requested group. The Jini service has now joined the group on the Lookup service. Figure 6-11 highlights the Jini runtime characteristics.

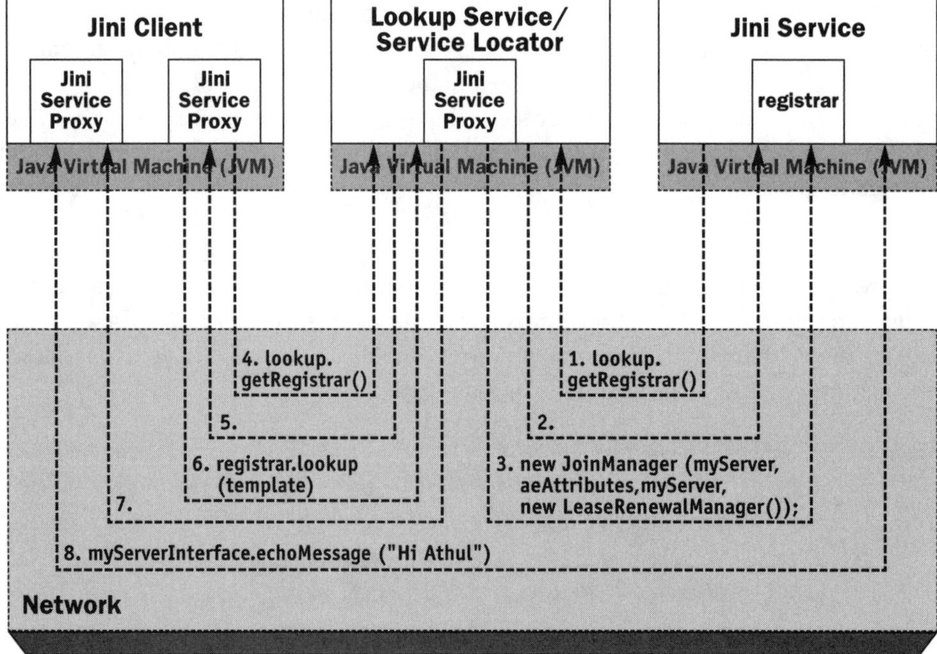

Figure 6-11: Runtime characteristics—discovery, join, and lookup

Lookup

A distributed Jini client looking up for a Jini service obtains a Jini service proxy from the Lookup service proxy it has. The client selects a template mask for its service and requests it from the Lookup service proxy. Only service proxies that match the mask template are returned. A typical piece of client code is shown in the following.

Listing 6-29: A Typical Source Module Used for Lookup

```
/*
    Perform a search on the lookup server to find the service
    that has the name attribute of "EchoServer". The lookup
    service returns an interface object to the service.
    ============================================================ */
    aeAttributes = new Entry[1];
    aeAttributes[0] = new Name ("EchoServer");
    template = new ServiceTemplate (null, null, aeAttributes);
    myServerInterface = (EchoInterface) registrar.lookup (template);
```

The template mask filled in by the client consists of the serviceID, service interfaces, and Entry sets. A wildcard value of null acts as a "do not care." The wildcard can be applied to any template field. The requested objects should match the interface exactly.

The echo service

Now we develop a Jini echo service. The client sends a message to the service and the server responds with the same message. The client finds the difference in time-stamps between the time it sent out the message and the time it took to receive it, and computes network latency.

The remote interface

Because remote interface is a Jini echo service, it simply echoes its input to its output. The interface is shown in the following. Note, the interface is explicitly marked public to prevent the IllegalAccessError on the client.

Listing 6-30: The EchoInterface Interface Definition

```
public interface EchoInterface extends java.rmi.Remote {
    String echoMessage (String message) throws java.rmi.RemoteException;
}
```

The Jini echo service

Notice we implement the echoMessage() method here, which sends its input back out. In our main() method, we first set the security manager. The service then creates the attributes (an array of entry objects) that describe this server and uses it to register this server with the Lookup service. The JoinManager finds and registers with the

Lookup service. We find the Jini Lookup service (reggie) and print its location. We also get the Lookup service's ServiceRegistrar (the class by which interaction with the Lookup service is possible). We then itemize the service items and the service objects available in the Lookup service.

Listing 6-31: The Echo Jini Service Class

```
import net.jini.core.entry.*;
import net.jini.core.lookup.*;
import net.jini.core.discovery.*;
import net.jini.lookup.entry.*;
import net.jini.discovery.*;
import com.sun.jini.lookup.*;
import com.sun.jini.lease.*;
import java.io.*;
import java.rmi.*;
import java.rmi.server.*;
// EchoServer -- The Jini Server Class
public class EchoServer extends UnicastRemoteObject
    implements EchoInterface, ServiceIDListener, Serializable {
    public EchoServer() throws RemoteException {
        super ();
    }
    // EchoInterface
    public String echoMessage (String message) throws RemoteException {
        System.out.println ("EchoServer: The method echoMessage()"+
                "in EchoServer was called");
        System.out.println ("EchoServer: Client says :" + message);
        return (message);
    }
    // ServiceIDListener
    public void serviceIDNotify (ServiceID idIn) {
    }
    public static void main (String[] args) {
        int iPort;
        String sHost;
        EchoServer myServer;
        LookupLocator lookup;
        Entry [] aeAttributes;
        JoinManager joinmanager;
        ServiceID id;
        ServiceMatches matches;
        ServiceRegistrar registrar;
        try {
```

Listing 6-31: continued

```
/*
Setting the security manager to allow the RMI class loader
to go to the codebase for classes that are not available
locally.
============================================================= */
System.setSecurityManager (new RMISecurityManager ());
/*
Create the attributes (an array of entry objects) that describe
this server and use it to register this server with the lookup
service. JoinManager finds and registers with the lookup
service.
============================================================= */
aeAttributes = new Entry [1];
aeAttributes[0] = new Name ("EchoServer");
myServer = new EchoServer ();
joinmanager = new JoinManager (myServer,aeAttributes,
                  myServer,new LeaseRenewalManager());
System.out.println ("EchoServer: JoinManager = " + joinmanager);
/*
Find the Jini lookup service (reggie) and print its location.
============================================================= */
lookup = new LookupLocator ("jini://" + args[0]);
sHost = lookup.getHost ();
iPort = lookup.getPort ();
System.out.println ("EchoServer: LookupLocator = " + lookup);
System.out.println ("EchoServer: LookupLocator.host = " + sHost);
System.out.println ("EchoServer: LookupLocator.port = " + iPort);
/*
Get the lookup service's ServiceRegistrar (the class by which
interaction with the lookup service is possible).
============================================================= */
registrar = lookup.getRegistrar();
id = registrar.getServiceID ();
System.out.println ("EchoServer: ServiceRegistrar = " + registrar);
System.out.println ("EchoServer: ServiceID = " + id);
/*
Itemize the service items and the service objects that are
available in the lookup service. Note: Sometimes this is
executed too quickly for the service that was registered above
to show up.
============================================================= */
try {Thread.sleep (2000);} catch (Exception e) {}
```

continues

Listing 6-31: continued

```
            matches = registrar.lookup(new ServiceTemplate (null, null, null),50);
            System.out.println ("EchoServer: ServiceMatches = " + matches);
            System.out.println ("EchoServer: num matches = "+
                matches.totalMatches);
            for (int i = 0; i < matches.totalMatches; i++) {
              System.out.println ("EchoServer: svc item " + i + ": " +
                matches.items[i]);
              System.out.println ("EchoServer: svc object " + i + ": "+
                matches.items[i].service);
            }
            System.out.println ("*----------------------------------------*");
          } catch (Exception e) {
            System.out.println ("EchoServer: EchoServer.main(): Exception ");
            e.printStackTrace ();
          }
      }
}
```

The echo client

The listing for the client is shown in the following. In our `main()` method, we first set the security manager. We find the Jini Lookup service (reggie) and print its location. We also get the Lookup service's ServiceRegistrar (the class by which interaction with the Lookup service is possible). Perform a search on the Lookup server to find the service that has the name attribute of "EchoServer." The Lookup service returns an interface object to the service. If the correct object was returned, call one of its methods.

Listing 6-32: The EchoClient Class

```
import net.jini.core.entry.*;
import net.jini.core.lookup.*;
import net.jini.core.discovery.*;
import net.jini.lookup.*;
import net.jini.lookup.entry.*;
import net.jini.discovery.*;
import java.rmi.*;
// EchoClient -- The Jini Client Class
class EchoClient {
    public static void main (String[] args) {
        int iPort;
        String sHost;
        Entry[] aeAttributes;
        LookupLocator lookup;
        ServiceID id;
```

Listing 6-32: continued

```
        ServiceRegistrar registrar;
        ServiceTemplate template;
        EchoInterface myServerInterface;
        try {
          /*
          Setting the security manager to allow the RMI class loader
          to go to the codebase for classes that are not available locally.
          ============================================================= */
          System.setSecurityManager (new RMISecurityManager ());
          /*
          Find the Jini lookup service (reggie) and print its location.
          ================================================================ */
          lookup = new LookupLocator ("jini://" + args[0]);
          sHost = lookup.getHost ();
          iPort = lookup.getPort ();
          System.out.println ();
          System.out.println ("client: LookupLocator = " + lookup);
          System.out.println ("client: LookupLocator.host = " + sHost);
          System.out.println ("client: LookupLocator.port = " + iPort);
          /*
          Get the lookup service's ServiceRegistrar (the class by which
          interaction with the lookup service is possible).
          ================================================================ */
          registrar = lookup.getRegistrar ();
          id = registrar.getServiceID ();
          System.out.println ("client: ServiceRegistrar = " + registrar);
          System.out.println ("client: ServiceID = " + id);
          /*
          Perform a search on the lookup server to find the service
          that has the name attribute of "EchoServer". The lookup
          service returns an interface object to the service.
          ============================================================= */
          aeAttributes = new Entry[1];
          aeAttributes[0] = new Name ("EchoServer");
          template = new ServiceTemplate (null, null, aeAttributes);
          myServerInterface = (EchoInterface) registrar.lookup (template);
          System.out.println ("client: ServiceTemplate = " + template);
          System.out.println ("client: Service object = " + myServerInterface);
          /*
          If the correct object was returned, call one of its methods.
          ================================================================ */
          if (myServerInterface instanceof EchoInterface) {
```

continues

Listing 6-32: continued

```
            long startTime = System.currentTimeMillis();
            System.out.println ("client: Time at server is " + startTime);
            String message = myServerInterface.echoMessage (args[1]);
            long stopTime = System.currentTimeMillis();
            System.out.println ("client: Time at client is " + stopTime);
            float difference= stopTime-startTime;
            System.out.println ("client: The Server echoed thus --->"
                        + message);
            System.out.println ("client: Time for message to traverse"+
                        "the net is --->"
                        + difference + " msecs<---");
        }
    } catch (Exception e) {
        System.out.println ("client: EchoClient.main() exception: ");
        e.printStackTrace ();
    }
  }
}
```

Compile the sources, generate stubs and skeletons, and run the server.

```
F:\MyProjects\EchoService>javac *.java
F:\MyProjects\EchoService>rmic EchoServer
F:\MyProjects\EchoService>start java -jar c:\files\jini1_0\lib\tools.jar -port 8080
        -dir C:\files\jini1_0\lib -verbose
F:\MyProjects\EchoService>start rmiregistry
F:\MyProjects\EchoService>start rmid
F:\MyProjects\EchoService>java -jar
     -Djava.security.policy=c:\files\jini1_0\example\lookup\policy.all
        c:\files\jini1_0\lib\r
eggie.jar http://localhost:8080/reggie-dl.jar C:\files\jini1_0\example\lookup\policy.all
     reggie_log public
using absolute dbdir path: F:\MyProjects\EchoService\reggie_log
F:\MyProjects\EchoService>java
        -Djava.security.policy=c:\files\jini1_0\example\lookup\policy.all
        -Djava.rmi.server.codebase=
http://localhost/ EchoServer localhost
EchoServer: JoinManager = com.sun.jini.lookup.JoinManager@1fcdd4c7
EchoServer: LookupLocator = jini://localhost/
EchoServer: LookupLocator.host = localhost
EchoServer: LookupLocator.port = 4160
EchoServer: ServiceRegistrar = com.sun.jini.reggie.RegistrarProxy@ee58c3bf
EchoServer: ServiceID = 191ef071-155c-4e2f-a94c-88304b56f5d1
```

```
EchoServer: ServiceMatches = net.jini.core.lookup.ServiceMatches@f41dd4c7
EchoServer: num matches = 2
EchoServer: svc item 0: net.jini.core.lookup.ServiceItem@10e1d4c7
EchoServer: svc object 0: com.sun.jini.reggie.RegistrarProxy@ee58c3bf
EchoServer: svc item 1: net.jini.core.lookup.ServiceItem@439d4c7
EchoServer: svc object 1: EchoServer_Stub[RemoteStub
    [ref: [endpoint:[130.151.68.179:3649](remote),objID:[0]]]]
*---------------------------------------*
=================================================================
EchoServer: The method echoMessage() in EchoServer was called
EchoServer: Client says :Hello... This is Gopalan
=================================================================
=================================================================
EchoServer: The method echoMessage() in EchoServer was called
EchoServer: Client says :Hi Athul...
=================================================================
=================================================================
EchoServer: The method echoMessage() in EchoServer was called
EchoServer: Client says :Hi Arjun...
=================================================================
```

Run multiple client sessions.

```
C:\jini\EchoServer\EchoService>java
    -Djava.security.policy=c:\files\jini1_0\example\lookup\policy.all
    -Djava.rmi.server.codebase=http://130.151.68.179/
    EchoClient 130.151.68.179 "Hello... This is Gopalan"
client: LookupLocator = jini://130.151.68.179/
client: LookupLocator.host = 130.151.68.179
client: LookupLocator.port = 4160
client: ServiceRegistrar = com.sun.jini.reggie.RegistrarProxy@b5244982
client: ServiceID = e78354c2-3881-4079-8a5a-bfafe07ce296
client: ServiceTemplate = net.jini.core.lookup.ServiceTemplate@1f21d3
client: Service object = EchoServer_Stub[RemoteStub [ref:
    [endpoint:[130.151.68.179:3813](remote),objID:[42ed2864:d7106f929a:-8000, 0]]]]
=================================================================
client: Time at server is 923695814890
client: Time at client is 923695814930
client: The Server echoed thus --->Hello... This is Gopalan
client: Time for message to traverse the net is --->40.0 msecs<---
=================================================================
C:\jini\EchoServer\EchoService>java
    -Djava.security.policy=c:\files\jini1_0\example\lookup\policy.all
    -Djava.rmi.server.codebase=http://130.151.68.179/
```

```
    EchoClient 130.151.68.179 "Hi Athul..."
client: LookupLocator = jini://130.151.68.179/
client: LookupLocator.host = 130.151.68.179
client: LookupLocator.port = 4160
client: ServiceRegistrar = com.sun.jini.reggie.RegistrarProxy@b5244982
client: ServiceID = e78354c2-3881-4079-8a5a-bfafe07ce296
client: ServiceTemplate = net.jini.core.lookup.ServiceTemplate@1f3ba4
client: Service object = EchoServer_Stub[RemoteStub [ref:
    [endpoint:[130.151.68.179:3813](remote),objID:[42ed2864:d7106f929a:-8000, 0]]]]
==============================================================
client: Time at server is 923698395130
client: Time at client is 923698395140
client: The Server echoed thus --->Hi Athul...
client: Time for message to traverse the net is --->10.0 msecs<---
==============================================================
C:\jini\EchoServer\EchoService>java
    -Djava.security.policy=c:\files\jini1_0\example\lookup\policy.all
    -Djava.rmi.server.codebase=http://130.151.68.179/
    EchoClient 130.151.68.179 "Hi Arjun..."
client: LookupLocator = jini://130.151.68.179/
client: LookupLocator.host = 130.151.68.179
client: LookupLocator.port = 4160
client: ServiceRegistrar = com.sun.jini.reggie.RegistrarProxy@b5244982
client: ServiceID = e78354c2-3881-4079-8a5a-bfafe07ce296
client: ServiceTemplate = net.jini.core.lookup.ServiceTemplate@e33b97
client: Service object = EchoServer_Stub[RemoteStub [ref:
    [endpoint:[130.151.68.179:3813](remote),objID:[42ed2864:d7106f929a:-8000, 0]]]]
==============================================================
client: Time at server is 923698442298
client: Time at client is 923698442328
client: The Server echoed thus --->Hi Arjun...
client: Time for message to traverse the net is --->30.0 msecs<---
==============================================================
C:\jini\EchoServer\EchoService>
```

The distributed programming model

The Programming Model is used by Clients to enlist the help of Jini services in achieving the client's goal. It consists of support for leasing, distributed events, and transactions.

Leasing

Access to any service is done through a leasing model, which imposes a time limit for the use of the service. This enabling any existing object references to be reclaimed safely in the case of network failures. Persistence of the held reference depends on renewed proof of interest expressed by renewing a lease. Lease holders can safely crash, get disconnected, or simply forget about a leased resource. Leases can be exclusive, thus effectively locking the service from use by others or it can allow multiple requesting services to share a given service. Once the lease expires, the service cannot be used by any other unless the lease is renewed.

In a distributed Jini system, the client "holder" requests a lease from a "grantor." The holder may negotiate a lease duration. The grantor decides whether to grant the lease for that lease duration. The grantor may then send the holder a `Lease` object. The `Lease` may be exclusive or nonexclusive. The grantor agrees to keep the resource available, to the best of its ability, until the lease is cancelled or expires. If the lease is cancelled or expires, the holder can dispose of the resource.

Distributed events

Jini enables communication between resources and services via an event notification mechanism derived from the JavaBeans event model. This distributed event model allows services to register with each other and receive notification—even across machine boundaries—in response to specific actions. The Event Generator generates remote events upon abstract state changes. The Event Listener registers interest in being notified of the abstract state changes in the Event Generator. The registration of the interest is lease-based. The remote event is passed from the Event Generator to the `notify()` method of the registered Event Listeners. Each `RemoteEvent` object contains an identifier for the kind of event, a reference to the Event Generator, a sequence number, and an object that was passed in as part of the registration of interest in the event. Objects that want to receive notification of a remote event, implement the `RemoteEventListener` interface. Unlike JavaBean events, Jini events are identified by an event identifier and the event source. An `UnknownEventException` is thrown if the event is unrecognizable.

Transactions

A transaction is essentially multiple atomic operations that can be treated as a single unit. The transaction is successful or can be committed, only if each of the discrete statements succeeds; it aborts if any one of those statements fail. The Jini transaction system is based on the two-phased commit model, which saves the system's state before and after the transaction is executed. Thus, if the transaction aborts, the system can perform a rollback or recreate the state the way it was before the transaction was initiated.

Jini transactions are managed and completed by the `TransactionManager`. The client hands a factory method a `TransactionManager` reference and a lease duration. The client receives a new `Transaction` object and a `Lease` object from the factory method. The client passes this Transaction object to participants when asking a participant to do a task "under the transaction." Participants must "join" the transaction before performing the task. If a client or a participant "aborts" the transaction, the TransactionManager instruct all participants to "rollback." If a client or a participant "commits" the transaction, the TransactionManager queries all participants. If all participants report either "prepared" or "no-change," the TransactionManager instructs all participants to "roll forward".

Comparing Jini with RMI

Although Jini technology has a lot in common with RMI, there are some important differences nonetheless. Table 6-2 draws a comparison between the main features of both technologies.

Table 6-2: Comparing Java/RMI and Jini

Java/RMI	Jini
The service storing information about other service providers is the RMI registry.	In Jini, the service storing information about other service providers is called Jini Lookup service.
RMI clients use the class Naming.Lookup() for locating the requested RMI service.	Jini clients use the discovery process to locate Jini Lookup services. Discovery is done through multicast requests to well-known addresses or ports.
The RMI client must know the RMI registry host explicitly. The same rule applies to RMI servers.	The Jini clients search for the Jini service without any service hosting knowledge.
The approach is more rigid because the client is dependent on a particular service provider.	The approach is more tolerant to service provider's faults and maximizes client independence on a particular service provider.
The RMI proxy-stub approach is strictly adhered to.	The Jini proxy concept is more protocol-independent because it does not rely on generated fixed-protocol stubs. The proxy fulfills requests by itself or uses either an RMI call or an internal proxy provider to fulfill a request.
No concept of built-in support for transactions, distributed events, or leasing.	Programming model provides for support for transactions, distributed events, and leasing.

Applying Jini Technology

What's possible with Jini? Consider the following scenario:

Assume your federation is on an enterprise WAN. Now, a colleague of yours looking at a spreadsheet halfway around the world, can easily print out a copy on the printer next to your desk. If this does not sound too impressive, consider the possibility that you may have just plugged in your Jini-enabled printer into the federation while you were on the phone with him—without any printer configuration or messy driver installation.

Although Jini technology may sound futuristic, it is both a reality and currently being beta tested by about 30 companies worldwide, including market leaders like Canon, Toshiba, Ericsson, Mitsubishi, Epson, and Quantum among others. Jini is not part of Java 2, but Sun is considering making the Jini code freely available in the future by placing it in the public domain. For more details on this rapidly evolving technology, check the Jini home page at `http://java.sun.com/products/jini/`.

Future Trends

RMI has had its critics ever since its introduction. Some developers have argued RMI is a superfluous technology, especially when compared with the more mature facilities available within the CORBA architecture. But critics notwithstanding, RMI has continued to evolve at a rapid pace. RMI technology, as found within Java 2, not only features significant performance improvements, but also has several enhancements,

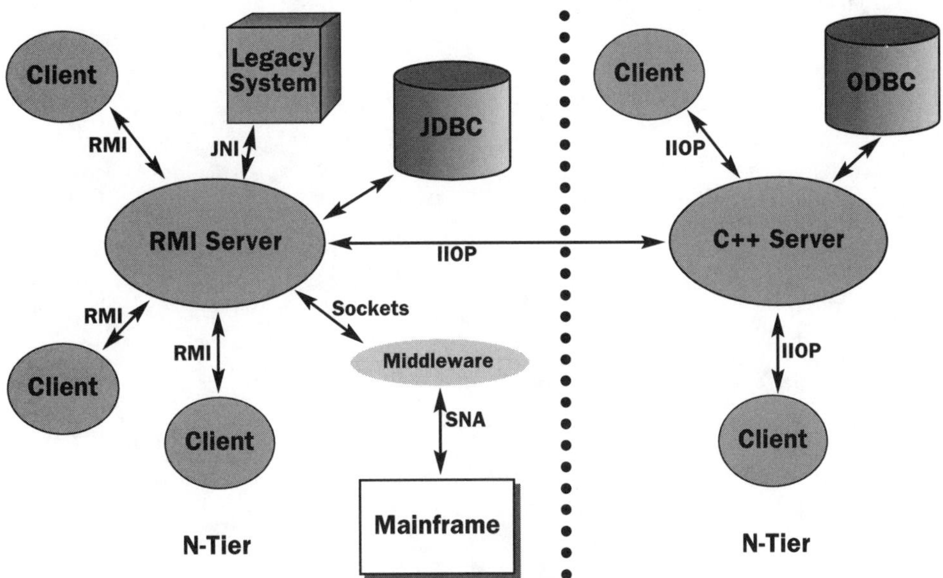

Figure 6-12: RMI in the future—*N-N* Tier computing

including custom sockets and remote activation. Additionally, Sun has released several new APIs, which run atop RMI for handling distributed events, leasing, and transactions. Although not currently included within Java 2, Sun has demonstrated the interoperability of RMI with CORBA objects by providing support for additional support to the IIOP protocol. When this is finally released, we should ultimately witness the integration of RMI and CORBA systems, leading to dynamic N-N tier computing architectures, as shown Figure 6-12:

Substantial industry momentum is also behind RMI—it is currently both an integral component of Sun's EJB technology and the bulwark of enterprise-wide frameworks like IBM's San Francisco project. From all indications, RMI appears to be the de facto technology for distributed object computing in a pure Java environment.

Summary

With RMI, Java objects can invoke the methods of methods of remote objects as if they were locally available – irrespective of the host or the JVM the remote object may be running on. Remote methods can send and receive any serializable object, and transparently use object serialization convert objects to a byte stream. RMI clients and servers communicate using the JRMP protocol, although it is certainly possible to enable them to use IIOP too. The Java 2 platform delivers some significant enhancements to RMI by allowing the default TCP-socket to be replaced with custom sockets implementing proprietary functionality like data encryption and compression. It also permits the dynamic instantiation of RMI servers at run-time.

Chapter 7

Java IDL: Java Meets CORBA

Distributed object computing extends an object-oriented programming system by allowing objects to be distributed across a heterogeneous network. Then each of these distributed object components interoperates as a unified whole. These objects may be distributed on different computers throughout a network and living within their own address space outside of an application, yet appear as though they were local to an application.

Three of the more popular distributed object paradigms are Microsoft's Distributed Component Object Model (DCOM), OMG's Common Object Request Broker Architecture (CORBA), and Sun's Java/Remote Method Invocation (Java/RMI). In this chapter, you learn about the CORBA architecture and the mechanics of developing CORBA clients and servers. The chapter concludes with a detailed comparison between CORBA and Java/RMI technologies.

The CORBA Distributed Computing Model

CORBA is a structural architecture designed to support heterogeneous object systems. CORBA achieves communication between different distributed objects while still allowing encapsulation and hiding of the internal object structure from external objects through *Indirection*. CORBA uses Indirection efficiently to achieve encapsulation preventing systematic recompilation.

CORBA defines a model that specifies interoperability between distributed objects on a network in a way that is transparent to the programmer. CORBA achieves this by defining ways for specifying the externally visible characteristics of a distributed object in a way that is implementation-independent.

This model is based on clients requesting the services from distributed objects or servers through a well-defined interface, by issuing requests to the objects in the form of events. An event carries information about an operation that needs to be performed, including the object name (called an *object reference*) of the service provider and the actual parameters, if any.

CORBA automatically handles a lot of network programming tasks, such as object registration, object location, object activation, request demultiplexing, frame and error-handling, marshaling, and operation dispatching.

CORBA objects are accessed through the use of an interface. OMG's Interface Definition Language (IDL, for short) is used to define interfaces, their attributes, methods, and parameters to those methods within the interface.

CORBA relies on a protocol called the *Internet Inter-ORB Protocol (IIOP)* for remoting objects. Everything in the CORBA architecture depends on an *Object Request Broker (ORB)*. The ORB acts as a central Object Bus over which each CORBA object interacts transparently with other CORBA objects located either locally or remotely. Each CORBA Server Object has an interface and exposes a set of methods. To request a service, a CORBA client acquires an object reference to a CORBA server object. The client can now make method calls on the object reference as if the CORBA server object resided in the client's address space. The ORB is responsible for finding a CORBA object's implementation, preparing it to receive requests, communicating requests to it, and carrying the reply back to the client. A CORBA Object interacts with the ORB, either through the ORB interface or through an Object Adapter, which comes in two flavors: Basic Object Adapter (BOA) or Portable Object Adapter (POA).

Some of the benefits of CORBA include, but are not limited to, the following:

1. CORBA forces a separation of an object's interface and its implementation.
2. CORBA's support for reuse is inherent to the technology.
3. CORBA is scalable.
4. CORBA enforces transparency of platforms and languages.
5. CORBA provides interoperability.
6. CORBA abstracts network communication from the developer.

Because CORBA is just a specification, it can be used on diverse platforms, including Mainframes, UNIX, Windows, AS/400, and so forth as long as an ORB implementation exists for that platform. Currently, major ORB vendors like Inprise and Iona offer CORBA ORB implementations for numerous platforms.

The Object Management Architecture

OMG, the industry consortium that created the CORBA standard, defines two basic models on which CORBA and all its standard interfaces are based. They are

- The Core Object Model and
- The Reference Model

The *Core Object Model* defines concepts that facilitate distributed application development using the Object Request Broker (ORB). It defines a framework for refining the CORBA model to a concrete form. The Core Object Model is an abstract specification that does not attempt to detail the syntax of object interfaces or any other part of the ORB. This model provides the basis for CORBA, but is more relevant to ORB designers and implementers than it is to application developers.

The Figure 7-1 shows the OMA Reference Model.

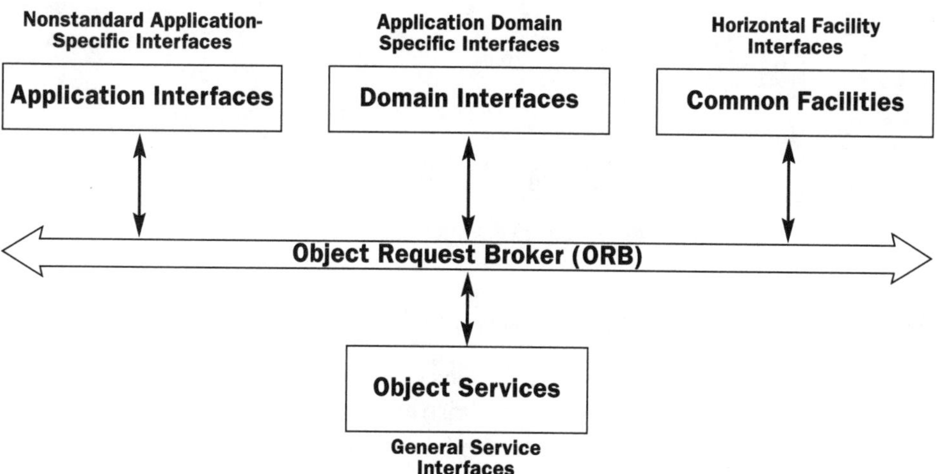

Figure 7-1: The Object Management Architecture Reference Model

The *Reference Model* defines a development model for CORBA and its standard interfaces through which developers can create and use frameworks, components, and objects. This model places the ORB at the center of a grouping of objects with standardized interfaces that provide support for application developers. In addition to the ORB, the Reference model identifies four groupings:

- *Object Services*, which provide the infrastructure.
- *Domain Interfaces*, which provide support for applications from specific industry domains.
- *Common Facilities*, which provide application-level services across domains.
- *Application Interfaces*, which is the set of objects developed for a specific application.

The CORBA 2.0 Architecture

Figure 7-2 shows the CORBA 2.0 architecture. In CORBA, the IDL compiler generates type information for each method in an interface and stores it in the *Interface Repository (IR)*. A client can thus query the IR to get run-time information about a particular interface and then use that information to create and invoke a method on the remote CORBA Server Object dynamically through the *Dynamic Invocation Interface (DII)*. Similarly, on the server side, the *Dynamic Skeleton Interface (DSI)* enables a client to invoke an operation of a remote CORBA Server Object that has no compile time knowledge of the type of object it is implementing.

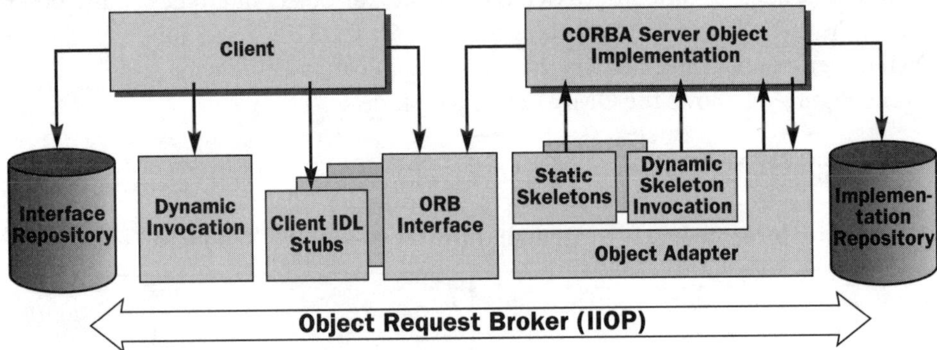

Figure 7-2: CORBA 2.0 architecture

The Object Request Broker (ORB)

The central component of CORBA is the Object Request Broker (ORB). This component provides all the communication infrastructure needed to identify and locate objects, handle connection management, and deliver data and request communication.

The Figure 7-3 shows a typical CORBA environment with the ORB facilitating communication between a Remote CORBA Server and a Client Application.

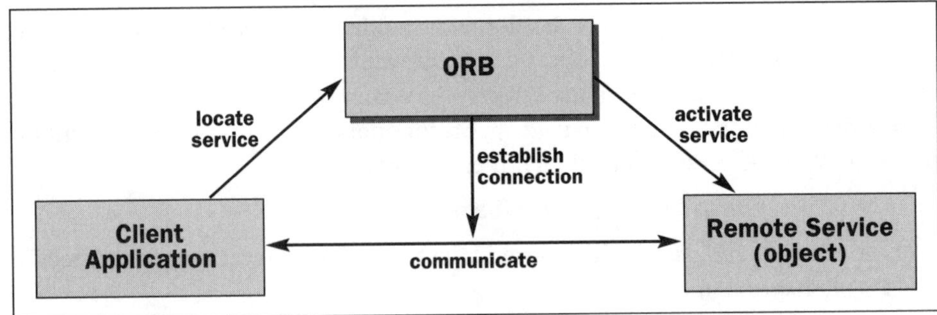

Figure 7-3: The Object Request Broker

One CORBA object never talks directly with another. Instead, the object requests for an interface to the ORB running on the local machine. The local ORB then passes the request to an ORB on the other machine. The remote ORB then locates the appropriate object and passes back an object reference to the requester.

The functions of the ORB are as follows:

- Lookup and instantiate objects on remote machines
- Marshal parameters from one application object to the other
- Handle security issues across machine boundaries
- Retrieve and publish data on objects on the local machine for another ORB to use
- Invoke methods on a remote object using static method invocation
- Invoke methods on a remote object using dynamic method invocation
- Automatically instantiate objects not currently running
- Route callback methods to the appropriate local object being managed
- Communicate with other ORBs using the Internet Inter-ORB Protocol (IIOP)

Object Adapters

An *Object Adapter* is a server-side facility that provides a mechanism for the CORBA object implementations to communicate with the ORB and vice versa. An Object Adapter also extends the functionality of the ORB. An Object Adapter is layered on top of the ORB Core to provide an interface between the ORB and the object implementation. Object Adapters can also be used to provide specialized services optimized for a particular environment, platform, or object implementation.

Some of the services provided by an Object Adapter are

- Registration of server object implementations with the Implementation Repository
- Activation and deactivation of object implementations
- Instantiation of objects at runtime
- Generation and management of object references
- Mapping of object references to their implementations
- Dispatching of client requests to server objects through a skeleton or the Dynamic Skeleton Interface (DSI)

While many object adapter implementations may exist for unique situations, the CORBA specification only requires implementations to provide a Basic Object Adapter (BOA) or a Portable Object Adapter (POA) which is a portable version of the BOA.

Basic Object Adapter (BOA)

The BOA is a pseudo-object and is created by the ORB, but it is invoked like any other object. The BOA provides operations the CORBA Server Object implementations can access. It interfaces with the ORB Core and with the skeletons of your object server implementation classes.

A BOA may be required to perform two types of activations on behalf of a client's request: implementation activation and object activation.

- *Implementation Activation*: This occurs when the implementation for the target object is unavailable to handle the request. This requires the use of a daemon that can launch a Java VM with the server's byte code. The information necessary to associate an object implementation with a Java class is stored in the Implementation Repository.
- *Object Activation*: This occurs when the target object is unavailable to handle the request.

The BOA is mandated by CORBA 2.0, but was recently deprecated in favor of a Portable Object Adapter (POA). Even though vendors, to support existing implementations, may support the BOA, OMG will no longer update the BOA specifications.

Portable Object Adapter (POA)

The POA addresses many problems found in applying the BOA. It mandates additional functionality and is tightly specified to increase portability. With the POA API, the interfaces between the ORB and the object's implementation have been standardized. Thus, CORBA services stand a fighting chance of being ORB-independent as well as interoperable.

The Implementation Repository

The Implementation Repository is an online database that contains information about the classes a server supports, the objects instantiated, and their IDs. Additional information about a specific ORB implementation may also sometimes be stored here.

The Dynamic Skeleton Interface (DSI)

For CORBA components that do not have an IDL-based compiled skeleton, the Dynamic Skeleton Interface (DSI) provides a runtime binding mechanism. The DSI determines the target object for which a message is meant by looking at the parameter values in an incoming message, so it can receive either static or dynamic client invocations. The DSI thus allows servers to dispatch client operation requests to objects that were not statically defined at compile time.

Interface Repository

The Interface Repository (IR) is an online database of metainformation about ORB object types. Metainformation stored for objects includes information about modules, interfaces, operations, attributes and exceptions.

The Dynamic Invocation Interface (DII)

During run time, the DII allows methods to be discovered dynamically so they can be invoked. Client programs can obtain information about an object's interface from the Interface Repository and dynamically construct requests to act on the object.

The Interface Definition Language (IDL)

Whenever a client needs some service from a remote distributed object, it invokes a method implemented by the remote object. The service the remote distributed object (server) provides is encapsulated as an object and the remote object's interface is described in an Interface Definition Language (IDL). The interfaces specified in the IDL file serve as a contract between a remote object server and its clients. Clients can thus interact with these remote object servers by invoking methods defined in the IDL. CORBA supports multiple inheritance at the IDL level and allows exceptions to be specified in the IDL definitions.

A typical CORBA IDL definition looks like Listing 7-1.

Listing 7-1: A Typical CORBA IDL

```
module SimpleStocks {
    interface StockMarket {
        float get_price( in string symbol );
    };
};
```

The CORBA IDL file shows a `StockMarket` interface with a `get_price()` method. When an IDL compiler compiles this IDL file it generates files for stubs and skeletons.

IDL to Java Mapping

The highlights of the IDL to Java mapping are as follows:

- An IDL module maps to a Java package of the same name.
- An IDL interface maps to a public Java interface with the same name.
- Inheritance of IDL interfaces is achieved through inheritance of Java interfaces.

- Nested IDL type definitions are mapped to Java classes using a scoped package name.
- IDL attributes are mapped to a pair of overloaded Java accessor and mutator methods.
- All IDL out and inout parameters require the use of a Holder class.

Identifiers, naming, and scope

Except where a conflict would result with a Java reserved word, IDL names and identifiers are mapped directly to Java with no modification. Where a name or identifier in IDL exactly matches a Java reserved word, the collision is resolved by prepending an underscore (_) in the mapped name. For example:

```
// in IDL
interface synchronized {};
```

maps to

```
// generated Java
public class _synchronized {}
```

Depending upon the IDL construct, the mapping may require more than one uniquely named Java construct. When such a situation occurs, additional constructs are tagged on to the Java names like Helper, Holder or Package. In case any of these still conflicts with standard Java constructs, the collision resolution rule (_) applies.

Generated classes

In addition to the Java class that maps directly from an IDL construct, helper and holder classes may be generated to aid the developer in the use of the class.

Holder classes

Because all parameters are passed by value in Java, a method may change only the state of an object passed to it, not the reference to the object itself. To allow IDL types to be used with out and inout parameter passing modes, additional holder classes are required. The holder classes provide a level of indirection and are passed instead of the actual type. The client instantiates a holder object and passes it in the operation invocation. The server may then set or modify the value member of the holder object. Because the encapsulated actual object is modified without affecting the holder object reference itself, the semantics of out and inout parameters are supported. Holder classes are available for all the basic IDL datatypes in the `org.omg.CORBA` package and are generated for all named user-defined types, except those defined by nonconstructed type typedefs.

Helper classes

All user-defined IDL types have an additional helper Java class with the suffix `Helper` appended to the mapped type name. A *helper class* contains convenience and utility methods for operating on the associated object. The purpose of the helper class is to prevent bloating of the mapped classes with methods that may not be needed. The class provides methods for reading and writing the object to a stream, obtaining the object's repository identifier, and casting the object to/from a CORBA `Any`. The helper classes for mapped IDL interfaces also have the `narrow()` method defined, which is used to cast the object reference of `org.omg.CORBA.Object` to the base type of the helper.

Mapping for basic types

Table 7-1 shows the mapping of the CORBA basic types to the corresponding Java class or type.

Table 7-1: The Mapping for Basic Types

IDL Type	Java Type	Exceptions
boolean	boolean	CORBA::DATA_CONVERSION
char	char	
wchar	char	
octet	byte	
string	java.lang.String	CORBA::MARSHAL CORBA::DATA_CONVERSION
wstring	java.lang.String	CORBA::MARSHAL
short	short	
unsigned short	short	
long	int	
unsigned long	int	
long long	long	
float	float	
double	double	

Mapping for enum

An IDL enumeration (*enum*) is mapped to a public Java final class. Each enumeration has two corresponding static class constants: one is a Java *int* named with a prepended underscore to the element identifier and the other is an instance of the mapped final class with the same name as the element that represents the element's value.

```
// in IDL
enum TrafficLight {red, yellow, green};
```

maps to

```
// generated Java
final public class TrafficLight {
    final public static int _red    = 0;
    final public static int _yellow= 1;
    final public static int _green = 2;
    final public static TrafficLight red = new TrafficLight(_red);
    final public static TrafficLight yellow= new TrafficLight(_yellow);
    final public static TrafficLight green= new TrafficLight(_green);
    public int value() {....}
    ........
}
```

Mapping for struct

An IDL struct maps to a final Java class containing one instance variable for each structure field. The class name is the same as the IDL structure name. Two constructors are provided: one takes the fields of the structure as arguments to initialize the instance variables and the other is a null constructor that initializes the instance variables to null or zero.

Mapping for union

An IDL *union* is mapped to a final Java class that has the following characteristics:

- Same name as the IDL identifier
- A default constructor
- An accessor method for the union's discriminant named discriminator()
- An accessor method for each variant
- A mutator method for each variant
- A mutator method for each variant that has more than one case label
- A default mutator method if needed

Mapping for ordered collections

CORBA provides two types of ordered collections: sequences and array. A *sequence* maps to a single dimensional Java array, which may be either bounded or unbounded. An *IDL array* is a multidimensional array whose size, in each dimension, must be fixed at compile time.

Mapping for attributes and operations

Attributes are mapped to a pair of overloaded Java accessors and mutator methods. These methods have the same name as the IDL attribute and differ only in their signature. No mutator method exists for IDL read-only attributes.

Parameter-passing modes

IDL in parameters, which implement call-by-value semantics, are mapped to normal Java actual parameters. The results of IDL operations are returned as the result of the corresponding Java method.

IDL out and inout parameters, which implement call-by-result and call-by-value/result semantics, cannot be mapped directly into the Java parameter-passing mechanism. This mapping defines additional holder classes for all the IDL basic and user-defined types used to implement these parameter modes in Java.

Table 7-2 shows the mapping of IDL type to Java for the different parameter modes.

Table 7-2: Mapping of CORBA IDL to Java for different parameter modes

IDL Type	In Mapping	In/out Mapping	Return Mapping
boolean	boolean	BooleanHolder	boolean
char	char	CharHolder	char
wchar	char	CharHolder	char
octet	byte	ByteHolder	byte
string	java.lang.String	StringHolder	java.lang.String
wstring	java.lang.String	StringHolder	java.lang.String
short	short	ShortHolder	short
unsigned short	short	ShortHolder	short
long	int	IntHolder	int
unsigned long	int	IntHolder	int
long long	long	LongHolder	long
unsigned long long	long	LongHolder	long
float	float	FloatHolder	float
double	double	DoubleHolder	double
enum	<enum>object	< enum >Holder	< enum >object
struct	<struct>object	< struct >Holder	< struct >object
union	<union>object	<union>Holder	<union>object
sequence	<sequence>object	<sequence>Holder	<sequence>object

continued

Table 7-2: continued

IDL Type	In Mapping	In/out Mapping	Return Mapping
array	<array>object	<array>Holder	<array>object
Any	Any	AnyHolder	Any
interface	<interface>object reference	<interface>Holder	<interface>object reference

Mapping for user-defined exceptions

A user-defined exception is mapped to a final Java class that extends `org.omg.CORBA.UserException`. The `UserException` class extends the standard `org.omg.CORBA.Exception` class. The mapping is identical to the IDL struct type, including generated Holder and Helper classes.

Mapping for system exceptions

The standard IDL system exceptions are mapped to final Java classes that extend `org.omg.CORBA.SystemException` and provide access to the IDL major and minor exception code, as well as a string describing the reason for the exception. Instantiating `org.omg.CORBA.SystemException` is impossible. Only classes that extend it can be instantiated.

Developing CORBA Servers and Clients

When developing distributed applications for CORBA using the Java IDL, you first identify the objects required by the application. Figure 7-4 denotes the Java IDL development lifecycle.

You are usually required to follow these steps:

1. Write a specification for each object using the IDL.
2. Use the IDL compiler to generate the client stub code and server skeleton code.
3. Write the client application code.
4. Write the server object code.
5. Compile the client and server code.
6. Start the server.
7. Run the client application.

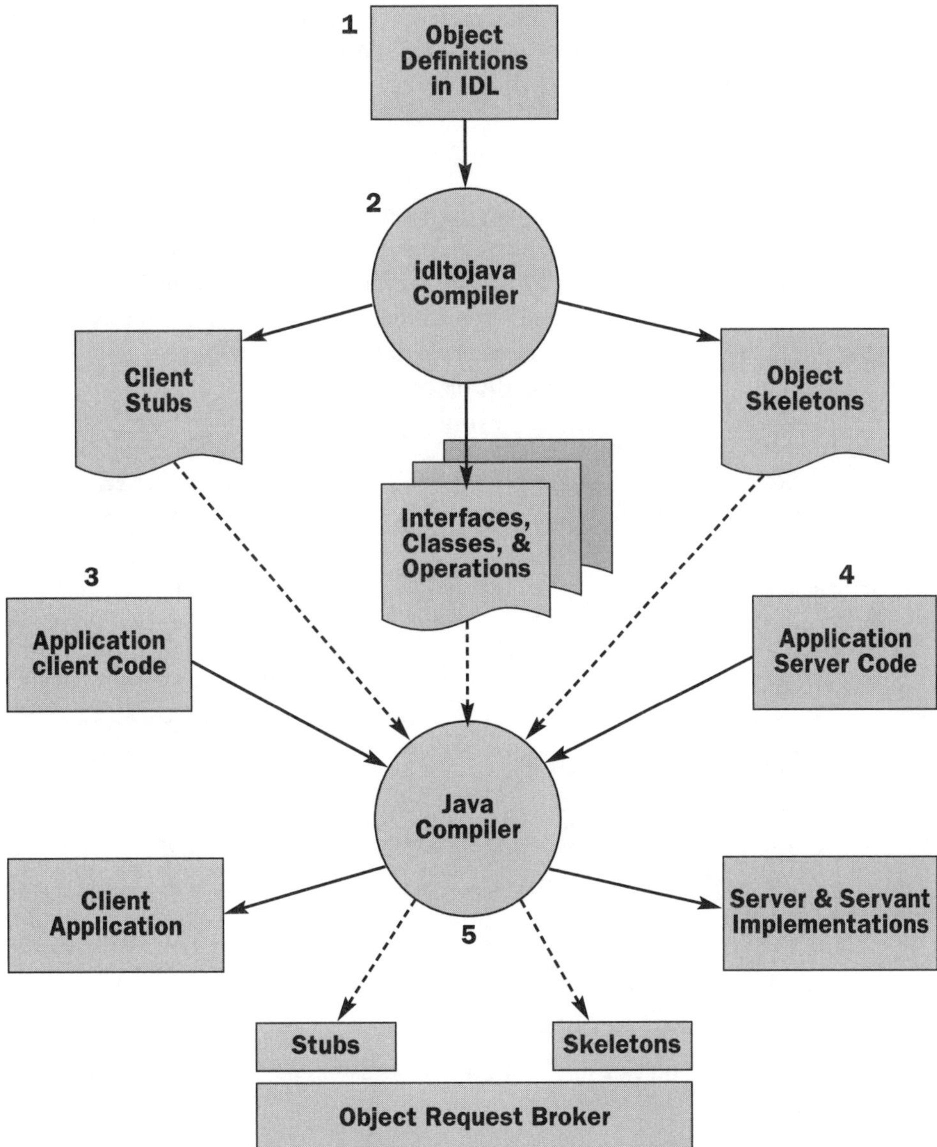

Figure 7-4: Java IDL Development Lifecycle

Before developing CORBA servers and clients, make sure you have Java 1.2 and the idltojava compiler installed on your machine. The JDK provides the API and ORB needed to enable CORBA-based distributed object interaction. The idltojava compiler uses the IDL-to-Java mapping to convert IDL interface definitions to corresponding Java interfaces, classes, and methods, which you can then use to implement your client and server code.

Also ensure your Path and Environment variables conform to what is specified in the JDK installation docs. For more information about setting up these environment variables, see the *JDK 1.2 Installation Guide.*

The TimeServer example

Now let's go through the tasks involved in building a CORBA-distributed application using Java IDL. We can build a Time Server program as a distributed application, with both applet and application clients. The Time Server program has a single operation, which returns the current time of a server machine to any client that requests it.

Figure 7-5 shows a diagramatic representation of what actually goes on the wire when a client calls our `TimeServer` CORBA object.

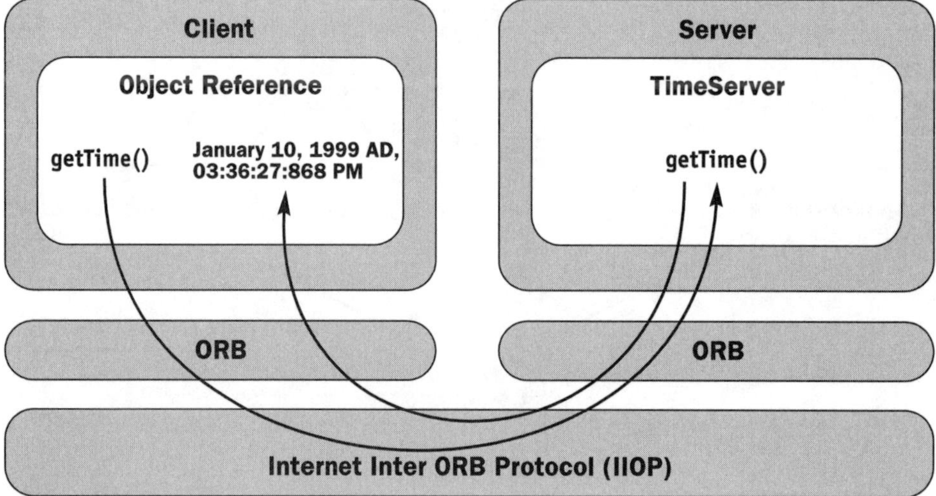

Figure 7-5: The TimeServer example

The operations involved are as follows:

1. The client (applet or application) invokes the `getTime()` operation of the `TimeServer`.
2. The ORB transfers that invocation to the `TimeServer` object registered for that IDL interface.
3. The `TimeServer` 's `getTime()`method runs, returning a Java `String`.
4. The ORB transfers that String back to the client.
5. The client prints the value of the String.

Defining the IDL

The OMG IDL is a purely declarative language designed for specifying programming-language-independent operational interfaces for distributed applications. OMG specifies a mapping from IDL to several different programming languages, including C, C++, Smalltalk, COBOL, Ada, and Java. When mapped, each statement in OMG IDL is translated to a corresponding statement in the programming language of choice. You can use the tool idltojava to map an IDL interface to Java and implement the client class. When you map the same IDL to C++ and implement the server in that language, the Java client and C++ server interoperate through the ORB as though they were written in the same language.

As was previously mentioned, the IDL interface defines a contract between the client and server parts of your application, specifying what operations and attributes are available. When you run the idltojava compiler on your IDL code, your IDL code is mapped to equivalent Java code automatically. You can then go about writing any of your implementation code.

Our IDL definition for the TimeServer object looks like Listing 7-2.

Listing 7-2: Time Tracker CORBA IDL

```
module Tracker {
    interface Time {
        string getTime();
    };
};
```

A CORBA module is a namespace that acts as a container for related interfaces and declarations. It corresponds closely to a Java package. Each module statement in an IDL file is mapped to a Java package statement. We have defined a module called Tracker.

Like Java interfaces, CORBA interfaces declare the API contract that an object has with other objects. Each interface statement in the IDL maps to a Java interface statement when mapped. When you compile the IDL, this statement generates an interface statement in the Java code. We have defined an interface called Time. Your client and server classes may implement this Time interface in different ways.

CORBA operations are the behavior that servers promise to perform on behalf of clients that invoke them. Each operation statement in the IDL generates a corresponding method statement in the generated Java interface. In the previous IDL, getTime() is one such operation.

The tool idltojava reads OMG IDL files and creates the required Java files. The idltojava defaults are set up so if you need both client and server files, you simply enter the tool name and the name of your IDL file. Compile the IDL from the command line.

```
F:\>idltojava Tracker.idl
```

Develop the client application

You start off by importing the required packages. The package containing our stubs is in package Tracker. Because our Client is using the Naming Service to get a reference to the server object, we need org.omg.CosNaming. Since All CORBA applications need org.omg.CORBA, we import that package too.

The listing of our Client program is shown in Listing 7-3.

Listing 7-3: The TimeServer CORBA Client

```
package cup.chap7.ex71;
import Tracker.*; // The package containing our stubs.
import org.omg.CosNaming.*; // Client will use the naming service.
import org.omg.CORBA.*;  // All CORBA applications need these classes.
public class Client {
      public static void main (String args[]) {
         try {
            // Create and initialize the ORB
            ORB orb = ORB.init (args, null);
            // Get the root naming context
            org.omg.CORBA.Object objRef =
                  orb.resolve_initial_references ("NameService");
            NamingContext ncRef = NamingContextHelper.narrow (objRef);
            // Resolve the object reference in naming
            NameComponent nc = new NameComponent ("TimeServer", "");
            NameComponent path[] = {nc};
            Time timeRef = TimeHelper.narrow (ncRef.resolve (path));
            // Call the time server object and print results
            String time = "Time on the Server is " + timeRef.getTime ();
            System.out.println (time);
         } catch (Exception e) {
            e.printStackTrace ();
         }
      }
}
```

Creating an ORB Object

A CORBA client needs a local ORB object to perform all its marshaling and IIOP work. Every client instantiates an org.omg.CORBA.ORB object and initializes it by passing to the object certain information about itself.

We declare and initialize an ORB variable:

```
ORB orb = ORB.init (args, null);
```

The call to the ORB's init method passes in your application's command line arguments, enabling you to set certain properties at runtime.

Finding the Time Server Object

Once the application has an ORB, it can ask the ORB to locate the actual service it needs, in this case, the Time Server. A number of ways exist for a CORBA client to get an initial object reference; our client application will use the COS Naming Service specified by OMG and provided with Java IDL.

The steps involved in finding a CORBA object,using the Naming Service, are as follows.

1. Obtain the Initial Naming Context
2. Narrow the object reference
3. Find the object service in Naming

Obtaining the initial naming context

The first step in using the Naming Service is to get the initial naming context. In the previous code , we call `orb.resolve_initial_references` to get an object reference to the name server.

```
org.omg.CORBA.Object objRef =
        orb.resolve_initial_references ("NameService");
```

The string `"NameService"` is defined for all CORBA ORBs. When you pass in that string, the ORB returns the initial naming context, an object reference to the name service.

Narrowing the object reference

As with all CORBA object references, `objRef` is a generic CORBA object. To use it as a `NamingContext` object, you must narrow it to its proper type. The call to `narrow` just following the previous statement does this for us.

```
NamingContext ncRef = NamingContextHelper.narrow (objRef);
```

Here you see the use of an `idltojava` -generated helper class, similar in function to `TimeHelper`. The `ncRef` object is now an `org.omg.CosNaming.NamingContext` and we use it to access the Naming Service and find other services. We do this in the next step.

Finding a Service in Naming

Names can have different structures depending upon the implementation of the Naming Service. Consequently, CORBA name servers handle complex names by way of `NameComponent` objects. Each `NameComponent` holds a single part, or element, of the name. An array of `NameComponent` objects can hold a fully specified path to an object on any computer file or disk system.

To find the `Time` server, you first need a `NameComponent` to hold an identifying string for the `Time` server. In the previous code, the call to `narrow` does this for us. This is discussed as we go along.

```
NameComponent nc = new NameComponent ("TimeServer", "");
```

This statement sets the id field of nc, the new NameComponent, to "TimeServer" and the kind field to an empty string.

Because the path to the Time object has just one element, we create a single-element array out of nc. The NamingContext.resolve method requires this array for its work:

```
NameComponent path[] = {nc};
```

Finally, we pass the path to the Naming Service's resolve method to get an object reference to the Time server and narrow it to a Time object:

```
Time timeRef = TimeHelper.narrow (ncRef.resolve(path));
```

Here you see the TimeHelper helper class at work. The resolve method returns a generic CORBA object as you saw previously when locating the name service itself. Therefore, we immediately narrow it to a Time object, which is the object reference needed to perform the rest of the work.

Invoking the getTime() operation

CORBA invocations look like a method call on a local object. The complications of marshaling parameters over the wire, routing them to the server-side ORB, unmarshaling, and placing the upcall to the server method are completely transparent to the client programmer. Because so much is done for you by generated code, invocation is the easiest part of CORBA programming.

1. Continuing with the try-catch block in Client.java, the following invocation following the call to the name service's resolve method, invokes the getTime() operation on the server

   ```
   String time = "Time on the Server is " + timeRef.getTime ();
   ```

2. Finally, we add code to print the results of the invocation to standard output

   ```
   System.out.println (time);
   ```

Develop the server application

Once again, the steps involved are more or less similar to what we did when we developed the client application. The steps involved are

- Importing Required Packages
- Declaring the Server Class
- Creating an ORB Object

All this was explained previously when we developed our client application.

Managing the servant object

A *server* is a process that instantiates one or more servant objects. The servant implements the interface generated by idltojava and actually performs the work of the operations on that interface. Our Server needs a TimeServer.

Instantiating the TimeServer servant object

Inside the try-catch block, just below the call to init, we instantiate the servant object.

```
TimeServer timeRef = new TimeServer ();
```

Next, we connect the servant to the ORB, so the ORB can recognize invocations on it and pass them along to the correct servant:

```
orb.connect (timeRef);
```

Defining the servant class

We define the class for the servant object as follows.

```
class TimeServer extends _TimeImplBase {
    public String getTime () {
        SimpleDateFormat formatter =
            new SimpleDateFormat ("MMMMM dd, yyyyy GGG, hh:mm:ss:SSS aaa");
        Date date = new Date ();
        return formatter.format ( date );
    }
}
```

The servant is a subclass of _TimeImplBase, so it inherits the general CORBA functionality generated for it by the compiler.

Working with COS Naming

Once again, the steps involved are similar to what we had to do when we developed our client application.

1. Obtaining the Initial Naming Context
2. Narrowing the Object Reference

Registering the servant with the Name Server

The only interesting piece of code here is where we pass path and the servant object timeRef to the Naming Service, binding the servant object timeRef to the "TimeServer" id.

```
NameComponent nc = new NameComponent ("TimeServer", "");
NameComponent path[] = {nc};
ncRef.rebind (path, timeRef);
```

Now, when the client calls resolve("TimeServer") on the initial naming context, the Naming Service returns an object reference to the Time servant.

Waiting for invocation

The server is ready; it simply needs to wait around for a client to request its service. The following piece of code achieves this for us:

```
Thread.currentThread ().join ();
```

This requires TimeServer to remain alive (though quiescent) until an invocation comes from the ORB. Because of its placement in main, after an invocation completes and getTime() returns, the server will wait again.

The complete server source listing is shown in Listing 7-4.

Listing 7-4: The TimeServer CORBA Server Code

```
package cup.chap7.ex71;
// The package containing our stubs.
import Tracker.*;
// Server will use the naming service.
import org.omg.CosNaming.*;
// The package containing special exceptions thrown by the name
// service.
import org.omg.CosNaming.NamingContextPackage.*;
// All CORBA applications need these classes.
import org.omg.CORBA.*;
import java.util.*;
import java.text.*;
class TimeServer extends _TimeImplBase {
    public String getTime () {
        SimpleDateFormat formatter =
            new SimpleDateFormat ("MMMMM dd, yyyyy GGG, hh:mm:ss:SSS aaa");
        Date date = new Date ();
        return formatter.format (date);
    }
}
public class Server {
    public static void main (String args[]) {
        try {
            // Create and initialize the ORB
            ORB orb = ORB.init (args, null);
            // Create the servant and register it with the ORB
            TimeServer timeRef = new TimeServer ();
            orb.connect (timeRef);
            // Get the root naming context
            org.omg.CORBA.Object objRef =
                orb.resolve_initial_references ("NameService");
            NamingContext ncRef = NamingContextHelper.narrow (objRef);
            // Bind the object reference in naming
            NameComponent nc = new NameComponent ("TimeServer", "");
            NameComponent path[] = {nc};
            ncRef.rebind (path, timeRef);
```

Listing 7-4: continued

```
                // Wait forever for current thread to die
                Thread.currentThread ().join ();
            } catch (Exception e) {
                e.printStackTrace ();
            }
        }
    }
```

Start the name service

Java 2 ships with a compliant implementation of the COS Naming Service, called tnameserv. The command-line syntax for running tnameserv is

```
tnameserv [-ORBInitialPort ####]
```

The tnameserv runs on port 900 unless specified otherwise using the -ORBInitialPort command-line parameter

```
F:\>
F:\>tnameserv
Initial Naming Context:
IOR:000000000000002849444c3a6f6d672e6f72672f436f734e616d696e672f4e616d696e67
    436f6e746578743a312e3000000000000100000000000000300001000000000000008686f6d
    655f
706300087400000000000018afabcafe000000025e1c358b00000008000000000000000
TransientNameServer: setting port for initial object references to: 900
```

Start the CORBA TimeServer

```
F:\>
F:\>java cup.chap7.ex71.Server
```

Execute the TimeServer client

```
F:\>
F:\>java cup.chap7.ex71.Client
Time on the Server is January 10, 1999 AD, 03:37:27:868 PM
F:\>
```

Stringified Object References

To invoke an operation on a CORBA object, a client application needs a reference to the server object. You can get such references in a number of ways, such as calling `ORB.resolve_initial_references()` or using another CORBA object (like the name service). Often no Naming Service is available in the distributed environment. In this situation, CORBA clients use a stringified object reference to find their first object.

Although CORBA provides myriad ways for locating CORBA server objects, only one mechanism works for all IIOP-compliant CORBA implementations, Interoperable Object References (IORs). When working in a multiple-ORB environment, an IOR usually provides the only means to obtain an initial reference to an object, be it a Naming Service, transaction service, or customized CORBA servant.

ORBs supporting IIOP identify and publish object references using IORs. An IOR contains the information required for a client ORB to connect to a CORBA object or servant. Specifically, an IOR contains the following:

- *IIOP version*—Describes the IIOP version implemented by the ORB
- *Host*—Identifies the TCP/IP address of the ORB's host machine
- *Port*—Specifies the TCP/IP port number where the ORB is listening for client requests
- *Key*—Identifies uniquely the servant to the ORB exporting the servant
- *Components* —Contains additional information applicable to object method invocations, such as supported ORB services and proprietary protocol support
- *Stringification* is the process of converting a servant reference to and/or from a string representation of an IOR. Once an object reference has been stringified, it can be used by other applications to obtain a remote servant reference.

An IOR thus specifies the wire protocol for talking to an object, as well as specifying the object's network location. The IOR structure isn't important to programmers because an IOR is represented through a `String` instance by the process of stringification. IORs are convenient because they are easy to use and ORB-implementation-independent.

The InterestRates Server Example

In this section, we create a stringified object reference as a part of the server startup and show how the client gets that reference and destringifies it for use as a real object reference.

Define the IDL

The InterestRates Server Program has a single purpose. From one centralized server machine, it returns the current interest rates of different types of accounts a particular credit union provides. Clients can use these rates to perform their own computations. The IDL is defined in Listing 7-5.

Listing 7-5: Int Interest Rates CORBA IDL

```
module Interest {
    interface Rates {
        float getPremiumChecking ();
        float getPremiumSavings ();
        float getEconomyChecking ();
        float getEconomySavings ();
    };
};
```

Code the server application

For a stringified object reference to be available to the client, the server must create the reference and store it somewhere the client can access. Our reference is written to disk in the form of a text file.

Because the new server will write a file to disk, the following import statement is added.

```
import java.io.*;
```

Define the servant class

We define the class for the servant object as shown in Listing 7-6.

Listing 7-6: Defining the InterestRates CORBA Server Class

```
class InterestRates extends _RatesImplBase {
    private static final float _premiumChecking = 0.55f;
    private static final float _premiumSavings  = 2.10f;
    private static final float _economyChecking = 0.20f;
    private static final float _economySavings  = 1.50f;
    public float getPremiumChecking () { return _premiumChecking; }
    public float getPremiumSavings ()  { return _premiumSavings; }
    public float getEconomyChecking () { return _economyChecking; }
    public float getEconomySavings ()  { return _economySavings; }
}
```

The servant is a subclass of `_RatesImplBase` so it inherits the general CORBA functionality generated for it by the compiler.

Making a stringified object reference

The new server won't use the Naming Service, so we don't need the CosNaming packages.

The call to the ORB's object_to_string method passes it the reference to the servant object. This returns the object reference in a string form that can be saved in a file on disk.

```
String str = orb.object_to_string (ratesRef);
```

We then build the path to the file that will be stored, using system properties to determine the path structure and syntax.

```
String filename = System.getProperty ("user.home")+
            System.getProperty ("file.separator")+"RatesIOR";
```

Use standard Java operations to write the stringified IOR to disk:

```
FileOutputStream fos = new FileOutputStream (filename);
    PrintStream ps = new PrintStream (fos);
    ps.print (str);
    ps.close ();
```

When the server runs, instead of calling the ORB and registering the InterestRates servant object with naming, it creates the text file RatesIOR containing a stringified reference to the servant. The file is stored in our home directory.

The complete source for the server is shown in Listing 7-7.

Listing 7-7: The InterestRates CORBA Server Class

```
// Server.java, stringified object reference versionpackage cup.chap7.ex72;
import java.io.*;
import org.omg.CORBA.*;
import Interest.*;
class InterestRates extends _RatesImplBase {
    private static final float _premiumChecking = 0.55f;
    private static final float _premiumSavings  = 2.10f;
    private static final float _economyChecking = 0.20f;
    private static final float _economySavings  = 1.50f;
    public float getPremiumChecking () { return _premiumChecking; }
    public float getPremiumSavings ()  { return _premiumSavings; }
    public float getEconomyChecking () { return _economyChecking; }
    public float getEconomySavings ()  { return _economySavings; }
}
public class Server {
    public static void main (String args[]) {
        try {
            // create and initialize the ORB
            ORB orb = ORB.init (args, null);
```

Listing 7-7: continued

```
            // create servant and register it with the ORB
            InterestRates ratesRef = new InterestRates ();
            orb.connect (ratesRef);
            // stringify the ratesRef and dump it in a file
            String str = orb.object_to_string (ratesRef);
            String filename =System.getProperty ("user.home")+
               System.getProperty("file.separator")+"RatesIOR";
            FileOutputStream fos = new FileOutputStream (filename);
            PrintStream ps = new PrintStream (fos);
            ps.print (str);
            ps.close ();
            // Wait forever for current thread to die
            Thread.currentThread ().join ();
         } catch (Exception e) {
            e.printStackTrace ();
         }
      }
   }
```

Code the client

Because the new server will write a file to disk, the following import statement is added.

```
import java.io.*;
```

Obtaining a stringified object reference

The new client won't use the Naming Service, so we don't need the CosNaming packages.

We use standard Java operations to read the file that has the object reference. Note, client and server programs must know the name of the file and where it is stored.

```
// Get the stringified object reference and destringify it.
   String filename=System.getProperty ("user.home")+ System.getProperty
   ("file.separator")+"RatesIOR";
   FileInputStream fis = new FileInputStream (filename);
   DataInputStream dis = new DataInputStream (fis) ;
   String ior = dis.readLine () ;
```

The client application now has a String object containing the stringified object reference.

Destringifying the Object Reference

To destringify the object reference in IOR, call the standard ORB method:

```
org.omg.CORBA.Object obj = orb.string_to_object(ior) ;
```

Finally, narrow the CORBA object to its proper type, so the client can invoke operations on it:

```
Rates ratesRef = RatesHelper.narrow(obj);
```

The rest of the client code is self-explanatory. The complete client code is shown in Listing 7-8.

Listing 7-8: The InterestRates CORBA Client

```
// Client.java, stringified object reference version
package cup.chap7.ex72;
import java.io.*;
import org.omg.CORBA.*;
import Interest.*;
public class Client {
    public static void main (String args[]) {
        try {
            // create and initialize the ORB
            ORB orb = ORB.init (args, null);
            // Get the stringified object reference and destringify it.
            String filename=System.getProperty ("user.home")+
                System.getProperty ("file.separator")+"RatesIOR";
            FileInputStream fis = new FileInputStream (filename);
            DataInputStream dis = new DataInputStream (fis) ;
            String ior = dis.readLine () ;
            org.omg.CORBA.Object obj = orb.string_to_object (ior) ;
            Rates ratesRef = RatesHelper.narrow (obj);
            // call the Interest server object and print results
            System.out.println ("Interest Rates provided by " +
                "The Lake Side Credit Union\n");
            System.out.println ("    Premium Checkings Interest = " +
                ratesRef.getPremiumChecking () + "%");
            System.out.println ("    Premium Savings Interest   = " +
                ratesRef.getPremiumSavings () + "%");
            System.out.println ("    Economy Checkings Interest = " +
                ratesRef.getEconomyChecking () + "%");
            System.out.println ("    Economy Savings Interest   = " +
                ratesRef.getEconomySavings () + "%");
        } catch (Exception e) {
            e.printStackTrace ();
        }
    }
}
```

Start the CORBA InterestRates server

```
F:\>
F:\>java cup.chap7.ex72.Server
```

Execute the InterestRates client

```
F:\>
F:\>java cup.chap7.ex72.Client
Interest Rates provided by The Lake Side Credit Union
     Premium Checkings Interest = 0.55%
     Premium Savings Interest   = 2.1%
     Economy Checkings Interest = 0.2%
     Economy Savings Interest   = 1.5%
F:\>
```

Common Object Services— The Naming Service

The COS Naming Service is an OMG-specified extension to the core CORBA standard, where COS stands for Common Object Service. This Naming Service allows an object to be published using a symbolic name and it allows client applications to obtain references to the object using a standard API. The COS Naming Service can reside on any host accessible within the network and enables applications to publish, lookup, and list CORBA object references from any network host.

A *namespace* is the collection of all names bound to a Naming Service. A namespace may contain naming context bindings to contexts located in another server. In such a case, the namespace is said to be a *federated namespace* because it is a collection of namespaces from multiple servers. An interesting point is the location of each context is transparent to the client applications; they have no knowledge that multiple servers are handling the resolution requests for an object.

Java 2 ships with a compliant implementation of the COS Naming Service, called `tnameserv`. The Java IDL COS Naming Service implementation supports transient bindings only, which means objects must be reregistered each time the Naming Service is restarted. The COS Naming Service implementations for Iona and Inprise are much more sophisticated and scalable because they support persistent bindings, load balancing, and customization. The JDK `tnameserv` Naming Service is more than adequate to get developers started on a project. When rolling out your applications, you want to purchase a commercial implementation to gain persistent naming and load-balancing capabilities.

A COS Naming Service stores object references in a hierarchical name space; much like a file system uses a directory structure to store files. Specifically, *bindings* maintain the association between a symbolic name and an object reference, while *naming contexts* are objects that organize the bindings into a naming hierarchy. Like the root directory in a file system, the *initial naming context* provides a known point to build binding hierarchies. To complete the file system analogy, a binding maps to a file and a naming context maps to a directory. Thus, a naming context can contain multiple bindings and other naming contexts.

Common Object Services— The Event Service

The Event Service package provides a facility that decouples the communication between objects. It provides a supplier-consumer communication model that allows multiple supplier objects to send data asynchronously to multiple consumer objects through an event channel. The supplier-consumer communication model allows an object to communicate an important change in state, such as a disk running out of free space, to any other objects that might be interested in such an event.

The flow of data into the event channel is handled by the supplier objects, while the flow of data out of the event channel is handled by the consumer objects. The event channel is both a consumer of events and a supplier of events. The data communicated between suppliers and consumers are represented by the `Any` class, allowing any CORBA type to be passed in a type-safe manner. Supplier and consumer objects communicate through the event channel using standard CORBA requests.

Proxy consumers and suppliers

Consumers and suppliers are completely decoupled from one another through the use of *proxy objects*. Instead of directly interacting with each other, they obtain a proxy object from the `EventChannel` and communicate with it. Supplier objects obtain a *consumer proxy* and consumer objects obtain a *supplier proxy*. The `EventChannel` facilitates the data transfer between consumer and supplier proxy objects.

Communication models

The Event Service provides both a pull and a push communication model for suppliers and consumers. In the *push model*, supplier objects control the flow of data by pushing it *to* consumers. In the *pull model*, consumer objects control the flow of data by pulling data *from* the supplier.

The `EventChannel` insulates suppliers and consumers from having to know which model is being used by other objects on the channel. This means a pull supplier can provide data to a push consumer and a push supplier can provide data to a pull consumer.

Push model

The push model is the more common of the two communication models. An example use of the push model is a supplier that monitors available free space on a disk and notifies interested consumers when the disk is filling up. The push supplier sends data to its ProxyPushConsumer in response to events it is monitoring.

The push consumer spends most of its time in an event loop, waiting for data to arrive from the ProxyPushSupplier. The EventChannel facilitates the transfer of data from the ProxyPushSupplier to the ProxyPushConsumer.

Pull model

In the pull model, the event channel regularly pulls data from a supplier object, puts the data in a queue, and makes it available to be pulled by a consumer object. An example of a pull consumer would be one or more network monitors that periodically poll a network router for statistics.

The pull supplier spends most of its time in an event loop, waiting for data requests to be received from the ProxyPullConsumer. The pull consumer requests data from the ProxyPullSupplier when it is ready for more data. The EventChannel pulls data from the supplier to a queue and makes it available to the ProxyPullSupplier.

Putting It All Together—The Bank Example

In this section, we build a sample client application that can query and perform operations on the balance in a bank checking account.

Define the IDL

The *Bank.idl file* defines the Bank module that contains two interfaces: The Account interface provides methods for setting and obtaining the current balance; the CheckingsAccount interface provides a method that opens, credits to, debits from, and creates accounts with a specified name, and returns an Account object reference. The Account object reference can then be used to obtain the balance in the account.

User-defined exceptions

The Bank.idl defines a user exception called InvalidTransaction. This exception is raised by many of the methods defined in this file in various interfaces. User-defined exceptions map to final Java classes that extend org.omg.CORBA.UserException. The idltojava compiler automatically generates a Java class for each exception you define in the IDL. The class generated by the idltojava compiler provides instance variables for the fields of exception, as well as constructors.

Listing 7-9: The Bank Account CORBA IDL

```
module Bank {
    exception InvalidTransaction {
      string explanation;
    };
    interface Account {
      float getBalance ();
      void  setBalance (in float balance) raises (InvalidTransaction);
    };
    interface CheckingsAccount {
      Account open(in string name);
      Account create(in string name, in float balance);
      Account credit(in string name, in float amount)
        raises (InvalidTransaction);
      Account debit(in string name, in float amount)
        raises (InvalidTransaction);
    };
};
```

Because the Bank.idl file requires no special handling, you can compile it by typing the following command:

```
F:\>idltojava Bank.idl
```

The generated code

Because Java allows only one public interface or class per file, compiling the Bank.idl file generates several java files. These files are stored in a generated subdirectory named Bank, which is the `module` name specified in the IDL file. IDL modules are mapped to Java packages, so all the files listed in the following will be part of the `Bank` package:

- `Account.java`—The `Account` interface declaration.
- `CheckingsAccount.java`—The `CheckingsAccount` interface declaration.
- `InvalidTransaction.java`—The `InvalidTransaction` interface declaration.
- `AccountHelper.java`—Declares the `AccountHelper` class, which contains an `AccountHelper`. This class defines helpful utility functions.
- `CheckingsAccountHelper.java`—Declares the `CheckingsAccountHelper` class. This class defines helpful utility functions.
- `InvalidTransactionHelper.java`—Declares the `InvalidTransactionHelper` class. This class defines helpful utility functions.
- `AccountHolder.java`—Declares the `AccountHolder` class, which provides a holder for passing parameters.
- `CheckingsAccountHolder.java`—Declares the `CheckingsAccountHolder` class, which provides a holder for passing parameters.

- InvalidTransactionHolder.java—Declares the InvalidTransactionHolder class, which provides a holder for passing parameters.
- _AccountStub.java—Stub code for the Account object on the client side.
- _CheckingsAccountStub.java—Stub code for the CheckingsAccount object on the client side.
- _AccountImplBase.java—Skeleton code (implementation base code) for the Account object implementation on the server side.
- _CheckingsAccountImplBase.java—Skeleton code (implementation base code) for the CheckingsAccount object implementation on the server side.

Develop the client

The Client class implements the client application that obtains the current balance of a bank account. The program performs the following steps:

1. Initializes the Object Request Broker.
2. Binds to a CheckingsAccount.
3. Requests the CheckingsAccount to open the Account with the specified name. If no account name is supplied, a default name is used.
4. Gets the balance of the Account using the object reference returned by the methods of the server.
5. Prints the balance.

Listing 7-10: The Bank Account CORBA Client

```
// Client.java
package cup.chap7.ex73;
public class Client {
    public static void main (String[] args) {
        try {
        // Initialize the ORB.
        org.omg.CORBA.ORB orb = org.omg.CORBA.ORB.init (args,null);
            // Get a reference to the Naming Service
            org.omg.CORBA.Object nameServiceObj =
            orb.resolve_initial_references ("NameService");
            if ( nameServiceObj == null ) {
                System.out.println ("nameServiceObj = null");
                return;
            }
            // Narrow the object
            org.omg.CosNaming.NamingContext nameService =
            org.omg.CosNaming.NamingContextHelper.narrow (nameServiceObj);
```

continues

Listing 7-10: continued

```
            if( nameService == null ) {
                System.out.println ("nameService = null");
                return;
            }
            // Locate an object called CheckingsAccount
            // relative to the initial namecontext
            org.omg.CosNaming.NameComponent[] accountName = {
                new org.omg.CosNaming.NameComponent ("CheckingsAccount", "")
            };
            Bank.CheckingsAccount checkingsAccount =
            Bank.CheckingsAccountHelper.narrow (
                nameService.resolve (accountName));
            nameService.rebind (accountName, checkingsAccount);
            // use args[1] as the account name, or a default.
            String op = args.length > 0 ? args[0] : "-c";
            String name = args.length > 1 ? args[1] : "Athul";
            float amount = args.length > 2 ?
                (new Float (args[2])).floatValue () : 1000;
            // Request the CheckingsAccount to open a named account.
            Bank.Account account = null;
            try {
                if (op.equals("-c"))
                account = checkingsAccount.create (name, amount);
                if (op.equals("-o"))
                    account = checkingsAccount.open (name);
                if (op.equals("-cr"))
                    account = checkingsAccount.credit (name, amount);
                if (op.equals("-db"))
                    account = checkingsAccount.debit (name, amount);
            } catch (Exception e) { e.printStackTrace (); }
            // Get the balance of the account.
            float balance = account.getBalance ();
            // Print out the balance.
            System.out.println ("The balance in " + name + "'s account is $" + balance);
        } catch (Exception e) { e.printStackTrace (); }
    }
}
```

Code the AccountImpl servant

The AccountImpl class in this file extends Bank._AccountImplBase class generated in the Bank package. This class contains methods to set or get an account Balance. If the Balance goes below zero, it throws an InvalidTransaction Exception.

Listing 7-11: The AccountImpl Class Definition

```
// AccountImpl.java
package cup.chap7.ex73;
import java.util.*;
public class AccountImpl extends Bank._AccountImplBase {
    private float _balance;
    public AccountImpl (float balance) {
        super ();
        _balance = balance;
        System.out.println ("Created Account Server");
    }
    public float getBalance () { return _balance; }
    public void setBalance (float amount)
        throws Bank.InvalidTransaction {
        if (amount < 0)
            throw new Bank.InvalidTransaction ();
        else
            _balance = amount;
    }
}
```

Code the CheckingAccountImpl servant

The CheckingsAccountImpl class in this file extends Bank._CheckingsAccountImplBase class generated in the Bank package. This class provides the actual implementation of the open, create, credit, and debit method used to obtain, create, credit, or debit an Account. The CheckingsAccountImpl uses a Dictionary to contain all the accounts.

When a request to create an account is received, the create method does the following:

- Looks for an Account with a matching name.
- If a match is not found, a new Account is created with that name and balance. A new object is activated.
- An object reference to the new or existing Account is returned.

All the other code is straightforward and needs no explanation.

Listing 7-12: The CheckingAccountsImpl CORBA Servant Class Definition

```
// CheckingsAccountImpl.java
package cup.chap7.ex73;
import java.util.*;
public class CheckingsAccountImpl
    extends Bank._CheckingsAccountImplBase {
    private Dictionary _accountsTable    = new Hashtable ();
    private Random    _random            = new Random ();
    public CheckingsAccountImpl () {
```

continues

Listing 7-12: continued

```
        super ();
        System.out.println ("Created CheckingsAccount Server");
    }
    public synchronized Bank.Account open(String name) {
        // Lookup the account in the account dictionary.
        Bank.Account account = (Bank.Account) _accountsTable.get (name);
        // Return the account.
        return account;
    }
    public synchronized Bank.Account credit(String name, float amount)
        throws Bank.InvalidTransaction {
        // Lookup the account in the account dictionary.
        Bank.Account account = (Bank.Account) _accountsTable.get (name);
        if (amount > 0)
            account.setBalance (account.getBalance ()+amount);
        // Return the account.
        return account;
    }
    public synchronized Bank.Account debit(String name, float amount)
        throws Bank.InvalidTransaction {
        // Lookup the account in the account dictionary.
        Bank.Account account = (Bank.Account) _accountsTable.get (name);
        if (amount > 0)
            account.setBalance (account.getBalance ()-amount);
        // Return the account.
        return account;
    }
    public synchronized Bank.Account create(String name, float balance) {
        // Lookup the account in the account dictionary.
        Bank.Account account = (Bank.Account) _accountsTable.get (name);
        // If the account is not in the dictionary, create an account.
        if (account == null) {
            // Create the account implementation, given the balance.
            account = new AccountImpl (balance);
            // Make the object available to the ORB.
            // Export the newly created object
            _orb ().connect (account);
            System.out.println ("Created " + name + "'s account: " + account);
            // Save the account in the account dictionary.
            _accountsTable.put (name, account);
        }
        // Return the account.
```

Listing 7-12: continued

```
            return account;
        }
    }
```

Develop the server class

Just as with the client, many of the files used in implementing the bank server are contained in the Bank package generated by the idl2java compiler. The program performs the following steps:

1. Initializes the Object Request Broker.
2. Initializes the Portable Object Adaptor.
3. Creates an CheckingsAccount object.
4. Activates the newly created object.
5. Prints a status message.
6. Waits for incoming client requests.

Listing 7-13: The Bank Account CORBA Server Application

```
// Server.java
package cup.chap7.ex73;
import org.omg.CosNaming.*;
public class Server {
    public static void main (String[] args) {
        try {
            // Initialize the ORB.
            org.omg.CORBA.ORB orb = org.omg.CORBA.ORB.init (args,null);
            System.out.println ("Orb Initialized.");
            // Create the account CheckingsAccount object.
            Bank.CheckingsAccount checkingsAccount = new CheckingsAccountImpl();
            if (checkingsAccount == null) {
                System.out.println ("CheckingsAccount = null");
                return;
            }
            // Export the newly created object
            orb.connect (checkingsAccount);
            System.out.println ("CheckingsAccountServer is connected.");
            // Get a reference to the Naming Service
            org.omg.CORBA.Object nameServiceObj =
            orb.resolve_initial_references ("NameService");
            if (nameServiceObj == null) {
                System.out.println ("nameServiceObj = null");
```

continues

Listing 7-13: continued

```
                return;
            }
            // Narrow the object
            org.omg.CosNaming.NamingContext nameService =
            org.omg.CosNaming.NamingContextHelper.narrow (nameServiceObj);
            if (nameService == null) {
                System.out.println ("nameService = null");
                return;
            }
            // bind the CheckingsAccount object in the Naming Service
            org.omg.CosNaming.NameComponent[] accountName = {
                new org.omg.CosNaming.NameComponent ("CheckingsAccount", "")};
            nameService.rebind (accountName, checkingsAccount);
            // Wait forever for current thread to die
            Thread.currentThread ().join ();
        } catch (Exception e) { e.printStackTrace (); }
    }
}
```

Run the Naming Service

```
F:\>
F:\>tnameserv
Initial Naming Context:
IOR:000000000000002849444c3a6f6d672e6f72672f436f734e616d696e672f4e616d696e67
    436f6e746578743a312e300000000000010000000000000030000100000000000008686f6d
    655f706300108c000000000018afabcafe000000025ddcc3cd00000008000000000000
    000
TransientNameServer: setting port for initial object references to: 900
```

Run the CheckingAccount server

When the Checkings Account server is up and running, a typical session shows up like this on the window:

```
F:\>
F:\>java cup.chap7.ex73.Server
Orb Initialized.
Created CheckingsAccount Server
CheckingsAccountServer is connected.
Created Account Server
Created Athul's account:
    cup.chap7.ex73.AccountImpl:com.sun.CORBA.idl.GenericCORBAClientSC@dc47ae34
```

```
Created Account Server
Created Arjun's account:
    cup.chap7.ex73.AccountImpl:com.sun.CORBA.idl.GenericCORBAClientSC@d08fae34
```

Run the client

When the client is executed, typical sessions show up like this on the window:

```
F:\>
F:\>java cup.chap7.ex73.Client
The balance in Athul's account is $1000.0
F:\>java cup.chap7.ex73.Client -c Arjun 2000
The balance in Arjun's account is $2000.0
F:\>e:\java\jdk1.2\bin\java cup.chap7.ex73.Client -o Arjun
The balance in Arjun's account is $2000.0
F:\>e:\java\jdk1.2\bin\java cup.chap7.ex73.Client -cr Arjun 100
The balance in Arjun's account is $2100.0
F:\>e:\java\jdk1.2\bin\java cup.chap7.ex73.Client -db Arjun 100
The balance in Arjun's account is $2000.0
F:\>
```

You can always refer to my Homepage at http://www.execpc.com/~gopalan for more CORBA source code. Another good resource is the comp-object-corba@omg.org mailing list from OMG. You can get the CORBA specs from http://www.omg.org.

Comparing CORBA and RMI

In this section, we examine the differences between these two models from a programmatic and architectural viewpoint. At the end of this section, you can better appreciate the merits and innards of each of the distributed object paradigms.

Application sample: the StockMarket server and client

The StockMarket Server reports the stock price of any given symbol. It has a method called get_price() to get the stock value of a particular symbol.

Each of these implementations defines an IStockMarket interface. They expose a get_price() method that returns a float value indicating the stock value of the symbol passed in. We list the sources from four files. The first set of files is the IDL and Java files that define the interface and its exposed methods. The second set of files shows how the client invokes methods on these interfaces by acquiring references to the server object. The third set of files shows the server object implementations. The fourth set of files shows the main program implementations that start up the remote server Objects for CORBA and Java/RMI.

Specifying the Remote Interface

Whenever a client needs some service from a remote distributed object, it invokes a method implemented by the remote object. The service the remote distributed object (server) provides is encapsulated as an object and the remote object's interface is described in an Interface Definition Language (IDL). The interfaces specified in the IDL file serve as a contract between a remote object server and its clients. Clients can thus interact with these remote object servers by invoking methods defined in the IDL.

Listing 7-14: (a) The SimpleStocks CORBA IDL and (b) the SimpleStocks RMI Interface Listing

(a) CORBA IDL

```
module SimpleStocks {
    interface StockMarket {
        float get_price(in string symbol);
        };
};

StockMarket.idl
```

(b) Java/RMI Interface Definition

```
package SimpleStocks;
import java.rmi.*;
import java.util.*;
public interface StockMarket extends
    java.rmi.Remote {
        float get_price(String symbol )
        throws RemoteException;
}
StockMarket.java
```

CORBA—Both CORBA and Java/RMI support multiple inheritance at the IDL or interface level. Both CORBA and Java/RMI can specify exceptions in the IDLs. In CORBA, the IDL compiler generates type information for each method in an interface and stores it in the Interface Repository (IR). A client can thus query the IR to get run-time information about a particular interface and then use that information to create and invoke a method on the remote CORBA Server Object dynamically through the Dynamic Invocation Interface (DII). Similarly, on the server side, the Dynamic Skeleton Interface (DSI) enables a client to invoke an operation of a remote CORBA Server Object that has no compile time knowledge of the type of object it is implementing. The CORBA IDL file shows the `StockMarket` interface with the `get_price()` method. When an IDL compiler compiles this IDL file, it generates files for stubs and skeletons.

RMI—Note, unlike CORBA, Java/RMI uses a .java file to define its remote interface. This interface ensures type consistency between the Java/RMI client and the Java/RMI Server Object. Every remotable server object in Java/RMI has to extend the `java.rmi.Remote` class. Similarly, any method that can be remotely invoked in Java/RMI may throw a `java.rmi.RemoteException`. `java.rmi.RemoteException` is the superclass of many more RMI-specific exception classes. We define an interface called `StockMarket`, which extends the `java.rmi.Remote` class. Also notice the `get_price()` method throws a `java.rmi.RemoteException`.

How remoting works

To invoke a remote method, the client makes a call to the client proxy. The client side proxy packs the call parameters into a request message and invokes a wire protocol like IIOP (in CORBA) or JRMP (in Java/RMI) to ship the message to the server. At the server side, the wire protocol delivers the message to the server side stub. The server side stub then unpacks the message and calls the actual method on the object. In both CORBA and Java/RMI, the client stub is called the *stub* or the *proxy* and the server stub is called the *skeleton*.

Implementing the Distributed Object Client

The **CORBA client** first must initialize the CORBA ORB by making a call to `ORB orb = ORB.init(args, null)`.

We will use the CORBA Naming Service to bind to the server object. We first look up a NameService and obtain a CORBA object reference. We use the returned `CORBA.Object` to narrow down to a naming context.

```
NamingContext ncRef = NamingContextHelper.narrow(
                          orb.resolve_initial_references("NameService"));
```

We now create a NameComponent and narrow down to the server object reference by resolving the name in the naming context that was returned to us by the COSNaming (Common Object Services—Naming) helper classes.

```
NameComponent path[] = {new NameComponent("NASDAQ", "")};
    StockMarket market = StockMarketHelper.narrow(ncRef.resolve(path));
```

Once the client has acquired a valid remote object reference to the CORBA Server Object, it can call into the server object's methods as if the server object resided in the client's address space.

Listing 7-15: The StockMarketClient Class, a CORBA Client Listing

```
// StockMarketClient
import org.omg.CORBA.*;
import org.omg.CosNaming.*;
import SimpleStocks.*;
public class StockMarketClient {
    public static void main (String[] args) {
        try {
            ORB orb = ORB.init (args, null);
            NamingContext ncRef = NamingContextHelper.narrow (
                        orb.resolve_initial_references("NameService"));
            NameComponent path[] = {new NameComponent("NASDAQ", "")};
            StockMarket market = StockMarketHelper.narrow(ncRef.resolve(path));
            System.out.println("Price of MY COMPANY is " +
                        market.get_price("MY_COMPANY"));
```

continues

Listing 7-15: continued

```
            }
            catch( SystemException e ) {
                e.printStackTrace();
            }
        }
    }
```

The **Java/RMI client** first installs a security manager before doing any remote calls. You do this by making a call to `System.setSecurityManager()`. As a convenience, JavaSoft has provided an `RMISecurityManager` so that you would not be required to write your own. JavaSoft does not force you to use its own `RMISecurityManager`, however. You can write your own security manager and install it if you choose.

Note

Setting a security manager for the use of Java/RMI is not mandatory. The reason to do this is so the Java/RMI client can handle serialized objects for which the client does not have a corresponding class file in its local CLASSPATH. If the security manager is set to the `RMISecurityManager`, the client can download and instantiate class files from the Java/RMI Server. This mechanism is actually fairly important to Java/RMI, as it allows the server to generate subclasses for any `Serializable` object and to provide the code to handle these subclasses to the client.

Using Java/RMI without setting the security manager is entirely possible, *as long as the client has access to definitions for all objects that might be returned.* Java/RMI has the ability to handle the passing of any object at any time using Serialization and class file download. This is possible only because the JVM provides a portable and secure environment for passing around Java byte codes. These Java Byte Codes form the Java executable from which Java objects can be reconstructed at run time, if required.

The Java/RMI client then instantiates a Java/RMI Server Object by binding to a server object's remote reference through the call to `Naming.Lookup()`.

```
StockMarket market = (StockMarket)Naming.lookup("rmi://localhost/NASDAQ");
```

Once the client has acquired a valid object reference to the Java/RMI Server Object, it can call into the server object's methods as if the server object resided in the client's address space.

Listing 7-16: The StockMarketClient RMI Client

```
// StockMarketClient
import java.rmi.*;
import java.rmi.registry.*;
import SimpleStocks.*;
public class StockMarketClient {
    public static void main (String[] args)throws Exception {
        if (System.getSecurityManager() == null) {
            System.setSecurityManager(new RMISecurityManager());
        }
        StockMarket market = (StockMarket)Naming.lookup("rmi://localhost/NASDAQ");
        System.out.println( "The price of MY COMPANY is "
                + market.get_price("MY_COMPANY") );
    }
}
```

Implementing the Distributed Object Server

All the classes required for CORBA are defined in the `org.omg.CORBA` package. The **CORBA Server Object** shown in the following extends the `_StockMarketImplBase` class that is a skeleton class generated by our CORBA IDL compiler. The `StockMarketImpl` class and the `get_price()` method are declared as public so they will be accessible from outside the package. The `StockMarketImpl` class implements all the operations declared in our CORBA IDL file. We need to provide a constructor that takes in a name of type `String` for our CORBA Object Server class. The reason is the name of the CORBA Server Class must be passed on to the `_StockMarketImplBase` class object, so it can be associated with that name with all the CORBA services.

Listing 7-17: The StockMarketImpl CORBA Server

```
// StockMarketServer
import org.omg.CORBA.*;
import SimpleStocks.*;
public class StockMarketImpl extends _StockMarketImplBase {
    public float get_price( String symbol ) {
        float price = 0;
        for(int i = 0; i < symbol.length(); i++) {
            price += (int) symbol.charAt( i );
        }
        price /= 5;
        return price;
    }
    public StockMarketImpl( String name ) { super( name ); }
}
```

All the classes required for Java/RMI are defined in the java.rmi package. The **Java/RMI Server Object** shown extends the UnicastRemoteObject class that has all of Java/RMI's remoting methods defined and implements the StockMarket interface. The StockMarketImpl class and the get_price() method are declared as public so, they will be accessible from outside the package. The StockMarketImpl class implements all the operations declared in our Java/RMI interface file. We need to provide a constructor that takes in a name of type String for our Java/RMI Object Server class because the name of the Java/RMI Server class is used to establish a binding and associate a public name with this Java/RMI Server Object in the RMIRegistry. The get_price() method is capable of throwing a RemoteException because it is a remotable method.

Listing 7-18: The StockMarketImpl RMI Server

```
// StockMarketServer
package SimpleStocks;
import java.rmi.*;
import java.rmi.server.UnicastRemoteObject;
public class StockMarketImpl extends UnicastRemoteObject
    implements StockMarket {
    public float get_price( String symbol ) {
        float price = 0;
        for( int i = 0; i < symbol.length(); i++ ) {
            price += (int) symbol.charAt( i );
        }
        price /= 5;
        return price;
    }
    public StockMarketImpl( String name ) throws RemoteException {
        try {
            Naming.rebind( name, this );
        } catch( Exception e ) { e.printStackTrace(); }
    }
}
```

The server main programs

The first thing to be done by the **CORBA server main** program is to initialize the CORBA ORB using ORB.init(). An Object Adapter (OA) sits on top of the ORB and is responsible for connecting the CORBA Server Object implementation to the CORBA ORB. Object Adapters provide services like generation and interpretation of object references, method invocation, object activation and deactivation, and mapping object references to implementations. You have to initialize the Portable Object Adapter (POA). We then create the CORBA Server Object with the call

```
StockMarketImpl stockMarketImpl = new StockMarketImpl("NASDAQ");
```

Note, we pass in a name "NASDAQ" by which our object is identified by all CORBA services. Because we are using the CORBA Object Service's Naming Service for our clients to connect to us, we must bind our server object with a Naming Service, so clients can find us. The following code helps us to do this:

```
NamingContext ncRef = NamingContextHelper.narrow(
            orb.resolve_initial_references("NameService"));
NameComponent path[] = {new NameComponent("NASDAQ", "")};
ncRef.rebind(path, stockMarketImpl);
```

The next statement ensures our main program sleeps on a daemon thread and does not fall off and exit the program.

```
// Wait forever for current thread to die
    Thread.currentThread().join();
```

We now enter into an event loop and we are in that loop until the main program is shut down.

Listing 7-19: StockMarketServer, The CORBA Server Main Program

```
// StockMarketServer Main
import org.omg.CORBA.*;
import org.omg.CosNaming.*;
import SimpleStocks.*;
public class StockMarketServer
{
    public static void main(String[] args) {
        try {
            ORB orb = ORB.init(args, null);
            BOA boa = orb.BOA_init();
            StockMarketImpl stockMarketImpl = new StockMarketImpl("NASDAQ");
            NamingContext ncRef = NamingContextHelper.narrow(
                    orb.resolve_initial_references("NameService"));
            NameComponent path[] = {new NameComponent("NASDAQ", "")};
            ncRef.rebind(path, stockMarketImpl);
            // Wait forever for current thread to die
            Thread.currentThread().join();
        }
        catch( Exception e ) { e.printStackTrace(); }
    }
}
```

Regarding the **Java/RMI server main**, the Java/RMI client will first have to install a security manager before doing any remote calls. You do this by making a call to System.setSecurityManager(). We then create the Java/RMI Server Object with the call

```
StockMarketImpl stockMarketImpl = new StockMarketImpl("NASDAQ");
```

and remain there until we are shut down.

Listing 7-20: StockMarketServer, The RMI Main Program

```
// StockMarketServer Main
import java.rmi.*;
import java.rmi.server.UnicastRemoteObject;
import SimpleStocks.*;
public class StockMarketServer {
    public static void main(String[] args) throws Exception {
        if(System.getSecurityManager() == null) {
            System.setSecurityManager(new RMISecurityManager());
        }
        StockMarketImpl stockMarketImpl = new StockMarketImpl("NASDAQ");
    }
}
```

Summary

The architectures of CORBA and Java/RMI provide mechanisms for transparent invocation and accessing of remote distributed objects. Although the mechanisms they employ to achieve remoting may be different, the approach each of them takes is more or less similar. Table 7-3 shows a detailed comparison of the CORBA and Java/RMI models.

Table 7-3: A Detailed comparison of the CORBA and Java/RMI models

CORBA	Java/RMI
Every interface inherits from CORBA.Object.	Every server object implements java.rmi.Remote (Note: java.rmi.UnicastRemoteObject is merely a convenience class that happens to call UnicastRemoteObject.exportObject(this) in its constructors and provide equals() and hashCode() methods).
Uniquely identifies remote server objects through object references (objref), which serves as the object handle at run time. These object references can be externalized (persistified) into strings, which can then be converted back into an objref.	Uniquely identifies remote server objects with the ObjID, which serves as the object handle at run time. When you .toString() a remote reference, there will be a substring, such as "[1db35d7f:d32ec5b8d3:-8000, 0]" which is unique to the remote server object.
Uniquely identifies an interface using the interface name and uniquely identifies a named implementation of the server object by its mapping to a name in the Implementation Repository.	Uniquely identifies an interface using the interface name and uniquely identifies a named implementation of the server object by its mapping to a URL in the Registry.
The remote server object reference generation is performed on the wire protocol by the Object Adapter.	The remote server object reference generation is performed by the call to the method UnicastRemoteObject.exportObject(this)
The constructor implicitly performs common tasks like object registration, skeleton instantiation, and so forth.	The RMIRegistry performs common tasks like object registration through the Naming class. UnicastRemoteObject.exportObject(this) method performs skeleton instantiation and it is implicitly called in the object constructor.
Uses the Internet Inter-ORB Protocol (IIOP) as its underlying remoting protocol.	Uses the Java Remote Method Protocol (JRMP) as its underlying remoting protocol (at least for now).
When a client object needs to activate a server object, it binds to a naming or a trader service. (Note: the client can get a server reference in other ways, but we won't go into that here.).	When a client object needs a server object reference, it has to do a lookup() on the remote server object's URL name.

continues

Table 7-3: continued

CORBA	Java/RMI
The mapping of Object Name to its Implementation is handled by the Implementation Repository.	The mapping of Object Name to its Implementation is handled by the RMIRegistry.
The type information for methods is held in the Interface Repository.	Any type of information is held by the Object itself, which can be queried using Reflection and Introspection.
The responsibility of locating an object implementation falls on the Object Request Broker (ORB).	The responsibility of locating an object implementation falls on the Java Virtual Machine (JVM).
The responsibility of locating an object implementation falls on the Object Adapter (OA)—either the Basic Object Adapter (BOA) or the Portable Object Adapter (POA).	The responsibility of activating an object implementation falls on the Java Virtual Machine (JVM).
When passing parameters between the client and the remote server object, all interface types are passed by reference. All other objects are passed by value, including highly complex data types.	When passing parameters between the client and the remote server object, all objects implementing interfaces extending `java.rmi.Remote` are passed by remote reference. All other objects are passed by value.
Does not attempt to perform general-purpose distributed garbage collection.	Attempts to perform distributed garbage collection of remote server objects using the mechanisms bundled in the JVM.
Complex types that will cross interface boundaries must be declared in the IDL.	Any Serializable Java object can be passed as a parameter across processes.
Will run on any platform as long as there is a CORBA ORB implementation for that platform (like Inprise's VisiBroker).	Will run on any platform as long as there is a Java Virtual Machine implementation for that platform (provided by many companies, including JavaSoft and Microsoft).
Because this is just a specification, diverse programming languages can be used to code these objects as long as there are ORB libraries you can use to code in that language.	Because it relies heavily on Java Object Serialization, these objects can only be coded in the Java language.
Exception handling is taken care of by Exception Objects. When a distributed object throws an Exception Object, the ORB transparently serializes and marshals it across the wire.	Allows throwing exceptions that are then serialized and marshaled across the wire.

Chapter 8

Enterprise JavaBeans

Writing distributed enterprise applications has always been a significant challenge, but this once Herculean task has been somewhat ameliorated with the advancement of component-based programming in general. For example, by increasing program modularity, you can now compose a behemoth application from multiple functionally independent modules. This not only enables you to assemble complex systems using an assembly-line approach, but also greatly increases the reusability of the modules themselves.

Although using components enhances the modularity and natural distribution of applications in general, they still present some interesting challenges. For example, in days of old, when a monolithic program failed, it was simply restarted as a unit. But, today, with a modular system, when a failure of any one component occurs, the challenge is to ensure faults are isolated to limit their propagation and that it does not corrupt others. This is more complicated than it sounds with distributed applications, however, as the components can reside anywhere on the network. In addition, because enterprises are essentially heterogeneous environments, the presence of multiple operating systems and platforms that host the different components adds a new level of complexity.

Clearly, a technology like Java, with its promise of the "write once run anywhere," can significantly mitigate many of the problems associated with enterprise distributed systems development. This chapter is devoted to understanding the implications and architecture of an enabling server-side component technology—Enterprise JavaBeans (EJBs)—and presents examples of how to use this technology to implement real-life, distributed enterprise solutions.

Backgrounder— The Relevant Technologies

Before we explore EJBs, you should first understand what enterprise applications are all about. Although covering the entire spectrum of details is impossible, we'll examine some of the more important concepts before going in for an enterprise solution.

What are Transactions?

A transaction is the most important concept you should be aware of when dealing with enterprise applications. To a user, a *transaction* is a single change event that either happens or doesn't happen. To system implementers, a *transaction* is a programming style that enables them to code modules that can participate in distributed computations. To illustrate this concept, assume you want to transfer money from a savings account into a checking account. In this scenario, it is critical that both the accounts are changed from a successful transaction and neither is affected from an unsuccessful one. You cannot afford to have your money vaporize if crediting your checking account fails for any reason after the debit on your savings account! Although this may sound like a fairly straightforward request, making this work in a distributed system without deploying some form of transaction control is hard—computers can fail and messages can easily get lost.

Transactions provide a way to bundle a set of operations into an atomic execution unit.

This atomic, all or nothing property is not new: it appears throughout life. For example, a minister conducting a marriage ceremony first asks the bride and groom, "Do you take this person to be your spouse?" Only if they both respond "I do" does the minister pronounce them married and *commit* the transaction. In short, within any transaction, several independent entities must agree before the deal is done. If any party disagrees, the deal is off and the independent entities are reverted back to their original state. In transactions, this is known as a *rollover operation.*

Transactions are essential for distributed applications. Further, transactions provide modular execution, which complements a component technology's modular programming.

The ACID properties

All transactions subscribe to the following "ACID" properties:

- *Atomicity:* A transaction either commits or rollbacks. If a transaction commits, all its effects remain. If it rollbacks, then all its effects are undone. For example, in renaming an object, both the new name is created and the old name is deleted (commit), or nothing changes (rollback).

- *Consistency:* A transaction always leads to a correct transformation of the system state by preserving the state invariance. For example, within a transaction adding an element to a doubly linked list, all four forward and backward pointers are updated.
- *Isolation:* Concurrent transactions are isolated from the updates of other incomplete transactions. This property is also often called *serializability*. For example, a second transaction traversing a doubly linked list already undergoing modification by a first transaction, will see only completed changes and be isolated from any noncommitted changes of the first transaction.
- *Durability:* If a transaction commits, its effects will be permanent after the transaction commits. In fact, the effects remain even in the face of system failures.

The application must decide what consistency is and bracket its computation to delimit these consistent transformations. The job of the transactional resource managers is to provide consistent, isolated, and durable transformations of the objects they manage. If the transactions are distributed among multiple computers, the two-phase commit protocol is used to make these transactions atomic and durable.

The Java Transaction Service

The Java Transaction Service (JTS) plays the role of a *transaction coordinator* for all the constituent components of the EJB architecture. In JTS terminology, the director is called the *transaction manager*. The participants in the transaction that implement transaction-protected resources, such as relational databases, are called *resource managers*. When an application begins a transaction, it creates a transaction object that represents the transaction. The application then invokes the resource managers to perform the work of the transaction. As the transaction progresses, the transaction manager keeps track of each of the resource managers enlisted in the transaction.

The application's first call to each resource manager identifies the current transaction. For example, if the application is using a relational database, it calls the JDBC interface, which associates the transaction object with the JDBC connection. Thereafter, all calls made over that connection are performed on behalf of the database transaction until it ends.

Typically, the application completes the transaction by invoking a `xa_commit()` method and the transaction is said to commit. If the application is unable to complete for any reason, it performs a rollover by calling the `xa_rollback()` method, which undoes the transaction's actions. If the application fails, the JTS aborts the transaction. When the application successfully completes the transaction's work, it calls the JTS to commit the transaction. The JTS then goes through a two-phase commit protocol to get all the enlisted resource managers to commit.

Two-phase commits

The *two-phase commit protocol* ensures all the resource managers either commit a transaction or abort it. In the first phase, the JTS asks each resource manager if it is prepared to commit. If all the participants affirm, then, in the second phase, the JTS broadcasts a commit message to all of them. If any part of the transaction fails—for instance, if a resource manager fails to respond to the prepare request or if a resource manager responds negatively—then the JTS notifies all the resource managers the transaction is aborted. This is the essence of the two-phase commit protocol.

What is a naming service?

A naming system provides a natural, understandable way of identifying and associating names with data. For example, the DOS file system uses a naming system for associating data with folder and file names, while a relational database uses a naming system for associating data with column and table names. Naming systems enable humans to interact with complex computer addressing systems by associating data and objects with simple, understandable names.

A *naming service* is a dedicated piece of software that manages a naming system or *namespace.* Naming services often run independently of the computer systems that use them. In other words, they provide the service of associating names with data or objects—a naming system—but are independent and can serve any system that understands their protocol and can connect to them.

Directory and naming services usually employ two layers: a client layer and a server layer. The server is responsible for maintaining and resolving the actual name—object bindings, controlling access, and managing operations performed on the structure of the directory service. The client acts as an interface that applications use to communicate with the directory service.

The Java Naming and Directory Interface

The Java Naming and Directory Interface (JNDI) shown in Figure 8-1 is a client API that provides naming and directory functionality. JNDI is specified in Java and is designed to provide an abstraction that represents those elements most common to naming and directory service clients. JNDI is not intended as an alternative to established naming and directory services. Instead, it is designed to provide a common interface for accessing existing services like DNS, NDS, LDAP, CORBA, or RMI.

JNDI provides an interface that hides the implementation details of different naming and directory services behind the JNDI API. This allows multiple directory services to coexist and even cooperate within the same JNDI client. Using JNDI, a user can navigate across several directory and naming services while working with seemingly only one logical *federated* naming service.

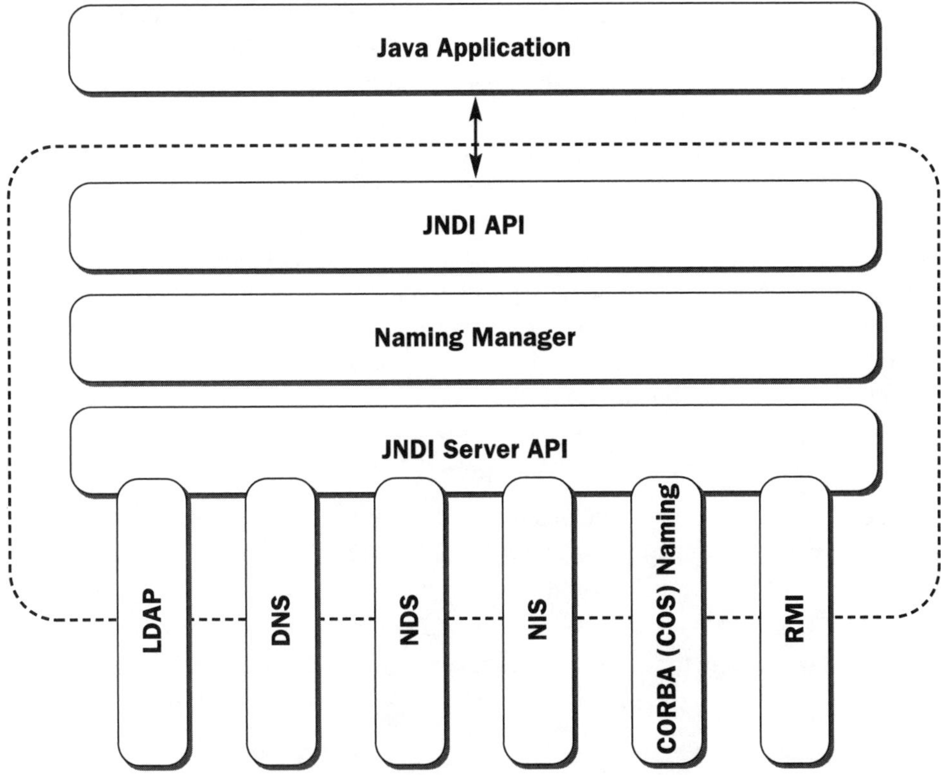

Figure 8-1: The Java Naming and Directory Interface

JavaBeans—the generic component model

A *component model* defines an environment that supports reusable application components. Java defines a generic component model called JavaBeans for linking together pieces of code like Lego building blocks, to form an applet or application. Today, hundreds of JavaBean components are readily available, with a number of tools supporting their use.

Any object that conforms to certain basic rules as defined in the JavaBeans API can be a JavaBean. In addition to having a default constructor and being serializable, a JavaBean exports properties, events, and methods. Properties indicate the internal state of a Bean and can be manipulated using a pair of get and set methods (getter/setter methods). A Bean is also capable of generating events and follows the Java 1.1 Delegation Event Model for generating them. A bean defines an event by providing methods for adding and removing event listener objects from a list of interested listeners for that event. Bean methods are any public methods the bean exposes (except the getter/setter methods) to change property values or the methods to register and remove event listeners.

In addition to this, JavaBeans also define indexed properties, bound properties, and constrained properties. An *indexed property* is a property that has an array value and methods to change the value of either an individual array element or the entire array. A *bound property* is one that sends out a notification event when its value changes. A *constrained property* is one that sends out a notification when its value changes and allows the change to be vetoed by its listeners.

A bean can also provide a `BeanInfo` class that provides additional information about the bean in the form of `FeatureDescriptor` objects, each of which describe a single feature of the bean. If a bean has complicated property types, it may need to define a `PropertyEditor` class that enables the user to set values for that property. A bean can also define a `Customizer` class, which creates a customized GUI that enables the user to configure the bean in some useful way.

Note

The acronym *EJB* is used interchangeably to denote a component and an architecture. Some confusion exists because, in the specification, EJB is used both as an acronym for an Enterprise JavaBean (EJB)—the component—and for Enterprise JavaBeans—the architecture.

A packaged EJB component is identified by multiple individual elements:

1. a. The home interface.
   b. The home object.
2. a. The remote interface.
   b. The EJB object—this is an implementation of the remote interface, which is referred to as the EJBObject to avoid confusion.
3. The actual Bean implementation—this is the piece that contains the actual implementation code for the business logic. I refer to this as an Enterprise Bean.
4. Its deployment descriptors.

An EJB component is specified as the combination of the three elements and its deployment descriptors. You can change any one of those elements and create a new and unique EJB (for example, in most servers, EJBs can differ by remote interface only or by Enterprise Bean class implementation only, or by deployment data only, and so forth). In that light, a descriptor uniquely specifies an EJB component.

Enterprise JavaBeans—Components at the Server

Enterprise JavaBeans (EJB) takes a high-level approach for building distributed systems. It frees the application developer to concentrate on programming only the business logic, while removing the need to write all the "plumbing" code required in any enterprise application development scenario. For example, the enterprise developer no longer needs to write code that handles transactional behavior, security, connection pooling, or threading because the architecture delegates this task to the server vendor.

The current version of EJB bears little relation to JavaBeans. The name "Enterprise JavaBeans," however, implies a relationship that doesn't really hold. Typically, JavaBeans are used in a manner similar to Microsoft's ActiveX components (to provide user-friendly controls for building user interfaces), whereas EJBs are used to implement transactional middleware and are decidedly nonvisual. In addition, EJB does not include things like `BeanInfo` classes, property editors, or customizers.

In essence, EJB is a *server component model* for Java and is a specification for creating server-side, scalable, transactional, multiuser, and secure enterprise-level applications. Most important, EJBs can be deployed on top of existing transaction processing systems including traditional transaction processing monitors, Web servers, database servers, application servers, and so forth.

Why use EJB?

In applications like Microsoft's Visual Basic, a *property window* exists, which can be used as a simple, code-free means of programming various objects that are part of an application. Similarly, Sybase's PowerBuilder, has a *data window,* which allows a code-free means of programming data access to database applications. EJB brings a similar concept to building enterprise applications. Users can now focus on developing business logic with ease, while being shielded from the nitty-gritty aspects of enterprise application development through the use of EJB components.

In an n-tier architecture, it does not matter where the business logic is, though in a typical 3-tier architecture, the business logic is normally in the middle-tier by convention. With EJB, however, you can now move your business logic wherever you want, while adding additional tiers if necessary. The EJBs containing the business logic are platform-independent and can be moved to a different, more scalable platform should the need arise. If you are hosting a mission-critical application and need to move your EJBs from one platform to the other, you can do it without any change in the business-logic code. A major highlight of the EJB specification is the support for ready-made components. This enables you to "plug and work" with off-the-shelf EJBs without having to develop or test them or to have any knowledge of their inner workings.

The primary advantages of going in for an EJB solution are

- *EJB provides developers architectural independence*—EJB insulates developers from the underlying middleware because the only environment an EJB developer sees is the Java environment. It also helps the EJB server/container vendor to change and make improvements on the underlying middleware layer without affecting a user's existing enterprise applications.
- *WORA for server-side components*—Because EJB is based on Java technology, both the developer and the user are guaranteed that their components are Write Once, Run Anywhere (WORA). As long as an EJB server faithfully conforms to the EJB specification, any third-party EJB component should run within that server.
- *EJB establishes roles for application development*—The EJB specification assigns specific roles for project participants charged with enterprise application development using EJBs. For instance, business developers can focus on writing code that implements business logic. Application deployers can take care of installation issues in a simple and portable fashion. The server vendor can take care of providing support for complex system services and make available an organized framework for a EJB to execute in, without assistance from the actual EJB developers.
- *EJB takes care of transaction management*—The EJB container vendor is required to provide transaction control. The EJB developer who is writing the business functionality need not worry about starting and terminating transactions.
- *EJB provides distributed transaction support*—EJB provides transparency for distributed transactions. This means a client can begin a transaction and then invoke methods on EJBs present within two different servers, running on different machines, platforms, or Java virtual machines. Methods in one EJB can call methods in the other EJB with the assurance they will execute in the same transaction context.
- *EJB helps create portable and scalable solutions*—EJBs conforming to the EJB API will install and run in a portable fashion on any EJB server.
- *EJB seamlessly integrates with CORBA*—EJB and CORBA are a natural combination that complement each other. For example, EJBs may provide CORBA/IIOP for a robust transport mechanism or pure CORBA clients can access EJBs as EJB clients. Currently, a highlight of OMG's CORBAServices is the wide range of features they provide to an enterprise application developer. In the future, rather than trying to rewrite these services, EJB server vendors may simply wrap them with a simplified API, so EJB developers can use them without being CORBA experts.
- *EJB provides for vendor specific enhancements*—Because the EJB specification provides considerable flexibility for the vendors to create their own enhancements, the EJB environment may end up being feature-rich.

Differences between JavaBeans and Enterprise JavaBeans

Table 8-1 summarizes some of the major differences between a JavaBean and an Enterprise JavaBean.

Table 8-1: Differences Between JavaBeans and Enterprise JavaBeans

JavaBeans	Enterprise JavaBeans
JavaBeans may be visible or nonvisible at runtime. For example, the visual GUI component may be a button, list box, graphic, or a chart.	An EJB is a nonvisual, remote object.
JavaBeans are intended to be local to a single process and are primarily intended to run on the client side. Although one can develop server-side JavaBeans, it is far easier to develop them using the EJB specification instead.	EJBs are remotely executable components or business objects that can be deployed only on the server.
JavaBeans is a component technology to create generic Java components that can be composed together into applets and applications.	Even though EJB is a component technology, it neither builds upon nor extends the original JavaBean specification.
JavaBeans have an external interface called the `Properties` interface, which allows a builder tool to interpret the functionality of the bean.	EJBs have a deployment descriptor that describes its functionality to an external builder tool or IDE.
JavaBeans may have `BeanInfo` classes, property editors, or customizers.	EJBs have no concept of `BeanInfo` classes, property editors ,or customizers and provide no additional information other than that described in the deployment descriptor.
JavaBeans are not typed.	EJBs are of two types—session beans and entity beans.
No explicit support exists for transactions in JavaBeans.	EJBs may be transactional and the EJB Servers provide transactional support.
Component bridges are available for JavaBeans. For example, a JavaBean can also be deployed as an ActiveX control.	An EJB cannot be deployed as an ActiveX control because ActiveX controls are intended to run at the desktop and EJBs are server side components. However, CORBA-IIOP compatibility via the EJB-to-CORBA mapping is defined by the OMG.

The EJB Model

A basic EJB architecture is shown in Figure 8-2 and consists of:

- An EJB server
- EJB containers that run within the server
- Home objects, remote EJBObjects, and enterprise beans that run within containers
- EJB clients
- Auxiliary systems like JNDI, JTS, security services, and so forth.

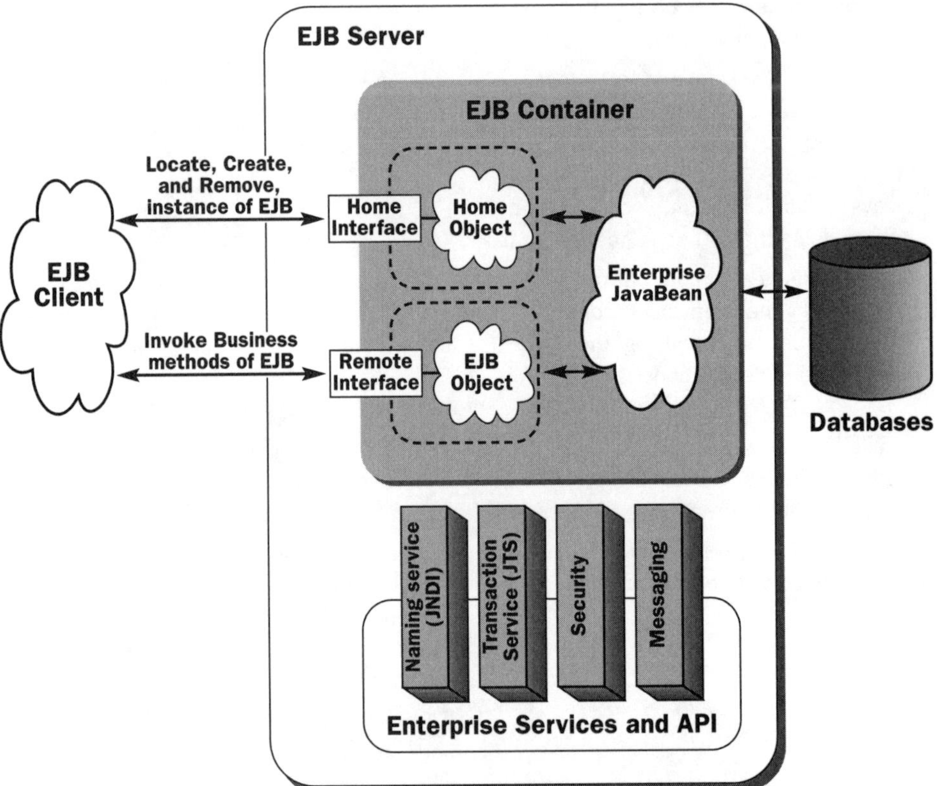

Figure 8-2: The basic Enterprise JavaBean architecture

Now, let's examine the primary components of the EJB architecture in greater detail:

EJB server

The *EJB server* provides an organized framework or execution environment in which EJB containers can run. It makes available system services for multiprocessing, load balancing, and device access for EJB containers. The EJB server also makes EJB containers running within them visible to the outside world. It may also provide vendor-specific features like an optimized data access interface, additional CORBAServices, SSL support, a JNDI-accessible naming service, and transaction management services.

In some respects, the EJB server is analogous to CORBA's Object Transaction Monitor (OTM). The OTM, too, provides an execution framework for running server side CORBA components.

EJB containers

An *EJB container* acts as the interface between an enterprise bean and low-level, platform-specific functionality that supports the bean. In essence, the EJB container is an abstraction that manages one or more EJB classes, while making the required services available to EJB classes through standard interfaces as defined in the EJB specification. The container vendor is also free to provide additional services implemented at either the container or the server level. An EJB client never accesses a bean directly. Any bean access is done through the methods of the container-generated classes, which, in turn, invoke the bean's methods.

Having the container interpose on all bean invocations allows the container to manage transactions, load bean instances, if necessary, and, in general, to do all the wonderful things EJBs do.

Two types of containers exist: session containers that may contain transient, non-persistent EJBs whose states are not saved and entity containers that contain persistent EJBs whose states are saved between invocations.

The home interface and home object

Factory methods for locating, creating, and removing instances of EJB classes are defined in the *home interface*. The *home object* is the implementation of the home interface. The EJB developer first has to define the home interface for his bean. The EJB container vendor provides tools that automatically generate the implementation code for the home interface defined by the EJB developer.

The remote interface and EJBObject

The *remote interface* lists the business methods available for the enterprise bean. The *EJBObject* is the client's view of the enterprise bean and implements the remote interface. While the enterprise bean developer defines the remote interface, the container vendor provides the tools necessary to generate the implementation code for the corresponding EJBObject. Note, however, the EJB container is still responsible for managing the EJBObject. Each time the client invokes the EJBObject's methods, the EJB container first handles the request before delegating it to the Enterprise Bean.

The Enterprise JavaBean

The real *enterprise bean* itself is contained within an EJB container and should never be directly accessed by anyone but the container. Although direct access may be possible, this is inadvisable as it breaks the contract between the bean and the container.

The EJB container should mediate all enterprise bean accesses. For this reason, the enterprise bean developer does not implement the remote interface within the enterprise bean itself. The implementation code for the remote interface is generated automatically by tools the container vendor provides, in the form of the EJBObject. This prevents inadvertent direct accesses from clients or other beans.

The EJB clients

EJB clients locate the specific EJB container that contains the enterprise bean through the Java Naming and Directory Interface (JNDI). They then make use of the EJB container to invoke bean methods. The EJB client only gets a reference to an EJBObject instance and never really gets a reference to the actual Enterprise Bean instance itself. When the client invokes a method, the EJBObject instance receives the request and delegates it to the corresponding bean instance while providing any necessary wrapping functionality.

The client uses the home object to locate, create, or destroy instances of an enterprise Bean. It then uses the EJBObject instance to invoke the business methods of a bean instance.

The EJB Lifecycle

In any enterprise development scenario, numerous complex programming issues are usually involved, which require the involvement of multiple domain experts. Without addressing all these issues and cohesive team-oriented approaches, it is impossible to create successful enterprise applications. To ease enterprise development, the EJB specification assigns responsibilities or roles. The EJB specification also specifies who is responsible for delivering what in an enterprise application that uses EJBs, as shown in Figure 8-3. Note, the EJB specification does not necessarily preclude the same person from carrying out more than one role.

Let's take a closer look at the different roles the EJB specification defines in greater detail:

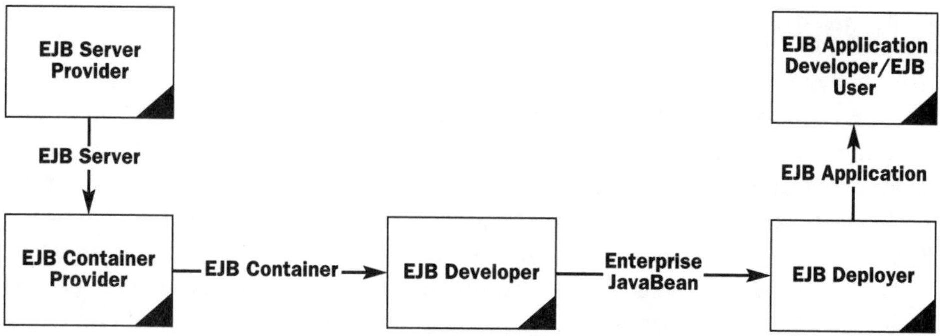

Figure 8-3: The lifecycle of a typical enterprise JavaBean

EJB server provider

The *EJB server provider* provides an organized application framework in which to run the EJB containers. The EJB server vendor implements and provides access to a JNDI-compatible naming service and a transaction service that is CORBA-OTS-compatible. Note, the EJB server vendor might also act as the EJB container vendor.

EJB container provider

The *EJB container provider* provides software to install an EJB with its supporting classes on an EJB server. The container vendor is also responsible for providing run-time classes that provide the required services to the EJB instances. These include the generation of stub and skeleton classes to provide access to the EJB instance's home object and EJBObject, installation of references to the home object in a JNDI-accessible namespace. Additionally, it also has to make available a suitable EJBObject implementation that can provide correct proxy services for the enterprise Bean class.

EJB developer

The *EJB developer* should have knowledge not only of the EJB specification, but also business needs because she or he is responsible for coding the business logic into server-side components. Basically, the developer implements EJB classes that focus on the business logic using the classes and interfaces defined in the EJB specification.

While the EJB container is responsible for handling all the transaction controls on behalf of the EJB instance, the EJB developer must understand how transactions work. Consequently, the developer is responsible for stipulating the transactional needs of the various methods in the EJB class to the EJB deployer. The EJB specification calls the EJB developer, the enterprise Bean provider.

EJB deployer

Although the *EJB deployer* may not be a Java developer or understand the business rules an EJB class implements, he or she should understand the application framework in which the EJB instance runs. Additionally, the deployer should have an in-depth understanding of the characteristics of the run-time server environment, such as database types, its location, and so forth. The deployer is responsible for taking the EJB and all its supporting classes and installing them correctly on the EJB server.

The deployer gets the EJB class requirements from the EJB developer, such as transactional needs, names, and descriptions of the required environment properties, and so forth. The deployer is responsible for making these properties, along with their correct run-time values, available to the EJB class at runtime. The deployer also has to ensure the home object for the EJB class is available in the namespace and is accessible through JNDI. The deployer and the developer must communicate clearly to ensure the EJB class is deployed with the correct deployment attributes.

Application developer

The *application developer* writes the client applications using pre-built EJB components. Here, a client is defined generally and can be a Java application, applet, servlet, a CORBA application, or even an ActiveX control connecting through a COM-CORBA bridge.

The application developer can thus plug-in ready-made EJBs without having to develop or test them, or without having any internal knowledge of how to integrate them. This frees the application developer to concentrate on high-level functionality, such as data presentation, without having to worry about how such data is actually obtained. The EJB specification calls the application developer, the *application assembler.*

EJB Components

In an earlier section, you saw the basic EJB model. Now, you have a more in-depth look at some of the major components of the EJB architecture, shown in Figure 8-4, so you can understand their run-time behavior.

The home interface and the home object

When an EJB client needs to use the services of an enterprise bean, it creates the EJB through its home interface. The client specifically uses one of the multiple `create()` methods the home interface defines. The implementation of the home interface is done through an object called the home object. An instance of this home object is created within the server and is made available to the clients as a factory for creating the enterprise bean.

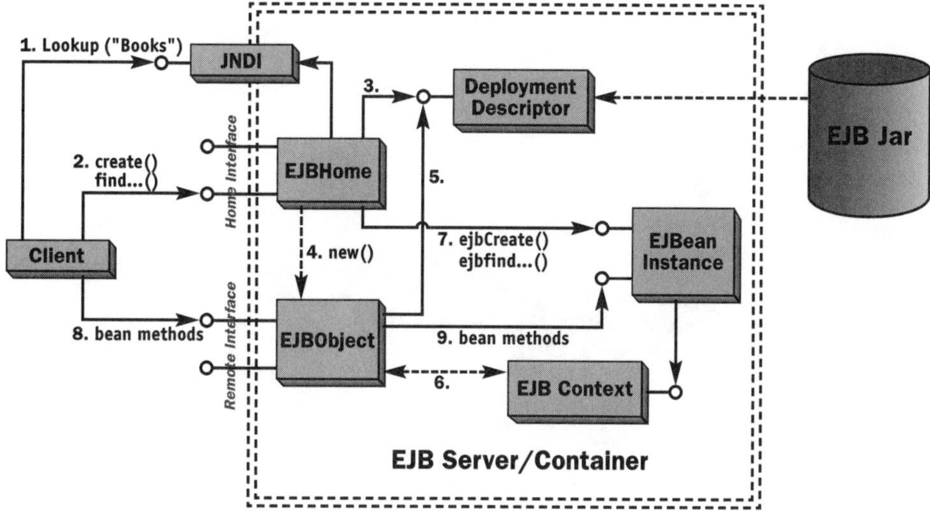

Figure 8-4: Major components of the EJB architecture

Finding the home object

The EJB client locates the home object through JNDI because a reference to the home object is placed in the naming service. The location of the namespace and the JNDI context factory class name are provided to the client initially. In addition to providing the location and class name, the client should also have some knowledge of how to locate the home object within the naming tree.

When an EJB deployer deploys an EJB onto an EJB server, he or she specifies a particular location in the naming tree such as "cup/chap8/Account." Then, the EJB client must be given this fully qualified pathname to locate and obtain a reference to the "Account" home object.

The code segment the client uses to create the bean through the home object looks something like Listing 8-1.

Listing 8-1: Client Code to Create an EJB

```
// get the JNDI naming context
Context initialCtx = new InitialContext ();
// use the context to lookup the EJB Home interface
AccountHome home =(AccountHome)initialCtx.lookup ("cup/chap8/Account");
// use the Home Interface to create a Session bean object
Account account = home.create (1234, "Athul", 1000671.54d);
```

Definition of the home interface

The home object is an implementation of an interface that extends the javax.ejb.EJBHome interface. It has the needed create(), find(), and remove() methods, each of these is matched with a corresponding ejbCreate(), ejbFind(), and ejbRemove()

method of the same signature in the actual enterprise Bean implementation being created. Methods also exist to obtain the metadata of the enterprise Bean. The EJBHome interface is defined in the specification illustrated in Listing 8-2.

Listing 8-2: The EJBHome Interface Definition

```
public interface javax.ejb.EJBHome extends Remote {
    public abstract void remove (Handle handle)
      throws RemoteException,RemoveException;
    public abstract void remove (Object primaryKey)
      throws RemoteException,RemoveException;
    public abstract EJBMetaData getEJBMetaData ()
      throws RemoteException;
}
```

The EJB developer has to define ejbCreate() methods in his enterprise beans. The EJB developer is also required to define corresponding create() methods that match the signatures in the EJB's home interface. If the developer is coding an entity bean, she or he may have to define finder methods in the home interface, which allows clients to locate existing entity beans based on their identity.

A typical home interface definition for an EJB may look something like Listing 8-3.

Listing 8-3: The AccountHome Interface Definition

```
import javax.ejb.*;
import java.rmi.*;
public interface AccountHome extends EJBHome {
    Account create(int accountNo, String customer)
      throws CreateException, RemoteException;
    Account create(int accountNo, String customer, double startingBalance)
      throws CreateException, RemoteException;
    Account findByPrimaryKey(AccountPK accountNo)
      throws FinderException, RemoteException;
}
```

The remote interface

The EJB developer must create a remote interface, which describes the business methods of the bean the EJB client would be able to invoke. The EJBObject will have the implementation code generated by the container tools for this interface.

The method names and the signatures listed in the remote interface must exactly match the method names and signatures of the business methods defined by the enterprise bean. This differs from the home interface, whose method signatures matched, but whose names were different.

A typical remote interface definition for an EJB may look like Listing 8-4.

Listing 8-4: The Account Remote Interface Definition

```
import javax.ejb.*;
import java.rmi.*;
public interface Account extends EJBObject {
    void credit (double amount) throws RemoteException;
    void debit (double amount) throws RemoteException;
    double getBalance () throws RemoteException;
}
```

The EJBObject

The EJBObject is a network-visible object with a stub and skeleton that acts as a proxy for the enterprise bean. The bean's remote interface extends the javax.ejb.EJBObject interface, making the EJBObject class specific to the bean class. For each enterprise bean, a custom EJBObject class exists.

Entity and session beans

Enterprise beans are building blocks that can be used alone or with other enterprise beans to build complete, robust, thin-client multitiered applications. An EJB is a body of code with fields and methods to implement modules of business logic. They can either be transient or persistent. Two types of enterprise beans can exist:

- *Entity beans*—These beans are generally used to model a business entity.
- *Session beans*—These are more general purpose server-side beans.

Figure 8-5 illustrates a high-level view of an EJB environment with session and entity enterprise beans.

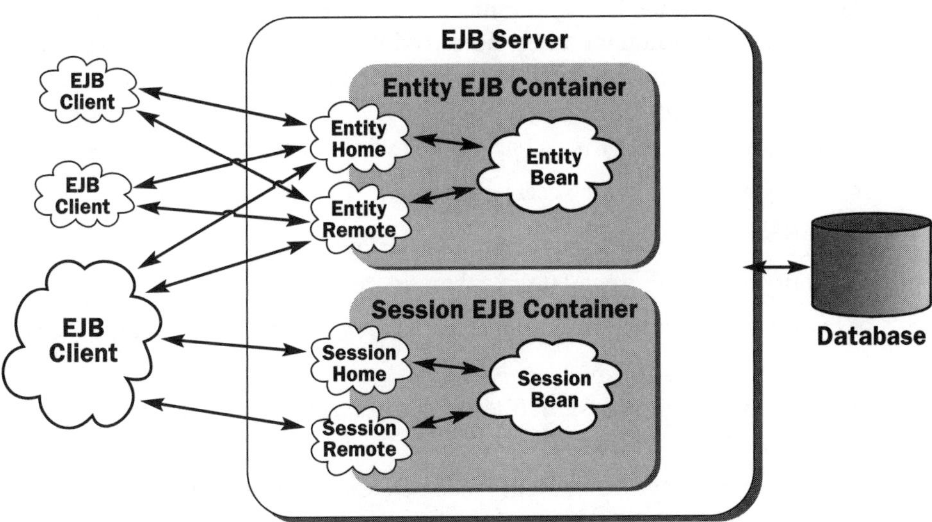

Figure 8-5: A typical EJB environment with entity and session beans

Before beginning a discussion of entity and session beans, you must understand the concept of *passivation* and *activation*. *Passivation* is the process by which the state of a bean is saved to persistent storage and then is swapped out. *Activation* is the process by which the state of a bean is restored by swapping it in from persistent storage.

Entity beans

An *entity bean* represents persistent data maintained in a domain model, as well as methods that act on that data. To be more specific, an entity bean maps to a record in your domain model. In a relational database context, one bean exists for each row in a table. This is not a new concept; this is how object databases have been modeled all along. A primary key identifies each entity bean. Entity beans are created by using an object factory `create()` method. Entity beans are also implicitly persistent, as an EJB object can manage its own persistence or delegate its persistence to its container.

Entity beans always have states, which can be persisted and stored across multiple invocations. Multiple EJB clients may, however, share an entity bean. The lifetime of an entity bean is not limited by the lifetime of the virtual machine within which it executes. A crash of the virtual machine may result in a rollback of the current transaction, but will neither destroy the entity bean nor invalidate the references that other clients have to this entity bean. Moreover, a client can later connect to the same entity bean using its object reference because it encapsulates a unique primary key allowing the enterprise bean or its container to reload its state. Entity beans can thus survive system shutdowns.

Persistence in entity beans is of two types:

Container-managed persistence: Here, the EJB container is responsible for saving the state of the entity bean. Because it is container-managed, the implementation is independent of the data source. All container-managed fields need to be specified in the deployment descriptor, however, for the persistence to be automatically handled by the container.

Bean-managed persistence: Here, the entity bean is directly responsible for saving its own state and the container does not need to generate any database calls. Consequently, this implementation is less adaptable than the previous one as the persistence needs to be hard-coded into the bean.

To summarize, every entity bean has the following characteristics:

- Entity beans can share access from multiple users.
- Entity beans can participate in transactions.
- Entity beans represent data in a domain model.
- Entity beans are persistent. They live as long as the data lives in the domain model.
- Entity beans can survive EJB server crashes. Any EJB server crash is always transparent to the client.
- Entity beans have a persistent object reference. The object reference encapsulates the persistent key for this bean.

Session beans

A *session bean* is created by a client and, in most cases, exists only for the duration of a single session. It performs operations on behalf of the client, such as database access or number crunching based on some formula. Although session beans can be transactional, they are not recoverable following a system crash. They can be stateless or they can maintain conversational state across methods and transactions. The container manages the conversational state of a session bean if it needs to be evicted from memory. A session bean must manage its own persistent data.

Each session bean is usually associated with one EJB client, which is responsible for creating and destroying it. Thus, session beans are transient and will not outlive the virtual machine on which they were created. A session bean can either maintain its state or be stateless. Session beans, however, do not survive a system shutdown.

Two types of session beans exist:

Stateless session beans: These types of session EJBs have no internal state. Because they are stateless, they needn't be passivated and can be pooled to service multiple clients.

Stateful session beans: These types of session beans possess internal states, hence, they need to handle activation and passivation. Because they can be persisted, they are also called *persistent session beans*. Only one EJB Client can exist per stateful session bean, however. Stateful session beans can be saved and restored across client sessions. The `getHandle()` method returns a bean object's instance handle, which can be used to save the bean's state. Later, to restore a bean from persistent storage, the `getEJBObject()` method can be invoked.

The characteristics of a session bean can be summarized as follows:

- Session EJBs execute on behalf of a single client. A session bean instance is an extension of the client that creates it.
- Session beans may be transaction-aware.
- Session beans can update data in an underlying database.
- Session beans are relatively short-lived. The lifetime of stateless session beans is limited to that of their client.
- Session beans may be destroyed when the EJB server crashes. The client has to establish connection with a new session bean object to resume any computation.
- Session beans do not represent data that must be stored in a database.

Every session bean can read and update a database on behalf of the client. Its fields may contain conversational state on behalf of the client. The state describes the conversation represented by a specific client/instance pair. Within a transaction, some of this data may be cached in the bean.

Session beans are supposed to be private resources, used only by the client that created it. For this reason, a session bean hides its identity and is anonymous, in sharp contrast to an entity bean that exposes its identity through its primary key.

Table 8-2 summarizes some of the major differences between a session bean and an entity bean.

Table 8-2: Differences Between a Session Bean and an Entity Bean

Session Bean	Entity Bean
The data members of the session bean contain conversational state.	The data members of the entity bean represent actual data in the domain model.
A session bean may handle database access for a single client.	Entity beans share database access for multiple clients.
Because session beans are about a conversation with a single client, session beans are allowed to store per-client state information.	Because entity beans are shared between multiple clients, they do not allow storage of per-client state information.
The relationship between a session bean and its client is one-to-one.	The relationship between an entity bean and a row in the domain model is one-to-one.
The life of the session bean is limited to the life of its client.	An entity bean persists as long as the data exists in the database.
Session beans can be transaction aware.	Entity beans are transactional.
Session beans do not survive server crashes.	Entity beans survive server crashes.

Developing an N-Tier EJB Application

How can you provide an EJB-based business solution by integrating session and entity beans? Assume you are a consulting firm that was just asked to develop an online store for a fictitious bookstore chain called Horses and Stable, Inc. This bookstore chain now wants to expand its business to the Web. Now suppose Horses and Stable Online carries about 5 million books and sells tens of thousands of copies of books every day.

Horses and Stable Online offers extensive book catalogs, as well as a variety of other resources including customer reviews, personal recommendations, and gift suggestions. When customers visit Horses and Stable Online, they should be able to:

- Browse for books in 28 subject areas and browse for music within hundreds of genres in 14 different browse rooms.
- Maintain a dynamic shopping cart by adding books and CDs, which they may opt to check out later.

While the previous scenario is hypothetical, you are likely to find similar requirements that need similar solutions in the real world. Throughout much of this chapter, we will gradually develop the functionality for this online bookstore, while explaining the concepts behind building and deploying powerful EJB applications

To develop the example, you must have the appropriate deployment tools and an EJB server. The deployment tools are used to generate enterprise bean containers, which are the classes that provide an interface to the low-level implementations in a given EJB server.

All the EJB source code follows certain naming conventions to help the EJB server find the application classes, containers, and database tables. For example, the source code that constitutes enterprise beans—the enterprise bean class, home interface, and primary key class names—use the remote interface name as a prefix. These naming conventions are discussed as we go along. While source file-naming conventions are standard across EJB server implementations, naming conventions used within the implementation sources are specific to the EJB server or other deployment tools.

All these examples make use of the EJB server "HomeBase" v0.5.1 (formerly called "EJBHome"—not to be confused with the `javax.ejb.ejbhome` interface) from Iona, the makers of the popular CORBA ORB Orbix. You can download a free implementation of HomeBase, as well as deployment tools for generating containers from `http://ejbhome.iona.com`. You can also, of course, opt to use any other EJB Server and deployment tools as long as you know how to modify your deployment descriptors to match the particular EJB server with which you are working. Similarly, you need a database and you should know how to set up the data source for your platform. The source code for all the examples can also be found in the accompanying CD-ROM, which came with this book.

Assuming you follow through, by the end of this chapter, you will have built an online store from which books and music CDs can be purchased over the Web.

The accompanying CD contains the following example code used for developing our online store:

1. A couple of *entity beans* (Books and Music entity beans).
2. A *session bean* (Cart session bean) that creates and manages the entities.
3. A *servlet client* (Online servlet) that creates a Cart and mimics an online store.
4. An entity bean client to test out our entities.
5. A session bean client to test out our session bean.
6. A Microsoft Access database (Shop.mdb) containing the store inventory.

The following Figure 8-6, shows the architecture for our online bookstore. The Web browser client starts the whole process by initiating a session and sending a `GET` message to the `Online` servlet, which resides on a Web server. The `init()` method of the `Online` servlet class looks up the `Cart` EJB from the EJB server and creates the `Cart` EJB. The `Cart` EJB, in turn, creates a `Books` Entity bean and a `Music` Entity bean that talk to the database to get the work done.

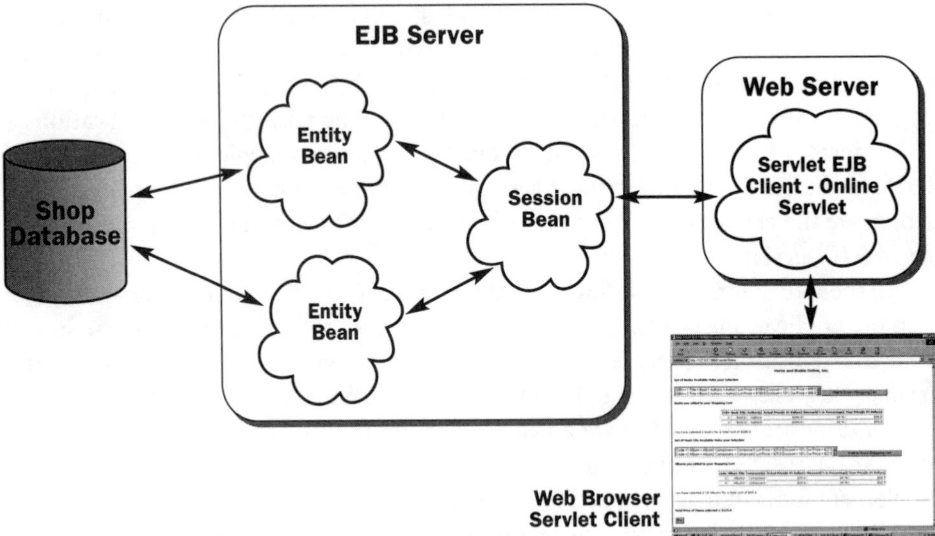

Figure 8-6: The four-tier architecture for our online bookstore

Developing entity beans

To develop the virtual Horses and Stable online bookstore example, the entity beans must be developed first. We develop an inventory entity bean to use later to build the shopping cart. Our inventory entity bean has methods to get and set the attributes of the various book titles our bookstore sells. It can also be queried for the price or other information on any given ISBN symbol.

Typically, when developing an entity bean, the steps to follow are as follows:

1. Set up the data source.
2. Define the EJB remote interface.
3. Define the EJB home interface.
4. Define the primary key class.
5. Implement the enterprise bean.
6. Compile the EJB classes.
7. Declare the security and deployment properties.
8. Generate the container classes using the tools supplied by the EJB server/container vendor, register the factory with the server, and deploy it.
9. Write the client code.
10. Compile the client code.
11. Start the client.

Now we'll examine each of these steps in greater detail:

Set up your data source

The example program requires a database table named BOOKS. The DML for the creation of such a table is given in Listing 8-5.

Listing 8-5: The DML for the BOOKS Table

```
CREATE TABLE BOOKS
    CODE        Number
    TITLE       Text
    AUTHORS     Text
    PRICE       Currency
    DISCOUNT        Number
    *primary key(CODE)
```

Define your EJB home interface

EJB clients do not work directly with the entity bean to create rows or access data but, rather, first create an instance of the home interface. The *home interface* extends `javax.ejb.EJBHome` and has methods that define how the entity bean is created and located in its container. It also follows the rules of RMI in that the arguments and return types for each method must be serializable and the methods should throw `java.rmi.RemoteException` as one of its exceptions, as illustrated in Listing 8-6.

Listing 8-6: The BooksHome Interface Definition

```
package cup.chap8.Shop.Books;
import javax.ejb.*;
import java.rmi.*;
public interface BooksHome extends EJBHome {
    Books create (int isbn, String title, String authors, double price, int discount)
        throws CreateException, RemoteException;
    Books findByPrimaryKey (BooksPK book)
        throws FinderException, RemoteException;
}
```

The `create()` method corresponds to the `ejbCreate()` method in the entity bean. The parameter sets of the two methods are identical. When the client calls `BooksHome.create()`, the container allocates an instance of the entity bean and calls `BooksHome.ejbCreate()`. For container-managed entity beans, `ejbCreate()`returns a `void`, unlike in the case of bean-managed persistence, where it returns a primary key object. The first thing a client does is to locate the home object for the required bean using JNDI. The `BooksHome` interface contains `create()` methods that will be invoked whenever a client requests a new bean. Note, this method is implemented in the `EJBHome` implementation and calls the `ejbCreate()` method in the bean class when invoked.

Define your EJB remote interface

When the home interface implementation is instantiated, the EJB server also creates the remote interface implementation and enterprise bean instances. The methods in this interface are the external interfaces of `BooksBean`. The signatures of the methods in this external interface are identical to those of the bean, except these methods throw a `java.rmi.RemoteException`. The entity bean does not directly implement this interface. The corresponding container-generated EJBObject code implements this interface and delegates to the enterprise bean. The EJBObject acts as a proxy, passing method invocations through to the bean instance installed in the server. The remote interface is shown in Listing 8-7.

Listing 8-7: The Books Remote Interface Definition

```
package cup.chap8.Shop.Books;
import javax.ejb.*;
import java.rmi.*;
public interface Books extends EJBObject {
    public int    getIsbn () throws RemoteException;
    public String getTitle () throws RemoteException;
    public String getAuthors () throws RemoteException;
    public double getPrice () throws RemoteException;
    public int    getDiscount () throws RemoteException;
    public double getDiscountedPrice () throws RemoteException;
    public void   setPrice (double cost) throws RemoteException;
    public void   setDiscount (int disc) throws RemoteException;
}
```

Notice the remote interface `Books` extends the `javax.ejb.EJBObject` and declares the `BooksBean`'s get/set methods. It also follows the rules of RMI in that the arguments and return types for each method must be `Serializable` and the methods should throw `java.rmi.RemoteException` as one of its exception.

Define your primary key class

The EJB server requires an entity bean to have a primary key class with a public primary key data member (or data members, if using composite primary keys). You can have the container manage an enterprise bean or write the code to manage the bean yourself. As shown in Listing 8-8, the bean is container-managed.

Listing 8-8: The BooksPK Primary Key Class Definition

```
package cup.chap8.Shop.Books;
public class BooksPK implements java.io.Serializable {
    public int code;
    public BooksPK (){}
    public BooksPK (int isbn) {
```

Listing 8-8: continued

```
            code = isbn;
        }
    }
```

The primary key class is shown in the previous example. The primary key in the BOOKS table is CODE and so code is defined as a public data member in this class, which is assigned a value when the class is constructed.

Implement the entity bean

The enterprise bean implements javax.ejb.EntityBean and the developer-defined interface methods. It should follow the rules of RMI in that the arguments and return types for each method must be serializable and the methods should throw java.rmi.RemoteException as one of its exceptions. See Listing 8-9.

Listing 8-9: The BooksBean Enterprise Bean Implementation Class

```
package cup.chap8.Shop.Books;
import java.rmi.*;
import javax.ejb.*;
public class BooksBean implements EntityBean {
    EntityContext entityContext;
    public int    code;    // CODE
    public String title;   // TITLE
    public String authors; // AUTHORS
    public double price;     // PRICE
    public int    discount; // DISCOUNT
    // Implementation for all the Remote Interface business methods
    public int    getIsbn () throws RemoteException {
       return code;
    }
    public String getTitle () throws RemoteException {
       return title;
    }
    public String getAuthors () throws RemoteException {
       return authors;
    }
    public double getPrice () throws RemoteException {
       return price;
    }
    public int    getDiscount () throws RemoteException {
       return discount;
    }
    public double getDiscountedPrice () throws RemoteException {
```

continues

Listing 8-9: continued

```
        double deduct = ((double)discount)/100;
        return ( price*(1-deduct) );
    }
    public void   setPrice (double cost) throws RemoteException {
        price = cost;
    }
    public void   setDiscount (int disc) throws RemoteException {
        discount = disc;
    }
    // Implementation for all the Home Interface methods
    public void ejbCreate (int isbn, String bookTitle, String author,
                double cost, int disc)
        throws CreateException, RemoteException {
        code    = isbn;
        title   = bookTitle;
        authors = author;
        price   = cost;
        discount= disc;
    }
    public void ejbPostCreate (int isbn, String bookTitle, String author,
                    double cost, int disc) {
    }
    // Implement all the mandatory methods required by the EJB Spec
    public void ejbActivate () throws RemoteException{}
    public void ejbLoad () throws RemoteException{}
    public void ejbPassivate () throws RemoteException{}
    public void ejbRemove () throws RemoteException, RemoveException{}
    public void ejbStore () throws RemoteException{}
    public void setEntityContext (EntityContext context)
        throws RemoteException {
        entityContext = context;
    }
    public void unsetEntityContext () throws RemoteException {
        entityContext = null;
    }
}
```

Much of the previous code should be self-explanatory. Notice all the business methods that constitute the remote interface and the creation and find methods that constitute the home interface have been implemented in the enterprise Bean.

Compile your EJB classes

You can now compile all the sources you developed. Go ahead and compile the code.

```
javac *.java
```

Declare the deployment descriptors

From here on, whatever is discussed is specific to the particular EJB server implementation. Iona's HomeBase server requires we specify our deployment descriptors in XML. (You can get information on XML from any good book on the subject. A detailed explanation of XML is beyond the scope of this chapter.) These properties are used both in the container class generation and in deployment. We need to define the various properties that help you to generate the container classes. In a properties file (call it `Shop.ejbml`), paste in the Listing 8-10

Listing 8-10: The Deployment Descriptor for the Books EJB

```
<!------------------------------------------------------------>
<!-------     Books Entity Bean           ---------------->
<!------------------------------------------------------------>
<ejbml>
     <entity-bean
        name="Books"
        descriptor="Books/BooksDeployment"
        package="cup.chap8.Shop.Books"
        home="cup.chap8.Shop.Books.BooksHome"
        remote="cup.chap8.Shop.Books.Books"
        bean="cup.chap8.Shop.Books.BooksBean"
        primary-key="cup.chap8.Shop.Books.BooksPK"
        tx-attribute="TX_SUPPORTS"
     >
        <property
           name="databasePassword"
           value="mouse"
        />
        <property
           name="dataSourceName"
           value="Shop"
        />
        <property
           name="databaseUser"
           value="user"
           />
        <property
           name="databaseTable"
```

continues

Listing 8-10: continued

```
            value="books"
        />
        <container-managed
            storage-helper=
                "com.ejbhome.generator.helpers.RelationalPersistenceCodeHelper"
            table="books"
            data-source="Shop"
            user="user"
            password="mouse"
        >
            <field
                name="discount"
            />
            <field
                name="price"
            />
            <field
                name="authors"
            />
            <field
                name="title"
            />
            <field
                name="code"
            />
        </container-managed>
    </entity-bean>
</ejbml>
```

The first few lines specify the name of our home and remote interfaces and that this is an entity bean. We also declare our Primary Key class in this file. Because this is a container-managed bean, we specify the fields in the database that are container managed. We also specify the enterprise bean supports transactions (TX_SUPPORTS) in its transaction attributes.

The different transaction attributes available that can be specified are shown in Table 8-3.

Because the enterprise bean is container managed, we specify the fields that are container managed so the tools can generate appropriate JDBC code. We then specify the data source name, the table name, the user name, and the password, which may be helpful in any JDBC calls the enterprise bean makes.

Table 8-3: Transaction Attributes that Can Be Specified

TX_BEAN_MANAGED	Enterprise bean starts and ends a transaction. It may use the javax.jts.UserTransaction interface to demarcate transaction boundaries.
TX_MANDATORY	Caller must start transaction. The bean is always invoked in the scope of the client's transaction. If the client does not have one, a javax.transaction.TransactionRequiredException exception is raised.
TX_REQUIRED	Enterprise bean requires a transaction. If the client is associated with a transaction context, the bean is invoked in the same context. Otherwise, the container starts a new transaction before invoking methods on the bean and commits the transaction before returning from them.
TX_REQUIRES_NEW	Enterprise bean requires a new transaction be created for each method call.
TX_NOT_SUPPORTED	Caller's transaction will be suspended before calling the enterprise bean. The bean is invoked without transactional scope.
TX_SUPPORTS	The caller's transaction is simply passed on by the EJB Container. If the caller does not have a transaction context, the bean methods are invoked without a transaction context.

Register and deploy the bean

This section is again specific to the EJB Server/container you are using. The EJBHome server defines a couple of files datasource.properties and ejbhome.properties in a directory named conf.

You need to modify the datasource.properties file to look like Listing 8-11.

Listing 8-11: The Datasource Definition for Deployment on HomeBase

```
# This is a list of datasource names with their respective JDBC databases URLs.
#
# For example:
#
# To map a datasource name of jdbc/Inventory to an Oracle lite database called test,
# you would use the following:
#
# jdbc/Inventory=jdbc:polite:test
#
Books=jdbc:odbc:Books,user=user,password=mouse
Music=jdbc:odbc:Books,user=user,password=mouse
```

Generate the container classes

The next step is to generate the container classes using the tools supplied by the EJB server/container vendor. When the entity and session beans are deployed, a number of container source and class files are generated with the following prefixes. A container is a set of classes generated by the deployment tool that manages an enterprise bean's persistence, transactional properties, and security. Now that we have our Shop.ejbml ready, we can generate and compile the container classes. For this, we need to execute the HomeBase server's deployer tool. We do this as follows:

```
java com.ejbhome.Deployer .\conf\Shop.ejbml
```

The following listing shows what our screen console would look like while we compile and deploy our files.

```
E:\>javac cup\chap8\Shop\Books\*.java
E:\>java com.ejbhome.Deployer .\conf\Shop.ejbml
EJBHome EJB Deployer version 0.5.1 (Scunthorpe)
(c) Copyright IONA Technologies PLC 1999.  All Rights Reserved.
Windows NT x86 4.0
A nonfatal internal JIT (3.00.072b(x)) error 'regvarHI' has occurred in :
    'com/ejbhome/Deployer.<init> (Ljava/util/Properties;Ljava/util/Vector;)V':
    Interpreting method.
    Please report this error in detail to http://java.sun.com/cgi-bin/bugreport.cgi
Deploying: Books...
Generating: IonaBooksHome...done.
Generating: IonaRemoteBooks...done.
Generating: IonaBooksBean...done.
Generating: IonaBooksContext...done.
Implementing Communications: Home Stubs & Skels...done.
Implementing Communications: Remote Stubs & Skels...done.
Compiling: IonaBooksHome.java...done.
Compiling: IonaRemoteBooks.java...done.
Compiling: IonaBooksBean.java...done.
Compiling: IonaBooksContext.java...done.
Compiling: IonaBooksHome_Stub.java...done.
Compiling: IonaBooksHome_Skel.java...done.
Compiling: IonaRemoteBooks_Stub.java...done.
Compiling: IonaRemoteBooks_Skel.java...done.
Deploying: Music...
Generating: IonaMusicHome...done.
Generating: IonaRemoteMusic...done.
Generating: IonaMusicBean...done.
Generating: IonaMusicContext...done.
Implementing Communications: Home Stubs & Skels...done.
Implementing Communications: Remote Stubs & Skels...done.
```

```
Compiling: IonaMusicHome.java...done.
Compiling: IonaRemoteMusic.java...done.
Compiling: IonaMusicBean.java...done.
Compiling: IonaMusicContext.java...done.
Compiling: IonaMusicHome_Stub.java...done.
Compiling: IonaMusicHome_Skel.java...done.
Compiling: IonaRemoteMusic_Stub.java...done.
Compiling: IonaRemoteMusic_Skel.java...done.
Deploying: Cart...
Generating: IonaCartHome...done.
Generating: IonaRemoteCart...done.
Generating: IonaCartBean...done.
Generating: IonaCartContext...done.
Implementing Communications: Home Stubs & Skels...done.
Implementing Communications: Remote Stubs & Skels...done.
Compiling: IonaCartHome.java...done.
Compiling: IonaRemoteCart.java...done.
Compiling: IonaCartBean.java...done.
Compiling: IonaCartContext.java...done.
Compiling: IonaCartHome_Stub.java...done.
Compiling: IonaCartHome_Skel.java...done.
Compiling: IonaRemoteCart_Stub.java...done.
Compiling: IonaRemoteCart_Skel.java...done.
E:\>
```

You can now start up the server with the command:

```
java com.ejbhome.Server
```

Write your client code

The client code for the entity bean is listed in the following. The client generally goes ahead and creates a set of records in the database and modifies the prices.

The client first does a `Naming.lookup()`and gets a reference to the `BooksHome` interface. It then goes about creating a whole bunch of entity bean instances and these records are created in the database. The client also exercises the various business methods of our `ShopBean` like getting and setting the prices of the book titles, as in Listing 8-12.

Listing 8-12: The BooksTest Entity Bean Client Application

```
package cup.chap8.Shop.Books;
import java.rmi.*;
import java.util.*;
public class BooksTest {
    static final int NUMBOOKS = 4;
```

continues

Listing 8-12: continued

```
    public static void main(String[] args) throws Exception {
        BooksHome home = (BooksHome)Naming.lookup ("Books");
        System.out.println ( "Naming.lookup successful..." );
        if (home == null) {
            System.out.println( "null BooksHome returned..." );
        }
        String title = "Book";
        String author= "Author";
        Vector v = new Vector ();
        for (int i = 0; i < BooksTest.NUMBOOKS; i++) {
            System.out.println ("ISBN = " +(i+1) +
                        " Book = " +title+(i+1) +
                        " Author = " +author+(i+1) +
                        " Creating home.create...");
            v.addElement (home.create ((i+1),title+(i+1),
                        author+(i+1),100.00,10));
        }
        for (int i = 0; i < BooksTest.NUMBOOKS; i++) {
            Books books= (Books) (v.elementAt (i));
            books.setPrice (books.getPrice ()+1);
            System.out.println ("Final Price of " + books.getTitle () +
                        " is "+ books.getPrice ());
        }
        System.out.println ("Books.setBooksPrice successful...");
        for (int i = 0; i < BooksTest.NUMBOOKS; i++) {
            Books books= (Books)(home.findByPrimaryKey (new BooksPK (i+1)));
            books.setPrice (books.getPrice ()+1);
            System.out.println ("Final Price of " + books.getTitle () +
                        " is "+ books.getPrice ());
        }
        System.out.println ("Books.findByPrimaryKey successful...");
    }
}
```

Compile and run the client. The client will create four records in the database. When session beans are discussed, you see how to model the session bean to be a client to our entity bean.

Developing session beans

You can create a session bean by implementing the following steps:

1. Define the EJB home interface.
2. Define the EJB remote interface.

3. Implement the enterprise Bean.
4. Compile the EJB classes.
5. Declare the security and deployment properties.
6. Generate the container classes using the tools supplied by the EJB server/container vendor.
7. Register the factory with the server.
8. Write the client code.
9. Compile the client code.
10. Start the client.

The session bean we are about to develop acts as a client to a couple of entity beans and manages the workflow between these entities. Session beans can be also be used to create new entity instances and their data in the database. Our shopping cart session bean implemented in the following has methods to help the user to shop for various items.

Define the home interface

We begin by defining our home interface. Only one create method is defined to help us create session bean instances, as seen in Listing 8-13.

Listing 8-13: The CartHome Interface Definition

```
package cup.chap8.Shop.Cart;
import javax.ejb.*;
import java.rmi.*;
public interface CartHome extends EJBHome {
    Cart create () throws RemoteException, CreateException;
}
```

Define the remote interface

Now to define the remote interface that will contain our business method interfaces. If you notice, we define two interfaces—createNewBook() and createNewAlbum() to help us create entity beans. We define methods like getBook()and getAlbum() to help us retrieve data. We define methods like addToBooksCart() and addToMusicCart() to help us build the shopping cart. The methods getNumberBooks(),getNumberAlbums(), getBooksTotal() getAlbumsTotal(),and getGrandTotal() help us get statistics we can provide to the user, as seen in Listing 8-14.

Listing 8-14: The Cart Remote Interface Definition

```
package cup.chap8.Shop.Cart;
import javax.ejb.*;
import java.rmi.*;
import java.util.*;
```

continues

Listing 8-14: continued

```
import cup.chap8.Shop.Books.*;
import cup.chap8.Shop.Music.*;
public interface Cart extends EJBObject {
    public Books  createNewBook (int isbn, String title, String authors,
                      double price, int discount)
       throws RemoteException, CreateException;
    public Music  createNewAlbum (int code, String album, String authors,
                      double price, int discount)
       throws RemoteException, CreateException;
    public Books  getBook (int isbn)
       throws RemoteException, FinderException;
    public Music  getAlbum (int code)
       throws RemoteException, FinderException;
    public void   addToBooksCart (int code) throws RemoteException;
    public void   addToMusicCart (int code) throws RemoteException;
    public void   flushBooksCart () throws RemoteException;
    public void   flushMusicCart () throws RemoteException;
    public int    getNumberBooks () throws RemoteException;
    public int    getNumberAlbums () throws RemoteException;
    public double getBooksTotal () throws RemoteException;
    public double getAlbumsTotal () throws RemoteException;
    public double getGrandTotal () throws RemoteException;
    public Vector getBooksList () throws RemoteException;
    public Vector getMusicList () throws RemoteException;
    public Vector getBooksCart () throws RemoteException;
    public Vector getMusicCart () throws RemoteException;
}
```

Implement the session bean

Our session bean invokes the home interfaces of two entity beans—the BooksBean and the MusicBean. The source code for the MusicBean, while not listed here, is similar to the BooksBean entity bean and is available on the accompanying CD along with all these sources. If you look at the setSessionContext()methods, you can see we get a reference to the home interface factory objects for the Books and Music bean. The setSessionContext() method is one of the first methods to be called when the container creates the session bean. This method also invokes our private init()method we use to initialize our data. Notice we cache data in the session bean. This ensures the entity bean is not invoked every time the client makes a call and minimizes our database access, thus, improving overall system performance. All the remote interfaces we defined for our business methods now have a body defined in the session bean.

When you read the listing, you find a certain ReturnSet class, which you will learn about soon.. The listing for the CartBean is shown in Listing 8-15.

Listing 8-15: The CartBean Enterprise Bean Implementation

```
package cup.chap8.Shop.Cart;
import java.rmi.*;
import javax.ejb.*;
import java.util.*;
import cup.chap8.Shop.Books.*;
import cup.chap8.Shop.Music.*;
import cup.chap8.Shop.Cart.ReturnSet;
public class CartBean implements SessionBean {
    SessionContext      sessionContext;
    public BooksHome  booksHome;
    public MusicHome  musicHome;
    public Vector       booksList = null, booksCart = null;
    public Vector       musicList = null, musicCart = null;
    int   totalBooks = 0, totalMusic = 0;
    double booksCost = 0, musicCost = 0, grandTotal = 0;
    void init () {
      booksList = new Vector ();
      booksCart = new Vector ();
      musicList = new Vector ();
      musicCart = new Vector ();
      ReturnSet result = null;
      for (int i=0; ;i++) {
        try{
          BooksPK key = new BooksPK (i+1);
          Books found = booksHome.findByPrimaryKey (key);
          if (null == found) {
            break;
          }
          result = new ReturnSet (key.code, found.getTitle (),
                found.getAuthors (),
                found.getPrice (),
                found.getDiscount (),
                found.getDiscountedPrice ());
          System.out.println ("isbn = "+ result.code +
                " Title = "+result.title+
                " Authors = "+result.authors+
                " Price = " + result.price);
          booksList.addElement (result);
          } catch (Exception e) { e.printStackTrace(); break; }
        }
      for (int i=0; ;i++) {
        try {
```

continues

Listing 8-15: continued

```
                MusicPK key = new MusicPK (i+1);
                Music found = musicHome.findByPrimaryKey (key);
                if (found == null) {
                break;
                }
                result = new ReturnSet (key.code, found.getAlbum (),
                        found.getComposers (),
                        found.getPrice (),
                        found.getDiscount (),
                        found.getDiscountedPrice ());
                System.out.println ("code = "+ result.code +
                        " Album = "+result.title+
                        " Composers = "+result.authors+
                        " Price = " + result.price);
                musicList.addElement (result);
            } catch (Exception e) { e.printStackTrace (); break; }
        }
    }
    // Implementation for all the Remote Interface business methods
    public Books createNewBook (int isbn, String title,
                        String authors,
                        double price, int discount)
        throws RemoteException, CreateException {
    Books book = booksHome.create (isbn, title, authors,
                        price, discount);
        if (null != book) {
            booksList.addElement (new ReturnSet(isbn, title,
                            authors,
                            price, discount,
                            book.getDiscountedPrice ()));
        }
        return book;
    }
    public Music createNewAlbum (int code, String album, String authors,
                        double price, int discount)
        throws RemoteException, CreateException {
        Music music = musicHome.create (code, album, authors, price, discount);
        if (null != music) {
            musicList.addElement(new ReturnSet(code, album, authors,
                            price, discount,
                            music.getDiscountedPrice ()));
        }
```

Listing 8-15: continued

```
        return music;
    }
    public void addToBooksCart (int isbn) throws RemoteException {
        try {
            Books book = getBook (isbn);
            if (null != book) {
                booksCart.addElement(new ReturnSet(isbn, book.getTitle (),
                                book.getAuthors (),
                                book.getPrice (),
                                book.getDiscount (),
                                book.getDiscountedPrice()));
                ++totalBooks;
                booksCost += book.getDiscountedPrice ();
                grandTotal+= book.getDiscountedPrice ();
            }
        } catch (Exception e) { e.printStackTrace (); }
    }
    public void flushBooksCart () throws RemoteException {
        grandTotal -= booksCost;
        totalBooks = 0;
        booksCost = 0;
        booksCart.removeAllElements ();
    }
    public void flushMusicCart () throws RemoteException {
        grandTotal -= musicCost;
        totalMusic = 0;
        musicCost = 0;
        musicCart.removeAllElements ();
    }
    public void addToMusicCart (int code) throws RemoteException {
        try {
            Music music = getAlbum (code);
            if (null != music) {
                musicCart.addElement(new ReturnSet(code, music.getAlbum (),
                            music.getComposers (),
                            music.getPrice (),
                            music.getDiscount (),
                            music.getDiscountedPrice()));
                ++totalMusic;
                musicCost += music.getDiscountedPrice ();
                grandTotal+= music.getDiscountedPrice ();
            }
```

continues

Listing 8-15: continued

```
        } catch (Exception e) { e.printStackTrace(); }
    }
    public Books getBook (int isbn)
        throws RemoteException, FinderException {
        return booksHome.findByPrimaryKey (new BooksPK (isbn));
    }
    public Music getAlbum (int code)
        throws RemoteException, FinderException {
        return musicHome.findByPrimaryKey (new MusicPK (code));
    }
    public Vector getBooksList () throws RemoteException {
        return booksList;
    }
    public Vector getMusicList () throws RemoteException {
        return musicList;
    }
    public Vector getBooksCart () throws RemoteException {
        return booksCart;
    }
    public Vector getMusicCart () throws RemoteException {
        return musicCart;
    }
    public int getNumberBooks () throws RemoteException {
        return totalBooks;
    }
    public int getNumberAlbums () throws RemoteException {
        return totalMusic;
    }
    public double getBooksTotal () throws RemoteException {
        return booksCost;
    }
    public double getAlbumsTotal () throws RemoteException {
        return musicCost;
    }
    public double getGrandTotal () throws RemoteException {
        return grandTotal;
    }
    // Implementation for all the Home Interface methods
    public void ejbCreate () throws RemoteException, CreateException {}
    // Implement all the mandatory methods required by the EJB Spec
    public void ejbActivate () throws RemoteException {}
    public void ejbPassivate () throws RemoteException {}
```

Listing 8-15: continued

```
        public void ejbRemove () throws RemoteException {}
        public void setSessionContext (SessionContext context)
            throws RemoteException {
            sessionContext = context;
            try {
                booksHome = (BooksHome)Naming.lookup ("Books");
                musicHome = (MusicHome)Naming.lookup ("Music");
                init();
            } catch (Exception ex) {
                throw new RemoteException ("Shop not found", ex);
            }
        }
}
```

To make working with vectors easier, we created a serializable ReturnSet class, which contains a member for each of the fields of the enterprise Bean in which we are interested. This enables us to store and retrieve each element of the Vector as a ReturnSet object. The listing for the ReturnSet class is shown in Listing 8-16.

Listing 8-16: The ReturnSet Class Definition

```
package cup.chap8.Shop.Cart;
public class ReturnSet implements java.io.Serializable {
      public intcode;
      public Stringtitle;
      public Stringauthors;
      public double   price;
      public intdiscount;
      public double   ourPrice;
      public ReturnSet(int no, String name, String author,
                     double cost, int disc, double cp) {
          code = no; title = name; authors = author;
          price = cost; discount = disc; ourPrice = cp;
      }
}
```

Compile the EJB classes

You can now compile all the sources you developed as:

```
javac *.java
```

Declare the deployment properties

From here on, whatever we talk about is specific to the particular EJB server implementation. The EJBHome server requires we specify properties in four different files.

These properties are used both in the container class generation and in deployment. We need to define the various properties that help you to generate the container classes. In a properties file, which we call Shop.ejbml, paste in Listing 8-17.

Listing 8-17: The Deployment Descriptors for the Cart EJB

```
<!------------------------------------------------------->
<!-------   Cart Session Bean          --------------->
<!------------------------------------------------------->
<ejbml>
     <session-bean
        name="cart"
        descriptor="Cart/CartDeployment"
        package="cup.chap8.Shop.Cart"
        home="cup.chap8.Shop.Cart.CartHome"
        remote="cup.chap8.Shop.Cart.Cart"
        bean="cup.chap8.Shop.Cart.CartBean"
        type="stateful"
        timeout="3600"
        tx-attribute="TX_SUPPORTS"
     >
     </session-bean>
</ejbml>
```

The first few lines specify the name of our interfaces and that this is a session bean. We also specify our generated code should belong to the cup.chap8.Shop.Cart package.

Generate the container classes

The next step is to generate the container classes using the tools supplied by the EJB server/container vendor. When the entity and session beans are deployed, a number of container source and class files are generated with the following prefixes. A *container* is a set of classes generated by the deployment tool that manages an enterprise bean's persistence, transactional properties, and security. Now that our Shop.ejbml file is ready, we can generate and compile the container classes. For this we need to execute the HomeBase server's deployer tool. We do this as follows from the command line:

```
java com.ejbhome.Deployer .\conf\Shop.ejbml
```

We can now run the server as:

```
java com.ejbhome.Server
```

A snapshot of the console when the server is running and ready to receive client connections is shown in the following.

```
E:\>java com.ejbhome.Server
com.ejbhome.server.EnterpriseServer, initializing.
com.ejbhome.server.EnterpriseServer.fireContainerAdded() at (Compiled Code)
```

```
com.ejbhome.VendorConfiguration.<init>() at (VendorConfiguration.java:57)
com.ejbhome.VendorConfiguration.getSystemCodeHelper() at
    (VendorConfiguration.java:174)
com.ejbhome.VendorConfiguration.getTransactionCodeHelper() at
    (VendorConfiguration.java:138)
com.ejbhome.VendorConfiguration.getCommsCodeHelper() at
    (VendorConfiguration.java:163)
com.ejbhome.VendorConfiguration.getTracingCodeHelper() at
    (VendorConfiguration.java:152)
com.ejbhome.VendorConfiguration.getPersistenceCodeHelper() at
    (VendorConfiguration.java:125)
com.ejbhome.VendorConfiguration.getSessionPassivationCodeHelper() at
    (VendorConfiguration.java:185)
com.ejbhome.VendorConfiguration.getVendorPrefix() at (VendorConfiguration.java:100)
starting RMI registry on port 1099...
RMI registry on port 1099, has started.
com.ejbhome.server.EnterpriseServer.bindDataSources() at (Compiled Code)
com.ejbhome.naming.spi.rmi.RMICtx.<init>() at (RMICtx.java:20)
registering XA data sources
com.ejbhome.sql.XADataSourceImpl.<init>(jdbc:odbc:Shop,{password=mouse, user=user})
    at (XADataSourceImpl.java:75)
com.ejbhome.naming.spi.rmi.RMICtx.bind() at (RMICtx.java:168)
com.ejbhome.server.EnterpriseServer.fireDataSourceAdded() at (Compiled Code)
    registered: Shop -> jdbc:odbc:Shop, as an XA pooled data source [main]
com.ejbhome.naming.spi.rmi.RMICtx.<init>() at (RMICtx.java:20)
loading beans from: Books.ejbml
com.ejbhome.server.EnterpriseServer$2.startElement(ejbml) at (EnterpriseServer.java:228)
com.ejbhome.server.EnterpriseServer$2.startElement(entity-bean) at
    (EnterpriseServer.java:228)
com.ejbhome.VendorConfiguration.getHomeContainerClassName() at
    (VendorConfiguration.java:226)
com.ejbhome.VendorConfiguration.getVendorPrefix() at (VendorConfiguration.java:100)
com.ejbhome.container.AbstractEJBHome.<init>() at (AbstractEJBHome.java:136)
com.ejbhome.naming.spi.rmi.RMICtx.<init>() at (RMICtx.java:20)
com.ejbhome.naming.spi.rmi.RMICtx.lookup("Shop") at (RMICtx.java:35)
com.ejbhome.naming.spi.rmi.RMICtx.bind() at (RMICtx.java:168)
registered cup.chap8.Shop.Books.IonaBooksHome, as: Books.
com.ejbhome.server.EnterpriseServer$2.startElement(property) at
    (EnterpriseServer.java:228)
com.ejbhome.server.EnterpriseServer$2.startElement(property) at
    (EnterpriseServer.java:228)
com.ejbhome.server.EnterpriseServer$2.startElement(property) at
    (EnterpriseServer.java:228)
```

```
com.ejbhome.server.EnterpriseServer$2.startElement(property) at
    (EnterpriseServer.java:228)
com.ejbhome.server.EnterpriseServer$2.startElement(container-managed) at
    (EnterpriseServer.java:228)
com.ejbhome.server.EnterpriseServer$2.startElement(field) at (EnterpriseServer.java:228)
com.ejbhome.server.EnterpriseServer$2.startElement(field) at (EnterpriseServer.java:228)
com.ejbhome.server.EnterpriseServer$2.startElement(field) at (EnterpriseServer.java:228)
com.ejbhome.server.EnterpriseServer$2.startElement(field) at (EnterpriseServer.java:228)
com.ejbhome.server.EnterpriseServer$2.startElement(field) at (EnterpriseServer.java:228)
finished loading beans from: Books.ejbml
loading beans from: Cart.ejbml
com.ejbhome.server.EnterpriseServer$2.startElement(ejbml) at (EnterpriseServer.java:228)
com.ejbhome.server.EnterpriseServer$2.startElement(session-bean) at
    (EnterpriseServer.java:228)
com.ejbhome.VendorConfiguration.getHomeContainerClassName() at
    (VendorConfiguration.java:226)
com.ejbhome.VendorConfiguration.getVendorPrefix() at (VendorConfiguration.java:100)
com.ejbhome.container.AbstractEJBHome.<init>() at (AbstractEJBHome.java:136)
com.ejbhome.naming.spi.rmi.RMICtx.bind() at (RMICtx.java:168)
 registered cup.chap8.Shop.Cart.IonaCartHome, as: cart.
finished loading beans from: Cart.ejbml
loading beans from: Music.ejbml
com.ejbhome.server.EnterpriseServer$2.startElement(ejbml) at (EnterpriseServer.java:228)
com.ejbhome.server.EnterpriseServer$2.startElement(entity-bean) at
    (EnterpriseServer.java:228)
com.ejbhome.VendorConfiguration.getHomeContainerClassName() at
    (VendorConfiguration.java:226)
com.ejbhome.VendorConfiguration.getVendorPrefix() at (VendorConfiguration.java:100)
com.ejbhome.container.AbstractEJBHome.<init>() at (AbstractEJBHome.java:136)
com.ejbhome.naming.spi.rmi.RMICtx.<init>() at (RMICtx.java:20)
com.ejbhome.naming.spi.rmi.RMICtx.lookup("Shop") at (RMICtx.java:35)
com.ejbhome.naming.spi.rmi.RMICtx.bind() at (RMICtx.java:168)
 registered cup.chap8.Shop.Music.IonaMusicHome, as: music.
com.ejbhome.server.EnterpriseServer$2.startElement(property) at
    (EnterpriseServer.java:228)
com.ejbhome.server.EnterpriseServer$2.startElement(property) at
    (EnterpriseServer.java:228)
com.ejbhome.server.EnterpriseServer$2.startElement(property) at
    (EnterpriseServer.java:228)
com.ejbhome.server.EnterpriseServer$2.startElement(property) at
    (EnterpriseServer.java:228)
com.ejbhome.server.EnterpriseServer$2.startElement(container-managed) at
    (EnterpriseServer.java:228)
```

```
com.ejbhome.server.EnterpriseServer$2.startElement(field) at (EnterpriseServer.java:228)
com.ejbhome.server.EnterpriseServer$2.startElement(field) at (EnterpriseServer.java:228)
com.ejbhome.server.EnterpriseServer$2.startElement(field) at (EnterpriseServer.java:228)
com.ejbhome.server.EnterpriseServer$2.startElement(field) at (EnterpriseServer.java:228)
com.ejbhome.server.EnterpriseServer$2.startElement(field) at (EnterpriseServer.java:228)
finished loading beans from: Music.ejbml
loading beans from: Shop.ejbml
com.ejbhome.server.EnterpriseServer$2.startElement(ejbml) at (EnterpriseServer.java:228)
com.ejbhome.server.EnterpriseServer$2.startElement(entity-bean) at
    (EnterpriseServer.java:228)
com.ejbhome.VendorConfiguration.getHomeContainerClassName() at
    (VendorConfiguration.java:226)
com.ejbhome.VendorConfiguration.getVendorPrefix() at (VendorConfiguration.java:100)
com.ejbhome.container.AbstractEJBHome.<init>() at (AbstractEJBHome.java:136)
com.ejbhome.naming.spi.rmi.RMICtx.bind() at (RMICtx.java:168)
java.rmi.AlreadyBoundException: Books
 registered cup.chap8.Shop.Books.IonaBooksHome, as: Books.
com.ejbhome.server.EnterpriseServer$2.startElement(property) at
    (EnterpriseServer.java:228)
com.ejbhome.server.EnterpriseServer$2.startElement(property) at
    (EnterpriseServer.java:228)
com.ejbhome.server.EnterpriseServer$2.startElement(property) at
    (EnterpriseServer.java:228)
com.ejbhome.server.EnterpriseServer$2.startElement(property) at
    (EnterpriseServer.java:228)
com.ejbhome.server.EnterpriseServer$2.startElement(container-managed) at
    (Compiled Code)
com.ejbhome.server.EnterpriseServer$2.startElement(field) at (Compiled Code)
com.ejbhome.server.EnterpriseServer$2.startElement(field) at (Compiled Code)
com.ejbhome.server.EnterpriseServer$2.startElement(field) at (Compiled Code)
com.ejbhome.server.EnterpriseServer$2.startElement(field) at (Compiled Code)
com.ejbhome.server.EnterpriseServer$2.startElement(field) at (Compiled Code)
com.ejbhome.server.EnterpriseServer$2.startElement(entity-bean) at (Compiled Code)
com.ejbhome.VendorConfiguration.getHomeContainerClassName() at
    (VendorConfiguration.java:226)
com.ejbhome.VendorConfiguration.getVendorPrefix() at (VendorConfiguration.java:100)
com.ejbhome.container.AbstractEJBHome.<init>() at (AbstractEJBHome.java:136)
com.ejbhome.naming.spi.rmi.RMICtx.bind() at (RMICtx.java:168)
 registered cup.chap8.Shop.Music.IonaMusicHome, as: Music.
com.ejbhome.server.EnterpriseServer$2.startElement(property) at (Compiled Code)
com.ejbhome.server.EnterpriseServer$2.startElement(property) at (Compiled Code)
com.ejbhome.server.EnterpriseServer$2.startElement(property) at (Compiled Code)
com.ejbhome.server.EnterpriseServer$2.startElement(property) at (Compiled Code)
```

```
com.ejbhome.server.EnterpriseServer$2.startElement(container-managed) at
    (Compiled Code)
com.ejbhome.server.EnterpriseServer$2.startElement(field) at (Compiled Code)
com.ejbhome.server.EnterpriseServer$2.startElement(field) at (Compiled Code)
com.ejbhome.server.EnterpriseServer$2.startElement(field) at (Compiled Code)
com.ejbhome.server.EnterpriseServer$2.startElement(field) at (Compiled Code)
com.ejbhome.server.EnterpriseServer$2.startElement(field) at (Compiled Code)
com.ejbhome.server.EnterpriseServer$2.startElement(session-bean) at (Compiled Code)
com.ejbhome.VendorConfiguration.getHomeContainerClassName() at
    (VendorConfiguration.java:226)
com.ejbhome.VendorConfiguration.getVendorPrefix() at (VendorConfiguration.java:100)
com.ejbhome.container.AbstractEJBHome.<init>() at (AbstractEJBHome.java:136)
com.ejbhome.naming.spi.rmi.RMICtx.bind() at (RMICtx.java:168)
 registered cup.chap8.Shop.Cart.IonaCartHome, as: Cart.
finished loading beans from: Shop.ejbml
```

The session bean client

The code to test out our session bean is given in Listing 8-18.

Listing 8-18: The CartTest Session EJB Client Application

```
package cup.chap8.Shop.Cart;
import java.rmi.*;
import java.util.*;
public class CartTest {
    static final int NUMITEMS = 2;
    public static void main (String[] args) throws Exception {
        CartHome home = (CartHome)Naming.lookup ("Cart");
        System.out.println ("Naming.lookup successful...");
        if (null == home) {
            System.out.println ("null CartHome returned...");
        }
        Cart cart = home.create ();
        String title = "Title";
        String author= "Author";
        for (int i = 0; i < CartTest.NUMITEMS; i++) {
            System.out.println ("code = " +(i+1) +
                        " Title = " +title+(i+1) +
                        " Author = " +author+(i+1) +
                        " Creating cart.create...");
            cart.createNewBook ((i+1),title+(i+1),author+(i+1),100.00,10);
            cart.createNewAlbum ((i+1),title+(i+1),author+(i+1),20.00,5);
        }
```

Listing 8-18: continued

```
        for (int i = 0; i < CartTest.NUMITEMS; i++) {
            cart.addToBooksCart (i+1);
            cart.addToMusicCart (i+1);
        }
        Vector bookList = cart.getBooksList ();
        System.out.println ("Book List of size "+
                        bookList.size ()+" is...");
        for (int i = 0; i < bookList.size(); i++) {
            ReturnSet set = (ReturnSet)bookList.elementAt (i);
            System.out.println ("code = " +set.code +
                            " Title = " +set.title +
                            " Author = " +set.authors);
        }
        Vector musicList= cart.getMusicList ();
        System.out.println ("Music List of size "+
                                musicList.size ()+" is...");
        for (int i = 0; i < musicList.size(); i++) {
            ReturnSet set = (ReturnSet)musicList.elementAt (i);
            System.out.println ("code = " +set.code +
                            " Title = " +set.title +
                            " Author = " +set.authors);
        }
        Vector bookCart = cart.getBooksCart ();
        System.out.println ("Book Cart of size "+
                        bookCart.size ()+" is...");
        for(int i = 0; i < bookCart.size (); i++) {
            ReturnSet set = (ReturnSet)bookCart.elementAt (i);
            System.out.println ("code = " +set.code +
                            " Title = " +set.title +
                            " Author = " +set.authors);
        }
        Vector musicCart = cart.getMusicCart ();
        System.out.println ("Music Cart of size "+
                        musicCart.size ()+" is...");
        for (int i = 0; i < musicCart.size (); i++) {
            ReturnSet set = (ReturnSet)musicCart.elementAt (i);
            System.out.println ("code = " +set.code +
                            " Title = " +set.title +
                            " Author = " +set.authors);
        }
```

continues

Listing 8-18: continued

```
        System.out.println ("Total Books = " +cart.getNumberBooks () +
                " Total Albums = " +cart.getNumberAlbums () +
                " Book Cost = " +cart.getBooksTotal () +
                " Album Cost = " +cart.getAlbumsTotal () +
                " Grand Total =" + cart.getGrandTotal ());
    }
}
```

Observe that we obtain a reference to our session bean's home interface by doing a Naming.lookup("Cart") and then create our session bean using home.create(). The new entities are then created, adding records to the database via cart.createNewBook(). We then add items to our shopping cart by invoking the cart.addToBooksCart() method and display the various lists we maintain.

The EJB servlet session bean client

The accompanying CD contains the source for an EJB Servlet client that talks to the Cart session EJB and enables clients to buy books and music albums on the Web. The entire code is not reproduced here, however, the servlet instantiates a Cart session bean in its init() method and communicates with the bean via the doGet() and doPost() methods.

The init() class method and class members of the Online servlet class are defined as shown in Listing 8-19.

Listing 8-19: Partial Listing of the Online Servlet Class

```
public class Online extends HttpServlet {
    CartHome home = null;
    Cart   cart = null;
    Vector   bookList = new Vector();
    Vector   musicList= new Vector();
    Vector   bookCart = new Vector();
    Vector   musicCart= new Vector();
    public void init (ServletConfig config) throws ServletException {
        super.init (config);
        System.out.println ("Called from Online::init...");
        try {
            home = (CartHome)Naming.lookup ("Cart");
            if (null == home) {
                System.out.println ("null CartHome returned...");
            }
            else {
                cart = home.create();
```

Listing 8-19: continued

```
                System.out.println ("Naming.lookup successful...");
                System.out.println ("home.create successful...");
            }
        } catch (Exception e) { e.printStackTrace (); }
    }
.... etc., etc.
```

As shown earlier in Figure 8-6, the browser client starts the whole process by sending a `GET` message to the `Online` servlet, which resides on a Web server. This causes the `init()` method of the `Online` servlet class to look up the `Cart` bean from the EJB server and to create it. The `Cart` EJB's `setSessionContext()` method, which is one of the first methods called when the session bean is created, looks up the `Books` entity EJB and the `Music` entity EJB and creates them. As mentioned earlier, entities are a direct mapping of the records in the domain model of the database `Shop`, which is associated with these entities. The entity EJBs (`Books` and `Music`) then interact with the database (`Shop`) to service requests from the session EJB (`Cart`).

I assume the servlet engine is obtained from Sun's Servlet Development Kit, although the example servlet should also run fine with any other engine. To run the servlet:

1. Copy the `Online.class` and the `servlet.properties` files to the root directory.
2. Make sure the EJB Server is up and running.
3. Start up the `servletrunner` with the command.

   ```
   servletrunner -p 6060 -d E:\ -s E:\cup\chap8\Shop\ServletClient\servlet.properties
   ```

The console screen should then resemble

```
E:\>copy .\cup\chap8\Shop\ServletClient\Online.class
        1 file(s) copied.
E:\>copy .\cup\chap8\Shop\ServletClient\servlet.properties
        1 file(s) copied.
E:\>servletrunner -p 6060 -d E:\ -s E:\cup\chap8\Shop\ServletClient\servlet.properties
servletrunner starting with settings:
    port = 6060
    backlog = 50
    max handlers = 100
    timeout = 5000
    servlet dir = E:\
    document dir = .\examples
    servlet propfile = E:\cup\chap8\Shop\ServletClient\servlet.properties
Online: init
Called from Online::init...
```

continues

```
Naming.lookup successful...
home.create successful...
Called from Online::doGet...
Called from Online::displayForm...
Book List of size 4 is...
code = 1 Title = Book1 Author = Author1
code = 2 Title = Book2 Author = Author2
code = 3 Title = Book3 Author = Author3
code = 4 Title = Book4 Author = Author4
Book Cart of size 0 is...
Music List of size 4 is...
code = 1 Title = Album1 Author = Composer1
code = 2 Title = Album2 Author = Composer2
code = 3 Title = Album3 Author = Composer3
code = 4 Title = Album4 Author = Composer4
Book Cart of size 0 is...
Called from Online::doPost...
Content Type =application/x-www-form-urlencoded
--------------------------------------------
name = BooksButton
The No. of Values selected are =1
--------------------------------------------
--------------------------------------------
name = BooksCombo
The No. of Values selected are =2
1
2
--------------------------------------------
Called from Online::displayForm...
Book List of size 4 is...
code = 1 Title = Book1 Author = Author1
code = 2 Title = Book2 Author = Author2
code = 3 Title = Book3 Author = Author3
code = 4 Title = Book4 Author = Author4
Book Cart of size 2 is...
code = 1 Title = Book1 Author = Author1
code = 2 Title = Book2 Author = Author2
Music List of size 4 is...
code = 1 Title = Album1 Author = Composer1
code = 2 Title = Album2 Author = Composer2
code = 3 Title = Album3 Author = Composer3
code = 4 Title = Album4 Author = Composer4
```

```
Book Cart of size 0 is...
Called from Online::doPost...
Content Type =application/x-www-form-urlencoded
--------------------------------------------
name = MusicCombo
The No. of Values selected are =2
2
4
--------------------------------------------
--------------------------------------------
name = MusicButton
The No. of Values selected are =1
--------------------------------------------
Called from Online::displayForm...
Book List of size 4 is...
code = 1 Title = Book1 Author = Author1
code = 2 Title = Book2 Author = Author2
code = 3 Title = Book3 Author = Author3
code = 4 Title = Book4 Author = Author4
Book Cart of size 2 is...
code = 1 Title = Book1 Author = Author1
code = 2 Title = Book2 Author = Author2
Music List of size 4 is...
code = 1 Title = Album1 Author = Composer1
code = 2 Title = Album2 Author = Composer2
code = 3 Title = Album3 Author = Composer3
code = 4 Title = Album4 Author = Composer4
Book Cart of size 2 is...
code = 2 Title = Album2 Author = Composer2
code = 4 Title = Album4 Author = Composer4
```

Now start your Web browser and access the servlet's URL:

```
http://127.0.0.1:6060/servlet/Online
```

Figure 8-7 shows a typical browser client session interacting with the server to purchase books and music CDs from our online bookstore.

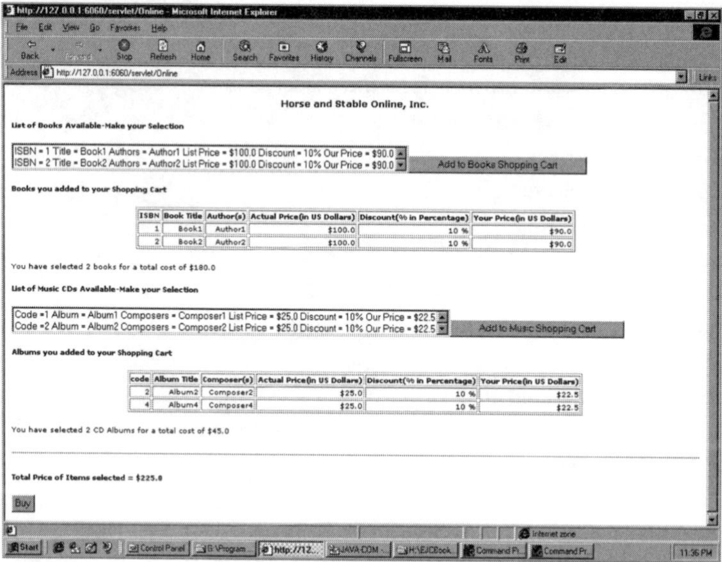

Figure 8-7: The client's view of the online bookstore

You can also refer to my Web site at http://www.execpc.com/~gopalan for more EJB source code. Another good resource is the EJB-INTEREST mailing group from Sun and Iona's EJBHome mailing list.

Modeling Using Session and Entity Beans

In general, session beans are about a conversation with a single client and entity beans are about records in the domain model.

- Use entity beans for a persistent object model (to act as a JDBC wrapper, for instance) giving the rest of your application an object-oriented interface to your data model. Session beans are for application logic. For example, use session beans to model the layer that interfaces with your object-model but normally should not go direct to your database. Thus, a set of session beans provide all the functionality for a particular application of which several could be communicating with the entity-based object model. It will be session bean's EJBObjects that communicate with the front-end GUI code (or servlets, and so forth). Be aware, however, that entity beans can also have an object model behavior. As always, no hard and fast rules exist about this; it depends on your particular scenario.
- Use session beans as the only interface to the client, providing a "coarse grained" facade to the underlying model. You should use entity beans to

enforce the accuracy/integrity of databases, not merely as an object representation of data. Then use session beans to run the processes that operate on the databases. This split reduces the pain of introducing new/changed processes because testing needn't be as stringent.

- Insist on reuse of entity beans. Although they may initially be hard to develop, over time they will prove a valuable asset for your company.
- Expect little reuse of session beans. Plan instead to discard them and create new ones quickly by building a RAD capability around them.
- Elevate entities to a much higher level. Entities are good candidates to model business objects/domain objects, which have a unique identity and need to be shared by various clients and be persisted over a longer time. They can also incorporate the business logic that goes on with their responsibility. Session beans can be used whenever a business method requires services from two or more entities. A good idea is to have all interfaces to the system through session beans.

To summarize:

- Use session beans for application logic.
- Use session beans as the only interface to the client.
- Expect little reuse of session beans.
- Use session beans to control the workflow of a group of entity beans.
- Use entity beans to develop a persistent object model (wrap all your JDBC code).
- Use entity beans to enforce accuracy/integrity of your database.
- Insist on reuse of entity beans.
- Use entity beans to model domain objects with a unique identity shared by multiple clients.

EJB Container

A container is a set of classes generated by the deployment tool that manages, among other things, an enterprise bean's persistence, transactional properties, and security.

Obtaining services from the container

The EJB container provides EJBs with a distributed object infrastructure. EJB assumes an underlying ORB that understands the CORBA/IDL or RMI/IDL semantics. The IIOP transport layer should be able to propagate CORBA OTS transactions.

The container helps in component packing and deployment. An EJB is packaged using manifests, JARs, and deployment descriptors. The container un-JARs the EJBs and then executes it based on the instructions it gets from the manifest file and deployment descriptors

EJB containers provide declarative transaction management by enabling you to define your transactional objects. Although EJB supports transactions built around the JTS service, your application need not make explicit calls to JTS to participate in a distributed transaction. The EJB container can explicitly manage the start, commit, and rollback of a transaction. It can also start a transaction if none exist and manage its completion using the underlying JTS services. You design the transactional attributes of the EJB at design-time (or during deployment) using declarative statements in the deployment descriptors. Optionally, EJBs can explicitly control the boundaries of a transaction using explicit JTS semantics.

EJB containers manage the entire lifecycle of a bean. As a bean provider, you are responsible for providing a remote interface for your EJB. You must also define a factory interface that extends the `javax.ejb.EJBHome` factory object. The interface should provide one or more `create()` methods, one for each way you create your `EJBObject`. The container provider automatically generates the factory implementation. However, your enterprise Bean must implement an `ejbCreate()` method for each `create()` method you defined in your factory interface. As a last step, you must register your factories with the container so clients can create new beans. The container also provides a finder interface to help clients locate existing entity beans.

As part of managing the lifecycle of an enterprise bean, the container calls your bean when it is loaded into memory (or activated) and also calls it when it is deactivated from memory (passivated). Your component can then use these calls to manage its state explicitly and allocate or release system resources.

EJB containers can manage both transient enterprise Bean and persistent enterprise Beans. Persistent or entity beans encapsulate in their object reference a unique ID that points to their state. An entity bean manages its own persistence by implementing the persistence operations directly. The container just hands down a unique key and tells it to load its state. The entity EJB can also direct the EJB container to manage its state. The container can do this simply by serializing the enterprise Bean's state and storing it in some persistent store. Or, it can be as sophisticated as to map the enterprise Bean's persistent fields to columns in an RDBMS. Alternately, the EJB container may choose to implement persistence using an embedded ODBMS. The more advanced EJB containers can load the state of an enterprise Bean from a persistent store and later save it on transactional boundaries.

EJB containers can provide metadata about the enterprise Bean they contain. For example, the EJB container can return the class name of the enterprise Bean with which this factory (`EJBHome`) interface is associated.

EJB containers automate the management of some of the security aspects of the enterprise Bean. The EJB developer gets to define the security roles for his EJB in a `SecurityDescriptor` object. The developer then serializes this object and puts it in his bean's JAR. The EJB container uses this object to perform all security checks on behalf of the EJB.

Relationship between EJB container and the server

The interface between the container and the server isn't specified yet, so it's impossible at this point to have a container without a server. EJBs are intended to exist within an EJB container; they don't run as standalone classes. The reason for this is the container provides the logical interface between the bean and the outside world; the server provides the implementation of the functionality the container requires (persistence, transactions, pooling, multiple instances, and so forth). The idea of the EJB architecture is the server and container are responsible for providing the hard stuff (transactions, persistence, and so forth), so you only have to write the business logic. With EJB, you don't have to implement your own persistence mechanisms or explicitly deal with multithreading. Using EJB helps you avoid the truly hard parts of building distributed systems.

Building customized EJB containers

The EJB specification allows customization of the container. Beans that use customized containers naturally cannot be deployed within "vanilla" EJB containers, whereas the reverse is true (for example, regular EJBs can be deployed within customized EJB containers.) Because the specification also does not define the contract between the container and the server, the interfaces are proprietary to each server. To build a custom container, therefore, you need to work with the specific EJB server vendor.

Multiple reasons may exist for extending the EJB model for a given enterprise and create customized containers, however. The three reasons that come to mind are

1. Extending the container-to-EJB contract for legacy integration or for including a service currently not modeled into EJB. An event service is one such glaring example.
2. Viewing the legacy application as a persistence provider. No change occurs to the container-to-bean and container-to-EJB client contracts.
3. Reimplementing the services used or provided by the EJB container. For example, integrating an organization's custom middleware requires the EJB server to use the appropriate middleware. Again, no change occurs to any of the contracts per se.

If you wish to achieve the componentization benefits of the EJB model, extension of the EJB contracts should be the recommended approach over writing custom containers from scratch. Theoretically, nothing is wrong with organizations implementing component models with entirely different interfaces/contracts other than the fact that the benefits that may stem from such componentization are limited to that organization.

Contract between the client and the EJB container

The EJB provider must adhere to two contracts: the client contract and the component contract. The *client contract* is between the EJB client and the EJB container, and is actually the view the client sees of the enterprise bean. It serves to establish a unique identity by defining the home interface and indicating how the class methods work. The JNDI defines how to search and identify the EJB and container objects uniquely. Within the container, a unique key identifies each EJB. The home interface is a basic description of how to create EJBs in various forms according to the different create() methods and how to destroy EJBs using the remove() method.

Two sides exist to the life cycle of an EJB client-server session:

- How the client sees the EJB
- How the EJB container and server facilitate the client

Figure 8-8 illustrates the classes involved in a typical EJB scenario. The sequence diagram is shown in the following

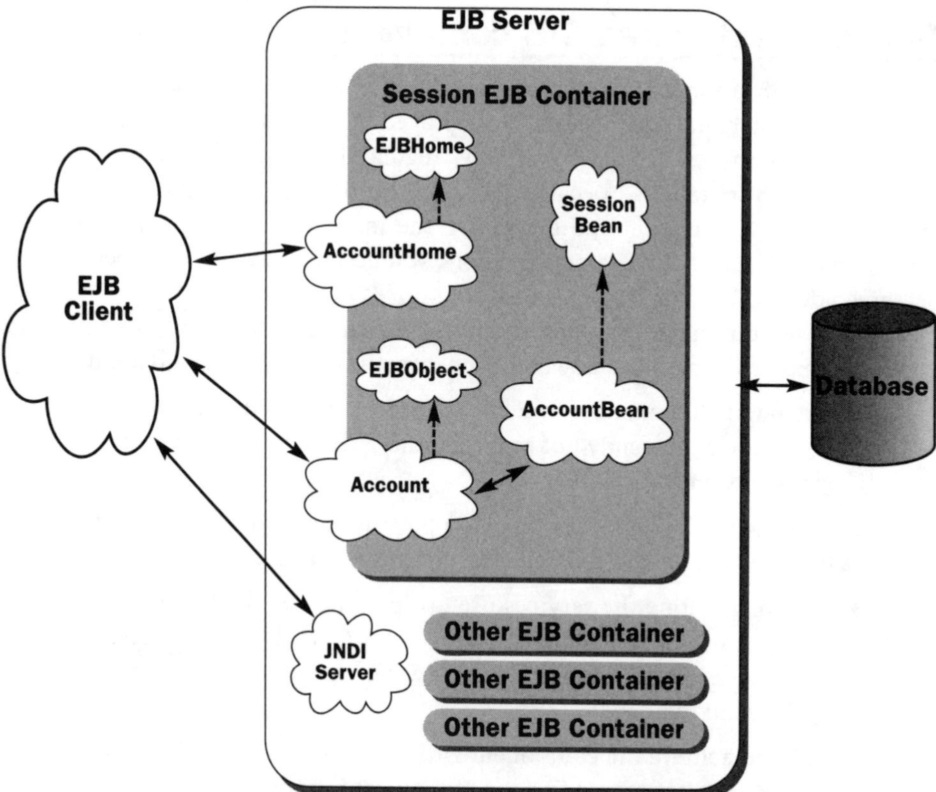

Figure 8-8: Classes available in a typical EJB scenario

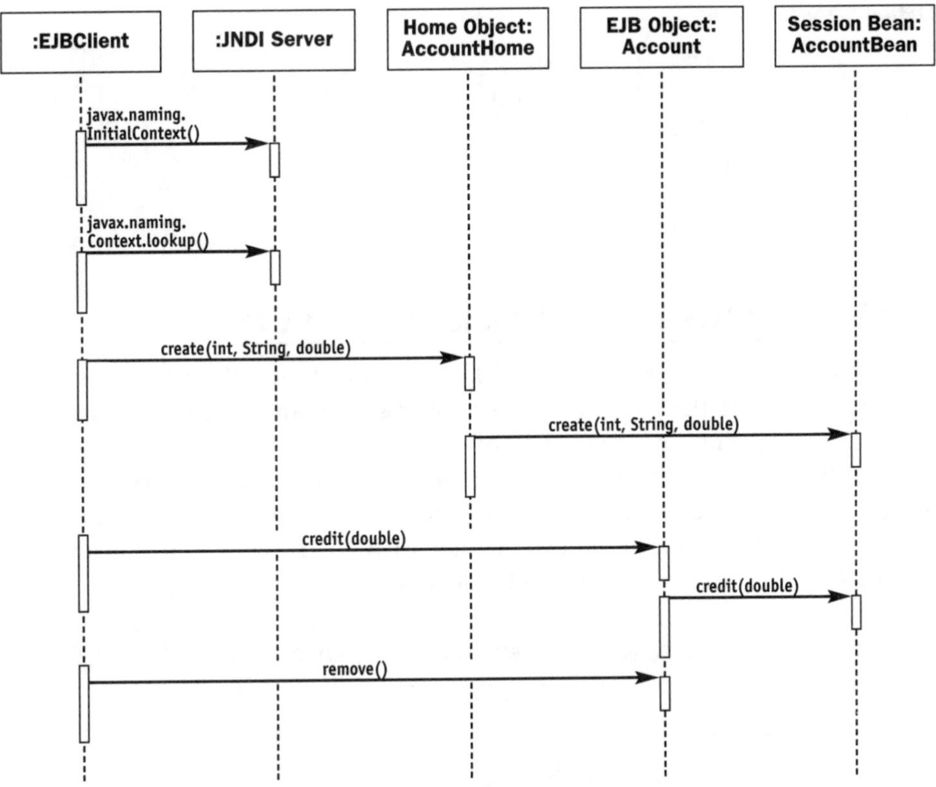

Figure 8-9: Client view of an enterprise JavaBean session

The point of view of the client is illustrated in Figure 8-9.

Starting at the top left of the image, the client first creates a new context to look up the EJBObject with the help of a JNDI server. Given this context, the client then creates an EJB using the home interface. The client can then call the available methods of the EJBObject. When all the activities are complete, the client calls the remove()method, also through the home interface, to terminates the session.

The equivalent code for the same looks like Listing 8-20.

Listing 8-20: The EJB Client Code to Talk to an EJB

```
import javax.naming.*;
public class EJBClient {
    public static void main (String[] argv) {
        // get the JNDI naming context
        Context initialCtx = new InitialContext ();
        // use the context to lookup the EJB Home interface
        AccountHome home=(AccountHome)initialCtx.lookup("Account");
        // use the Home Interface to create a Session bean object
        Account account = home.create (1234, "Athul", 1000225.28d);
```

continues

Listing 8-20: continued

```
            // invoke business methods
            account.credit (1000001.55d);
            // remove the object
            account.remove ();
        }
    }
```

Contract between a container and an EJB

The *component contract* is between an EJB container and the EJB and defines a call-back mechanism to the EJB instance for object state-management purposes. This allows the container to inform the EJB of events in its life cycle.

The EJB object and container's point of view is shown in Figure 8-10 in simplified form. Both the EJB server and container perform actions, which are invisible to the client. The container allocation is a function of the EJB server and is neither the responsibility of the client nor the EJB programmer.

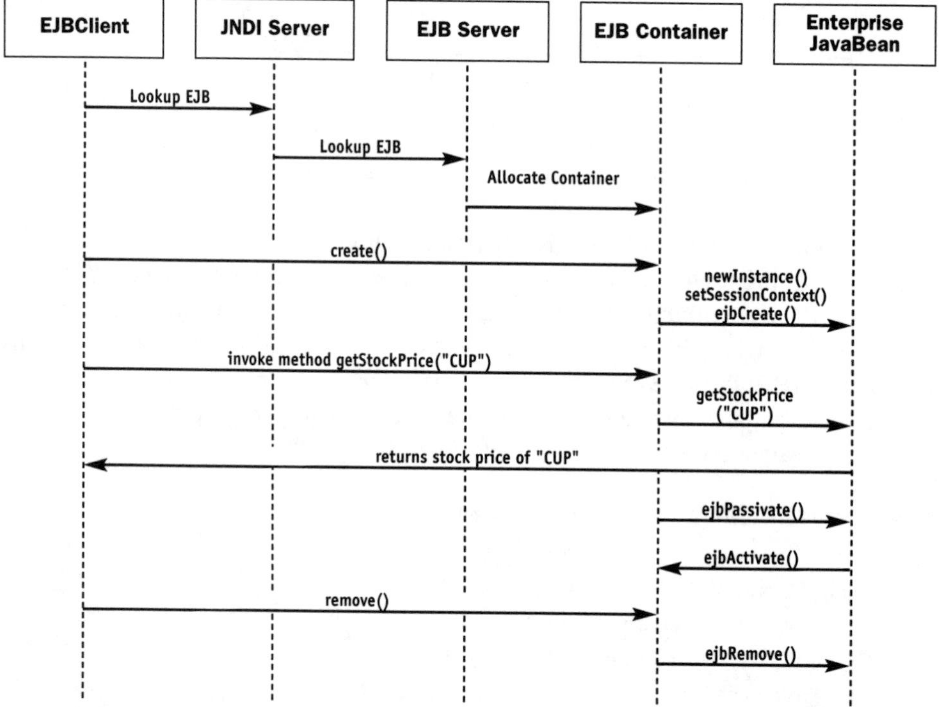

Figure 8-10: The container and enterprise JavaBean point of view of a session

The client begins a new session by sending the create() command. The container then creates a new enterprise bean using the newInstance() call and proceeds to define the context in which the enterprise bean will run with setSessionContext(). Elements of the context include: information about the container, the environment, and the calling client's identity. Finally, it sends the ejbCreate() call, which contains the input parameters as sent by the client. This creates a new enterprise bean whose methods can be accessed directly without any interference from the container.

In some cases, the container may choose to push EJB instances into a secondary cache when they are idle, using the ejbPassivate() call. When the EJB session object is needed again, it is recalled with ejbActivate(). When the client has completed its session, it sends the destroy() call, which is intercepted by the container. The container, in turn, sends a ejbDestroy() call to the EJB instance, allowing it to clean up any pieces as needed.

The container can do a lot more than just pass operations safely to an EJB instance. Where many session objects exist in parallel, for example, the container can manage concurrency for maximum efficiency service. The container can cache an EJB instance in secondary memory if it is idle for too long. This reduces the overall memory usage while preserving the EJB session and its state. The container can also use the number of incoming connections to predict how many additional sessions may be needed in the future and allocate them ahead of time, thus saving on connection setup time.

The capability to cache an EJB session object is not the same as with a persistent object. This cache is lost when the EJB server is shut down or crashes, or if the container is destroyed. It's a temporary cache system that exists only to enhance performance when the program has to handle a large number of session objects.

The container manages this working set of session objects automatically without the client or server's direct intervention. There are specific callback methods in each EJB which describes how to passivate (store in cache) or activate (retrieve from cache) these objects. When the ejbPassivate() call is made, the EJB is serialized using the Java serialization API or other similar methods and stored in secondary memory. The ejbActivate() method causes just the opposite.

EJB Servers

An EJB application server is a prerequisite for using EJBs. It is an integral component of the EJB architecture—the EJB containers run within the application server. Generally speaking, the primary goals of an application server are to improve performance and to simplify development. An application server combines the capabilities of a TP monitor with distributed object technology.

The most important feature in a TP monitor and, likewise, within an application server, is efficient resource management. Application servers pool and recycle expensive system resources such as network connections, processes, threads, memory, and database connections. As a developer, you don't want to write your own thread management and synchronization services within your application code. You don't want to write code within your application to initialize database connections, cache them

Note

Notice I have not talked about database connection pooling in the previous paragraph. While the current EJB specification does talk about instance pooling, it has nothing to say about connection pooling.

To see how these instance management algorithms work, think about the EJB component instance as living inside the EJB container. When a method request travels from the client outside the container to the component instance, it must travel through the container. The container intercepts the method before it is delivered to the enterprise bean. This gives the container an opportunity to participate in the delivery of that request. And one of the ways the container can participate is by injecting an instance management algorithm into that delivery.

Instance management is about faking out the client. The client code thinks it has a dedicated middle-tier instance, just waiting for the next client request. But the client has no idea whether an actual middle-tier instance really exists. All the client knows is this: By the time the method is actually delivered by the container, something needs to be there to receive that method.

Instance Pooling and EJB

EJB uses an instance management algorithm called *Instance Pooling* (IP). In the IP algorithm, the middle-tier instances are themselves pooled, not the database connections. After the method has been intercepted by the container, and before it has been delivered to the enterprise bean instance, the container does not create a brand new instance to process the request—it uses one from a pool of instances. When the instance has finished processing the method, the container does not destroy it. Instead, it is returned to the pool.

in a pool, and then allocate them to other applications as needed. You want the application server to do that for you.

EJB increases the simplicity level even more than a plain application server. EJB automates complicated middleware services such as transactions, security, state management, and persistence.

Distributed objects need to know where to find each other using naming services, whom to trust using appropriate security, and how to manage their life cycles. Services such as naming services, distributed transaction control, security mechanisms, remote access, persistence, resource pooling or threading, instance pooling and concurrency issues, and so forth are automatically handled (and built into) by the EJB server. Additionally, EJB also defines some design patterns and naming conventions.

Every EJB server implementation needs a runtime system, although the specification does not prescribe which one. It could be a database, it could be a legacy transaction system, or it could be CORBA-based. Currently, most EJB server implementations are based on JTS. JTS is to a large extent the Java mapping around CORBA's Object Transaction Service (OTS) and takes care of the "plumbing" that

Because the IP algorithm does not constantly create and destroy instances, it needn't worry about the efficiency of creating and destroying database connections. Certainly, the actual creation of the instance may sometimes be slow, but that happens infrequently.

The IP code moves the creation and destruction of the database connection out of the business logic and into the methods executed when the instance is first created during `ejbActivate()` and finally destroyed during `ejbPassivate()`. This simplifies the business logic code because you can take out the lines shown in brackets:

[1. Acquire a database connection.]

2. Read the component's state from the database.
3. Execute the business logic.
4. Write the component's changed state, if any, back to the database.

[5. Release the database connection.]

6. Return to the client.

IP is conceptually simple and has less algorithm dependent code in the business logic. In fact, even the read and write of the component state can be moved out of the business logic if this algorithm is coupled with transactional notification.

This is where the JDBC 2.0 specification could help because within it you'll find built-in support for database connection pooling. This means any EJB product can use JDBC 2.0 for relational database access and the connection pooling can be portable across EJB container products.

needs to be accomplished when coming up with distributed enterprise solutions. We hope someday the server vendors will give us the best of both worlds by directly layering EJB servers on top of CORBA OTS/SSL. This should give us direct access to the myriad services of the CORBA platform via the easy-to-use APIs of the EJB specification.

Server infrastructure

The EJB server provides an organized framework for EJB containers to execute in. Some of the important services EJB servers typically provides are as follows:

Distributed transactional support

Distributed transaction management involves two possible layers of distribution: multiple application participants and multiple data resource managers. Each layer must be managed separately. JTS/OTS focuses on managing the multiple application participants, while XA and DTC focus on managing the multiple data resource managers.

In a distributed object environment, a single transaction may involve a number of different objects. One object starts the transaction and then it calls some number of methods in other objects to perform some work. When everything is complete, it commits the transaction. JTS/OTS defines an object, called the *transaction context,* which keeps track of all the object participants in the transaction. When the transaction commits, the OTS forwards the commit request to a transaction coordinator (TC) to manage the data resource managers. An OTS can provide its own TC or it can delegate it to a third party—either the transaction coordinator in a database or a separate distributed transaction coordinator (such as Microsoft's DTC or an XA-compliant transaction coordinator like Encina or Tuxedo). Most EJB implementations (for example,, WebLogic, Bluestone, Novera, Persistence, Oracle AS, and Oracle8i) use the database delegation approach and don't support heterogeneous transactions. As of now, GemStone, Inprise, Secant, OrchidSoft, and IBM WebSphere are the only EJB servers that provide an integrated distributed TC service.Although EJBs can be used to implement nontransactional systems, the model was designed to support distributed transactions. EJB requires the application server to use a distributed transaction management system that supports two-phase commit protocols. EJB transactions are based on JTS. Individual enterprise beans do not need to specify transaction demarcation code to participate in distributed transactions. The EJB environment automatically manages the start, commit, and rollback of transactions on behalf of the enterprise bean. Transaction policies can be defined during the deployment process using declarative statements. Optionally, transactions can be controlled by the client application.

EJB transaction management

Each transaction is a set of atomic operations. In methods that have transactions in them, the method executes completely and *commits* or returns a failure notice. It's also possible to undo the action using a *rollback mechanism*. These kinds of transactions are common in the database world because they help maintain coherency of content data. Each executed method functions as a separate transaction. Figure 8-11 shows how transactions are handled.

The basics of transactional programming are the same, except when calling the EJB's methods. Figure 8-11 is a sequence diagram, which corresponds to the following code and shows what happens when the `getStockPrice()` method is invoked.

Listing 8-21 is important because not only does it show how to build transactional code into your beans, but it also shows how to connect to a remote CORBA server object using EJBs.

Listing 8-21: How the QuoteBean Session EJB Acts as a CORBA Client

```
import javax.ejb.*;
import javax.jts.UserTransaction;
import java.rmi.*;
import org.omg.CORBA.*;
```

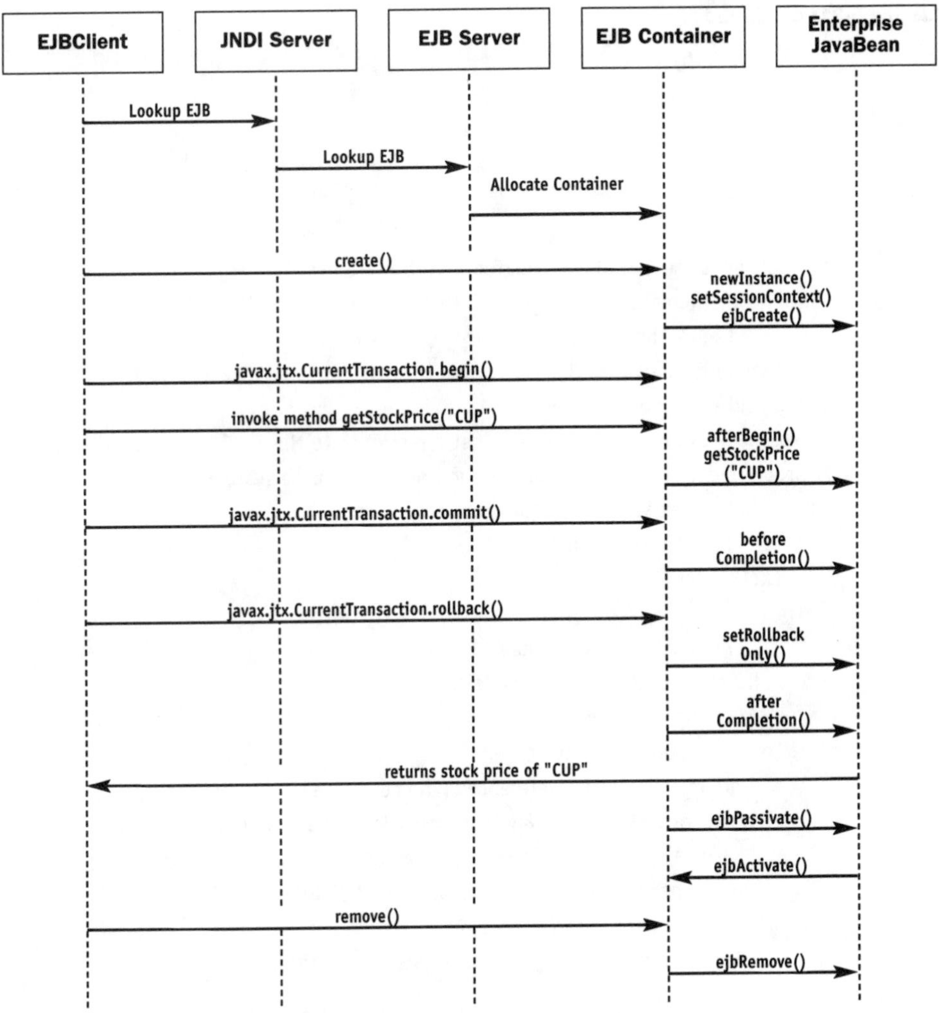

Figure 8-11: Transactional sessions

Listing 8-21: continued

```
import org.omg.CosNaming.*;
import Trader.*;
public class QuoteBean implements SessionBean {
    SessionContext ctx;
    public StockTrader trader;
    public double getStockPrice (String company)
    throws RemoteException {
    // Code for Transactions in the enterprise bean
        UserTransaction tx = ctx.getUserTransaction ();
        tx.begin ();
        double value = trader.getStockPrice (company);
```

continues

Listing 8-21: continued

```
            if (value > 0)
                tx.commit ();
            else
                tx.rollback ();
            return value;
        }
        // Implement the methods mandated by the EJB Spec
        public void ejbCreate ()  {}
        public void ejbActivate () {}
        public void ejbPassivate (){}
        public void ejbRemove ()  {}
        // Set the Session context and also get a reference to the
        // Stock Trader CORBA server object running on a remote system.
        public void setSessionContext (SessionContext ctx)
            throws RemoteException {
            this.ctx = ctx;
            try {
                // Create and initialize the ORB
                ORB orb = ORB.init (args, null);
                // Get the root naming context
                org.omg.CORBA.Object objRef =
                    orb.resolve_initial_references ("NameService");
                NamingContext ncRef = NamingContextHelper.narrow (objRef);
                // Resolve the object reference in naming
                NameComponent nc = new NameComponent ("NASDAQ", "");
                NameComponent path [] = {nc};
                trader = TraderHelper.narrow (ncRef.resolve (path));
            } catch (Exception e) {
                e.printStackTrace ();
            }
        }
}
```

Before a method is called, the client needs to indicate a new transaction is starting using the `javax.jts.UserTransaction.begin()` call.

When a method is called by the client, the container signals the EJB instance with the `afterBegin()` call. The EJB then begins processing the method call.

At this point, one of two things can happen: The client may request the method call be committed or change its mind and execute a rollback. When the client requests the method be committed to action, the container informs the EJB it is ready to receive the information with the `beforeCompletion()` signal. When the EJB's processing of the method call is complete and the action has been committed, the EJB first sends a response back to the client (if there is a response) and then the container sends the `afterCompletion()` signal, as `True`, to the EJB.

If the client changes its mind, it can execute a rollback call after the method call is started. The container sends a `setRollbackOnly()` signal to the EJB to undo whatever it may have done. When the rollback is complete, the container sends the `afterCompletion()` signal, as `False`, indicating to the EJB that it should reinitialize itself.

The passivation and activation methods defined in the EJB interface to the container work just the same as before with the exception that an EJB instance cannot be made passive while a transaction is in progress. One additional thing to note is that a transaction does not have to be limited to just one method call. In fact, typically a number of method calls are packaged inside a single transaction. This allows the client to execute complex operations while still reserving the ability to roll them all back in case of partial failure.

Multithreading and resource pooling

An enterprise bean is not allowed to use thread synchronization primitives. Hence, the keyword `synchronized` should never appear in an enterprise Bean implementation code.

The EJB specification allows the server to passivate an entity bean between methods—even within a transaction. This is to allow the server to perform scalable state management and resource pooling. When the container passivates bean *X,* it first calls `ejbStore()` to allow the bean to synchronize its updated state with the underlying database. When the container reactivates bean *X* in the future, it will `ejbLoad()` the state stored in the database. The *loaded state* is the state saved at the most recent `ejbStore()` by the transaction. Note, the database is doing all the necessary synchronization with other transactions free.

As far as threading is concerned, the EJB specification makes it explicitly illegal for an enterprise bean to start new threads. To ensure the system is manageable, the EJB server must control all thread creations. Allowing enterprise beans to start threads would lead to serious problems. For example, imagine two concurrent threads running with the same transaction context trying to access an underlying database. If one thread is reading data while the other thread is updating the data, it would be difficult to predict what data the first thread would read. Another problem is the EJB server will be unable to guarantee the X/Open checked transaction semantics because it would have little knowledge of whether all the threads involved in a transaction have terminated before the transaction's commit starts.

Security

EJB server implementations may choose to use connection-based authentication in which the client program establishes a connection to the EJB server and the client's identity is attached to the connection at connection establishment time.

The communication mechanism between the client and the server propagates the client's identity to the server. However, the EJB specification does not specify how the EJB server should accomplish this. The `getCallerIdentity()` method should always retrieve the identity of the current caller.

The EJB/CORBA mapping prescribes this mechanism—it specifies the CORBA principal propagation mechanism be used. This means the client ORB adds the client's principal to each client request.

If two EJB servers, *X* and *Y*, from two different vendors, both implement the EJB/CORBA mapping, it is possible for enterprise beans running on system *X* to access enterprise beans running on system *Y*, as if they were local enterprise beans (and vice versa). The transaction context will be properly propagated using the OTS propagation protocol between the transaction managers running at the two sites. The same applies to security, although one of the systems must provide mapping of principals.

The same level of interoperability exists between client systems and a server system. If both systems implement the EJB/CORBA mapping, they can interoperate even if they are from different vendors. This means, for example, if the EJB/CORBA client runtime becomes part of the JRE, and JRE is part of a browser, then the browser can run applets that are clients to any EJB server that implements the EJB/CORBA mapping. The downloaded applet only includes the application-specific client stubs, but not a server-specific ORB, transaction proxy, or EJB runtime. This level of interoperability was the primary motivation for doing the EJB/CORBA mapping.

CORBA/IIOP compatibility

While the EJB specification allows the EJB server implementers to use any communication protocol between the client and server, the EJB/CORBA mapping document is prescriptive with respect to what goes on the wire. This allows both system-level and application-level interoperability between products from vendors who choose to implement the EJB/CORBA protocol as the underlying communication protocol.

For example, Java clients have a choice of APIs—either the Java RMI or Java IDL. Non-Java clients can communicate with the server components using IIOP and the appropriate IDL language mapping. Clients using Microsoft's COM+ protocol can also communicate with the server component through a COM-CORBA bridge. Interesting to note is the client of an EJB can itself be a server component when, for example, it is a servlet. In this case, even a browser client can make EJB invocations by means of an HTTP connection to the servlet.

Deploying EJBs

EJBs are deployed as serialized instances (`*.ser` files). The manifest file is used to list the EJBs. In addition to this, a deployment descriptor has to be supplied along with each `.ser` file. *Deployment descriptors* are serialized instances of a class. They are used to pass information about an EJB's preferences and deployment needs to its container. The EJB developer is responsible for creating a deployment descriptor along with the bean. In this case, the deployment descriptors contain a serialized instance of an EntityDescriptor or SessionDescriptor.

A typical EJB manifest entry looks like Listing 8-22.

Listing 8-22: A Typical EJB Manifest Entry

```
Name: ~gopalan/BankAccountDeployment.ser
Enterprise-Bean: True
```

The Name line describes a serialized deployment descriptor. The Enterprise-Bean line indicates whether the entry must be treated as an EJB.

Future Trends

Currently, the EJB specification is Version 1.0 and provides an excellent architectural foundation for building distributed enterprise-level business systems. Although the specification authors did well to delegate lots of low-level details to specific implementers, some areas need to be addressed. For instance, the EJB model for handling persistent objects can be improved. Standardizing the contract between development tools and systems to provide a uniform debugging interface for all development environments may also be considered. The most significant issue that needs further clarification is one of compatibility, however. Compatibility is currently an issue in two areas. The first area relates to what actually constitutes an "EJB compatible" server. The second area is guaranteeing that EJB servers from different vendors seamlessly interoperate. No doubt exists that the current specification will go though some iteration to address some of these issues.

Summary

Enterprise JavaBeans is the cornerstone of what Sun terms as the "Java Platform for the Enterprise" (JPE). This platform consists of a suite of standard specifications for back-end services that deliver the required functionality for developing truly scalable, multithreaded, transaction-oriented, and distributed enterprise server applications. In this context, Enterprise JavaBeans has currently become one of the hottest technologies within the Java umbrella. As you learned in this chapter, EJB makes it easier for the developer to write business applications as reusable server components without having to worry about the nitty-gritty details. The Enterprise JavaBeans component architecture represents a giant step forward in simplifying the development, deployment, and management of enterprise applications.

Index

E

L

M

T

U

V

W

X

End-User Agreement